Development Challenges in the 1990s
Leading Policymakers Speak from Experience

Development Challenges

in the 1990s

Leading Policymakers
Speak from Experience

Edited by
Timothy Besley and Roberto Zagha

A copublication of the World Bank and Oxford University Press

Contents

Tables and Figures

Foreword

TWENTY YEARS AGO THE WORLD BANK INVITED A SELECT GROUP OF DEVELOPMENT economists—among them Lord P. T. Bauer, Albert Hirschman, Sir Arthur Lewis, and Gunnar Myrdal—to celebrate and critique their seminal contributions to the field. Each scholar delivered a lecture at Bank headquarters in Washington, D.C., and submitted an accompanying essay. The resulting two-volume *Pioneers in Development* provided a rich history of thinking on development.

This volume was inspired by *Pioneers*, but with a twist. Instead of intellectuals, this time the Bank invited prominent policymakers—though many are also first-rate scholars—focusing on those from developing regions. (Larry Summers and John Williamson are not from developing regions, but their vast experience with development issues merits their inclusion here.) The goal was to gain insights into the political dimensions of development policymaking, as well as pick up on the intellectual history of development where *Pioneers* left off. The policymakers were asked to assess their experiences and consider what they would have done differently had they known then what they know now. They rose to the challenge—filling their reflections with the development ideas that have influenced history as well as providing a feel for the blood, sweat, and tears of policymaking.

This book is part of a larger project undertaken by the Bank in 2003–05 to understand the development experiences of the 1990s, an extraordinarily eventful decade. Each of the project's three components serves a different purpose. *Economic Growth in the 1990s: Learning from a Decade of Reform* provides comprehensive analysis of the decade's development experiences, while *At the Frontlines of Development: Reflections from the World Bank* considers the decade's operational implications for the Bank. This volume offers insights on the practical concerns facing policymakers. Each of the policymakers represented here delivered a lecture to a Bank audience in 2003 or 2004; those lectures or related essays are contained here, along with a set of comments on each from experts in the areas discussed.

What arises most forcefully from the presentations has little to do with the widely debated policy matters of the 1990s—such as privatization, macroeconomic stabilization, and capital account liberalization—though the policymakers are eloquent on these issues. Instead, the policymakers are most insightful when they discuss the process of policy reform. Beyond the requisite analytical rigor, the lectures make clear three additional considerations for crafting sound policy. First, economic reforms are also inherently social reforms, and policymaking must reflect this social dimension. Second, each country's social, political, and institutional constraints and opportunities make home-grown solutions critical to success. And third, policy continuity and credibility strongly affect expectations, and hence influence reform outcomes.

Another striking aspect of the policymakers' contributions involves the learning process that emerges in their descriptions of the policy dilemmas they faced. To name just a few, there is Fernando Henrique Cardoso, who first made his mark as a leading dependency theorist, but later institutionalized fiscal responsibility through legislation and practice (among other significant reforms) as president of Brazil. His transformation reflects a fundamental shift in development thinking since the time of *Pioneers*. There is Mario I. Blejer, who speaks candidly about the challenges, adjustments, and mistakes he encountered as Central Bank governor during Argentina's recent crisis. There is Rima Khalaf Hunaidi, who explains how Jordanian policymakers learned from their failures to account for the social costs of reforms. And there is Yegor Gaidar, former minister of economy and finance and deputy prime minister of Russia, who says pointedly of his country's transition from communism: "Were I czar of Russia at the end of 1991, I would do everything differently. But if I were deputy prime minister or minister of finance of a government that lacked the support of the parliamentary majority and had to maneuver to implement any kind of policy—in other words, if I were in the same position—I would do things more or less the way I did."

In transforming the political, economic, and social landscapes of their countries, the policymakers were transformed as well. Each describes instances when they were forced to question assumptions, refine their thinking, or change course. Though they struggled to influence events with their ideas, and met with some success, they inevitably found their ideas influenced by events—whether crisis, transition, regime change, or volatile growth. Accordingly, this is a book about ideas but also about leadership—how to transform ideas into practice. The learning process that they describe is not just their own, but also a reflection of the learning that their societies underwent in the 1990s. With their lectures, the policymakers extended this learning process to the World Bank staff who heard them speak—and with this volume, to the rest of the world as well.

Gobind Nankani
Former Vice President
and Head of Network,
Poverty Reduction and
Economic Management
Network; now
Vice President, Africa Region

Frannie A. Leautier
Vice President
and Head of the
World Bank Institute

François J. Bourguignon
Senior Vice President and
Chief Economist

Washington, D.C
March 2005

Acknowledgments

THIS VOLUME WAS PREPARED UNDER THE GENERAL DIRECTION OF GOBIND NANKANI and benefited from his support, guidance, and advice while he was Vice President of the World Bank Poverty Reduction and Economic Management Network (PREM). Current PREM vice president Danny Leipziger's support and encouragement made it possible to complete this volume. Frannie Leautier, vice president and head of the World Bank Institute and Nicholas Stern, former vice president, development economics provided numerous suggestions and help in the formulation of the lecture series on which this book is based. François Bourguignon, who succeeded Nicholas Stern, continued to support the series. Paul Holtz skillfully edited the volume, patiently sifting through numerous drafts and transcripts to capture the essence of each contributor's thinking. Nathalie Tavernier, Rafaela Reff and Muriel Darlington capably handled many logistical challenges. Indermit Gill provided useful comments. Ravi Kanbur provided numerous and constructive criticism to the authors. Alfred Friendly edited portions of the book. Todd Pugatch contributed both with substantive editing and organizational support. The authors and commenters themselves deserve many thanks for engaging in the honest and critical thinking that made this project successful. Last but not least, Nancy Lammers, Stephen McGroarty, and Mark Ingebretsen shepherded the manuscript to publication with infinite patience.

1 Introduction

Timothy Besley

It is ideas, not vested interests, which are dangerous for good or evil.
— John Maynard Keynes (1883–1946)

LORD KEYNES' MUCH-QUOTED EPIGRAM SERVES ON THREE LEVELS AS A PROLOGUE TO the essays gathered in this volume. Like the authors, Keynes was an economist turned practitioner—the leading one of his day. A pioneer in moving between the worlds of ideas and policies, he was an architect of the Bretton Woods system—and thus of the World Bank, which fostered these contributions. More immediately, his observation gives special relevance to this collection's raison d'être: the presentation of ideas within a debate on their relevance in the modern world.

Among those ideas, the Washington consensus stood out at the start of the 1990s as a view of what constituted good policies for growth and development. Both the International Monetary Fund (IMF) and World Bank pushed elements of the consensus, particularly the virtues of openness through tariff cuts and privatization, as preconditions for adjustment assistance. The practitioners whose essays appear in this volume were asked to reflect on the lessons of the 1990s and to apply critical analysis to their experiences during the decade dominated by the Washington consensus. Having had the opportunity to put its ideas into practice, they are well placed to describe what worked and, as policymakers at the highest levels, help readers judge whether the prevailing ideas of the 1990s were indeed "for good or evil."

The organizers of the lecture series that spawned this book made no attempt to set the agenda for these practitioners, coordinate their contributions, or make them representative geographically or in terms of the policy challenges of the era. This introduction—by an academic economist—aims to bring together some of the contributors' themes. It also seeks to provide a context for the essays, relating them to some of the major academic and policy themes from the 1990s onward and connecting the specific contributions to broader debates.

This group of practitioners comes from the mainstream development community—part of the international elite, many of whom are educated at a small number of top institutions.[1] They share an exposure to mainstream thinking in economics and a common set of international institutions (including the World Bank and IMF) often viewed as guardians of the policy paradigm dominated by the Washington consensus. Accordingly, their essays contain little in the way of radicalism or criticism of the world order.[2] For the most part that sense is reinforced by the discussants of the lectures, whose comments are also printed here.

This volume is not just about the nuts and bolts of policymaking; the essays are equally about ideas. In addition to dealing with important economic issues, they reinforce the importance of thinking about history, politics, and institutions in understanding development. This broadly based approach to development thinking sits well with the *Pioneers in Development* volume published 20 years ago.

The essays reflect each contributor's style and expertise. They draw on experiences from all over the world and deal with a variety of policy issues, among which two overall modes can be distinguished. The first is proactive policymaking, cases where policy—as with China's gradualist pursuit of economic reform—fosters internally motivated, purposive change. The second mode is reactive, a description of policymaking episodes in response to specific events, such as in Russia after the fall of communism.

The first two essays, by Lawrence H. Summers and John Williamson, are not based on specific country experiences, but are the fruit of wide-ranging experience with international policymaking by two former academic economists. The remaining authors draw largely from their country-specific policy experiences. There are two such essays on Europe: Yegor Gaidar on Russia and Kemal Derviş on Turkey. From Latin America come Fernando Henrique Cardoso on Brazil, Eduardo Aninat and Alejandro Foxley on Chile, and Mario I. Blejer on Argentina. Derviş and Blejer deal with crisis management, while Foxley discusses more general themes of macroeconomic management. Aninat and Cardoso are more concerned about social development and its link to economic development. Gaidar discusses Russia's transition from a socialist to capitalist economy.

Asia is represented by its two giants. Montek S. Ahluwalia surveys India's economic reform, while Zhou Xiaochuan does the same for China. These case studies are extremely important because sustained economic growth in these countries is likely to have a major impact on global poverty. Both countries have pursued gradualist paths toward economic reform starting from highly complex, heavily regulated initial conditions. Both have also sought greater integration with the global economy. But the political and social institutions of these countries are very different, and it is clear from the essays that these structures have profoundly influenced the policy process. Nonetheless, both countries are generally considered success stories, even if they face significant policy challenges in the years ahead.

Finally, three essays offer more as much in the way of comparative experience as analysis of specific countries. Although Leszek Balcerowicz is from Poland, his essay looks at the broad experience of postsocialist transition in Eastern Europe, drawing lessons for this whole group of countries. Rima Khalaf Hunaidi reviews the development experience of Jordan from her perspective as a former minister of planning, and of the Arab world as a whole from her work coordinating the U.N.'s Arab human development reports. Similarly, Kwesi Botchwey takes a broad perspective on development issues in Africa from his Ghanaian vantage point.

In his opening essay, Williamson offers a retrospective on the Washington consensus—a term he coined to describe a set of economic policies on which he perceived agreement among the World Bank, IMF, and U.S. Treasury in the late 1980s. As Williamson makes clear, the term has been widely abused. Many commentators have taken the license of attributing to the consensus some policies that were not on Williamson's original list. Moreover, in some quarters "Washington consensus" has become a pejorative term used to describe a certain kind of free market economics often (misleadingly) referred to as neoliberal.

Many elements of the Washington consensus are anodyne. Few, if any, can doubt the importance of sound fiscal and monetary policies. That said, important questions remain about the right means to achieve those ends. It needs to be remembered that the consensus was formulated after a period when rich countries began to pull back from flirtations with Keynesian demand management. During the 1970s these countries had experienced bouts of stagflation that had dented confidence in the postwar Keynesian consensus. These episodes lead to pessimism about the capacity of government to fine-tune the economy and fueled the more classical view on the role of monetary policy, which was given its intellectual underpinnings by Milton Friedman and Robert Lucas. The consensus tried to distill these lessons on a more global scale.

Intellectual fashion may play a role here. But serious macroeconomic imbalance has repeatedly proven to be the handmaiden of economic crises and social unrest throughout the developing world. The experiences described by Derviş and Blejer show just how hard it is for a country emerging from a period of sustained macroeconomic imbalance to concentrate on issues of long-run development. During such times the energy of policymakers is absorbed by issues of immediate relevance. The discussions here underscore the need to avoid key vulnerabilities that precipitate crises, such as overvalued exchange rates, excessive fiscal deficits, and poorly regulated financial systems. Only when crises are avoided can essential issues of long-run development take center stage in the policy arena.

Apart from macroeconomic and monetary stability, a central ingredient of the policy recipe advocated by the Washington consensus was the need to strengthen property rights as a means of improving the investment climate. Although it can be overstated as a sufficient condition for growth, this precept, too, is fairly uncontroversial.[3] A large body of empirical work, both microeconomic and macroeconomic, bears out the links between stronger property rights and better economic performance.

The Washington consensus also offered fairly uncontentious recommendations on taxation and public spending—emphasizing the merits of broadly based taxation in financing public spending targeted toward poor people. In hindsight, this recommendation lacked any engagement with the challenges of service delivery to ensure that poor people benefit from public spending. At the time the more technocratic notion of targeting was riding high. As discussed below, this technocratic view of policy is symptomatic of a more general weakness of the Washington consensus approach that focused on policies rather than institutional solutions. The institutional foundations of effective service delivery have since taken the spotlight, not least as the subject of the World Bank's *World Development Report 2004*. Cardoso's discussion of social policies in Brazil emphasizes the kind of compact between civil society and state governance that underpins the modern consensus on building effective services that work in the interests of the poor.

All the elements of the Washington consensus mentioned so far are broadly in step with mainstream economic views as they stood then and have remained. None of the policymakers herein takes issue with them.

The two most controversial elements of the consensus were its emphases on openness and privatization. The value of being open to trade in goods and services is not hugely controversial. Moreover, the experiences of China and India in integrating with the world economy, following on the East Asian miracle, illustrate the power of openness. Arguably these bouts of global integration have resulted in the most rapid, sustained fall in global poverty that the world has ever seen (see Besley and Burgess 2003). But current Chinese and Indian efforts toward global integration are not experiments in wholesale trade liberalization. Rather, they are efforts to generate carefully managed paths toward greater openness.

Just how such integration should occur still provokes debate. The Washington consensus reflected skepticism about the usefulness of infant industry protection as a means of pursuing economic development. In the early postwar era such protection was a key part of the mainstream approach to development. But in many ways the consensus formulation marked the end of naïve, state-led development strategies that had dominated for a generation. This reversal was largely fueled by the concern that controlled trade regimes created rents and fostered political opportunism. Although such influential commentators as Peter Bauer, Jagdish Bhagwati, and Anne Krueger were wise to this defect early on, it took a while for their views to become accepted. The Washington consensus marked the watershed.

This point is not necessarily at odds with assigning the state an important role in promoting development. Indeed, there are powerful theoretical arguments for government intervention based on imperfect information and coordination failure. But putting them into practice is not easy. One key issue is how to deal with incentive problems in government, so that policy choices conducive to economic development are implemented. For this, the political and administrative prerequisites to economic development need to be understood. Amsden (1989) and Wade (1990) provide insightful commentaries on East Asia's experience and the way that the state fostered development in these cases. But despite such case studies, knowledge of how to build a successful developmental state remains quite limited. Generalizing from this, Hausmann and Rodrik (2002) argue that the key feature of trade policy in successful economies is the way it is conditioned on performance.

Even if openness to trade is broadly accepted, whether countries should pursue capital market liberalization is more controversial. But as Williamson notes in his essay, this policy approach was not part of the original Washington consensus. Nonetheless, it became a widely accepted part of the "augmented" consensus that gained prominence and significant policy influence in the 1990s. The subsequent economic crises in East Asia, Russia, and Latin America were often attributed to unwarranted pursuit of capital market liberalization.

Given the controversies surrounding capital market liberalization, it is striking that the policymakers in this volume do not give this issue a huge amount of play. It surfaces in only three essays. Summers observes that many of the problems attributed to capital market openness are really symptoms of policy errors that subsequently fueled private speculation. This general theme is echoed in Blejer's discussion of the background to the 2002 Argentine crisis and in Derviş's description of the structural weaknesses underpinning the problems that confronted Turkey. Summers makes some important observations on the need to develop more appropriate institutional arrangements for international capital markets.

Endorsement of privatization was one of the more controversial parts of the original Washington consensus. Above all, it created an association between Reaganite and Thatcherite policies—dubbed neoliberal in some quarters—and the consensus. But it is important to realize that two somewhat distinct privatization agendas were taking root during this period, each with its own controversies.

By the early 1990s privatization strategies were being pursued throughout OECD and a number of developing countries. In most cases this amounted to divestment of private goods production where the theoretical case for public ownership was weakest. Calls for privatization also reflected political difficulties in managing public enterprises. Janos Kornai developed the notion of the "soft budget constraint" to describe the difficulties that politicians had in trying to impose financial discipline on public firms. If anything, democratic government made such problems even more severe, and governments privatized as a form of self-denying ordinance.

But the thrust of privatization goes much deeper. In large parts of the economy— education, health care, pensions, airlines, railways—the divergence between private and social returns may indeed speak in favor of some form of public ownership. In such contexts the assertion of the primacy of private ownership is much more ideological, not based on any strong theoretical or empirical case. The cause of the Washington consensus was damaged by being associated with those who pushed privatization in the social sphere. In places like Chile this effort was pushed hard, with mixed success.

The second (and largely distinct) set of privatization policies came into play after the collapse of communism in Eastern Europe, where the issues faced had little to do with the Washington consensus. Given the extent of public ownership, privatization was inevitable, and the main issues concerned the structure, speed, and form that it would take. In this case—one of reactive policymaking par excellence—there was little experience to guide mass privatization. And there is much debate about which countries in Eastern Europe got it right. Balcerowicz's essay offers some provocative suggestions. He argues that, after taking into account initial conditions, the countries that reformed fastest fared best. But Gaidar reminds us that the pace of reform is not

always something over which policymakers have complete control, given other
events in the economy.

Both Balcerowicz and Gaidar emphasize the importance of the institutional context in which privatization occurs. The market operates well only when supported
by a wide variety of institutions—particularly judicial and regulatory systems—many
of which work poorly and take time to develop. It seems likely that the size of the
postprivatization recession in Europe's transition economies was related to institutional shortcomings. Moreover, gains from privatization in the production of private
goods require a reasonable degree of competition in product markets, and the extent
of competition that emerged varied greatly.

The discussion of privatization hints at a more general theme pervading these
essays: the importance of institutions and institutional change in fostering development. This subject is a central theme of Summers's contribution, which cites institution building and efficient political administration as key factors in the development
process. He recognizes that these are difficult issues, but sees grappling with them as
unavoidable. In a similar vein, Williamson considers insufficient attention to the
importance of institutions a deficiency in his formulation of the Washington consensus. This oversight is not surprising, but over the past 15 years the development
literature has paid far more attention to these issues.

During the 1990s debates about institutional reforms and governance issues became
increasingly central in mainstream economics and the policy sphere. Indeed, the idea
that development is about getting institutions right is now widely accepted. There is
nothing particularly new in the idea that development and institutional change are
closely linked. It was at the heart of the Nobel Prize–winning work of Douglass North.
The current preoccupation with good institutions builds on North's insights.[4]

Even so, the term *institution* is often used quite loosely in policy discussions. What
is meant by a good institution is vaguer still. Nonetheless, the mantra of good institutions has come to dominate thinking on development. It crops up throughout the
contributions to this book. But the literature is only just coming to grips with how
to think about institutional change and build good institutions. Thus, as Summers
notes, "It is a huge challenge for development experts…to build on the recognition
of the importance of institutional capacity and to think as constructively as possible
about how to develop it. Too often the insight is recognized, platitudes are delivered
about transparency and integrity, and little more is done." This truth presents a huge
challenge for future progress.

Even so, the focus on institutions shifts debates about development in useful ways.
It gets away from discussions about the specific policies that were at the core of the
Washington consensus. Thus it is more easily reconciled with the notion that a wide
variety of approaches can be used to achieve growth and reduce poverty. In that sense
it is aligned with Dani Rodrik's influential work on growth strategies (see, for example, Rodrik 2004 and Rodrik, Subramanian, and Trebbi 2002).

Rodrik has argued persuasively that by being couched in the language of policies,
the Washington consensus failed to communicate the broader message that what
matters to economic success is creating good incentives for the production and dis-

tribution of public and private goods. There are many ways—and many policy measures—to achieve this broad goal. The policies of the Washington consensus irritated those who thought that it was trying to build a monolithic path. Moreover, the history of postwar development illustrates a wide variety of development paths. For example, the path being pursued in China follows no conventional model. East Asian economies grew using an entirely different model. And successful transition economies have used different strategies still.

But in all cases, there is no mystery from an economic point of view. The structural transformation that is economic development can be achieved only by a sustained process of change based on actors who perceive their interests in making that change work through a combination of appropriate public and private incentives tailored to the history and institutions of the country in question. While some of the key elements of the Washington consensus would be part of any such strategy, it came up short as a blueprint for economic development.

The institutional approach puts a lot more weight on policy implementation, not just policy choice. As Summers notes, "strong institutions, and the closely related issue of efficient political administration, are essential to effective development. Well-executed policies that are slightly misguided are much more effective than absolutely correct but poorly executed ones."

This is a reaction to mainstream economic policies that had traditionally taken a rather technocratic view of government. The process of policymaking, then given little attention, has become a central concern of the so-called new political economy literature. The drawbacks of ignoring incentive problems in government became increasingly apparent as the lessons of the 1990s unfolded. Many of the essays here lay bare the nontechnocratic aspects of policymaking. For example, Foxley and Ahluwalia provide vivid illustrations of the political preconditions for reform in Chile and India, respectively.

An approach that gives institutions due weight also makes clear why good policies are not always enough. One key illustration throughout this volume is the need to make policies credible. Having a good policy today may be fine, but the real issue often centers on maintaining that policy stance going forward and convincing both the private sector and other branches of government to back the effort. This theme of credible commitment is a persistent theme in North's original work on institutions.

How to establish credibility in practice is far from clear. One possibility is to create institutions, such as independent central banks, that are under more limited state control and hence less susceptible to opportunistic behavior by politicians. Another is to structure the political system with an appropriate separation of powers and with the right structure of "veto players"—that is, those who hold countervailing authority over policy decisions.[5]

But while institutions are undoubtedly important, the game theory literature has also emphasized the potential for many different outcomes (so-called multiple equilibria). This can explain how what Summers calls "bank run mentalities" can have policy consequences. In the classic example of a bank run, a bank collapses as investors withdraw their funds even though there is no fundamental problem with the bank's lending portfolio. The collapse becomes a self-fulfilling prophecy. Similar logic has been used to explain balance of payments crises. Policymakers wishing to achieve credibility then have to shift expectations to deal with the problems, possibly requiring that they do much more than initiate a policy reform.

Blejer, Derviş, and Foxley all discuss their attempts as policymakers to establish credibility by affecting expectations. As Foxley says, "It was clear that our first challenge was to build trust and credibility in the new administration's ability to govern responsibly and effectively. To achieve that goal, we had to prove that our economic program…was guided by sound policies." This was a particular challenge in Chile, where the transition to democracy created a weight of expectation among citizens. Foxley also emphasizes the importance of credibility in maintaining an ongoing program of policy change, especially in the public sector.

Credibility in the face of a crisis is also an important theme in Derviş' discussion of his policymaking experience in Turkey. He mentions in particular the difficulties of enhancing credibility by getting key private sector actors—organized labor and private investors—to believe that the policy responses to the Turkish crisis could be sustained.

A focus on institutions also helps in understanding inertia in policymaking. Institutions are harder to change than policies and have strong historical roots, as Gaidar notes in the Russian context. The functioning of institutions is embedded in social structures, such as traditional relationships of trust between actors. Such trust relationships can be valuable in some institutional settings and counterproductive in others, for example if they lead to organized crime. Thus institutional change is more complex than policy change. It needs to work with history and culture; it certainly cannot ignore them.

Human capital is also important in shaping institutional capabilities (see Djankov and others 2003). Yet the role and importance of human capital formation do not get much play in this volume, the main exception being Aninat's essay on education reform in Chile. It is increasingly clear that the traditional role for human capital formation in increasing labor market productivity sells short its contribution to the economic development process. Human capital also makes important contributions to social development (especially health) and political development.

Giving a central role to the institutional setting in economic development is consistent with recent cross-country evidence. Acemoglu, Johnson, and Robinson (2001) and Hall and Jones (1999) are important examples.[6] Both create measures of institutional quality that they show to be strongly related to aggregate economic performance. Acemoglu, Johnson, and Robinson relate this measure to colonial settlement patterns. They find that countries with more European settlers enjoy better institutional quality today, and argue that short-term colonizers had incentives to set up "extractive" institutions that ultimately inhibited development.

Recognizing the historical roots of institutional structures gives further support to Rodrik's contention that each country needs to find its own growth strategy, a theme borne out by the essays on China and India in this volume. Both countries have pursued policy paths that reflect the circumstances they faced at the outset. Zhou's discussion of the Chinese experience emphasizes the legacy created by the peculiar set of institutions that China inherited through the Great Leap Forward (and

before).The move toward reform required a strategic disempowerment of state structures to provide incentives for enterprise. In line with North's views, institutional
change—in the form of decentralization—was used to reduce the possibility of state
predation by creating competition between localities.The results have been dramatic,
ushering in one of the most dynamic periods of poverty reduction that the world has
seen. In China good economic incentives have been provided without democratic
institutions and private property rights. But it is hard to draw general conclusions
from this accomplishment, and Zhou does not try to do so.

The importance of institutional structures is also clear in Ahluwalia's discussion of
India's liberalization.The country's policy history created powerful vested interests in
the status quo. Given the democratic setting, there was a need to build sufficiently
broad consensus for reform. Thereafter, the reform strategy had to be sustained
through democratic institutions. And despite changes in political administration,
there are now clear signs of such continuity.

In contrast to many other countries, India's economic reforms have been less
about institutional changes and more about policy reforms in a stable institutional
environment. Although the country's 1990–91 crisis accelerated the reform process,
internally motivated deregulation had begun in the mid-1980s. Given the strength of
Indian democracy, the liberalization program is more typical of policy reforms in
richer countries. As such India's reform process is atypical of the major policy transitions experienced throughout most of the developing world and discussed by many
of the other practitioners.

The essays in this volume deal not only with policy design and implementation
but also with the authors' contributions to these processes.This dual perspective creates important links to the political economy issues that now play a central role in
mainstream economic analysis. At the heart of this literature is a desire to understand
how political forces shape policy choices and their implementation.

The essays are full of examples of political forces shaping policymaking—clear
instances of economic reforms occurring on the back of coalition building, with
attendant compromises sometimes required. Ahluwalia says that in India inaction was
often due to lack of consensus between technocrats and politicians. Foxley's discussion of the bargain struck between Chilean unions is an example of the importance
of coalition building in advancing reform. Botchwey, Derviş, and Gaidar echo this
theme. More generally, Cardoso attributes Brazil's focus on social development to the
action of democratic institutions in creating incentives that forced politicians to pay
greater attention to what the public wanted.

The political economy approach is a useful antidote to the technocratic view traditionally taken in mainstream economics. As noted, the Washington consensus is
mostly couched in terms of policies. But as Summers mentions, the realization that
the policy process matters has been increasing among mainstream economists. He
refers specifically to policy administration, but policy formulation is important too.

In assessing and pursuing these concerns, however, it is necessary to distinguish
between normal politics—the cut and thrust of political competition through the
ballot box, where some benefit at the expense of others—and more malign elements

such as special interest politics and problems of corruption. Normal democratic policies must deal with the political incentives that lead to some groups gaining an upper hand in the political process. Democracy has often imposed patterns of trade protection that do not lead to patterns of redistribution corresponding to reasonable notions of social justice.[7] As India's experience illustrates, policymakers often find themselves dealing with vested interests created by past policy favors. Ahluwalia stresses the power that open debate in India had in overcoming this and therefore helping in reaching consensus on the path to reform.

Concerns about corruption often take pride of place in debates on governance. Given that emphasis, it is somewhat surprising that corruption receives so little attention in this volume's essays. That may be because such problems are of less concern to policymakers than to international institutions. There is a sense from Botchwey that corruption has gained too much focus in discussions of governance. He sounds a cautionary note about paying too much attention to problems of state failure: "By reducing the problems to almost sui generis corruption and predatory behavior by politicians and other public sector actors, it diverted attention from the real causes of market failure and of what was needed to improve the efficiency of nonmarket institutions." More generally, it not clear whether corruption is a symptom or a cause of underdevelopment. The large body of evidence demonstrating a negative correlation between corruption and economic performance (see, for example, Mauro 1995) is consistent with either conclusion.

Whichever way the causality runs, corruption is symptomatic of resource misallocation. Moreover, there is now less acceptance of the more benign view of corruption as grease for wheels frozen by overbearing bureaucrats and practices. Corruption can have a corrosive effect on the conduct of policy and politics. It undermines faith in government to resolve problems and can lead to arbitrary redistribution of the costs and benefits from state intervention. That said, Botchwey is reminding us that it should be tackled in the context of trying to strengthen public institutions rather than promoting cynicism.

Many recent policy discussions have looked for ways to reorganize government to limit corruption, alter policies in ways that anticipate corrupt behavior, or both. Making transparency and accountability the motherhood and apple pie of good governance also places weight on the roles of civil society and the media in holding government in check[8] and suggests a role for effective political competition as a means of improving accountability.

Better governance also refers importantly to a broader effort to improve the role of the state in delivering public services. Not just directly important constituents of well-being, these services are important inputs into enhancing productivity. As argued by Cardoso, effective delivery of social policies is a key aspect of building a stable coalition for growth. This issue is particularly important in a country like Brazil, with its historical legacy of inequality. Cardoso recognizes the difficulties that arise when economic growth does not bring demonstrable social progress. Similar concerns are echoed in Ahluwalia's discussion of whether India's economic growth has led to sustained poverty reduction. Khalaf Hunaidi also discusses the need to ensure that the growth performance in Jordan was mirrored in human development achievements. She emphasizes the importance of participatory decisionmaking in achieving this goal. All of this illustrates the interplay between governance issues and improvements in public service delivery.

An important related proposal stems from efforts to decentralize public service delivery. The main goal is to enhance accountability by strengthening local decision-making—reducing waste and corruption as well as allowing better targeting of the neediest groups. Decentralization is also part of a wider theme of empowerment, providing poor people with a greater say in how the state operates.

The 1990s saw many decentralization experiments around the globe. But while proponents can muster some promising evidence, the jury is still out. Concerns have been raised about the potential ability of local elites to capture local governments. There is also evidence that the degree of fragmentation in society crucially affects public service delivery (see Easterly 2001).

Some parallels characterize current discussions of decentralization and privatization. There is no sensible answer to the question, "should an economy privatize?" It depends on the good or service being privatized, the objective being pursued, and the array of complementary institutions in place. Similarly, there is no sensible answer to the question, "should government be decentralized?" Again, the answer will depend on what is being decentralized, the objectives of policymaking, the institutional structure, and the economic and social development of the country in question.

In tune with Rodrik's work on growth strategies, the political economy literature does not suggest that there is a uniquely optimal set of political institutions, and the practitioners in this volume spend little time debating the relative merits of alternative political institutions. But even among the world's advanced democracies, a wide variety of options operate. And as recent literature has demonstrated, there is good reason to believe that they can shape the policy process.

Cross-country data show little convincing evidence on the merits of democratic settings for economic policy outcomes. This is true despite broad consensus on the importance of representative democracy after what Samuel Huntington has called "democracy's third wave." Democracy is no panacea for the problems of economic management. Indeed, many of the dilemmas faced by the policymakers in this volume arose because they operated under democratic constraints.

Much of the policymaking discussed here is in response to crises. As Blejer points out, policymaking in normal times and in crisis situations is quite different—both in terms of the speed of responses needed and the type of medicine administered. More generally, the practitioners draw important lessons about crisis management. First, there is a need to monitor critical vulnerabilities and to spot them before they reach crisis proportions. Second, it is vital to develop a strategy and persist with it. Blejer cautions against always listening to external actors; both he and Derviş discuss how they stood up to the IMF at the height of their crises.

Derviş proffers the bold suggestion that crises are the time to push for fundamental reform. There may be a paradox here, heightening the tension between economic and political necessity. Any economist would say that economic reform is most important when it avoids the onset of a crisis. But the ability to push a reform through the political process is greatest after a crisis occurs. The question is how to resolve such a real and theoretical tension.

So, what are the main lessons?

First and foremost, there is a need to avoid economic crises. Crises may occasionally prompt radical policy reform that would otherwise be resisted, but for the most part they are a tax on the energy of policymakers and citizens alike. The aspects of the Washington consensus that emphasize sound macroeconomic management are as relevant today as when it was formulated.

Second, the policymakers' reflections show the importance of focusing on specific issues in the policy process to deal with binding constraints. These will vary by country and over time, but the successes described here demonstrate focus and an eye toward developing a proactive strategy—not just reacting to events.

Third, the essays illustrate the complexity of policy reform and show how there is rarely a simple, stylized fix to problems of economic reform. In coping with complexity, learning is important—as is understanding how an economy gives information about what is being achieved and what further policy changes are needed.

Fourth, the essays illustrate that policy reform depends on process as much as substance. Effective reform involves much more than creating "political will"—it also requires strategic management of the policy process.

Fifth, each country must find its own growth strategy based on an internally driven process responsive to its institutional capacity and economic conditions. The principal failure of the Washington consensus was to suggest—perhaps unintentionally—a monolithic view of development strategy. The discussions in this volume of postcommunist transition in Eastern Europe and the ongoing transformations of China and India drive home the message that paths to development need to be tailored to country-specific institutional capacity. Without the development of a suitably nuanced growth strategy for each country, Africa's growth (and humanitarian) tragedy will continue to haunt humanity, and the sequence of international initiatives that Botchwey discusses will generate little progress.

Sixth, the authors' reflections show that institutions matter both as constraints and defining opportunities. But it would be a mistake to couch this doctrinairely as defining uniquely good institutions for all contexts. To the contrary, history and circumstance matter far more than easy generalization.

Finally, the power of ideas is striking—ideas taught in the classroom to generations of students—in the thinking of the practitioners. They provide a vivid illustration of the increasingly porous boundary between academia and policymaking, across which economic ideas travel easily and influence the world. These essays make plain just how extensive and vigorous this commerce has become. But these ideas are constantly being refined in light of experience (albeit in many cases with a lag). It is to this back and forth between ideas and experience that these essays make a distinctive contribution.

Notes

1. Although it is apparent that the policymakers entered the fray with many shared convictions, it is less clear how much their views have been changed by what they have seen. Insights into such epiphanies are only occasional, and in general it is striking how little self-criticism the essayists voice. No authors say that they got it wrong, and reference to policy error is largely muted.

2. That said, Derviş does note the problems, as a practitioner, of dealing with the Bretton Woods institutions when they are seen primarily as agents of the G-7 countries. There is also a note of skepticism in Botchwey's assessment of the array of initiatives for Africa that have, so far, made little headway against poverty in the region.

3. Even though China does not have a formal system of private property, many of the institutional reforms used in China have replicated the incentives for investment afforded with private property.

4. *Institutions* is used here in the sense first suggested by North as the humanly devised constraints that shape social interaction (or, more succinctly, as the "rules of the game").

5. Classic examples are the separation of powers between a president and legislature or a bicameral parliamentary system.

6. Some of this empirical work is summarized and some broader themes developed under the heading of "New Comparative Economics" in Djankov and others (2003).

7. Recent advances in political economy have suggested that political systems that make greater use of proportional representation are less likely to use selective redistribution policies; see Persson and Tabellini (1999).

8. For example, Djankov and others (2003) argue that greater state ownership of the media is associated with higher corruption.

References

Acemoglu, Daron, Simon Johnson, and James A. Robinson. 2001. "The Colonial Origins of Comparative Development: An Empirical Investigation." *American Economic Review* 91 (5): 1369–1401.

Amsden, Alice. 1989. *Asia's Next Giant: South Korea and Late Industrialization.* New York: Oxford University Press.

Besley, Timothy, and Robin Burgess. 2003. "Halving Global Poverty." *Journal of Economic Perspectives* 17 (3): 3–22.

Djankov, Simeon, Edward Glaeser, Rafael LaPorta, and Florencio Lopez-de-Silanes. 2003. "The New Comparative Economics." Harvard University, Cambridge, Mass.

Djankov, Simeon, Caralee McLeish, Tatiana Nenova, and Andrei Shleifer. 2001. "Who Owns the Media?" Harvard University, Cambridge, Mass.

Easterly, William. 2001. *The Elusive Quest for Growth—Economists' Adventures and Misadventures in the Tropics.* Cambridge, Mass.: MIT Press.

Hall, Robert E., and Chad Jones. 1999. "Why Do Some Countries Produce So Much More Output per Worker than Others?" *Quarterly Journal of Economics* 114: 83–116.

Hausmann, Ricardo, and Dani Rodrik. 2002. "Economic Development as Self-Discovery." NBER Working Paper 8952. National Bureau of Economic Research, Cambridge, Mass.

Mauro, Paulo. 1995. "Corruption and Growth." *Quarterly Journal of Economics* 110 (3): 681–712.

Persson, Torsten, and Guido Tabellini. 1999. "The Size and Scope of Government: Comparative Politics with Rational Politicians." *European Economic Review* 43 (1): 699–735.

Rodrik, Dani. 2003. "Growth Strategies." Harvard University, Cambridge, Mass.

———. 2004. "Getting Institutions Right." Harvard University, Cambridge, Mass.

Rodrik, Dani, Arvind Subramanian, and Francesco Trebbi. 2002. "Institutions Rule: The Primacy of Institutions over Geography and Integration in Economic Development." Harvard University, Cambridge, Mass.

Shleifer, Andrei, and Robert Vishny. 1998. *The Grabbing Hand: Government Pathologies and Their Cures*. Cambridge, Mass.: Harvard University Press.

Wade, Robert. 1990. *Governing the Market: Economic Theory and the Role of the State*. Princeton, N.J.: Princeton University Press.

Williamson, John [2000], "What should the Bank think about the Washington Consensus?", Background Paper for 2000 World Development Report, available at http://www.iie.com/papers/williamson0799.htm.

World Bank. *World Development Report 2004*. New York: Oxford University Press.

Lawrence H. Summers

President, Harvard University;
Former U.S. Secretary of Treasury

Born in New Haven, Connecticut, in 1954, Larry Summers received his Ph.D. in Economics from Harvard University in 1982. By that time he had spent three years as Professor of Economics at the Massachusetts Institute of Technology. He then became a Domestic Policy Economist for the U.S. President's Council of Economic Advisers. In 1983 he returned to Harvard as Professor of Economics, becoming one of the youngest people in recent history to be named a tenured member of the University's faculty. In 1987 he was named Nathaniel Ropes Professor of Political Economy. In 1993 he received the John Bates Clark Medal, awarded every two years to the most outstanding U.S. economist under age 40.

   In 1991 Summers became Vice President of Development Economics and Chief Economist of the World Bank. In 1993 he was named U.S. Under Secretary of the Treasury for International Affairs, with broad responsibility for assisting then Secretary Lloyd M. Bentsen in formulating and executing international economic policies. In 1995 then Secretary Robert E. Rubin promoted Summers to the Department's second-highest post, Deputy Secretary of the Treasury. Over the next few years Summers worked closely with Rubin and Alan Greenspan, Chairman of the Federal Reserve System, in crafting government policy responses to financial crises in major developing countries. In 1999 Summers became Secretary of the Treasury, where he led efforts to enact the most sweeping financial deregulation in 60 years, reform international financial architecture and the International Monetary Fund, secure debt relief for the world's poorest countries, and combat international money laundering. After leaving the Treasury Department in early 2001, Summers became Arthur Okun Distinguished Fellow in Economics, Globalization, and Governance at the Brookings Institution. In July 2001 he took office as 27th president of Harvard University. His many publications include *Understanding Unemployment* (1990) and *Reform in Eastern Europe* (written with others, 1991), as well as more than 100 articles in professional economics journals.

2 Development Lessons of the 1990s

Lawrence H. Summers

When I was appointed chief economist of the World Bank in 1991, I embarked on a profound personal adventure that would ultimately become the most satisfying professional experience of my life. It was at the Bank that I began my close involvement with international economics and development, providing the basis for the lessons I offer here based on my evolving views on these issues.

Of course, memories are selective, and I am sure that some people remember moments of breathtaking naiveté—moments that I have blotted out of my mind—from my tenure at the Bank. For example, within my first month here I traveled to India with D. C. Rao to begin acquainting myself with the developing world. During the trip D. C. made two powerful comments that I have come to fully appreciate only with the passing of time.

At one point in the trip there was quite a bit of disorganization: appointments were being postponed and our transportation was not working quite the way it was supposed to. And when I expressed my frustration with the disorganization, D. C. responded, "Larry, if everything worked the way it did in Boston, it wouldn't be a developing country—and we wouldn't be here." I return to that point below, because it says something powerful about institutions and societies.

The other important thing that D. C. said was in response to various problems we encountered with Bank-supported projects, such as elements not entirely consistent with loan conditions or sector plans. He said, "Larry, in every sector in every developing country, it is easy to think of reasons why things are unsatisfactory, and why not all aid will be used effectively. But the challenge is not to figure out reasons to not be constructive. The challenge is to figure out ways to be constructive—and to make a big difference."

Over time I have come to realize that it is crucial to keep in mind those two perspectives—on the overwhelming importance of institutional capacity and on the challenges facing donors—when analyzing and debating development issues. Yet I suspect that they are neglected by many people with professional backgrounds similar to mine.

The Importance of Institutional Capacity

In reviewing the development experiences of the 1990s, five observations are clear. I have already stated the first one: strong institutions, and the closely related issue of efficient political administration, are essential to effective development. Well-executed policies that are slightly misguided are much more effective than absolutely correct but poorly executed ones.

Myriad examples support this point. Consider the transition economies that emerged in the early 1990s. Almost immediately it became clear that such countries' success depended on their institutional capacity to perform functions taken for granted in advanced market economies.

For example, not long after Robert Rubin became secretary of the U.S. Treasury, I was telling him about a trip I had taken to Russia. One of the stories I shared was about visiting a project designed to help establish custody arrangements for the Russian stock exchange, and hearing about some of the difficulties. After discussing it briefly, Bob said, "You know, Larry, I worked at Goldman Sachs for 26 years, and I was on the board of the New York Stock Exchange for 9 years. And the 5-minute conversation we just had doubles the cumulative amount of time I have spent in my entire lifetime thinking about custody."

Such issues arise throughout an economy, and their importance becomes clear in analyses such as those in the Bank's Doing Business Survey. Part of the survey compares countries with different cultural backgrounds and shows which legal frameworks work best in different contexts. The variations are enormous. In many countries it is not possible to collect on a bounced check. Similarly, in many countries landlords cannot evict tenants who do not pay their rent: not in a week, or a month, or even a year.

So, institutional capacity to conduct basic functions is far more intrinsic to success—or failure—in economic development than many analysts have historically suggested. And over the past decade the Bank has rightly placed enormous emphasis on this difficult issue.[1] It is easy for outside observers to debate more concrete issues, such as tariff rates, budget deficit targets, or approaches to bank supervision. But acquiring the ability to do things in effective, directed, coherent ways is central to successful development, and it is extremely difficult to figure out ways to build that capacity.

I wish I had solutions to this challenge. I support the idea that building such capacity requires strengthening linkages, supporting institutions, and learning to transcend what governments can do by working through all the institutions of society.[2] But I also remember listening to Pedro Malan, when he was Brazil's minister of finance, complain about why, in the name of popular enfranchisement, the political opposition to the program he was implementing—with the strong support of international financial institutions—had to be celebrated by visiting bureaucrats from the U.S. Agency for International Development, World Bank, and other international institutions.

So, although institutional development raises extremely difficult issues, grappling with them is essential. While I was at the Bank, I once made a comment that I no longer think is as clever as I did then, which was that institutional development is a popular topic for Bank papers because it is a great equalizer. My point was that, to discuss which health intervention will be most cost-effective in a given situation, people have to know a lot about health. But if the discussion is about institutional development, every senior manager can provide some off-the-cuff insight. As a result there is a tendency to talk about institutional development.

Though there is some truth to that observation, the problem—which I did not appreciate then in the way I do now—is that the cost-benefit analysis I was applauding will not be very helpful without successful institutional development. Thus it is a huge challenge for development experts—at the Bank, at places like Harvard University, and elsewhere—to build on the recognition of the importance of institutional capacity and to think as constructively as possible about how to develop it. Too often the insight is recognized, platitudes are delivered about transparency and integrity, and little more is done.

Managing Crises and Capital Markets

My second observation from the 1990s is that financial crises have more powerful, long-lasting effects than was previously believed. During the decade many emerging market countries experienced significant market distress. Nearly all these crises were due to a combination of policy errors and bank run mentalities. They were not the result of bank runs in countries pursuing sound financial policies.

In every case, however, the punishment was highly disproportionate to the policy crime. Moreover, the challenge of averting financial crises should be at the fore of the development agenda. Indeed, averting such crises is more important than improving strategies for mitigating them when they occur.

One of the main problems related to such crises involves international capital markets. At any time several dozen countries are borrowing or have borrowed money at spreads of 3, 4, or even 6 percentage points above the standard borrowing rate. A basic fact about pricing is that if countries borrow money at spreads of 3 percentage points, the market is saying that the odds are even that they will default within a decade. If they borrow at spreads of 4 percentage points, the market is saying that they will default within a decade. And if they borrow at spreads of 6 percentage points, their odds of defaulting are even higher.

A healthy capital market can function in two ways. One is the way that the U.S. municipal bond market functions, where no one borrows money at large spread. People borrow money at small spreads, and every so often they default or are on the verge of doing so. But defaults are extremely rare, and when they occur considerable efforts are made to resolve them. That is one way for a healthy capital market to function: planning for safety, and experiencing few actual or even potential defaults.

The second way is the way that high-yield junk bond markets function in Europe and the United States. People issue bonds with various spreads: 4 percentage points, 6, 8, 10. There is no certainty that bondholders will be paid off in full: the principal and interest stated on bonds are the maximum possible payoff, and bondholders realize that they will likely receive less. And when that happens, arrangements are renegotiated and business continues as usual.

But in the world's emerging markets, capital markets are akin to former U.S. President John F. Kennedy's joke about Washington, D.C. being a city that combines southern efficiency with northern charm. Pricing assumes that crises will be likely and that efforts to resolve them will be ineffective.

Yet it does not make much sense for investors to look at a country with a 5 or 6 percentage point spread on its bonds and conclude that that the bonds cannot or will not be paid in full—and then act like that outcome reflects extreme malfeasance by the authorities or a dramatic change in global economic circumstances that has victimized the country. When such bonds are issued, everyone who buys and sells them only has to look at their pricing to know that such an outcome was likely.

The question is which way such markets should be pushed: toward easier workouts or toward less cross-border, high-yield debt. And until that decision is made, it will be difficult to make much progress on financial crises and capital market weaknesses.

I believe that it would be preferable to push toward lower-yield debt, given the lack of evidence that high-yield debt is consistently used in ways that generate returns equal to its cost. Still, I am not certain that is the right approach. The problem is clear; the solution much less so.

There have been many claims, including by one of my successors as the Bank's chief economist, that crises in developing countries result from weaknesses due to financial liberalization imposed by industrial countries. Certainly, maintaining a healthy banking and financial system is crucial as liberalization occurs, and no one has ever suggested otherwise. But the major financial crises of the 1990s did not occur because innocent countries were overwhelmed by capital inflows from herds of speculators. Rather, they happened because country policies actively encouraged "dining with the devil" of speculators—and the countries ended up on the menu.

For example, Mexico's *tesobono* was a financial instrument tailored to short-term speculators. Thailand's offshore banking facility, which received favorable tax treatment, aimed to attract short-term interbank credit. Republic of Korea's capital control regime explicitly sought to ensure that capital inflows were short-term rather than longer-term. And Brazil's financial strategy involved issuing debt instruments carefully designed to meet the needs of hedge funds.

Under these circumstances the question is not, shouldn't those countries have had some kind of capital controls like those in Chile? Not only did they not have such controls, they were actively seeking short-term capital. And to my knowledge, such an approach has never been advocated by international financial institutions or industrial country governments. In that regard, maintaining a fixed exchange rate with the implied option value for those holding foreign currency to always get out at a fixed price represents a particularly pernicious kind of subsidy to short-term capital.

Finally, on the policy response to short-term capital and to financial crisis, in every case there has been more policy flexibility in the year after a crisis than in the preceding or succeeding decade. So it seems appropriate that efforts at policy reform be concentrated in such periods, and I hope that as the Bank conceptualizes its future role—and recognizes that fewer countries should need its finance because of their access to private markets—emergency lending at times of major malleability will play a larger role in its operations.

Facing Uncertainties and Questions

My third observation is that it is impossible to predict economic and other developments, and that countries should be careful what they wish for. In the wake of the East Asian financial crisis, many analysts—including me—recommended that emerging market economies build up reserves to reduce the risks of future crises. I still think that was good advice.

But in today's international financial system the largest net flow comes from the world's richest, most powerful country borrowing on a massive scale from countries containing a significant portion of the world's poorest people. And those loans, with a 1 percent interest rate ex ante, have a negative effective rate when likely currency movements are taken into account. Having such a huge flow of borrowing from the world's richest country, at interest rates below 1 percent, raises questions about how well the international financial system is working.

Recognizing the Fungibility of Aid

My fourth observation from the 1990s is that careful attention should be paid to the implications that fungibility has for development assistance. When I began working at the Bank, I realized that when it came to truly important projects, developing country governments would pursue them with or without Bank support. So, I concluded, what Bank support is really doing is providing budget support for marginal projects that otherwise would not occur. And I found that Bank staff generally agreed with me.

That attitude made me a bit frustrated, so I called Stanley Fischer, my predecessor, and asked how he felt about fungibility. He paused in a judicious way and said, "Well, Larry, when I first got to the Bank, I was really worried about it, and I used to ask people about it all the time. But eventually I sort of got used to it and stopped asking people about it. And when we analyze our projects, they're good—so I guess we're doing good things."

Joking aside, fungibility raises serious issues that the Bank and other donors tend to lose sight of as they go about their business. For example, at the International Monetary Fund (IMF) it is standard doctrine that sterilized intervention does not work, and that IMF funds should not be used for direct budget support. Yet the IMF still engages in sterilized intervention.

Similar issues arise with Bank funds. For example, I recall negotiations involving the IMF, the Bank, and Pedro Malan, and the IMF officials had set a budget target for Brazil and were trying to develop a financing plan, and they wanted the Bank to provide money according to the plan. But the Bank officials were hesitant, because they wanted to ensure that any new financing from the Bank was clearly tied to its development objectives and activities. So, for example, for $1 in Bank loans, they wanted to have $2 of social safety net activities, because Bank funds are supposed to be catalytic.

Then I spoke with Pedro, who wanted to secure as much financing as possible. I think that his strategy was to promote great innovation in some social safety net programs so that the Bank would achieve its desired development impact and the IMF would meet its budget target. And thanks to Pedro's leadership, very good things happened in Brazil. Still, questions about fungibility and the use of aid money require a lot of further reflection.

Building a Constituency for Development

My final observation is that there is a profound need in the United States to build a constituency for development and for meeting the needs of the world's poorest people. Over the past decade the Bank has done good work in this area, as has the United Nations. I also tried to advance this goal when I was at the U.S. Treasury.

Yet it is a continuing mystery and major problem that if one speaks with young people at different levels—from my daughter's classmates in junior high school to students at Harvard—they are seized by the real and enormous problem of species becoming extinct. And by the very real problem of global warming. And increasingly, by the problem of AIDS and its potential consequences.

But the problem of the 1 billion people living on less than $1 a day does not evoke their passionate interest in the same way as environmental issues. I am not in any way denying the importance of environmental issues. Rather, I am identifying an enormous political challenge for those of us who care about development. Moreover, much of today's concern about development is defined as much by an anticapitalism and antimarket attitude as it is by a genuine desire to help the world's poorest people.

Such short-sighted views are a huge problem, because mobilizing energy around the development agenda is crucial to continuing the great work that the Bank does, to enlisting the support needed for the Bank to maintain its scale in a growing global economy, and to mobilizing the intellectual, moral, and financial support required to achieve the Millennium Development Goals.

I do not know how to build such support. It may be that the developments related to the Millennium Challenge Account and other things that have occurred in recent years—even if one does not always like the method—represent progress in raising consciousness. Again, though, my final observation from the 1990s is the need to strengthen political support in rich countries for development efforts in poor ones.

Notes

1. Bank President James Wolfensohn did the developing world a major service early in his tenure when he placed corruption and related issues at the top of the Bank's development agenda. The once-common view, that corruption greases wheels that would otherwise grind to a halt, captures a small truth. But the much larger truth recognizes the damage done by corruption and the opportunities lost through the rent seeking associated with it.

2. Although I believe that nongovernmental organizations (NGOs) should be more active in providing services as a way of developing institutional capacity, that approach also has short-comings. I will never forget an African health minister who, after hearing me praise a project being conducted by an NGO in his country, agreed that the project was remarkable. But he also told me that 6 of his 10 most competent employees had left the ministry to work for the project, at salaries four times what he could pay them.

Comment

Pedro Malan

IT IS A PLEASURE TO BE HERE, AND IT IS ALWAYS EXTREMELY REWARDING TO LISTEN to Larry Summers—something I have been doing for many years, as well as sharing many experiences with him, good and bad. Speakers in this series were asked to address the development issues of the 1990s, which along with the 1980s is often viewed as a lost decade for development. But that view is too negative, and risks overlooking some important lessons from these so-called failed decades.

International Aspects of Development

Larry touches on this point when he recounts some conversations with D. C. Rao. It is easy to take a cynical view of development, but doing so can undermine prospects for change. So, though it is crucial to raise questions and apply intellectual reasoning—as Larry has shown his ability to do—we must not lose compassion for the deprived people who are the focus of development efforts.

The challenge, as Larry says, is to be constructive. For example, during the 1980s and 1990s some developing countries claimed that their enormous debts were due to external events beyond their control, and said that they were victims of biased international trade and financial systems. In response, industrial countries blamed debtor countries for following the wrong policies, and argued that adopting the right policies would lead to better results.

One of the positive outcomes of these often heated discussions was a recognition that developing countries cannot claim to be passive victims. At the same time, domestic policies cannot solve all problems. We live in an international system, and though the initial conditions in developing countries are important, so are the trade and financial links between countries.

I fully agree with Larry's final point on the need for more support from rich countries to reduce the appalling poverty and deprivation in poor ones. To solve these problems, we must understand them better. But as World Bank research has found, the solutions must be found by those working in a given country or system: they cannot be imposed from afar. Thus aid donors and recipients must work together in a comprehensive, constructive way—building on experience—or there will continue to be many countries with incomes lower than they were 20 years ago. I hope that the Bank will continue to play a central role in such efforts.

Such efforts must also recognize the essential role of trade. The 2001 World Trade Organization meeting in Doha, Qatar, committed all countries to reducing (with a view to eliminating) trade-distorting subsidies on domestic production, reflecting the importance of increasing market access and reducing protectionism. Yet such import obstacles remain strong in some key countries, especially around elections, often based on the argument that jobs must be preserved. This is a challenge for countries both rich and poor. Given the importance of trade for development, I hope that the progress made at Doha and at the U.N. Conference on Financing for Development (held in Monterrey, Mexico, in 2002) will not be lost, and I count on the Bank to help sustain it.

Domestic Concerns

I will now shift my focus from international concerns, because my many years of experience in Brazil have taught me that when push comes to shove, the fundamental battles of development are fought on the domestic front. Here I will discuss four achievements that were essential to the success of Fernando Henrique Cardoso's administration in Brazil, and that are crucial to economic and social development in Brazil and many other developing countries.

The first is macroeconomic stability: the notion that any government, regardless of its ideology, must be committed to maintaining fiscal balance, controlling inflation, and ensuring the intertemporal solvency of the public sector.

The second achievement is institutional, political, administrative, and judicial stability, including predictable rules and transparent, high-quality, well-functioning government. Moreover, the quality and efficiency of government cannot be dissociated from the quality and efficiency of its institutions. In addition, a country's civil society must be able to express itself effectively.

The third achievement is creating a basis for sustained growth. Long-term economic and social development requires increasing labor productivity over time. A country's ability to raise productivity depends not only on its capital, the strength of its capital accumulation, and the quality of its most important asset—its people—but also on its ability to innovate and introduce technological change into productive and economic activities. Essential to this is expanding the size of the tradable sector as a share of GDP. That share provides an objective measure of a country's productivity: its ability to compete in international and domestic markets. Increasing productivity also requires investing in people and education.

The final achievement is sustained improvement in living standards for the majority of a country's people. The three other achievements are not really ends in themselves, but are essential for achieving other goals. This one is an end in itself. Still, it is difficult to significantly reduce poverty and income inequality without sustained progress in the three other areas.

Higher living standards should be a central, long-term objective of any economic policy, and in many countries offer the most promising avenue for reducing poverty and inequality. For example, they provide a starting point for serious discussions on the level and composition of government social spending, with a view to making programs more efficient and developing mechanisms for society to supervise and assess them. Nongovernmental organizations (NGOs) have an important role to play here.

But the experiences of Brazil and many other countries show that an effective long-term attack on poverty and inequality requires more than the achievements above. It also requires financing: without it, there is no hope for serious change. This view is being recognized by the international community, including the World Bank. Achieving economic and social change and development will also require continuing efforts by international institutions and continuing honest discussions between these institutions and industrial and developing countries—both their governments and their people.

Moving forward, one of the most important things is to be forward looking, and to look to the future with confidence. But to avoid creating unrealistic expectations about short-term change, our visions of the future must be grounded in lessons from the past. Otherwise we risk generating a lack of interest in and dedication to development, instead of a desire for and commitment to change. My hope and expectation is that Brazil and most other countries will continue to make progress in achieving three basic features that make a society worth living in: individual liberties, social justice, and increased efficiency in both the private and public sectors.

Comment

Michael Mussa

I HAVE KNOWN LARRY SUMMERS FOR MANY YEARS. I THINK I FIRST MET HIM WHEN he came for a job interview at the University of Chicago. Quite rightly, the Economics Department was eager to hire him. But, probably wisely, he turned down that offer. In 1991, when I joined the International Monetary Fund (IMF) as economic counselor, Larry had recently been appointed the World Bank's chief economist. We met to discuss coordinating our departments' research agendas but, both being sensible, quickly concluded that we should instead focus on doing what we each thought best.

Several traits set Larry apart from many other high-ranking public officials. First, he is willing to listen to an argument based on logic and fact and, if that argument is persuasive, to alter his position. Second, though he is extremely intelligent, he does not believe that he knows all the answers—or even understands all the important questions. Finally, Larry understands, as Abraham Lincoln put it, that few things are wholly evil or wholly good. Almost everything, especially in government policy, is an inseparable compound of the two. On many public policy issues it is difficult to distinguish the right from the wrong and the right step in the wrong direction from the wrong step in the right direction. Yet throughout his career, Larry has maintained a remarkably open mind and considerable humility in the face of daunting problems.

Institutions and Development

In his lecture Larry first addresses the same issue that I would have put first in discussing development challenges of the 1990s: the transcendental importance of strong institutions and efficient political administration in implementing policies, economic and noneconomic. Although this issue was not entirely new, it came to the fore in the 1990s because of the transition of Central and Eastern Europe and the former Soviet Union from centrally planned to market economies. That situation focused attention on institutional development in a way that had not been as dramatic in earlier discussions.

But the importance of institutions has long been recognized. Indeed, after I joined the IMF and began to have some involvement with these issues—particularly relating to transition economies—I reread the famous address that George Marshall (author of the Marshall Plan) delivered at Harvard University in 1947. There Marshall said that in assessing Europe's needs after World War II, the loss of life and the destruction of cities, factories, mines, and railroads had been estimated correctly. But it had become obvious that this visible destruction was probably less serious than the damage done to the entire fabric of the European economy. Thus, Marshall said, rehabilitating Europe's economic structure would require much more time and effort than had been foreseen.

That outcome was the result of 10 years of Nazi dislocation in Europe. After 70 years of the Soviet Union and 40 years of Soviet occupation of Central and Eastern Europe, transition economies faced a far greater challenge, because much of the institutional basis for a modern economic system had been destroyed.

The absence of stable institutions that provide reasonable security to people and property destroys all aspirations for economic development. Indeed, in *The Wealth of Nations* Adam Smith concludes that commerce and manufacturing seldom flourish in any state where justice is not administered consistently, where people do not feel secure in the possession of their property, where contracts are not enforced by law, and where the authority of the state is not used to enforce payments of debt from those able to pay. In short, commerce and manufacturing seldom flourish where there is not a certain degree of confidence in the justice of government.

Thus the role of institutions in economic development has long been recognized, and in the 1990s it was right to emphasize their importance. James Wolfensohn at the World Bank and Michel Camdessus at the IMF were entirely justified in focusing on corruption, disruption, and the like as key impediments to economic progress in many countries. When ownership and control of a society's wealth and productive assets are up for grabs, economic development will be limited. That is a crucial lesson, and Larry is right to emphasize it.

Varying Patterns of—and Responses to—Financial Crises

Larry's second observation involves financial crises, which were certainly common in the 1990s. But again, financial crises did not begin in the 1990s, and they have not been limited to emerging market economies.

For example, the U.S. Panic of 1837 was a financial crisis that resulted from a relaxation of financial discipline and an explosion of borrowing by state-chartered banks to finance canals and other infrastructure investments. That panic, which would now be called a recession or depression, was similar to many emerging market crises in the 1990s. Many other industrial countries have also experienced financial crises at various points in history.

What makes industrial countries today less subject to the damage from international financial crises than they were 75–150 years ago? Since the early 1990s, for example, Japan's economy has suffered from financial excesses in the late 1980s and the subsequent collapse of the asset bubble. But unlike the United States during the Great Depression, where nominal GDP fell by 45 percent between 1929 and 1933, Japan has not experienced an economic catastrophe. Similarly, aside from a mild recession in 2001, the United States has survived a deflating of the NASDAQ asset bubble without major long-term damage.

A key part of the reason industrial countries are less subject to the damage from financial crises is that their economic policies are much better able to ameliorate the effects of economic declines, including asset price declines, than are policies in emerging market economies. In the U.S. recession of 2001, the government was able to shift its budget position from a surplus of 2 percent of GDP to a deficit of more than 4 percent—resulting in a shallow, short recession. If Brazil had tried to massively increase its budget deficit in 2002 in the face of pressure in its financial markets, domestic and international markets would have responded with alarm and doubt, and interest rate spreads would have risen 20–30 points higher than they did.

There are many other similar examples. Emerging market economies simply do not have the same flexibility to use fiscal policy to combat recessions or deal with economic crises. This same is true for monetary policy. Between late 2001 and 2003 the U.S. Federal Reserve dramatically eased monetary policy, cutting the interest rate on federal funds from 6.5 percent to 1.0 percent. But when Brazil tried to cut the SELIC rate by half a point during its 2002 crisis, from 18.5 to 18.0 percent, the market did not buy it. Indeed, after the new administration entered office, the Central Bank had to raise interest rates from 18 percent to 28 percent to reestablish monetary control.

Some analysts argue that such patterns are inevitable: that when a country has a long history of financial mismanagement, markets—domestic and international—will be suspicious of its future performance. And many emerging market economies have long histories of financial instability. It will take time and consistently good policies to overcome this problem.

Another difference between the two groups of countries is that industrial countries, such as the United States, conduct their domestic business using domestic currency, and can also (to the extent that they desire) conduct most of their international business in domestic currencies. If IBM, a U.S. multinational corporation, wants to deal in euros in Europe, it can. If it wants to borrow dollars in the United States, it can. It can conduct its business in whatever currency is most convenient.

But that is typically not the case for emerging market economies. When governments and companies in these countries access international credit markets, they almost always have to borrow in one of the major international currencies. Similarly, if companies in these countries want to conduct international business, most of it must be done in international currencies. Indeed, in countries with long histories of financial turbulence, a good deal of domestic business must also be done in international currencies.

Thus the international community needs to maintain a facility that, in the event of a financial crisis, can provide substantial monetary assistance in the form of international currencies. Because unlike in the United States, where the Federal Reserve can print as many dollars as it feels may be needed to deal with a financial crisis, Brazil cannot do so if it faces a shortage of foreign currency. So, part of the solution to potential crises in emerging market economies should be—in addition to limiting the risks that give rise to such crises—developing better mechanisms to provide financial support for countries taking actions to deal with the problems that gave rise to those crises.

John Williamson

Senior Fellow, Institute for International Economics

John Williamson has enjoyed a long and storied career as an academic, practitioner, and commenter on development economics. After obtaining his Ph.D. from Princeton University in 1963, he served as Professor of Economics in a number of academic appointments, including at Princeton (1962–63), University of York (1963–68), Massachusetts Institute of Technology (1967, 1980), University of Warwick (1970–77), and Pontificia Universidade Católica do Rio de Janeiro (1978–81). During this period he also served as Economic Consultant to the U.K. Treasury (1968–70) and Adviser to the International Monetary Fund (1972–74). Williamson first made his mark as an academic by advocating the adoption of a *crawling peg* for exchange rates, a term he coined that has since become common parlance in the economics profession. He has continued to write about exchange rate policy throughout his career.

After a successful career in academia, in 1981 Williamson joined the newly formed Institute for International Economics as Senior Fellow, a position he still holds today. Through his work at the Institute he has written or edited numerous studies on international monetary issues and developing country debt, including *Dollar Adjustment: How Far? Against What?* (with C. Fred Bergsten, 2004), *After the Washington Consensus: Restoring Growth and Reform in Latin America* (with Pedro Pablo Kuczynski, 2003), *Delivering on Debt Relief: From IMF Gold to a New Aid Architecture* (2002), *Exchange Rate Regimes for Emerging Markets: Reviving the Intermediate Option* (2000), *The Crawling Band as an Exchange Rate Regime* (1996), *What Role for Currency Boards?* (1995), *Estimating Equilibrium Exchange Rates* (1994), *The Political Economy of Policy Reform* (1993), *Economic Consequences of Soviet Disintegration* (1993), *Currency Convertibility in Eastern Europe* (1991), *Latin American Adjustment: How Much Has Happened?* (1990), and *Targets and Indicators: A Blueprint for the International Coordination of Economic Policy* (with Marcus Miller, 1987).

Williamson's best-known contribution to economics is his description of the *Washington consensus*, a term he coined in a 1990 paper. Though the term has since taken on a life of its own, Williamson's original paper had the humble goal of describing 10 economic policies about which there was considerable agreement in Washington, D.C. policy circles. During the 1990s the Washington consensus became the central point of debate about development policy, and continues to inspire lively discussion today.

3 The Washington Consensus as Policy Prescription for Development

John Williamson

THE WASHINGTON CONSENSUS AS I ORIGINALLY FORMULATED IT WAS NOT A POLICY prescription for development. It was a list of policies that I claimed analysts in Washington, D.C., considered widely desirable for Latin American countries at the time, in the second half of 1989. Although development was the main objective of the countries in question, the point is that my agenda excluded policies even if I believed they would promote development, unless I was also convinced that they commanded consensus.

But the Washington consensus has been widely interpreted—including by sympathetic observers such as Fischer (2003), not just by critics—as offering a policy prescription (and as having broader application beyond Latin America). That is sufficient to make it of interest to ask whether it was a good prescription. Asking that question also provides the occasion to ask what a good policy prescription would be.

What Is (or Was) the Washington Consensus?

As I have complained on innumerable occasions, the term *Washington consensus* has been used in very different ways. One can distinguish at least three distinct meanings:

- My original usage: a list of 10 policy reforms that I argued were widely agreed in Washington to be desirable for just about all Latin American countries as of 1989. That is how the consensus acquired "Washington" in its title, which was unfortunate because it suggested to the conspiratorially minded that this was a list of policies that Washington was seeking to impose on the world, and to some reformers that Washington was seeking to take credit for the reforms they were implementing. I first described the Washington consensus in a background paper for a conference, and one of the purposes of the conference was to explore how much Washington's views on development had changed in the 1980s. Focusing on Latin America, we concluded that there the changes were significant. We at the Institute for International Economics like to think that we helped this process along, principally through a tract that Bela Balassa took the lead in writing for us in his year off from the World Bank (Balassa and others 1986).

- A set of economic policies advocated for developing countries in general by official Washington—meaning international financial institutions (primarily the International Monetary Fund and the World Bank) and the U.S. Treasury. Dani Rodrik (2002, table 1) provides a convenient summary of what he conceived this to consist of in 1999. The original 10 points were augmented with another 10, with a heavy emphasis on institutional reforms and some recognition of social concerns. This is also the flavor of the eligibility requirements for the Millennium Challenge Account, which is the main attempt by the Bush administration to help low-income countries.

- Critics' beliefs about the policies that international financial institutions are seeking to impose on their clients. These vary by critic but usually include the view that international financial institutions are agents of "neoliberalism" and so are seeking to minimize the role of the state. An odd feature of this literature is that it almost never includes any citations to substantiate the views that the authors attribute to the international financial institutions. Indeed, many of these authors are out of touch with reality. For example, they often claim that international financial institutions are pushing cost recovery in primary education—a terrible policy that was pursued in the early 1980s but was progressively abandoned in subsequent years following the admirable report *Adjustment with a Human Face* (Cornia, Jolly, and Stewart 1987).

In this lecture I use *Washington consensus* in the first sense, but let me briefly comment on the differences between the three meanings. To the extent that I was an accurate reporter of the Washington scene in 1989, the first two meanings should have coincided. But in fact, I allowed wishful thinking to cloud my judgment of what commanded consensus in one respect, and that involved exchange-rate policy. I doubt whether even at that time the overwhelming bulk of Washington opinion would have endorsed a competitive exchange rate (which implies an intermediate exchange rate regime dedicated to limiting misalignments) rather than one or another of the two poles (free floating or firmly fixed, both of which are liable to generate misalignments).

This remains an issue between the original and "augmented" versions of the Washington consensus.[1] In later years a further divergence emerged, as the IMF (supported by the U.S. Treasury) often pressed its clients to quickly dismantle capital controls. I believed at the time that this was playing with fire, and since the East Asian crisis that view is no longer sacrilegious—at least within the international financial institutions, whose position can reasonably be summarized à la Rodrik as favoring "prudent" opening of the capital account.[2] There are also ways in which the positions of the Bretton Woods institutions changed with the times, in ways that I would endorse, of which the most notable was the emphasis on institution building (so-called second generation reforms).

I do not see any close connection between the third concept of the Washington consensus and the first two. It seems to me that since the word consensus implies a wide measure of agreement, there is an obligation on those who use the term in this way (the most intellectually eminent being Joseph Stiglitz) to demonstrate that the views they subsume under the term are indeed widely held in Washington, or at least in the international financial institutions. This they have notably failed to do, for the compelling reason that these views are not widely endorsed even in the IMF, let alone the World Bank. Accordingly I regard this usage of the term as mischievous.

Evaluating the Ten Commandments

In this section I discuss whether each of the 10 policy reforms that made up the original Washington consensus was a good tool for promoting development. I then assess—in very broad terms—where and how widely the reforms were adopted. In the next section I consider whether they collectively amounted to an adequate program for accelerating development. The descriptions of the 10 points are taken from Williamson (1994, pp. 26–28).

1. "Budget deficits…small enough to be financed without recourse to the inflation tax."

The view was widely held in the late 1980s that macroeconomic stability was an indispensable precondition for growth, that reasonable price stability was an essential aspect of macroeconomic stability, and that in most Latin American countries (except Chile and Colombia) price stability had been undermined by excessive budget deficits. Thus it was essential to restore fiscal discipline. My formulation focused on the need for sufficient fiscal discipline to avoid the need to resort to the inflation tax.

I am unimpressed by Stiglitz's argument (citing Bruno and Easterly 1998) that because moderate price inflation has no measurable growth effect, it has no serious welfare consequences—so one should be prepared to accept higher inflation and the larger budget deficits it would permit. I do not agree with that argument primarily because of evidence that, at least in Latin America, inflation is a regressive tax (see, for example, Cardoso, Pães de Barros, and Urani 1995). Because I am also persuaded by the evidence that the Phillips curve is vertical in the long run, permanent acceptance of more than a minimal inflation rate strikes me as misguided.

I find two other criticisms of my formulation far more compelling. The first is that it focuses only on inflation as the ill consequence of an excessive deficit. In Latin America in the 1980s, where few countries had much capacity to finance deficits by issuing domestic debt, that might have been reasonable. But the crises of the past few years have made it abundantly clear that inflation is by no means the only misfortune that a country risks by allowing an excessive fiscal deficit: excessive debt creation can also lead to unsustainable debt dynamics. Note that this criticism reinforces rather than undermines the case for fiscal discipline. It merely says that the criterion of fiscal discipline that I specified needs to be supplemented.

The second criticism is that this point focuses exclusively on stabilizing inflation, and neglects the Keynesian case for stabilizing the real economy. In another lecture in this series, Alejandro Foxley (in this volume), Chile's first minister of finance after the restoration of democracy in 1990, describes how the government of which he was part ran budget surpluses and restricted foreign capital inflows when the economy was booming and foreign capital was trying to flood in.[3] The democratic government had inherited a high inflation rate (more than 20 percent a year), and it neither decided to live with this permanently nor focus on rapidly establishing price stability. Instead it lowered inflation gradually over the 1990s. I believe that wise macroeconomic policies were an important cause of Chile's success during that decade, and I worry that the Central Bank's current exclusive focus on stabilizing inflation makes it unlikely that the country will enjoy similar success in the current decade. But again, this criticism does not make a case for looser fiscal policy. It says that fiscal policy should be tight during booms so that it can be easy during recessions.

Even if Robert Lucas (2003) is right in his argument that the welfare gains from better stabilization are derisorily small in the United States—and I will be surprised if he is not challenged on that contention—I doubt that anyone would argue the same in the context of developing countries. The wasted resources that are underused during recessions continue to be massive. But the potential benefit of keeping economies operating close to capacity is not simply the difference between an exogenous level of full capacity output and the actual path of output, unless one is prepared to argue that the path of full capacity output is indeed exogenous. If one believes rather that investment raises output capacity,[4] and one also accepts the strong evidence that investment is responsive to the pressure of demand on capacity (the capacity accelerator), then successful stabilization will have the additional benefit of leading to faster supply-side growth. That is surely an important part of success stories such as Chile and East Asia: full employment and continued growth increased incentives to invest and so reinforced growth.

2. "Redirecting [public] expenditure from politically sensitive areas…[that] receive more resources than their economic return can justify…toward neglected fields with high economic returns and the potential to improve income distribution, such as primary health and education, and infrastructure."

Contrary to charges leveled by most critics, my version of the Washington consensus did not call for general cuts in public spending. I would not deny that there are people in Washington who share the *Wall Street Journal's* attitude on this issue, but I did not feel that they commanded a consensus. By the late 1980s—after *Adjustment with a Human Face*—there was, instead, substantial support—especially in the World Bank—for redirecting public spending in a pro-poor and pro-growth way, from things like nonmerit subsidies[5] to basic social services and infrastructure. So that is what I put in the Washington consensus (though most of its critics seem completely unaware of that fact).

Subsequent events have only reinforced my belief that the attitude expressed in this policy reform is thoroughly correct. Unfortunately, there has not been much progress in this area since 1989. I have never thought, for example, that the Bank's Public Expenditure Reviews have much effect on countries' public spending priorities.

I fear that many public spending decisions are not based on what economists consider rational criteria. Moreover, sharp cuts in public spending do not raise the average quality of spending or eliminate waste. On the contrary, my impression is that worthwhile spending typically gets cut by as much as waste. I believe that efficient public spending requires establishing a chain of command of people in the public administration who believe in the ends of the programs being pursued. I see no short cuts.

3. "Tax reform...[to broaden] the tax base and cut...marginal tax rates."

The ideal for this proposal was the Bradley-Kemp tax act enacted in the United States in 1986. Whether or not people believe that public expenditures are important enough to justify relatively high taxes (as Bill Bradley did and Jack Kemp did not), almost everyone agrees that needed taxes should be raised efficiently, without a panoply of distorting exemptions that force high marginal tax rates on things that are not exempted.

This was not the consideration that drove tax reform in most developing countries during the 1990s. The dominant reform was the introduction or extension of a value added tax (VAT), driven by the desire for a resilient, broadly based (and thus relatively nondistorting) revenue source, partly to offset the revenue loss resulting from tariff reductions. The main problem with a VAT is that it is regressive, and for reasons I have never understood the international financial institutions have tended to be hostile to correcting this weakness by exempting basic necessities like food and medicine.

My basic purpose in this lecture is to ask whether the recommendations in my version of the Washington consensus make sense as policy prescriptions for development. Given that my formulation missed the basic objective that drove tax reform in the 1990s, I find it difficult to give myself high marks—even though the point I made is perfectly sensible. A policy agenda for development should have focused on how additional revenue should be raised, given the widespread need to correct budget deficits, increase public spending (in many countries), and replace revenue lost through trade reform. That approach would have compelled recognition that increased use of VATs would be regressive, and invited discussions on how to correct that.

4. "Financial liberalization, [with] an ultimate objective...of market-determined interest rates."

In the late 1990s, when Molly Mahar and I wrote a survey of the subject, we distinguished six dimensions of financial liberalization: whether credit is allocated by government or the market, whether interest rates are set by government or the market, whether government imposes entry barriers to the financial sector, whether government regulates bank operations or allows banks to operate autonomously,[6] whether government owns banks, and whether international capital flows are regulated or liberalized (Williamson and Mahar 1998). But in 1989 I still thought of financial liberalization primarily in terms of moving to market-determined interest rates, with what I saw as a corollary of allowing banks or markets, rather than government, determine who receives credit—that is, in terms of the first two dimensions of my later taxonomy. I did not, however, argue for liberalization of the capital account.

The case for financial liberalization had been persuasively argued by Ronald McKinnon (1973) and Edward Shaw (1973). But the first experiences in applying it, in the Southern Cone countries in the late 1970s, had been disastrous. Subsequent postmortems by economists yielded two explanations. One was sequencing: conventional wisdom came to hold that one of the last things that should be done in a liberalization program is to open the capital account, and that one of several preconditions for this should be a liberalized, robust banking system capable of intermediating capital inflows to where the social returns would be highest. This reasoning suggested that the Southern Cone countries had liberalized capital inflows prematurely.

The second explanation involved financial supervision. Because of the temptations posed by asymmetric information, a liberalization program that allows the private sector to decide who receives credit needs to be accompanied by measures that ensure lenders make decisions based on tradeoffs between social returns and risks. Temptations to engage in insider lending and gambling for redemption must be disciplined by imposing on bankers the potential obligation to explain their decisions to supervisors. This reasoning suggested that the Southern Cone countries had liberalized their financial systems before satisfying necessary institutional preconditions.

The past decade has provided substantial evidence that financial liberalization can yield real social benefits in terms of better allocations of investment (Bekaert, Harvey, and Lundblad 2001; Caprio and Honohan 2001; Rajan and Zingales 2003; Williamson and Mahar 1998)—but also that it can be dangerous. The crises that have engulfed so many developing countries are testimony to that. To me this implies that the objective of liberalization makes sense, but that it needs to be qualified in two important ways. One is delaying capital account liberalization until many other reforms have been successfully completed; since my version of the Washington consensus did not call for capital account liberalization in (see the discussion of point 7 below), I got that point right. Where I failed was in not emphasizing the need to accompany financial liberalization with the creation of appropriate supervisory institutions.

5. "A unified…exchange rate…at a level sufficiently competitive to induce a rapid growth in non-traditional exports."

As noted, this is the subject on which I feel I did the least adequate job as a reporter of the Washington scene. I consider myself very much a disciple of Bela Balassa in believing that export growth is key to igniting a general growth process and that a competitive exchange rate is key to export growth, or at least growth of nontraditional exports.[7] If one worries about having an exchange rate sufficiently competitive to induce rapid export growth, then one will be driven to support some type of intermediate exchange rate, because both fixed and floating rates imply government acquiescence in whatever real exchange rate happens to result from market forces. But in fact most of Washington, like most of the economics profession, seems content with one or the other of these polar positions. Indeed, a couple years ago it seemed to be widely believed that supporting anything else was a mark of mental imbecility.

Although I fear that my version of the Washington consensus was bad reporting of the Washington scene, I still think it was an admirable prescription for development. I do not believe that Washington institutions or the economics profession did a service to development through their infatuation with the bipolar solution. Fortunately, support for that approach seemed to disappear after the recent Argentine crisis.

6. "Quantitative trade restrictions should be rapidly replaced by tariffs, and these should be progressively reduced until a uniform low rate of 10 [to 20] percent is achieved."

It seems sensible to initiate trade liberalization by eliminating quantitative restrictions and replacing them with high tariffs, because doing so channels rents to the government instead of privileged importers and allows imports to expand in response to shocks that increase the need for them. It also seems sensible to progressively reduce tariffs until there is ambiguity about whether the benefits of freer imports are outweighed by a terms of trade cost, loss of bargaining power in the World Trade Organization, or both. I asserted that would happen with a uniform tariff in the range of 10 or at most 20 percent. That was admittedly a guess, but it was intentionally above the 0 percent that many trade economists would argue to be appropriate for a small country. Two issues on which my formulation deliberately did not take a stand were how quickly to reduce protection and whether to make the speed of dismantling protection endogenously dependent on the strength of the balance of payments, as in Western Europe after World War II.

Most critics of this point have been noneconomists who believe that reducing protection threatens jobs. There are two ripostes to that claim. One is that higher prices for imported intermediate goods will reduce jobs in end use industries even at a constant exchange rate, and that this effect may outweigh the direct effect of the increased number of jobs in intermediate goods industries. (This effect dominated recent steel protection in the United States; see Hufbauer and Goodrich 2003.)

The other retort is that the real exchange rate may adjust to a reduction in protection. Indeed, this is the standard assumption implicitly or explicitly used by economists analyzing this issue, and implies that whatever else it may do a reduction in protection will not cause a net loss of jobs. But one of the problems with trade liberalization in the 1990s, especially in Latin America, was that no attempt was made to ensure that this assumption was satisfied. Capital inflows were often allowed to appreciate real exchange rates to the point where there was indeed a net loss of jobs in tradable goods industries.

Another common critique is that an obligation to liberalize trade precludes a country from using protection to nurture infant industries. I imagine that most of us here have at some point made jokes about infant industries that failed to grow up, and in most cases such remarks are justified. But there are also occasional cases, such as Brazil's automobile industry, where an industry nurtured by protection has grown up to be internationally competitive. If a country is going to subsidize an industry for that type of reason, the theory of optimal intervention says that such support is better provided by a direct subsidy than by a tariff. But many developing countries are subject to fiscal pressures that preclude that possibility.

So, perhaps there should be a mechanism in the World Trade Organization allowing developing countries to nurture infant industries using temporary protection as long as they announce and register their intentions—and simultaneously announce and register timetables under which the protection will be phased out. If a country failed to abide by its declared intentions, it could face sanctions similar to those used to enforce other World Trade Organization rules. (It might also be necessary to craft rules to limit the extent of the temporary protection, in terms of its duration and the size of the initial tariff, but I will not address that issue here.)

7. "Barriers impeding the entry of foreign [direct investment] should be abolished."

In 1989 many developing countries were still reluctant to accept foreign investment, including foreign direct investment. That did not make economic sense. Even those of us who have emotional reservations about the global spread of Mickey Mouse and McDonalds can have sufficient respect for consumer sovereignty to accept that others should be allowed to consume such products if they wish.

In most cases a company will invest abroad—with all the costs and risks of operating in an unfamiliar cultural and legal environment—only if it commands some form of intellectual property that compensates for its disadvantage relative to local competitors. Making that intellectual property available in a developing country is likely to contribute to its development (though perhaps least in the case of consumer products like those produced by Disney and McDonalds). Since 1989 this logic seems to have been widely accepted. The more important problem now is restraining countries competing for foreign direct investment from offering excessive investment incentives, thereby handing back an undue proportion of the benefits of investments to the companies that make them.

One advantage of foreign direct investment that has been strongly emphasized—especially since the East Asian crisis—is that it is much more stable than portfolio investment and certainly bank loans. Note that my version of the Washington consensus spoke specifically about liberalizing foreign direct investment—not general liberalization of capital inflows (let alone capital outflows). That was because I did not believe there was (or, for that matter, should have been) consensus about the desirability of capital account liberalization.

Stanley Fischer, commenting on my original paper while chief economist of the World Bank, questioned my judgment on this point. He asserted that there was strong sentiment in Washington favoring capital account liberalization. Whether or not he was correct on that in 1989, it was certainly true by the mid-1990s, with Fischer—who had expressed reservations about the wisdom of such liberalization in 1989—being perceived as strongly in favor of it in the position he then held of first deputy managing director of the IMF.[8]

Along with the bipolar exchange rate regime, this seems to me one of the key respects in which the second perception of the Washington consensus—as the conventional wisdom of the Bretton Woods institutions—came to differ from my original list. I believe that in both cases my formulations were a much better prescription for development than the advice proffered by the Bretton Woods institutions, or at least by the IMF. I hold premature capital account liberalization to have been primarily responsible for the catastrophic crisis that in 1997 interrupted the East Asian miracle.

8. "Privatization of state-owned enterprises."

Privatization was U.K. Prime Minister Margaret Thatcher's principal contribution to economic policy worldwide. It is the only doctrine with a specifically neoliberal[9] origin that made my list of 10 desirable reforms. Neither minimalist government, nor supply-side economics, nor monetarism, nor the treatment of income redistribution as an assault on property rights or a threat to incentives made the list. These doctrines were also promulgated by the quintessentially neoliberal Reagan and Thatcher administrations, but my list was intended to include what had outlasted them and entered mainstream thinking by 1989. (It was, after all, supposed to consist of doctrines on which there was consensus.) I concluded that privatization fell in that category, while the other doctrines with a neoliberal origin did not.

The bulk of economic evaluations of privatization conclude that it has succeeded in two dimensions: increasing the efficiency and profitability of privatized enterprises and improving the coverage of and access to privatized utilities. But in other dimensions the outcomes have varied enormously. Privatization appears to have had no consistent effect on wages, prices, output quality, or employment. (In some cases the firings due to higher productivity are more than compensated by increased output, and in other cases they are not; Megginson and Netter 2001 and Nellis 2003.)

Despite the fact that economists tend to regard its successes as providing an endorsement of its utility, the fact is that—at least in Latin America, where Latinobarometro provides regular, reliable evidence on public attitudes—privatization is intensely and increasingly unpopular. One can understand why privatization has evoked public hostility in some cases, especially when it has been suspected of being corrupt or privatized enterprises have been allowed to retain monopolies and no adequate regulatory mechanisms have been established. Still, its unpopularity seems more general than can be explained this way.

Part of the problem may be the arousal of nationalist sensibilities when enterprises have been sold to foreign buyers, especially those from neighboring countries seen as historical rivals. And perhaps economists tend too readily to dismiss public concerns about corruption in the privatization process as fuss about "mere" distribution effects;[10] perhaps the public would actually prefer to see wealth destroyed than transferred to those who acquire it by illicit means. If we believe that democratic proprieties oblige us to respect public preferences, we need to be extra careful that all future privatizations are squeaky clean.

9. "[Abolition of] regulations that impede the entry of new firms or restrict competition."

The word *deregulation* has sometimes been used to defend the emasculation of regulations intended to protect public health, the environment, or consumers. That was not the sense I intended when I included deregulation in the Washington consensus. Rather, the purpose was to recommend the removal of constraints on entry and exit, to make the economy more competitive. The U.S. model was deregulation of the trucking and airline industries, not gutting the Endangered Species Act.

Is this a reform that can be expected to travel well—that is, to be appropriate if implemented in developing countries? There have been some excellent examples of such reforms in developing countries, as with India's extremely successful deregulation of its trucking industry in the 1980s (Williamson and Zagha 2002). Moreover, few examples of perverse regulation have struck me more than when I visited an African country and discovered that the only legal passenger transport was that provided by a parastatal bus company running pollution-belching behemoths three-quarters empty.

One of the best services that the World Bank has provided in recent years has been to create a Web site where developing countries can see how difficult they make it for new firms to enter the formal sector relative to best-practice countries such as Canada (where registering a new firm requires two procedures taking three days and 0.6 percent of the country's per capita income, and demands zero minimum capital).[11] Besley and Burgess (2003, p. 17) provide emphatic support for making "appropriately structured deregulation…part of the antipoverty agenda." So I think that deregulation is an excellent candidate for inclusion in a policy prescription for development.

10. "The legal system should provide secure property rights without excessive costs, and make these available to the informal sector."

This was the one institutional reform that I included in the original Washington consensus. The impetus for its inclusion came from Hernando de Soto (1989), who made the case for granting secure, affordable property rights to informal Peruvian enterprises. He argued that allowing such enterprises to formalize cheaply was in their best interests because it would reduce the costs of defending their property and ensure them that they would benefit from their investments—as well as empower them to access credit from the formal sector. It would simultaneously increase the government's tax base, so it was also in the wider public interest.

Soon after I wrote the 1989 paper on the Washington consensus, I became interested in the transition from a communist to market economy that was then in its early stages. It soon became clear that institutional issues were, or at least should be, at the heart of the transition—and that defining property rights was one of the most critical actions. But in developing countries property rights have rarely received much emphasis, and apart from de Soto (2000) I can think of no systematic attempt to examine the payoffs from such reforms as have occurred. I believe that this remains an extremely worthwhile area for action.

The extent of implementation

Though it is not possible to provide a systematic survey of the extent to which my version of the Washington consensus has been implemented over the past 15 years, a few remarks are in order. Among regions, Latin America and transition economies have moved furthest in terms of stabilization, liberalization, and integration with the world economy. East Asia has moved much less, and some of its movements have been a mistake—such as rapid capital account liberalization. But it started off with much less divergence from OECD countries in its policy stance, especially on the stabilization front. China and South Asia have both moved rather gradually, but the direction of the movement has been unambiguous. Sub-Saharan Africa has moved spottily and grudgingly, too often under foreign pressure rather than out of conviction.

Argentina has often been described as a poster child for the Washington consensus, and indeed it implemented many excellent liberalizing reforms in the 1990s (for which it was rewarded by its fastest growth since at least the 1920s). But it also failed to do two crucial things: maintain a competitive exchange rate and get its fiscal policy in order. Because both of these issues were included in my version of the Washington consensus—and it was the failure to address them that led to the country's 2001 crisis—I find it a bit rich when people blame the consensus for Argentina's implosion.

In terms of which reforms were most widely implemented, there have been widespread attempts to tighten fiscal policy, introduce extensive financial and trade liberalization, eliminate restrictions on foreign direct investment, and promote privatization and deregulation. Most neglected have been efforts to reform public spending priorities, maintain a competitive exchange rate, and extend property rights to the informal sector. And as noted, my formulation of tax reform failed to address the main issue. I should emphasize, too, that the 10 reforms on my list were not everywhere the 10 most important or urgent issues.

What Would a Good Policy Prescription Look Like?

My review of the 10 prescriptions that made up my version of the Washington consensus has not, I trust, given the impression that I believe they embodied the whole truth and nothing but the truth about development policy. Still, in light of experiences since 1989, there is not much that I think requires retraction. Most countries would have benefited from doing more of these reforms rather than fewer, and from doing them of their own volition rather than because someone from Washington told them they should be done. The big changes in development thinking underlying the Washington consensus—recognition of the importance of macroeconomic discipline, trade liberalization rather than import-substituting industrialization, development of a market economy rather than reliance on a leading role for the state—were as valid in developing countries as they had long been in OECD countries. The end of the intellectual apartheid that used to divide the globe into the first, second, and third worlds, each with its own economic laws, is something to be celebrated rather than mourned.

But that is not the same as saying that the Washington consensus, either in my version or as the policy stance of the Bretton Woods institutions, provides an adequate policy agenda for development. In this section I outline how a group of colleagues and I have updated an agenda for development in light of changing times and in the absence of an obligation to stick to proposals that have achieved broad consensus. I then discuss two leading critiques of the original Washington consensus—by Joseph Stiglitz (1998) in a lecture to the World Institute for Development Economics Research (WIDER) and by Dani Rodrik (2002, 2003)—assessing how well our new proposals stand up against them.

"After the Washington consensus…"

Our new strategy, presented in Kuczysnki and Williamson (2003), suggests what Latin American countries should do to advance development. This strategy is summarized under four headings. First, governments should aim to avoid crises and stabilize the macroeconomy. This still involves stabilizing inflation—the focus of most policy discussions a bit more than a decade ago and the element that I included in the Washington consensus—but it also requires stabilizing the real economy à la Keynes. The new strategy also discusses issues such as exchange rate policy, where we emphasize the importance of flexibility in most cases while acknowledging that there might be circumstances where fixed rates make sense, as well as the importance of avoiding currency misalignments and mismatches.

Second, we argue for completing rather than reversing the liberalizing reforms of the Washington consensus. We place particular emphasis on the desirability in most Latin American countries of liberalizing the labor market, to price more of the labor force back into formal sector jobs where they will get at least minimal social protections. We also argue for complementing the import liberalization that has already occurred with better access to export markets in industrial countries, and urge continuing the privatization programs that have already been undertaken in Latin America.

Third, we join the general chorus urging reforming countries to recognize that strong institutions are needed to make good policies effective. For example, a reformed tax code will not be much use if the tax administration remains mired in corruption. Our strategy discusses some of the institutional strengthening that we would like to see, but this covers a vast area, and the most urgent needs vary a lot by country. This is an important change from the Washington consensus, which was not ahead of its time in that it focused on policies rather than institutions. Recognition of the importance of institutions was perhaps the key innovation in development economics in the 1990s.

Fourth, we urge that the goal of economic policy should not be just to increase the growth rate, important as that is, but also to make governments recognize that it matters profoundly who receives an increase in income. We suggest that there might be some scope for pushing further the traditional mechanism for improving income distribution—namely, levying higher taxes on rich people to increase social spending that disproportionately benefits poor people—but acknowledge that it would not be practical to push this approach very far, because too many of Latin America's rich people have the option of placing too many of their assets in Miami. Thus we conclude that major improvements in the region's highly skewed income distributions will take a long time, since the alternative approach has to be to build up the assets that will enable poor people to earn their way out of poverty. That would require above all better education opportunities so that poor people can accumulate more human capital, but we also mention the potential of microcredit, land reform, and asset titling.

Stiglitz's critique

In his WIDER lecture Stiglitz relied on what I have dubbed the third concept of the Washington consensus, interpreting it as a neoliberal manifesto. But the "post–Washington consensus" that he sketched in his lecture is not based on Washington, for an essential feature is that it be owned by developing countries. Moreover, he evidently assumed that a new consensus is emerging, and that is what he was seeking to help mold. This new consensus is focused on achieving a broader range of goals than just economic growth: it also pursues equitable development, sustainable development, and democratic development. Accordingly, it encompasses a broader range of instruments than those embodied in the Washington consensus:

- It aims at stabilizing the real economy as well as inflation.
- It tries to improve financial sector regulation, rather than assuming that liberalization is the only game in town.
- It includes competition policy.
- It consider various mechanisms for improving government efficiency, rather than seeking to minimize government's role. (Remember that Stiglitz interprets the Washington consensus as advocating minimal government.)
- It focuses on improving human capital formation.
- It seeks to increase the transfer of technology to developing countries.

When I review this list I am impressed by how much of it is incorporated in Kuczynski and Williamson (2003). We certainly focus on the desirability of stabilizing the real economy as well as inflation. Although we do not discuss amending financial sector regulation, we do address the need to strengthen prudential supervision—so, despite taking a more charitable view of financial liberalization than does Stiglitz, we too recognize that the state plays a key role in making a liberalized financial system work. We do not specifically call for competition policy, but we do emphasize that a privatized monopoly requires a strong regulatory mechanism. There are important parallels between our thoughts on strengthening institutions and his call for state reform. We also emphasize the importance of human capital formation. And our call for a national innovation system is intended to facilitate technology transfer. In terms of objectives, we share his concern that development be equitable, and we acknowledge the importance of environmental and democratic dimensions, although we do not interpret our mandate as implying an obligation to focus on those issues. The main difference between us seems to be semantic: what we mean by the Washington consensus and therefore whether we think that it is a bad thing.

Where Stiglitz strikes me as sadly naïve is in imagining that the world is on the road to a new consensus incorporating concerns about equity, sustainability, and democracy as well as growth. One may want to discuss whether there was really a consensus in 1989—indeed, more than one person has quipped that the notion of a Washington consensus is an oxymoron. But 1989 came closer to consensus than ever before and probably than we will ever see again. (After all, that was the year that history was ending.) It strikes me as fantasy to imagine that we are on the cusp of a new consensus embracing equity and sustainability when the world's leading economic power has recently unbalanced its budget with the most inequitable tax cuts in living memory and denounced the Kyoto protocol.

Rodrik's critique

Rodrik (2002, 2003) claims that recent economic developments in most developing countries have hardly been encouraging in terms of growth, crises, income inequality, poverty, and economic security (just as Kuczynski and Williamson 2003 do, though our discussion focuses on Latin America and the message of gloom is quite unjustified when one includes Asia). He says that the few developing countries that have done well (such as Chile, China, India, and Vietnam) "have marched to their own drummers and are hardly poster children for neoliberalism" (Rodrik 2002, p. 1).[12] He asserts that the augmented Washington consensus is just as bound to disappoint as its predecessor, because it offers too broad an agenda for institutional reform that is insensitive to local contexts and needs. Moreover, it describes what advanced countries look like, rather than prescribing a practical path for getting there. Rodrik argues that the aim should be to provide an alternative set of policy guidelines for promoting development, while avoiding promoting another impractical blueprint that is supposed to be right for all countries at all times.

With most of that I wholeheartedly agree.[13] I especially applaud Rodrik's call to avoid jettisoning all the useful insights in mainstream economics, such as the importance of property rights, the rule of law, and incentives, the need to worry about debt sustainability, prudential principles, and sound money, the desirability of growth, and the benefits of globalization. He makes a very interesting argument (though he carries it a bit too far; see below) that such "universal principles of good economic management" (Rodrik 2002, p. 2) do not map uniquely into particular institutional arrangements or policy prescriptions. Debt sustainability, fiscal prudence, and sound money are, he asserts, compatible with many institutional arrangements other than independent central banks, flexible exchange rates, and inflation targeting. The need to align private incentives with social costs and benefits does not translate into unconditional support for trade liberalization, deregulation, and privatization.

Rodrik argues that transitions to high growth are usually sparked by a few policy changes and institutional reforms, which typically combine elements of orthodoxy with heterodox institutional innovations that are unlikely to travel well. Countries need both a short-run investment strategy to kick-start growth and a longer-run institution-building strategy to give the economy resilience in the face of volatility and adverse shocks, and thus keep growth going once it has been initiated. The investment strategy needs to combine a carrot to promote investments in nontraditional areas with a stick to weed out investment projects that fail. The key challenge is to learn what a country is (or can be) good at producing: investment that contributes to this has social value that can far exceed its private value, and thus will be undersupplied in the absence of subsidies of some type. But countries also need a mechanism to terminate investment projects that do not pan out, as with the Republic of Korea's willingness to cut off companies that did not succeed in the export market. Latin America lacked such a mechanism in the era of import substitution, and when it was introduced in the early 1990s countries dropped the carrot—whereas the carrot and the stick are needed in tandem.

Exactly what form of institutions will best serve a country cannot be pinned down by economic analysis. Discovering what works requires experimentation. Rodrik drives this point home with a brilliant thought experiment. He asks us to imagine the program that a Western economist would have recommended to China in 1978, and it turns out to be the quintessential "big bang." But fortunately that is not what Chinese reformers did. Instead they introduced the household responsibility system, two-track pricing, and township and village enterprises. I was told over dinner in Beijing recently that none of these was introduced as a result of analysis conducted by a local think tank. Each was legitimized by the leadership after emerging spontaneously—and working—at the local level.

If reforms need to differ by country, then a general blueprint such as the Ten Commandments of the Washington consensus sends the wrong message. Moisés Naím (2000) explains the success of the Washington consensus as providing an ideology for a world pining for something to replace the god of socialism that had just failed. An ideology, he elaborated, is a thought-economizing device. Follow the Ten Commandments and thou shalt grow, I suppose. My immediate reaction was that the world needs policymakers who think rather than those who economize on thought (Williamson 2000). I now feel even more uncomfortable with the realization that I may inadvertently have encouraged people to think that they did not have to adapt the Washington consensus to local circumstances, but could use the same blueprint everywhere.

But Rodrik takes too far the argument that agreement on the characteristics of good economic management does not map into endorsement of particular policies or institutional arrangements. He appears to think, for example, that one can dismiss the case for trade liberalization because his graduate students are capable of writing a model in which trade restrictions are welfare-enhancing. The argument in favor of liberal trade is essentially empirical, involving formal econometric evidence where available but also less formal attempts to make sense of what we see in the world around us.

We must always keep our minds open enough to recognize that standard arguments may not apply, but we should also try to discover the standard case. Indeed, the basic purpose of thinking about development strategy is to identify regularities about policies and institutional arrangements that suggest what might be useful in other countries. We would seriously shortchange our clients if we were to go no further than the sort of questions that Rodrik poses, such as "What is the appropriate regulatory apparatus for the financial system?" and "What is the appropriate exchange rate regime?" We must also offer some answers, even if we expect these only to be standard answers, from which actual answers may differ in certain situations.

How adequate do the Kuczynski and Williamson (2003) proposals appear as a strategy for development in light of the Rodrik critique? First, I do not believe that this time round it will be seen as a neoliberal formula, partly because it includes concern for income distribution and the social agenda, and partly because the summary version is in less danger of being mistaken for the Ten Commandments. But then, I never expected the original version to be interpreted that way either. And the new version still reflects a conviction that any country seeking to develop would be well advised to build a market economy rather than one where the state plays the leading role in the productive sector.

Second, I would maintain that the new strategy strikes a better balance than Rodrik's approach in terms of offering substantive advice on the strategic issues confronting developing countries. We do not leave readers pondering questions such as "What types of financial institutions are most appropriate for mobilizing domestic savings?" and "Should fiscal policy be rule-bound, and if so what are the appropriate rules?" Instead we outline what we believe the answers to be. We emphasize that we would expect the optimal sequencing of reforms to differ by country, and suggest that successful reformers are less countries that identify the right reforms than those that identify where constraints are binding and thus implement the right reforms at the right time.

Third, however, our new strategy does not address the issue of igniting an investment boom that Rodrik regards as key, except by emphasizing the importance of a competitive exchange rate and the advantages of a national innovation system. Can one argue that in Latin America, as opposed to Africa, countries have passed the stage where this is important? I think not; they may have had a healthy rate of investment at some time in the past, but investment rates now need boosting just about everywhere. Rodrik makes a persuasive argument that there is an important benefit external to the firm in identifying new export products that a country is capable of producing. But that does not make a convincing case for subsidizing all investment, or for thinking that governments will be capable of sorting out ex ante cases where subsidies are required.

Stimulating investment is a key to faster growth that probably got shorter shrift than it should have both in the original Washington consensus (see the critique in Malan 1991) and in our new strategy, but that may be partly because the best way to stimulate investment varies even more than Rodrik acknowledges. For example, in Brazil I would hate to see the government start subsidizing specific investments rather than get the real interest rate down from the double-digit stratosphere where it has been ever since the Real Plan, and indeed long before. So while it may be right to leave the door slightly open for measures to subsidize investment, I have yet to observe such measures—beyond competitive exchange rates and national innovation systems—that I would feel confident recommending to all countries.

Conclusion

Was the Washington consensus a good policy prescription for development? That depends on how one interprets a phrase whose meaning has become hopelessly compromised in public debate. The specific proposals to which I originally applied the term describe a sensible, if incomplete, reform agenda. But two of the ways in which much of Washington subsequently departed from this agenda were misguided. Today I would go further and argue that in the second sense the Washington consensus has evaporated, because of the profound gulf between the Bush administration and the international financial institutions on fiscal policy (see IMF 2003, p. 22), income distribution (contrast the World Bank's *World Development Report 2000/2001* and the Bush administration's tax cuts), and capital account convertibility (see note 2). And I can understand why anyone who has been brainwashed into thinking of the term in its third sense, as a neoliberal agenda, would reject it as unhelpful.

I have also sketched the outlines of a new strategy for development that I developed last year with some other economists, and compared it with critiques of the Washington consensus made by Joseph Stiglitz and Dani Rodrik. As far as Stiglitz is concerned, our new agenda incorporates most of his substantive points, and our main disagreement is semantic. Rodrik's disagreement is much more with the notion of formulating a program that might apply to many countries, rather than with specific policy proposals. I have some sympathy with this critique: I certainly believe that every country must decide on sequencing in light of its circumstances, and I understand that countries may sometimes have good reasons for doing heterodox things. But I believe that Rodrik is too nihilistic in implying that the most that economists can usefully do is spell out the questions to be asked, rather than marshalling the evidence for expecting particular answers to be the norm. Sadder and wiser 15 years later, I no longer expect those particular answers to command a consensus.

Notes

The author is indebted to colleagues at the Institute for International Economics for comments on a previous draft.

1. Items 5 and 17 of Rodrik's (2002, table 1) list strike me as contradictory, rather than the latter elaborating on the former.

2. However, judging from its insistence that the bilateral free trade agreements between the United States and Chile and Singapore emasculate their ability to use capital controls in the future, the U.S. Treasury continues to believe in rapid capital account liberalization.

3. See also Ffrench-Davis (2000) for an elaboration of Chile's attempt to stabilize the real economy.

4. Easterly (2001) gives the impression that investment is irrelevant to growth. If it were true that investment does nothing to raise capacity, then it would be a waste of resources. What Easterly presumably really believes is that higher investment is not sufficient to permit higher capacity growth, a position that is not hard to endorse.

5. This is the admirable Indian terminology for subsidies that cannot be rationalized in terms of offsetting externalities or improving income distribution.

6. This concerns "matters such as how managers and staff are appointed and what they are paid, where branches may be opened or closed, and in which types of business the bank may engage" (Williamson and Mahar 1998, p. 2), not issues that are typically the concern of bank supervisors.

7. I formalized these ideas in a recent paper (Williamson forthcoming). The basic idea is to ask what exchange rate will maximize the growth rate, given that a more competitive rate will promote investment but will also reduce the resources available for investment (because the current account deficit will be lower). A different, also important question is whether the government has policy weapons that would allow it to achieve the growth-maximizing exchange rate.

8. See Fischer (1997) or his contribution to Fischer and others (1998) for expositions of his position at the time. These statements suggest considerable enthusiasm for the goal, though qualified by concerns about the potential danger posed by an economy's increased vulnerability to shifts in market sentiment.

9. I use the term in its original sense, to refer to the doctrines propagated by the Mont Pelerin Society.

10. Megginson and Netter (2001, p. 329) are typical in dismissing such issues: "we ignore the arguments regarding the importance of equitable concerns such as income distribution."

11. The site is http://rru.worldbank.org/DoingBusiness/SnapshotReports/EntryRegulations.aspx

12. Rodrik uses the word *neoliberalism* to describe the policy stance that has been dominant in the United States in recent years, not in its original sense referring to the doctrines espoused by the Mont Pelerin Society.

13. In particular, I agree that countries can sometimes benefit from heterodox proposals. We at the Institute for International Economics once sponsored a conference when the ideas that ultimately flowered into the Real Plan first took form, with the objective of trying to ensure that if Brazil did implement the plan it would not be sabotaged by the IMF's dinosaurs; see Williamson (1985). To my mind the Real Plan was one of the most brilliant heterodox plans about which Rodrik enthuses, and was totally country-specific. (Its essence

was not the use of the exchange rate as a nominal anchor, which was an unfortunate belated add-on, but the use of the indexation unit as the new monetary unit following monetary reform.)

References

Balassa, Bela, Gerardo M. Bueno, Pedro Pablo Kuczynski, and Mario Henrique Simonsen. 1986. *Toward Renewed Economic Growth in Latin America*. Mexico City: El Colegio de Mexico and Washington, D.C.: Institute for International Economics.

Bekaert, Geert, Campbell R. Harvey, and Christian Lundblad. 2001. "Does Financial Liberalization Spur Growth?" Working Paper 8245. National Bureau of Economic Research, Cambridge, Mass.

Besley, Timothy, and Robin Burgess. 2003. "Halving Global Poverty." *Journal of Economic Perspectives* 17 (3): 3–22.

Bruno, Michael, and William Easterly. 1998. "Inflation Crises and Long-run Growth." *Journal of Monetary Economics* 41 (February): 3–26.

Caprio, Gerard, and Patrick Honohan. 2001. *Finance for Growth: Policy Choices in a Volatile World*. Washington, D.C.: World Bank.

Cardoso, Eliana A., Ricardo Pães de Barros, and André Urani. 1995. "Inflation and Unemployment as Determinants of Inequality in Brazil: The 1980s." In Rudiger Dornbusch and Sebastian Edwards, eds., *Reform, Recovery, and Growth*. Chicago: University of Chicago Press for the National Bureau of Economic Research.

Cornia, Giovanni Andrea, Richard Jolly, and Frances Stewart. 1987. *Adjustment with a Human Face*. Oxford: Clarendon Press for the United Nations Children's Fund (UNICEF).

De Soto, Hernando. 1989. *The Other Path*. New York: Harper & Row.

———. 2000. *The Mystery of Capital: Why Capitalism Triumphs in the West and Fails Everywhere Else*. London: Black Swan.

Easterly, William. 2001. *The Elusive Quest for Growth: Economists' Adventures and Misadventures in the Tropics*. Cambridge, Mass.: MIT Press.

Ffrench-Davis, Ricardo. 2000. *Reforming the Reforms*. London: Macmillan.

Fischer, Stanley. 1997. "Capital Account Liberalization and the Role of the IMF." Paper presented to the International Monetary Fund seminar on "Asia and the IMF," 19 September, Hong Kong.

———. 2003. "Globalization and Its Challenges." *American Economic Review* 93 (2): 1–30.

Fischer, Stanley, Richard N. Cooper, Rudiger Dornbusch, Peter M. Garber, Carlos Massad, Jacques J. Polak, Dani Rodrik, and Savak S. Tarapore. 1998. "Should the IMF Pursue Capital-Account Convertibility?" Princeton Essays in International Finance 207. Princeton University, Princeton, N.J.

Hufbauer, Gary Clyde, and Ben Goodrich. 2003. "Next Move in Steel: Revocation or Retaliation?" Policy Brief 03-10. Institute for International Economics, Washington, D.C.

IMF (International Monetary Fund). 2003. *World Economic Outlook* (May). Washington, D.C.

Kuczynski, Pedro-Pablo, and John Williamson. 2003. *After the Washington Consensus: Restarting Growth and Reform in Latin America.* Washington, D.C.: Institute for International Economics.

Lucas, Robert E. 2003. "Macroeconomic Priorities." *American Economic Review* 93 (1): 1–14.

Malan, Pedro S. 1991. "Critique to the Washington Consensus." *Revista de economia política* 2 (3).

McKinnon, Ronald I. 1973. *Money and Capital in Economic Development.* Washington, D.C.: Brookings Institution.

Megginson, William L., and Jeffry M. Netter. 2001. "From State to Market: A Survey of Empirical Studies of Privatization." *Journal of Economic Literature* 39 (2): 321–89.

Naím, Moisés. 2000. "Fads and Fashion in Economic Reforms: Washington Consensus or Washington Confusion?" *Foreign Policy* 118 (86).

Nellis, John. 2003. "Privatization in Latin America." Center for Global Development, Washington, D.C.

Rajan, Raghuram G., and Luigi Zingales. 2003. *Saving Capitalism from the Capitalists.* New York: Crown Business.

Rodrik, Dani. 2002. "After Neoliberalism, What?" Remarks at the Banco Nacional de Desenvolvimento Economico e Social (BNDES) seminar on "New Paths of Development," 12–13 September, Rio de Janeiro, Brazil.

————. 2003. "Growth Strategies." Harvard University, Cambridge, Mass.

Shaw, Edward S. 1973. *Financial Deepening in Economic Development.* New York: Oxford University Press.

Stiglitz, Joseph E. 1998. "More Instruments and Broader Goals: Moving toward the Post-Washington Consensus." United Nations University/World Institute for Development Economics Research (WIDER), Helsinki.

Williamson, John, ed. 1985. *Inflation and Indexation: Argentina, Brazil, Israel.* Washington, D.C.: Institute for International Economics.

————. 1990. *Latin American Adjustment: How Much Has Happened?* Washington, D.C.: Institute for International Economics.

————. 1994. *The Political Economy of Policy Reform.* Washington, D.C.: Institute for International Economics.

Williamson, John. 2000. "What Should the World Bank Think about the Washington Consensus?" *The World Bank Research Observer* 15 (2).

————. Forthcoming. "Exchange Rate Policy and Development." In a book sponsored by the Institute for Policy Dialogue.

Williamson, John, and Molly Mahar. 1998. "A Survey of Financial Liberalization." Princeton Essays in International Finance 211. Princeton University, Princeton, N.J.

Williamson, John, and Roberto Zagha. 2002. "From Slow Growth to Slow Reform." Paper presented at the Third Annual Stanford Economic Conference on Indian Economic Reform, June, Palo Alto, Calif.

World Bank. 2001. *World Development Report 2000/2001: Attacking Poverty.* New York: Oxford University Press.

Comment

Alice H. Amsden

IT IS A PLEASURE TO BE HERE AND, AS ALWAYS, TO HEAR JOHN WILLIAMSON SPEAK. I THINK that his conceptualization of the Washington consensus is terrific, because it makes us recognize its enormous influence. As he says, he cannot control the differences between the policies applied in the name of the consensus and the policies he identified when he proposed it. Regardless, for the past 15 years the neoliberal approach embodied by the consensus has dominated economic policies in both industrial and developing countries.

The Two Patterns of Postwar Development

The Washington consensus has caused huge changes in how countries see themselves, how they manage their economies, and how they function. This new paradigm was preceded by a period, say from 1945 to 1980, that was Keynesian, interventionist, and flexible. And comparing some basic economic data for these two periods, such as national growth rates, generates rather astonishing results.

These data, compiled by the World Bank, show that since 1980 most developing countries—especially those that have followed the Washington consensus and neoliberal policies—have suffered tremendous declines in growth and development. Nearly all grew faster growth in the Keynesian, interventionist period, sometimes referred to as the golden age of capitalism.

There are, of course, different ways of examining these data. Some analysts argue that they should be weighted, but I do not see the point of that approach. Weighting them would show how every person did instead of every country, and I want to know how every country did.

The data may also reflect different starting points. But both periods had difficult starting periods. Many developing countries had severe balance of payments problems just after World War II. And in the 1980s many experienced a crippling debt crisis because of neoliberal policies introduced in the 1970s. Mexico, for example, liberalized all of its financial controls, and as a result ran into debt problems.

The fact remains that all countries tended to grow faster in the first period and slower in the next. Moreover, during the first period developing countries were the world's fastest-growing economies. What explains these differences in growth rates?

First, during the earlier period two participants were extremely active in fostering world development. One consisted of elites from developing countries, who were fed up with colonialism and tired of slow growth. They formed developmental states: disciplined, with well-organized institutions and effective rules of the game.

The second major participant was the United States, which played a major role by teaching these countries about the importance and the problems of free trade. Although it had free trade agreements, it did not necessarily enforce them. It also had the General Agreement on Tariffs and Trade (GATT), which allowed for flexibility and choice—whereas today, countries that join the World Trade Organization (WTO) must sign all of its protocols.

Thus during the earlier period there was much more flexibility. And I believe that if we want to restore growth in the global economy, we should move back from the WTO to the GATT. That would be a progressive, positive step.

I also think that, just looking at the United States, the first few decades after World War II were great in terms of foreign aid. Although U.S. aid was often tied, that did not impede developments such as the green revolution—which was extraordinarily important. And it was important because it tied aid to production, and did not make a distinction between aid for alleviating poverty and aid for creating productive assets. I think that approach is very different from how the World Bank now thinks of aid, and from the approach taken by the Washington consensus.

I think that growth has slowed since 1980 because there are no longer engines of growth in many developing countries. There is nothing to drive these economies further in investment, trade, or anything else. The idea seems to be that if a free market is put in front of them, they will export. But many of them have nothing to export. I do not believe that free markets alone will stimulate people's entrepreneurial spirit, because it is not enough of an incentive. Similarly, few countries have introduced successful industrial policy.

The Future of Development

I think that the Washington consensus and its neoliberal approach to development are collapsing. I do not think that the consensus is collapsing just because people say that it is not working—though that is evident—but also because countries recognize that depending on it creates big problems.

Thus many countries have decided to reduce their dependence on the U.S. market. For example, the Republic of Korea used to send 65 percent of its exports to the United States, but today 60–65 percent go to other Asian countries. There is enormous intra-Asian trade, which I think is wonderful because it creates competition for the ideas underlying the Washington consensus.

It is great for Asia to have a big economy of its own, independent of the United States. It would be wonderful for the Middle East and Latin America to have such markets as well. Free trade agreements that exclude the major European and U.S. powers are wonderful because they give developing countries more leeway and flexibility—as opposed to the often crippling requirements of the WTO. For example, alliances are being made between developing countries, such as between India and Iran, and between Brazil and India. Such arrangements are great because they diffuse power, increase flexibility, and introduce the idea that policies are improved when countries have a reasonable model to emulate.

Comment

Ricardo Ffrench-Davis

I APPRECIATE THIS OPPORTUNITY TO DISCUSS JOHN WILLIAMSON'S INTERESTING presentation, and his evaluation of the results achieved by the so-called Washington consensus. Despite some significant successes—such as the eradication of hyperinflation, replaced by single-digit inflation—in Latin America the net balance of reforms implemented in the name of the consensus has been disappointing. Even after 15 years, significant privatization of public firms, and widespread liberalization of trade and capital markets, the region's GDP growth has averaged just 2.5 percent a year.

By the late 1980s Latin America needed tough reforms. But given their poor results, there has been something wrong with the way reforms have been implemented. In the limited space available here, I will focus on a few strategic issues.

The Goal Must Be Growth with Equity

The goal is not reforms by themselves, but sustained growth with equity. Latin America's GDP per capita (measured in purchasing power parity, or PPP, terms) is about one-fifth that of industrial countries. Moreover, the average Latin American country exhibits an equity gap between rich and poor households that is about twice that of rich countries.

To achieve both growth and equity, a market economy must be truly market-friendly and have truly "right" prices—outcomes both anticipated by the reforms of the 1990s. Instead, reforms made under neoliberal prescriptions have typically failed on both fronts.

Actual Outcomes

During the 1990s most Latin American countries achieved single-digit inflation and vigorous export growth (8–9 percent a year). In addition, until the contagion of the East Asian crisis, public sector deficits had fallen to about 1.5 percent of GDP.

But performance has been poor on growth and equity. Between 1990 and 2004 annual GDP rose scarcely 2.5 percent. Output per worker stagnated, job instability rose, and average incomes fell among nonwage workers. This worsening was partly associated with a low investment ratio (paradoxically, while financial investment was rising) and the weak role assigned to labor training and access to capital markets by small and medium-size enterprises. Indeed, the distribution of opportunities and productivity became even more skewed than before reforms—very unfriendly developments for most firms and workers (see Ffrench-Davis 2002).

What Went Wrong?

A common feature of underdevelopment is that there are many absent or incomplete markets. Complete markets do not emerge spontaneously with naïve, across the board liberalization. So, for several years some segments of markets required for growth and equity have not been in place. Timing, doses, and sequencing are also crucial. Indeed, liberalization helps expedite the development of some market segments. For others it can make the task more difficult or delay achievements. And it can create losers—as when the number of poor people increases or the income distribution worsens.

My interpretation is that implementation of the Washington consensus in Latin America involved too much of the third interpretation identified by John: the neoliberal version. Some of the more pervasive features of this include:

- Acting as if the same economic laws apply everywhere. (They do not, especially when crucial market segments are missing or the heterogeneity of agents is huge, implying large diversity in capacity to respond to abrupt changes or instability.)

- Acting as if liberalizing reforms were ends in themselves, and not inputs for growth and equitable markets.

- Assuming that more of the same, if it implies liberalization, is always better—no matter what the speed, the sequencing, and the missing ingredients (for instance, under "incomplete" financial markets). Outcomes have not been market friendly and have generated very distorted macro prices (such as outlier exchange rates).

Macroeconomics and Development

I agree with John that real macroeconomic balances are extremely important. I share his criticism of overemphasis on low inflation at the expense of balances in the real economy; simply look at Argentina, which had negative inflation in 1995–2001. I agree with his view that Chile's limits on foreign inflows were notably positive, and that for most of the 1990s Chile applied an unorthodox mix of macroeconomic policies that played a crucial role in its exceptional performance during that decade.

Growth implies that producers (capital and labor) face an environment stimulating for accumulating factors of production, increasing quality, and investing energy and knowledge in innovation. The aggregate demand faced by Latin American producers has been terribly unstable. Although inflation has been low and fiscal budgets have improved, macroeconomic policies have been such that the private sector has been forced to stop and go three times over the past 15 years. Capital flows have been the main variable behind this stop and go in aggregate demand. In fact, swings in aggregate demand were mainly responding to swings in capital flows.

Macroeconomic instability implies lower total factor productivity, lower profits, and lower businesses savings, and discourages capital formation and productive employment. In such an environment the approach to macroeconomics must be corrected to make the market friendly for producers and foster growth. There is a need for macroeconomic management that allows market agents to be placed in the production function (rather than below the transformation curve), using all installed economic capacity or potential GDP.

Moving toward a macroeconomic environment that supports growth requires making a clear differentiation between what is economic recovery and what is generation of additional productive capacity. Macroeconomic policies—monetary, exchange rate, and fiscal policies, and regulation of capital flows—should be guided by sharp distinctions between creating capacity and using existing capacity.

The Capital Account

John has been an outstanding, articulate, pioneering proponent of countercyclical, prudential management of the capital account as a crucial ingredient in sound macroeconomic balances. Full opening of the capital account may deter domestic macroeconomic mismanagement and encourage good macroeconomic fundamentals in cases of domestic sources of instability—such as large, irresponsible fiscal deficits. But lax demand policies or exchange rate overvaluation has been encouraged by financial inflows during booms, while excessive punishment during crises has forced authorities to adopt overly contractionary policies.

Opening of the capital account has led emerging market economics (EEs) to import financial instability, with capital inflows leading to a worsening of macroeconomic fundamentals. Financial operators, with their herd-prone expectations, have contributed to increasing financial flows to "successful" countries during capital surges—facilitating rapid increases in prices of financial assets and real estate, and sharp exchange rate appreciation. John's excellent publications on intermediate exchange rate regimes are closely linked to this issue.

An outcome of globalization has been that experts in financial intermediation—a microeconomic endeavor—have become determinants of the evolution and volatility of domestic macroeconomic balances. To achieve the macroeconomic balances needed for sustainable growth, economic authorities should make real macro fundamentals prevail (sustainable external deficit; moderate external liabilities, with a low liquid share; reasonable matching of terms and currencies; crowding in of domestic savings; limited real exchange rate appreciation; effective demand consistent with the production frontier, together with contained inflation and responsible fiscal policies). That appears to be an impossible challenge under capital surges and fully open capital accounts in developing economies.

In brief, there appears to be widespread misunderstanding about an adequate definition of "sound fundamentals." The inappropriate conventional definition, together with "irrational exuberance"(the explanation offered by U.S. Federal Reserve Chairman Alan Greenspan), is what led to high positive grades for Chile just before its crisis in 1982, for the Republic of Korea and Thailand in 1996, for Mexico and Argentina in 1994, and for all emerging market economies in Latin America in 1996–97. Thus something "fundamental" was missing in market evaluations of market fundamentals. The resulting crises were the result of a worsening of crucial components of a comprehensive set of fundamentals—a worsening led by massive capital inflows.

Domestic Financial Reforms

For economic growth to become vigorous and sustained, all the factors in the production function are also necessary: high physical capital formation, trained labor, availability of technological change, and capacity of labor and small and medium-size entrepreneurs to adapt and absorb it. Here I will focus on domestic finance. Latin America's reforms in the 1990s were similar to Chile's in the 1970s and early 1980s— which ended in 1982 with a 15 percent drop in GDP, a crowding out of domestic savings, a dive in domestic savings, and low capital formation.

Better allocation of resources requires better price signals and higher savings. Across Latin America there was a large increase in financial savings but not national savings, because markets received strong signals to allocate savings from savers to consumers. What the region needs is a financial sector that helps capture savings and allocates them mostly to productive investment. That is the main role of the capital market if the goal is growth and equity, yet this has been a big failure.

A Final Message

Latin America needs to redirect, rectify, and complement the reforms it has made. Some of the missing ingredients for sustainable development include labor training, long-term segments of domestic capital markets, systematic prudential regulation of capital accounts, and much better macroeconomic policies.

Reference

Ffrench-Davis, Ricardo. 2002. *Economic Reforms in Chile: From Dictatorship to Democracy.* Ann Arbor: University of Michigan Press.

Yegor Gaidar

Former Minister of Finance and Deputy Prime Minister,
Russian Federation

Yegor Gaidar was born in Moscow in 1956, and received his Ph.D. in Economics from Moscow State University in 1980. He began his career as a Research Fellow, first at the All-Union Institute for Systemic Research, and later at the Institute for Economic Forecasting, a division of the Central Economics and Mathematics Institute. Starting in 1987, he spent three years as a journalist. From 1990–91 he was Director of the Institute of Economic Policy under the Academy of National Economy of the Soviet Union.

When the Soviet Union dissolved in 1991, Gaidar began a distinguished career in government in the Russian Federation. He served in numerous positions from 1991–93, including Deputy Chairman (responsible for matters of economic policy), Minister of Economy and Finance, Acting Chairman, Counselor to the President, and First Deputy Chairman. During this time Gaidar contributed to the flurry of economic and political reforms undertaken during Russia's tumultuous transition from communism.

In 1993 Gaidar moved from the executive to the legislative branch of government, serving as Deputy of the State Duma, and began a five-year stint as Chairman of the Democratic Choice of Russia Party. He left the government in 1996, serving as Director of the Institute for the Economy in Transition until 1999, though he remained active in party politics. In 1999 Gaidar was elected Member of the State Duma, where he served until 2003. After his service in the Duma, he returned as Director of the Institute for the Economy in Transition, where he remains today. Gaidar has published several books and more than 100 articles on economic reform and postcommunist transition.

4 Russia's Transition Experience

Yegor Gaidar

IT IS A PRIVILEGE TO ADDRESS THIS ESTEEMED AUDIENCE. JUST BEFORE THIS LECTURE, I was interviewed by three extremely qualified Bank staff, and that gave me a good basis for understanding the main questions associated with the postsocialist and especially Russian transition. So, during this lecture I will focus on those issues.

Approaches to Transition

Transition economies have taken many approaches in their moves from plan to market. Although their shared history of socialism provided some common ground, efforts and outcomes have reflected a variety of domestic concerns and ideologies, as well as foreign pressures.

Russia's approach

Many analysts have asked why Russia did not follow China's path of a gradual transition to a market economy—an approach that has been less painful, has not involved a drastic drop in production, has been compatible with economic growth, and so on. The answer lies in the close interconnections in a socialist economy between the political regime and the functioning of the economic system.

With a functioning totalitarian regime it is possible to implement various types of economic systems. And as has been seen in China, Hungary, Yugoslavia, and to a less successful extent Poland, a totalitarian regime is not incompatible with the introduction of market mechanisms. But when such a regime collapses, it immediately undermines the basic functions of economic life. For those who have not lived under a socialist system and a totalitarian regime, it is difficult to understand all these interconnections.

(For instance, in late 2003 I was invited by the temporary administration leading Iraq to discuss the problems it faces. And I was struck by how difficult it is for people living in stable market economies to understand how closely a totalitarian regime is connected with everyday life—and why, when you destroy even a terrible totalitarian regime, law and order disappear, and you must confront the terrible problems associated with harm done to infrastructure, electricity systems, hospitals, and many other things.)

So, in the Soviet Union the political system and political repression were closely integrated with the functioning of the day-to-day economy. For instance, the chairman of a collective farm did not deliver grain to the state procurement agency because he needed the money. He delivered it—at a price much lower than the market price—because he knew that if he did not, he would be put in jail.

Such a system functions only until the moment when such economic agents are sure that they will not be put in jail if they do not do what they are told. When Russia's political system collapsed with the August 1991 coup—leading to the disappearance of the KGB, the Communist Party, and so on—the first economic consequence was that procurement of grain by the state grain agency collapsed within a week. As a result the supply of grain (and so bread) was severely cut in urban areas because the old administrative system was no longer being enforced and there was not a functioning market to fill the gap.

Such a situation is extremely dangerous because it risks a radical economic collapse. Russia was not prepared for such a crisis. It did not have the right institutions or experiences on which to draw. In addition, the government only had enough grain reserves to last six months. Of course, this situation was not limited to grain: it applied to all aspects of the economy.

So, Russia really did not have a choice between a rapid and a gradual transition. Obviously gradual, efficient transformations are less painful. Whether they are possible depends on the existing regime and whether it has been sensible enough to start preparing for such a transformation. But if the regime has collapsed, it is no longer a matter of choice. Thus the economic transformation in the former Soviet Union was really a response to the collapse of the previous regime. Moreover, what happened was more than an economic transformation: it was a revolution. No one anticipated, or even imagined, the simultaneous collapse of the regime, the state, and the economy.

The role of institutions

There have been claims that many of the mistakes associated with the early stages of transition were due to the fact that reformers did not sufficiently understand the role of and need for institutions in a market economy. I do not agree with this point.

When a country does not have a functioning central bank, it does not forget about it, and think that a central bank is unimportant. When a country does not have a functioning customs service, it does not forget about it. When the tax system is not adjusted to market realities, it does not forget about it. These are crucial elements of everyday life. Even if we had been complete fools, we could not have forgotten that all these institutions are necessary.

From the beginning, all the governments guiding the transition tried to create the institutions needed for a market economy. But there were several problems. The first was that when a regime collapses, it takes time to create new institutions: a functioning central bank cannot be developed overnight, even though it is needed immediately. Some analysts believed that it was possible to maintain or modify institutions of the previous regime. For example, the Soviet Union had 100 branch ministries responsible for various parts of production. But keeping all those ministries would in no way have helped resolve the institutional problems associated with the new environment. A new, functioning commission for securities could not be created from a ministry in charge of machine building or food production.

Another problem was that we underestimated the time needed to create market institutions and the problems connected with importing them. It is fairly easy to adopt new, pro-market legislation, and even to create formal market structures. But effective market institutions involve more than just legislation and formal structures. They also involve tradition. And after 75 years of socialism, these traditions were nonexistent in Russia. Thus time was needed to build them.

Lessons of Postsocialist Recessions

Looking back, many lessons are clear from the recessions experienced by Russia and other transition economies. Here I focus on their unexpected depth and duration, their drivers, and things that I would have done differently had I known then what I know now.

Depth and duration

One common mistake among reformers is easy to understand, but had severe consequences. From the outset, transition economies seriously underestimated the depth and duration of the depression that followed the collapse of socialism.

I have discussed this with many of my colleagues who initiated reforms. At the beginning almost all of us anticipated problems with falling production. We also recognized the need for far-reaching financial and monetary stabilization programs. But because the market system is supposed to be more efficient than the socialist system, we thought that the economic slowdown would be relatively brief, and that it would be followed by a strong recovery in production.

In hindsight, however, we had no real reason to expect such outcomes. The transition was a unique experience: no one had ever confronted the collapse of a socialist system. So while we could make assumptions, we could not have clear knowledge. And as it turned out, the economic and political results of this experience were unexpected—and unpleasant.

Poland's transition, led by Leszek Balcerowicz (who also appears in this volume), is considered one of the most successful. Even still, in 1991 evaluations of its efforts were extremely negative. Recall, for instance, the title of a book published in autumn 1991 by Grzegorz Kolodko, who had recently been Poland's minister of finance: it was *Chance Lost*.

In summer 1990 there was already a strong feeling among Polish elites that something was going terribly wrong and that the country was pursuing the wrong strategy. As a result the first weakening of budgetary and monetary policy in transition economies—repeated many, many times elsewhere—occurred in Poland at that time. As we now know, such efforts never help. Weakening policy simply prolongs inflation and undermines confidence in the domestic currency. But at the time that was not universally clear.

When we began economic reforms in Russia, we were obviously aware of Poland's experience. So we knew that we would experience a serious drop in production. But we also knew that an economic recovery had started in the third year of Poland's transition. So we thought that we would have a similar decline in production, followed by a recession of similar duration. But that is not what happened. Relative to most Eastern European transition economies, Russia's recession was deeper and lasted longer.

Drivers

From today's perspective the main drivers of the postsocialist recession are clear. Among the most obvious was the disorganization of the economic ties between enterprises in transition economies. Under socialism there was one system, which although inefficient was functional. When that system collapsed, time was needed to adjust to new realities, and to find ways of getting needed imports and selling outputs. Some friction was inevitable in this process.

An even more important cause of economic turmoil involved the notion of GDP. Economists have used GDP for decades, but I think that we sometimes forget the basic—and sometimes strange—assumptions held by those who created this concept. The concept was derived by market economists who assumed a limited role for government, with government usually organized as a system of democratic governance accountable to taxpayers. So the basic concept is that if someone is paying for a good, either in the market or as a taxpayer, then the good is sensible and needed. This view is logical under market economies and democracies. But it makes less sense under socialism, where it is not clear who is buying what, democracy is not in place, and there are no taxpayers in the traditional sense.

I could provide many examples about how the notion of GDP is strange in a socialist economy. To name just one: the level of the Caspian sea fluctuates for reasons that are not well understood, but that are most likely related to its ecology. Over the centuries the Caspian has risen and fallen, and in the 1970s it was falling. To prevent that, Russia launched a huge irrigation project, bringing water from northern rivers to the Volga river and then to the Caspian.

When that project was completed, the Caspian started to rise. But then we faced the opposite challenge: limiting its increase. So the Russian authorities introduced a project that diverted water from the Volga, to prevent the Caspian from rising too high. And in both cases we were technically creating GDP. Other areas of the socialist economy, such as military production and agricultural achievement, also show how strange it is to apply the notion of GDP to a socialist economy.

In a market economy, even in a newly formed and inefficient democracy, no one can pay for all these activities. Moreover, it is unrealistic to expect an overnight conversion, moving people from inefficient irrigation and other projects to activities that can be sold in markets. So essentially, the period of postsocialist recession and recovery is when resources are redistributed from activities with no market potential to activities with results that can be sold in markets or to taxpayers. During the first part of this process the decline in inefficient, nonmarket activities is higher than the increase in the new activities. But at some point the new activities start to exceed the old ones.

Because these features were especially entrenched in the Soviet economy, they help explain why we were wrong to assume that our postsocialist recession would be of the same duration as those in Eastern Europe—especially given the 75-year history of socialism in the Soviet Union, compared with 40 years in Eastern Europe. In Eastern Europe at the start of the transition, there were many people who had lived under a market economy, and the political elite were the sons of those who worked under the market. In addition, civil society was much more developed there, even under socialism. And the militarization of the economy was much lower. I believe that Irma Adelman and Dusan Vujovic were the first to predict, in 1995, that the duration of socialism would be the most important factor determining the dynamics of transition and the related drop in production (later published in Adelman and Vujovic 1998). That is a logical expectation, and today is widely accepted.

Different approaches

In considering, in hindsight, what I would do differently in response to some of the challenges of Russia's transition, a lot depends on the capacity in which I found myself. Were I czar of Russia at the end of 1991, I would do everything differently. But if I were deputy prime minister or minister of finance of a government that lacked the support of the parliamentary majority and had to maneuver to implement any kind of policy—in other words, if I were in the same position—I would do things more or less the way I did.

There are a lot of technical mistakes that I would not repeat; such as the hard currency regulation introduced in January 1992. At the same time, that regulation was not implemented in the way it was intended. Similarly, our options were limited in other areas. For example, in late 1993, after intense—and almost violent—debates about the division of power between the president and parliament, we adopted a new constitution. At that point the pro-reform party was the largest faction in parliament, and it was possible to make changes. Indeed, given the high price we had paid for political stabilization, it seemed crucial to start doing a lot of the things that we were unable to do in 1992–93: implementing structural reforms, tightening budgetary and monetary policy, fighting inflation, and so on. But an opposing view said that society was tired of reforms, and that we should slow things down—and that view prevailed. So we lost a lot of time and possibilities and were then in a much more difficult position when we later tried to make changes.

Another area common to transition, and seemingly ripe for revision, is privatization. I do not know of any postsocialist country where the population is satisfied with how privatization took place. I had been a fan of Hungary's approach, but I recently discussed it with the former chairman of its central bank—and he told me that he hated how Hungary's privatization was done. So I do not know what I would do if it were 1995 and I had to decide how to pursue privatization. Still, the experiences of transition economies show that privatization works. It just takes time to see the intended results, as with Russia's oil sector.

Russia's Recent Growth

Since 1999 Russia has seen strong growth, inspiring much debate. Those who are loyal to the current government attribute this growth to the reforms that the new president, Vladimir Putin, and his administration introduced in 2000. Those who are less enthusiastic about the current government believe that recent growth is due to the radical devaluation of the ruble in 1998 and relatively high international oil prices.

The problem with both explanations is that they regard Russia as being somehow unique. When discussing transition, most analysts rely on comparative studies, meaning that they consider what has happened in the Czech Republic, in Hungary, in Poland, and so on. Yet most of the people writing about Russia act as if it has experienced problems completely unlike those in other postsocialist countries.

One only has to consider the history of other former Soviet republics to see the similarities. Between 1991 and 1995 all these countries saw a decline in production. Then between 1995 and 1999 there was unstable growth, with shocks and variations. But since 1999 all of these countries have been growing except Ukraine, and since 2000 all of them including Ukraine. The Kyrgyz Republic had some temporary technical problems related to oil and gold production, but they have been resolved.

That is not to say that all these countries have shared the same economic experiences. Some are heavy importers, and some heavy exporters. Some have experienced serious currency devaluations over the past 5–10 years, while some have had serious revaluations. Still, the similar overall trends across these countries suggest that they are all undergoing the same process of postsocialist recovery. When the postsocialist recession ended everywhere, it created conditions for recovery and growth. That does not mean that institutions or economic policies are not important: they obviously are. But everywhere, this growth has been based on the general recovery.

In Russia the essence of this growth is that it is based on existing facilities and the previously prepared labor force. That is, workers who were out of factories are back in them, and machinery that was not being used is being used for other kinds of production. So that points to some of the features of this growth—some of which are very pleasant for the authorities, and some of which are not. One pleasant feature is that these developments emerged unexpectedly and very rapidly. No enormous investment was required; companies just had to bring the same people to the same factories and change their structure of production a bit, and it resulted in high growth.

In 2000 the Russian government anticipated economic growth to be about zero, while the International Monetary Fund (IMF), which made its forecast in May (when it was evident what was happening), projected growth of about 2.5 percent.

And in fact, growth was 10 percent that year. Obviously such growth, in its early stages, is splendid for economic policymakers.

Soon, though, this type of rapid, recovery-based growth creates a problem—which is that these growth rates usually fall fairly quickly, because there is a limited amount of prepared equipment and trained workers. The easiest resources are used first, but then you run into constraints, as became apparent to those conducting economic research in 2001 and 2002. Despite government efforts to implement various reforms, the high growth rates start to fall. So, believing that something is seriously wrong, the government feels compelled to do more: perhaps weaken monetary policy or push state investments. And enormous efforts are made to restore the recent high growth rates that are evidently unsustainable under current policies.

Those developments led to intense debates among Russian policymakers in 2002 and 2003, though fortunately they did not cause any serious damage to the government's practical policies. During that time the government was trying to support a transition from recovery-based to investment-based growth—meaning growth based not on the use of existing facilities but on the creation of new facilities.

Investment-based growth requires a much higher level of institutional development, because it is one thing to go to an existing factory, use its equipment, and earn a profit. It is quite different to invest your own money for a few years and only then hope to earn a return. To do that you must be sure that the political regime is stable and property rights are protected, and that no one will suddenly come and appropriate your investment. And the government took some of the right steps in that direction, introducing new land legislation, agricultural land improvement and protection of property rights legislation, legislation connected with the protection of shareholders, and radical tax reform.

One problem with such steps is that you need a lot of them, given the range of issues involved. Another is that you need supporting legislation and institutions. It is splendid to have sensible legislation governing joint stock companies. But it does not help much without a functioning court system that can protect property rights.

Still, in 2003 there were strong signs that recovery-based growth was being complemented by investment-based growth. First, economic growth was considerably higher than in recent years. Second, investment increased considerably. Third, there was rapid growth in the machine-building sector. Fourth, there was high growth in machine-building imports, which are usually associated with investment-based growth. And finally, in the first half of the year it looked like there was a reversal in the direction of capital flight. So, although the future is uncertain and obstacles will undoubtedly emerge, all of this has created hope that investment-based growth is possible in Russia.

Reference

Adelman Irma, and Dusan Vujovic. 1998. "Historical, Institutional and Policy Aspects of Transition: An Empirical Analysis." In A. Levy-Livermore, ed., *Handbook on the Globalization of the World Economy.* Northhampton, Mass.: Edward Elgar.

Comment

Gur Ofer

I AM HONORED TO HAVE BEEN INVITED TO SPEAK AT THIS EVENT. YEGOR GAIDAR'S lecture opens up wide horizons, both across space and over time—past and future. This lecture series is called *Practitioners in Development*, but in his presentation Gaidar goes far beyond his role as a key practitioner at a crucial moment in Russia's history, into the realm of academia. That makes sense, because his solid base in economics has provided Gaidar with both ammunition and a shield in his long struggle for reform in Russia.

I first met Gaidar at Arkhangelskoe, an estate south of Moscow, in fall 1991. I was told by telephone late one night to wait the next morning in the lobby of my hotel, from where I was driven to a mysterious hideout of the reform team. I must admit that the situation felt very Soviet.

My first question to Gaidar was, "What is the reform plan?" His response surprised me: "There is no plan; we are going to liberalize prices and wages and then work from there." We briefly discussed the need for some constraint that would stop prices from getting out of control. In retrospect this meeting seems to have been a sort of test of me. In the afternoon Gaidar offered me a ride back to town. He was going to see President Boris Yeltsin, and if I remember correctly that was when Gaidar was officially offered the position of deputy prime minister.

Today when I see Gaidar it usually involves issues related to Moscow's New Economic School, where Gaidar—and many other members of the original reform team—is a member of the Russian Advisory Board. (The school is an example of the kind of institutional buildup with a long gestation period that he advocates for Russia in his lecture.) On such occasions Gaidar never fails to update the rest of us on the status of Russia's reforms, and in most cases his main complaint is that in recent years they have been moving much too slowly.

Gaidar mentions 1992, the year when he was at the helm as deputy prime minister and then acting prime minister, only in passing in his lecture, and mainly in connection with the claim that reformers did not pay enough attention to institution building at that time. Indeed, he mentions 1992 only in order to draw attention to the future, a point that I return to below. When I was asked to be a commentator here, I assumed that 1992 would be at the center of the discussion, so I reread Gaidar's *Days of Defeat and Victory* (1999). I am among those who think that there may have been a better approach to the early reforms, including privatization and the dialogue with the rest of society. But I must confess that when one reads the detailed account of that period in Gaidar's book, it takes at least a few hours to reassure yourself that you might have been right on this issue.

Soviet and Russian Growth Patterns and Strategies

The rest of my discussion will focus on an issue that permeates Gaidar's lecture: the cyclical nature of the growth history and development strategies of the Soviet Union and Russia. These cycles have usually started with a burst of acceleration or catching up, then been interrupted by years of stagnation, and finally followed by a recovery that filled in the excess capacity left behind during the stagnation. The last major episode was the communist experiment, followed by the recent transition. This pattern is the reason the Soviet Union and Russia have achieved only the average global growth rate since 1820—a rather modest achievement—and lagged considerably behind the growth of the world's economic leaders: today's advanced, democratic, market economies.

Gaidar warns against repeating this development pattern, as manifested in President Vladimir Putin's recurring demand to double Russia's GDP within a few years. Instead Gaidar advocates a strategy of balanced, stable, sustained growth based on continuing reforms and institution building and at growth rates consistent with this strategy. Such reforms take longer to translate into growth, a fact that most people fail to recognize. True, important reforms have already occurred, including under Putin. But Gaidar sees many more that are pending and so observes Russia as being at best in the midst of its transition, and far from being a "normal country" as defined by Shleifer and Treisman (2003) and Åslund (in this volume).

The Russian case, as discussed in Gaidar's lecture, fits very well into the recent literature on development. Earlier theories of a uniform development pattern for all developing countries have been replaced by theories that emphasize, especially with respect to the initial period of takeoff, a plurality of growth strategies and the centrality of institutional changes. This new literature can be called the "new development economics," a combination of the "new comparative economics" (the title of a paper by Djankov and others 2003) and "growth strategies" (as according to Rodrik 2003). To this should be added a recent book by Easterly (2001) and papers by Hall and Jones (1999), Acemoglu, Johnson, and Robinson (2001), Acemoglu, Aghion, and Zilibotti (2002), Iyigun and Rodrik (2004), and many others.

Only at a later stage do most successful countries converge on the Kuznets model of (sustained) "modern economic growth" following the patterns of the growth leaders. One consequence of a two-stage development strategy is the high cost of the transition from one stage to the next. Gaidar mentioned how expensive (in terms of lost growth) such transitions have been in Russian history, including the current one. I will elaborate on this issue.

At a session on the new development theories mentioned above at the January 2004 American Economic Association meetings in San Diego, California, I presented a paper on the Soviet Union, Russia, and the communist experiment (Ofer 2004) that fits nicely into the historical picture presented by Gaidar. The theoretical and empirical question presented was, to what extent could an initial big push or takeoff, based on the use of extraordinary institutions and tools, pay off when one adds the costs of transition to the common strategy of modern economic growth?

The ancient Hebrew *Talmud* tells a story about a man looking for a way to a town. A boy he meets at a crossroads points in one direction and tells the man that it is "a short but long way," then points in another direction and says that it is "long but short." The man follows the short way and gets entangled in orchards and fences. When he comes back to the boy complaining, the boy responds, "didn't I also tell you it was long?"

The development record of many countries illustrates this story. Import substitution may have been an effective way to take off and grow fast for some time in Latin America, Central Asia, and elsewhere. But when the time came for a shift in strategy, misguided institutions and vested interests joined forces to delay the change, despite a sharp decline in growth. Then when the change came, the transition turned out to be extremely difficult, costly, and long. In these cases the Olsonian "sclerosis" that usually awaits aging societies attacked prematurely. Even Japan has found itself in this trap (those fences and orchards), so that despite its better initial growth strategy—of export-led growth, accompanied by heavy government intervention—it has been unable to avoid the same syndrome, and has endured more than a dozen years of stagnation. As a result Japan's healthy 5.5 percent growth in GDP per capita following World War II reconstruction falls to 4.0 percent when the period since 1991 is included.

The Soviet Union and Russia are an extreme example of this syndrome. It started with a long debate among economists in the 1920s about the best way to industrialize. The virtues and drawbacks of balanced growth, not far from the classical and evolutionary strategy of modern economic growth, were weighed against rapid industrialization and collectivization. The decision in favor of the second approach (the short way) was partly based on political considerations and power struggles, but it also promised fast results.

The regime that followed, led by Josef Stalin, was much more coercive, cruel, and therefore wasteful than required even by the drastic economic strategy. Still, it produced relatively impressive rates of growth (though much lower ones for consumption), with GDP per capita rising by more than 3 percent a year during 1928–73 (excluding the war years), as well as radical changes in the Soviet Union's industrial structure. But while growth was high, most observers do not believe that it was worth the enormous price paid in human life and strife and in forgone freedoms.

Costs of Transition

The focus on this occasion, however, is on what happened later. Growth rates started to fall in the mid-1960s, reaching virtual stagnation in the 1980s. The collapse of the Soviet Union and the subsequent transition produced another extended drop in output. Growth did not resume until 2000. But as Gaidar emphasizes, this may still be recovery-based growth—not the kind of sustained growth Russia needs—and the transition is far from over.

Russia's transition has been extremely costly for several reasons. The first was the delay in implementing reforms. Given the relative thaw after Stalin—with some reforms and open economic discussions under Nikita Khrushchev (1953–64), accompanied by a fair amount of disorganization—it is possible to imagine a shift starting then. Economists and leaders alike recognized most if not all of the problems that eventually led the Soviet Union to a dead end. One approach to reform at that time could have been to follow the Chinese approach, introducing gradual changes from above (starting with decollectivization) as a "new" Soviet model of communism. Alternatively, the situation could have deteriorated due to the growing disorganization caused by partial administrative and other reforms under Khrushchev, forcing a system change—and resembling the causes of the collapse under Mikhail Gorbachev (Ellman and Kontorovich 1997).

Instead the Cold War, the Sputnik space exploration program, and the conservatism and vested interests of the leadership and the elites brought about the modest Kosygin reforms, nearly all of which were watered down by Leonid Brezhnev (1964–82), and then caused the economic stagnation that led to the Soviet Union's collapse. But the energy crises of 1973 and 1979 generated substantial (though temporary) economic benefits for the Soviet economy, helped disguise the real situation, and created an optimistic (though false) view about the country's economic prospects, further postponing needed reforms. During 1973–90 annual growth of per capita GDP averaged a mere 1 percent—a high price to pay for delayed reforms.

The second reason was the enormous cost of the transition itself, in terms of suffering and lost output. Although this story is well known, I want to emphasize two clusters of related factors (in addition to the delayed reforms) that made the transition especially costly. The first is the "debt" accumulated under the old strategy of "haste" (catching up)—that is, the push for higher growth rates early at the expense of lower rates in the future. On the face of it the socialist strategy seemed to place a low discount rate on the future, investing early and postponing consumption. But in terms of growth, the regime's main goal, this haste meant the opposite: impatience and a high discount rate for future growth. Haste was manifested in the rapid depletion of natural and environmental resources and of social capital (through the establishment of enterprises in noncompetitive locations), in inadequate development of infrastructure (for communications, transportation, urban infrastructure and services, and so on), in the extensive mode of growth (which quickly consumed capital and labor inputs and reserves, the fuel of the model), and in the crowding out of technological development and productivity growth. Haste also required the early drafting of women into the labor force, a move that—combined with low consumption and poor housing and household services—rapidly reduced fertility and thus future growth in the labor force (Ofer 1987; Ofer and Vinokur 1992, ch. 7). The separation of Muslim states where fertility was high caused population decline and labor shortages in Russia, similar to conditions in advanced European countries. Like those advanced countries, Russia has had to reconsider its immigration policy.

The second cluster of factors responsible for Russia's costly transition is the contrast between the economic and political institutions of the old regime, both formal and informal, and those required for the new. The new institutions define the culture of economic and political behavior and the rules of the game so important to a well-functioning economy. Transition from communism involves creating a new set of formal institutions, and most have to be imported and transplanted. The formation of consistent informal institutions usually lags behind that of formal ones, especially if the latter are imported. Thus every transition must address the conflict between new formal institutions and informal institutions and modes of behavior inherited from the old regime.

In Russia this task is especially difficult due to the conflict between the formal and informal institutions that existed under and was inherited from the old regime. Unlike in most economic regimes, the authoritarian regime and central planning resulted in a culture of informal tools and rules designed to circumvent formal institutions. These informal institutions initially may have helped "lubricate" the old, rigid system, but they gradually contributed to its collapse through cynicism, shirking, diverted output and income, and destroyed solidarity, civic society, and social capital. The phenomena dubbed the "virtual economy" (Gaddy and Ickes 2002) is one manifestation of this contradiction. One of the challenges of the transition has been how to uproot this mentality of defying new formal institutions and exploiting them through rent-seeking and self-serving activities, and replace them with proper patterns of behavior.

In 1973–2003, during the latter period of delayed reforms in the Soviet Union and the early transition period in Russia, annual per capita GDP growth was about zero. And since the introduction of the socialist experiment, from 1928–2003 (excluding the war years), it was just 2 percent. Was it worth it? Could an evolutionary "classical" strategy starting in 1928—or better yet, 1913—have achieved at least that, and with less collateral damage? And what would the outcomes have been if reforms had "only" started under Khrushchev?

This point brings me back to Gaidar's emphasis on the hard work that remains for institutional reform in Russia and on the long-term nature and benefits of this process, as well as his warning against a new wave of haste, through industrial and other interventionist policies, to obtain higher growth in the short run at the cost of institutional deterioration. In some sense this is a lesson that Gaidar has drawn, or should have, from his experiences in the 1990s. For example, problematic privatization deals, especially in 1996, brought about the risky Yukos conflict of 2003—which has shaken faith in doing business in Russia and undermined the credibility of the political regime. Thus I share Gaidar's call for a long-term strategy of stable, moderate, open growth through steady institution building, while avoiding authoritarian tendencies. If that happens, Russia stands a chance of reaching the current income levels of today's global leaders within 50 years.

References

Acemoglu, Daron, Phillipe Aghion, and Fabrizio Zilibotti. 2002. "Distance to Frontier, Selection, and Economic Growth." NBER Working Paper 9066. National Bureau of Economic Research, Cambridge, Mass.

Acemoglu, Daron, Simon Johnson, and James A. Robinson. 2001. "Colonial Origins of Comparative Development: An Empirical Investigation." *American Economic Review* 91: 1369–1401.

Allen, C. Robert. 2003. *From Farm to Factory: A Reinterpretation of Soviet Industrial Revolution.* Princeton, N.J.: Princeton University Press.

Djankov, Simeon, Andrei Shleifer, Edward L. Glaeser, Rafael La Porta, and Florencio Lopez de Silanes. 2003. "The New Comparative Economics." *Journal of Comparative Economics*, 31 (4): 595–619.

Easterly, William. 2001. *The Elusive Quest for Growth: Economists' Adventures and Misadventures in the Tropics.* Cambridge, Mass.: MIT Press.

Ellman, Michael, and Vladimir Kontorovich, eds. 1997. "The Collapse of the Soviet System and the Memoir Literature." *Europa-Asia Studies* 49 (2): 259–79.

Gaddy, Clifford G., and Barry W. Ickes. 2002. *Russia's Virtual Economy.* Washington, D.C.: Brookings Institution Press.

Gaidar, Yegor. 1999. *Days of Defeat and Victory.* Seattle: University of Washington Press.

Hall, Robert E., and Charles I. Jones. 1999. "Why Do Some Countries Produce So Much More Output per Worker than Others?" *Quarterly Journal of Economics* 114 (February): 83–116.

Iyigun, Murat, and Dani Rodrik. 2004. "On the Efficiency of Reforms: Policy Tinkering, Institutional Change and Entrepreneurship." Paper presented at the American Economic Association meetings, January, San Diego, Calif.

Ofer, Gur. 1987. "Soviet Economic Growth: 1928–85." *Journal of Economic Literature* 25 (4): 1767–1833.

———. 2003. "Switching Development Strategies and the Costs of Transition: The Case of the Soviet Union and Russia." Paper presented at the American Economic Association meetings, January, San Diego, Calif.

Ofer, Gur, and Aaron Vinokur. 1992. *The Soviet Household under the Old Regime: Economic Conditions and Behavior in the 1970s.* Cambridge: Cambridge University Press.

Rodrik, Dani. 2003. "Growth Strategies." Harvard University, John F. Kennedy School of Government, Cambridge, Mass.

Shleifer, Andrei, and Daniel Treisman. 2004. "Normal Country." *Foreign Affairs* 83 (March/April): 20–38.

Vandenbussche, Jerome, Philippe Aghion, and Costas Meghir. 2004. "Distance to Technological Frontier and Composition of Human Capital." Paper presented at the American Economic Association meetings, January, San Diego, Calif.

Comment

Anders Åslund

I AM GREATLY HONORED TO BE COMMENTING ON YEGOR GAIDAR'S LECTURE. FEW if any other individuals have meant so much to the postsocialist economic transformation. My first experience with Gaidar came in the mid-1980s, when I was working at the Swedish embassy in Moscow and closely following the Soviet Union's economic development.

Then, out of the blue, in January 1987 there was a stunning article in the theoretical organ of the country's Communist Party (*Kommunist*), providing an economic analysis of the past year written by Gaidar. The surprising thing was that it was a completely accurate, Western-style analysis of the Soviet economy, with greater insight into national statistics than was usually made available to us foreigners at the time. The article pointed out, for example, that the Soviet Union had a large and rising budget deficit that posed a big danger of macroeconomic destabilization.

I tried to meet Gaidar, which was extremely difficult in those days because foreigners were not allowed to see almost anyone—particularly younger people. We were only allowed to see old Communist academics. Accordingly, I did not meet Gaidar until June 1991, when I organized a delegation from Sweden to visit his newly founded institute at the Academy of Sciences.

To our surprise and delight, we saw that Gaidar was engaged in absolutely the right activities. He had set up an institute to guide the country's transition to capitalism and had even managed to do so under the auspices of the Academy of Sciences and the National Academy. As a result I had no doubt who would lead Russia's transition. Indeed, I even told my Swedish friends that Gaidar would be the next prime minister of Russia. Although that prediction proved inaccurate, it does not make Gaidar's achievements any less impressive. Because at the time there were few people in Russia who understood what needed to be done, who understood the economy, and—perhaps most important—who dared to speak.

Developments in Russia

Russia is in the midst of a postrevolutionary stabilization, to quote Vladimir Mau and Irina Starodubrovskaya (2001). Capitalism has won, and for the time being democracy seems to have failed. Russia today is best described as a mildly authoritarian state. What explains these developments?

The transition generated sharply diverging outcomes. Economic transformation was due to a tightly knit group of reformers, led by Gaidar, who knew what they wanted and pushed it through. They had an economic reform program that President Boris Yeltsin announced to Parliament in October 1991 and that Parliament approved with a massive majority. The program also received, after some hesitation, strong international support. Led by the International Monetary Fund (IMF) and the World Bank, the international community came out strongly for the reform program and provided substantial financial support for it.

There was no such program for democracy. No one had a clear idea what kind of political structure Russia should have, and no group really pushed a specific initiative. The outside world also did not have a clear concept. And without a program, without domestic consensus, and without international support, massive reform is unlikely to succeed.

On the economic side everything was in place for needed reforms. In Russia and other transition economies, the Washington consensus (see Williamson in this volume) has worked where its tenets have been implemented as intended. Today 25 of 28 formerly communist countries can be described as capitalist. Thus, in terms of economic reforms, transition has largely been a success.

But what about political reforms? About half of these countries are not democracies. Thus economists have done a much better job than political scientists. And that is very much thanks to Yegor Gaidar, Leszek Balcerowicz (in Poland), Vaclav Klaus (in the Czech Republic), and a few others.

When reformers are thinking clearly and know what they want, they often achieve it. As John Maynard Keynes emphasized, nothing in the world is as important as ideas. But in too many transition economies, too little thought and energy were devoted to achieving democracy.

Weaknesses in Data on Transition

Any discussion of growth in transition economies must emphasize the weaknesses of the relevant data. Among members of the Commonwealth of Independent States, Russia probably has the best statistics. Even so, the estimated drop in its GDP between 1989 and 1994, though recently lowered to 44 percent, is probably only half that.

The exaggerated fall in GDP is much higher in Ukraine, and even more so in Moldova, the Caucasus, and Central Asia. To get a clear understanding of these issues, a major organization such as the World Bank—which is in the best position to sort out such discrepancies—should review and revise these data using Western methods, including adjusting statistics from the final year of communism. By doing so the Bank can determine actual output levels during those years, which are much lower than is widely believed.

The move to capitalism did not produce declines in GDP nearly as large as have been reported. I have tried to produce such evidence, but people have not liked my work. Although it is extremely difficult to reach agreement on how to do this kind of work, it is vital that it be done. Gaidar's lecture wisely relies on historical GDP per capita and purchasing power parities to escape the illusion of a massive drop in Russia's output.

The big question is the one that Gaidar poses: whether Russia and other transition economies are experiencing recovery-based growth or real, endogenous (investment-based) growth. Recovery-based growth occurs when a critical mass of good economic policies comes together and there is free capacity.

Divergences in Development Outcomes

The postcommunist world shows an interesting division. On the one hand are the four Central European countries usually considered the greatest transition success stories—the Czech Republic, Hungary, Poland, and the Slovak Republic. For the past five or so years these countries have had steady growth of about 3 percent a year. But this is not success: they should be growing by 6–8 percent a year. Why should they be doing worse than Ireland? They should catch up.

Average per capita GDP in these four countries is about 40 percent of the EU average, even when measured using purchasing power parities. At current growth rates they are not catching up to their Western neighbors. This is a miserable failure that should cause great concern.

Then there are the transition economies considered unsuccessful, such as the 12 members of the Commonwealth of Independent States (CIS). Here I will focus only on the reformers, leaving aside the nonmarket economies of Belarus, Turkmenistan, and Uzbekistan. For the past five years the reformers have achieved average growth of 6.0–6.5 percent a year. Though this performance is not quite as good as it should be—these countries should be growing by 8 percent—several countries in this group are doing quite well. For example, over the past four years Kazakhstan's GDP growth has averaged 10.5 percent. Though some of this growth has been due to the country's oil reserves, there are other reasons.

Some of the strong outcomes in CIS countries are due to recovery-based growth, because they saw larger declines in output than their Central European neighbors. Thus there is enormous free capacity. CIS countries are also benefiting from a laggard effect that could, all else being equal, account for an extra 1 percentage point in annual growth. Still, there is more to their better performance.

Unemployment is high in Central Europe, running 18 percent in Poland and the Slovak Republic. In Russia it is half that, which is indicative of levels throughout the CIS. Similarly, budget deficits in Central Europe are 5–6 percent of GDP, and even 9 percent in Hungary two years ago, while CIS countries have almost balanced their budgets.

In Central Europe public spending averages nearly 50 percent of GDP, and in Hungary it was 54 percent last year. Taxes are also high, with payroll taxes around 50 percent and progressive income taxes of 40 percent or more. Central European countries also provide huge social transfers—in particular, high pensions—and impose a lot of regulation on their labor markets.

These are not good economic policies, and there is nothing like them in the CIS. Payroll taxes have been falling in CIS countries; in Kazakhstan, for example, they are 20 percent. Kazakhstan has also been a leader in pension reform, introducing Chilean-style privatization of its pension system in 1997. In addition, Kazakhstan has implemented New Zealand–style deregulation of its labor market—a move that would be impossible in Central Europe. (Estonia and Latvia have done so, but that was before they had advanced too far in their accession to the European Union.) Moreover, Russia has introduced a landmark flat income tax of 13 percent, a move followed by Ukraine.

Thus Central European and CIS countries are developing completely different economic models. Emulating its EU neighbors, Central Europe has taken a social welfare approach. But as János Kornai pointed out in 1992, that approach is premature. Although good for stability, it does not generate much growth—which is what these countries need.

By contrast, former Soviet countries are rather taking their cue from the Washington consensus, from East Asia, and from economic theory. Perhaps the most remarkable difference between the two groups of countries involves public spending or redistribution. Among reforming CIS countries it has fallen to 26 percent of GDP. And in Kazakhstan, the growth leader, redistribution is probably 23 percent of GDP.

Given the enormous variations in outcomes between Central European and CIS countries, it seems crucial to determine the effects of their different economic models. These developments have two disturbing features. One is that in recent years there has been a perfect positive correlation between corruption and growth. The other is that there is a strongly negative correlation between democracy indicators (as measured by Freedom House) and growth.

These are big changes from earlier findings. In the 1990s there were almost perfect positive correlations between democracy, financial stabilization, liberalization, privatization, and growth—no matter how the variables were measured or manipulated. Today, especially in Central Europe, democracy is associated with budget deficits, high unemployment, and slow growth. So the EU model is also good for democracy but, again, bad for growth. And that is even clearer outside than inside the European Union.

While visiting Moscow in October 2003 I heard, to my surprise, Presidential Economic Adviser Andrei Illarionov ask why Russia should look to the West for economic guidance. Instead, he said, it should look to the East: Kazakhstan has almost the same economic structure as Russia, yet its growth rate is almost twice as high.

Illarionov did not mention that Kazakhstan is extremely corrupt and mildly authoritarian. Its leaders argue that there is no need to fight corruption because it does not harm growth. Nor do they see any economic need for a more democratic system. These views are the main challenges that the European Union needs to confront.

I think that discussions of transition economies should share Gaidar's focus—growth beyond recovery. From that perspective, transition indicators such as those produced by the European Bank for Reconstruction and Development (EBRD) are rather meaningless. Moreover, many analyses of transition lack a clear understanding of what generates growth at this stage. I am arguing for a fairly free market approach. Although it is difficult to prove all the benefits of this model in regression analysis, it would be even harder to prove the opposite.

Reference

Mau, Vladimir, and Irina Starodubrovskaya. 2001. *The Challenge of Revolution: Contemporary Russia in Historical Perspective*. Oxford: Oxford University Press.

Kemal Derviş

Former Minister of Treasury and Economic Affairs, Turkey

Born in Istanbul in 1949, Kemal Derviş earned an M.Sc. in Economics from the London School of Economics in 1970 and a Ph.D. in Economics from Princeton University in 1973. He was Assistant Professor at the Middle East Technical University (Turkey) and Princeton University before joining the World Bank in 1978. Derviş held a number of positions at the Bank, including Director for Central Europe, Vice President for the Middle East and North Africa, and Vice President for Poverty Reduction and Economic Management. He has coauthored a book on general equilibrium models, published by Cambridge University Press, and written various articles on economic policy and development economics published in Turkish, English, French, and German. A new book, titled *A Better Globalization*, is about to be published by the Center for Global Development (Washington, D.C.).

In early 2001, during a financial crisis in Turkey, Derviş was appointed Minister of Economic Affairs and assigned responsibility for defusing the crisis. He did so admirably, setting the country back on a path to stability by the time he left office in August 2002. Later in 2002 he was elected to the Turkish National Parliament, where he represents Istanbul as a member of the Social Democrat Party. He has also been a member of the European Constitutional Convention and participates in various international task forces, including one on Global Public Goods and one on the Future of the Balkans.

5 Returning from the Brink
Turkey's Efforts at Systemic Change and Structural Reform

Kemal Derviş

Between the early 1950s and late 1980s Turkey's performance on growth and development put it in the middle range of World Bank borrowers. Although it developed faster than most countries in Latin America, the Middle East, and South Asia, Turkey's performance fell short of Southern Europe's—and especially East Asia's. Still, per capita growth averaged about 2.5 percent a year, social indicators improved, and in the 1980s Turkey became a star performer in terms of growth in manufactured exports.

But in the 1990s performance worsened, with per capita growth close to zero between 1991 and 2001. As a result Turkey continued to lose ground to East Asia and Southern Europe. In addition, its growth rate fell below that in South Asia. Since World War II Turkey has experienced years of very rapid growth—sometimes 6–7 percent per capita—revealing the economy's inherent dynamism. But growth has been interrupted by a series of crises, causing severe contractions and slowing development.

A marked increase in such crises was what made the 1990s such a dismal decade, economically speaking. In 1994, 1999, and 2001 output fell by more than 6 percent. Two of these crises (1994 and 2001) were associated with exchange rate appreciation, followed by sharp devaluation. The negative growth in 1999 reflected fiscal and debt concerns as well as the effects of a devastating earthquake. Together these three years lowered real per capita income by about 30 percent.

A comprehensive, quantitative analysis of Turkey's development experience is beyond the scope of this lecture. Instead I highlight some key lessons from the 2001 crisis and the effort to overcome it, emphasizing aspects that have wider significance for middle-income countries and focusing on the role played by the Bretton Woods institutions: the International Monetary Fund (IMF) and World Bank. Topics covered include the strategy and political economy of crisis management, the exchange rate regime, the debate on debt sustainability, fiscal policy, and the macroeconomic framework, wage policy and labor relations, and Turkey's interactions with the IMF and the Bank. Detailed treatment of important related issues—such as banking sector reform, technical aspects of monetary policy, issues in areas such as agriculture and energy, and privatization policy—falls beyond the scope of this lecture.

The Making of a Severe Crisis

The February 2001 crisis was a rather typical result of the interaction between a nominal anchor exchange rate policy, an extremely weak banking sector (including ineffective supervision), and insufficiently strong fiscal policy. Table 5.1 summarizes some key economic indicators in the years preceding the crisis. A quasi currency board exchange rate regime was incompatible with active monetary policy. Fiscal policy was the only macroeconomic instrument available to ensure consistency between the preannounced exchange rate and balance of payments developments, as well as between real interest rates on government debt and public sector debt indicators. Structural improvements in the economy—such as better public administration and rapid reforms in sector policies—could also have contributed to macroeconomic consistency by creating positive expectations, although their impact on real variables (such as productivity) is more medium term in nature.

Neither the strength of fiscal policy nor the pace and quality of structural reforms was sufficient to prevent a rapidly growing current account deficit in the second half of 2000. The large deficit reflected inconsistency between the path set for the nominal exchange rate and the path of domestic prices, which include many relatively nontradable products. By September 2000 the markets had started to view this widening deficit as a threat.

Banking sector weaknesses interacted with these macroeconomic developments to create the conditions for the major crisis that ensued. Throughout the 1990s Turkish banks had grown accustomed to holding balance sheets with a large share of government debt on the asset side, mostly denominated in domestic currency but often largely financed by liabilities in foreign currency, taking advantage of the large interest rate differential. Real domestic interest rates tend to be much higher than foreign

TABLE 5.1
Economic Indicators in the Years Preceding Turkey's February 2001 Crisis

Indicator	1998	1999	2000
Current account balance (percentage of GNP)	1.0	−0.7	−4.9
Change in real effective exchange rate, December–December [a] (percent)	4.1	6.2	15.5
Inflation [a] (percent), end of year	69.7	68.8	39.0
Central Bank reserves (billions of U.S. dollars), end of year	19.7	23.2	22.2

a. Based on consumer price index.
Source: Central Bank of Turkey, Turkey Undersecretariat of the Treasury, and IMF data.

TABLE 5.2

Indicators of the Early 2001 Attack on the Turkish Lira

Indicator	February 16	19	20	21	22	23	26	March 2
Exchange rate (thousands of liras/ U.S. dollar)	686	688	686	691	689	963	1,080	916
Overnight rate (percent)	40	44	2,056	4,025	1,221	568	102	86
Central Bank reserves (billions of U.S. dollars)	27.9					22.6		21.5

Note: Reserves figures are end-of-week data.
Source: Central Bank of Turkey, Turkey Undersecretariat of the Treasury, and IMF data.

interest rates (minus ongoing exchange rate depreciation) in regimes that roughly target a fixed real exchange rate, reflecting different inflation rates and significant differences in risk premiums.

Turkey had essentially practiced an exchange rate regime where the Central Bank allowed the exchange rate to depreciate more or less in line with differential inflation prior to the reform program introduced in 2000. But the difference between domestic and foreign interest rates was much larger than the devaluations taking place. Although the quasi currency board regime in place in 2000 led to lower real domestic interest rates, incentives for short-term capital inflows grew stronger because the Central Bank made an explicit commitment to the path of the nominal exchange rate to reduce exchange rate uncertainty. Moreover, this path was leading to real exchange rate appreciation because of insufficiently strong fiscal policy, making it even more attractive to build open foreign exchange positions.

Thus the stage had been set for a major crash. The large current account deficit was financed by short-term capital inflows that took advantage of the interest rate differentials in a type of Ponzi scheme. The size of these flows gradually undermined the medium-term credibility of the exchange rate peg.

In such a situation a loss of confidence immediately leads to a reversal in short-term flows, resulting in higher domestic interest rates and lower domestic reserves. Higher interest rates cause losses for banks holding large amounts of government bonds. These losses undermine confidence in the banking system, leading to further net outflows and setting off a vicious circle that makes it increasingly difficult to defend the fixed nominal exchange rate. If the exchange rate eventually gives, banks and other players with open positions will incur large balance sheet losses as their net debt positions worsen. This makes it difficult for these players to finance their cash flows, leading to further losses in the banking system as nonperforming assets explode. The entire economy goes into a tailspin as high interest rates, bank failures, and contractions in output lead to ever worsening debt indicators—with the danger of having what starts as a liquidity crisis end in a solvency crisis for many economic actors and a default on government debt.

This is what happened in Turkey when confidence in the reform program started to decline in fall 2000. The first major shock occurred in November with the failure of a medium-size bank that had too much exposure to government bonds and could not withstand a sudden rise in interest rates. That failure led to a further loss of confidence and reserve losses by the Central Bank as it defended the nominal anchor. Only an immediate augmentation of IMF financial support stabilized the situation, but merely for another three months. In February 2001 a total collapse occurred, triggered by a dispute between the president and the prime minister related to concerns about bank supervision and accusations of regulatory irregularities—but reflecting inconsistent policies and the underlying weakness of the coalition government. It was then that the prime minister asked me to become governor of the Central Bank. The previous governor, along with the undersecretary of the treasury, had just resigned in the face of the catastrophe.

I did not accept the offer. This was not a crisis that could be overcome by the Central Bank. The ratio of debt to GDP was bound to rise dramatically as the state was forced to recognize its contingent liabilities in the banking system and as interest rates skyrocketed. Already many domestic and foreign analysts questioned Turkey's ability to roll over its debt. The balance of payments was in shambles, and the exchange rate in a free fall (table 5.2). Large parts of the banking system were decapitalized, and the payments system was not functioning. Perhaps more important than all of this was a deep loss of public confidence in the government and the entire political system. Again, this was not a situation that the Central Bank could salvage.

In fact, I was not sure how it could be salvaged. The more I learned—particularly about the situation facing public banks and the complete lack of coordination between various ministries influencing economic policy, such as treasury, finance, foreign trade, planning, privatization, and industry—the worse it looked. And though I had always kept in close contact with my native country, I had been abroad 25 years (first teaching and then working at the World Bank) and was not at all sure how Turkey's political system and bureaucracy worked and what levers could be mobilized to start the recovery. On the other hand, many friends in Turkey offered me their support, and I felt that my experience at the Bank and my academic work on economic policy was relevant.

I concluded that in responding to the crisis, a unified strategy and close coordination among decisionmakers would be essential to increasing the chances of success. So, in my response to the government I argued that only a minister of economic affairs with strong coordinating powers would have any chance of succeeding, and that I would accept a position only if the government ensured that I could play such a role.

I did not get what I wanted. The government was a coalition of three parties, and everyone jealously guarded their turf. After the coalition leaders consulted among themselves, I was offered the position of minister of the treasury, as well as coordinating responsibilities for the Central Bank and Banking Regulation and Supervision Agency and responsibility for negotiations with the IMF and World Bank—but no oversight over the ministries of finance (responsible for taxation), planning, foreign trade, or privatization. I accepted this offer on March 2 (probably too quickly), traveled back to Washington, D.C., to resign from the Bank, packed two suitcases and returned to Turkey. Once back I formed a small core team—including the new governor of the Central Bank (whom I had just convinced the prime minister to appoint) and the new, highly regarded undersecretary of the treasury (whom I was also able to appoint)—and hired as my chief of staff a dynamic young woman with infectious enthusiasm who had worked closely with me at the World Bank.

These were the most urgent appointments, followed later by new managers at state banks and a new head of the Banking Regulation and Supervision Agency. I must add that most of the department managers at the treasury, including the deputy undersecretaries, were excellent and had spent long, difficult years struggling for reform. In just a few days I felt at home and in a professional structure that I enjoyed and trusted.

The Strategy and Political Economy of Crisis Management

At the heart of Turkey's difficulties was a rent-seeking socioeconomic system where governments had for decades promised and attempted to distribute more resources than they could raise. The private sector, encouraged by the political class, spent enormous effort capturing rents in exchange for support to various political groups. As early as the 1960s Anne Krueger had described how the political economy of rent seeking undermined what was otherwise a remarkably dynamic society with great growth potential. Krueger also emphasized the negative consequences of what was at the time excessive protectionism.

The nature of rent seeking changed in the 1980s in response to a shift to export promotion under Prime Minister Turgut Özal. But the economy remained strongly influenced by rent-seeking mechanisms, now focused on export subsidies, cheap bank credit, and opportunities created by privatization rather than the quotas and tariffs of the past. The situation worsened in the 1990s because of an extreme fragmentation of the political system, with one unstable coalition succeeding another, the tenure of the average minister lasting just over one year, and decisionmaking on economic matters spread over a growing number of ministries and competing political parties. This situation led to chronically high inflation—averaging nearly 70 percent in the 1990s—and public debt rising from 28 percent of GDP at the beginning of the decade to about 60 percent in 1999, not counting the state's contingent liabilities accumulating in the private and public banking system, the social security system, and the energy sector.

As noted, the shock in November 2000 and the collapse in February 2001 came in the form of severe liquidity crises triggered by a bank failure in November and a political dispute in February. But the crisis was waiting to happen, because Turkey's political and economic structure had become unsustainable. Taking into account the state's contingent liabilities even before the crisis, debt had risen to about 70 percent of GDP, and the average maturity of this huge domestic and foreign debt was less than three years. This resulted in constant rollover fears and the looming threat of a "debt event."

Thus the first strategic decision we made in response to the crisis was that deep structural reforms—aimed at changing the basic nature of the socioeconomic system—were essential to a real and durable recovery. The task was not simply one of achieving stabilization or restoring liquidity. (It is distressing that some people who held influential positions in the 1990s still argue that the Central Bank could have avoided the crisis if it had provided liquidity to the banking system. They obviously do not—or do not want to—understand the implications of a debt to GDP ratio of more than 70 percent, combined with the short maturities on that debt and the fact that it reflected substantial state contingent liabilities in the banking sector.) What we had to achieve in Turkey was systematic economic change: shifting from a rent-seeking society to a modern, competitive economy with much greater autonomy for the economic sphere, greater separation of politics and markets, greater transparency, and less privilege and therefore a better distribution of income, which would also lead to greater legitimacy of governance and decisionmaking.

The next, and related, question involved sequencing. Should we spend the first few months addressing purely macroeconomic concerns, such as ensuring an adequate primary budget surplus and making the new flexible exchange-rate work? Or should we, simultaneously and without delay, try to implement many of the structural reforms that together would amount to systemic economic change? Some argued that we should not spend all our political capital upfront, that Turkey, having waited for some of these structural reforms for decades, could wait another six months. Strongly supported by the new undersecretary of the treasury, my view was that the crisis provided a unique opportunity to push reforms through Parliament that otherwise might take years to enact. Open heart surgery was necessary, but habits also had to change: the patient could not be allowed to continue smoking two packs of cigarettes a day.

This all or nothing kind of approach has its drawbacks. I know that Alejandro Foxley, discussing Chile in the first lecture of this series, emphasized the importance of not spending precious political capital all at once (see Foxley in this volume). There is much truth in this, and I think that in normal times the only possible course of action is to advance step by step, building required coalitions one or a few at a time. But a severe crisis creates a different situation. First, the need for reform is more urgent. The message that reform is under way must be stronger and more immediate for markets and citizens to respond. Such a crisis also creates opportunity. Vested interests have a lot to lose in a severe crisis. Thus they are more likely to accept reform even if it means a long-term loss of advantage and privilege—because with further deepening of the crisis they could lose almost everything.

Such was the situation in Turkey in spring 2001, and is why we chose and were able to frontload structural reforms. In less than a year Parliament passed 19 important structural reform laws or regulations, the most important of which were a law granting full independence to the Central Bank, a banking law, a complete reorganization of state banks (including substantial downscaling), an overhaul of agricultural policies (moving from distorting price supports to direct income support), a civil aviation law, a telecommunications law, a tobacco law, a law on sugar industry regulation, a public procurement law, and a law on public debt management. More than half of the 19 new laws were passed in the four months following the February crisis.

I believe that Turkey's experience in 2001 shows how reformers can seize the moment at a time of crisis and achieve structural reforms that would be extremely difficult in more normal times—contrary to the view expressed by, for example, Peter Kenen (2001) that such an approach will overload the system. Kenen's view, convincingly argued, is shared by many, particularly in evaluating the IMF's insistence on structural reforms during the East Asian crisis. The difference in Turkey may have been due to fairly strong domestic ownership of the reforms and our ability to mobilize much of civil society in support of them.

The reforms sent markets and citizens a strong message of radical change and were instrumental in the relatively rapid restoration of confidence. Independent regulatory agencies were strengthened at the expense of line ministries, reducing the ability of party politics to influence regulatory decisions. The reforms also strengthened the potential effectiveness of fiscal policy by making it much harder for the state to accumulate contingent liabilities. In addition, transparency was increased (for example, procurement, banking, and debt management), limiting opportunities for corruption and special privileges.

Did we succeed with this systemic change? Are the reforms irreversible? Only time will tell. I resigned from the government in August 2002 due to increasing strains within the governing coalition. When this lecture was written in fall 2003, the basic reforms were still in place despite a general election (in November 2002), which led to a completely new government, and the Iraq crisis, which was a serious shock to the system. It is worth emphasizing that the public generally understood the link between the structural reforms and the rebound that started in early 2002, as well as the long-term benefits that the reforms could provide.

There is reason to be cautiously optimistic about the continued success of the reforms. Still, two years is not enough for a new system to gain deep roots, and the danger remains of a return to many of the old rent-seeking ways. The reforms were pushed through by a group of economists and technicians with support from civil society but without organized political support. Debt started to decline significantly in mid-2002 but was still nearly 70 percent of GDP at the end of 2003 (after having peaked at more than 90 percent at the end of 2001). It remains to be seen whether the political system will continue to forgo the short term benefits of excessive rent-seeking populism and begin to truly own the new economic system. Short-term macroeconomic management also remains important, including the need to fight volatility of expectations and of short-term capital flows and portfolio shifts.

The Exchange Rate Regime

The 2001 crisis started when Turkey had to abandon its preannounced nominal anchor exchange rate regime in the face of a massive attack on the lira triggered by a dispute between the president and the prime minister on February 19, 2001. The IMF advised the government to float the lira, which it did on February 22. After I joined the government in early March, one of our first tasks was to formally commit Turkey to a new exchange rate regime. Given our need for its backing, this had to be done as part of a letter of intent that would form the basis for IMF support. Table 5.3 shows the exchange rate, inflation, and Central Bank reserves in the critical months of February–August 2001.

All of us on the economic team realized that a return to some kind of exchange rate peg—even a band with upper and lower limits—was impossible in the short term. As long as serious doubts remained about Turkey's ability to roll over its public debt, it would remain vulnerable to an attack on the lira triggered by fear of a "debt event." Moreover, the Central Bank had lost about $6 billion in reserves between mid-February and early March 2001 (see table 5.2), and the current account deficit had reached nearly 5 percent of GNP in 2000 (see table 5.1). The question was not whether to have a floating exchange rate, but how "clean" our floating rate regime would be.

There were three competing views. One, essentially the IMF's, argued for a completely clean float, with interventions by the Central Bank strictly limited to preventing excessive daily movements in the nominal exchange rate (with "excessive" defined as more than 5 percent a day), without any attempt to manage the exchange rate in the short or medium term. Another view, prevalent in academic circles in Turkey and to some extent among Central Bank staff, was that the Central Bank should retain the freedom to intervene directly in markets and use such interventions to give the markets a sense of direction. The goal here was to move the regime as quickly as possible to a kind of managed float where the Central Bank would take into account balance of payments, reserve, and debt indicators in helping it deter-

TABLE 5.3

Turkey's Exchange Rate, Inflation, and Central Bank Reserves, January–August 2001

Indicator	January	February	March	April	May	June	July	August
Nominal exchange rate (thousands of liras/ U.S. dollar), monthly average	670	749	953	1,197	1,127	1,208	1,316	1,395
Nominal exchange rate (thousands of liras/ U.S. dollar), end of month	682	910	1,061	1,166	1,162	1,273	1,326	1,375
Inflation (percent, based on consumer price index)	2.5	1.8	6.1	10.3	5.1	3.1	2.4	2.9
Reserves (billions of U.S. dollars), end of month	25.7	22.6	18.4	18.2	20.5	16.5	17.2	18.7

Source: Central Bank of Turkey, Turkey Undersecretariat of the Treasury, and IMF data.

mine the extent of desirable intervention—without making any commitment to a certain exchange rate and, in particular, no real exchange rate targeting.

The third view, increasingly defended by the governor of the Central Bank and supported by the Banking Regulation and Supervision Agency, stressed the dangers of a large overshooting type of depreciation for the balance sheets of many banks and corporations holding debt denominated in foreign currency. There was a scary prospect that a wave of bankruptcies would be triggered throughout the economy if the exchange rate lost another 30–40 percent of its value in spring 2001. I quickly came to support this third, intermediate view. The challenge was to slow further downward movements in the value of the Turkish lira without giving the impression that we were trying to move back to some kind of pegged rate and without losing too much reserves. So we embarked on an imperfect free float, using Central Bank interventions and attempts to "talk up" the exchange rate to limit the excessive over-shooting that has characterized the aftermaths of acute crises in most emerging market economies.

We had considerable success with this approach in April and May (see table 5.3). The Central Bank intervened rather heavily in late March and in April, and then again in June when there were intermittent panic attacks. The exchange rate reached a temporary peak of 1,285,000 liras to the U.S. dollar on April 11, testing the 1,300,000 level in some trades around that time. An interesting episode during this period was that I had declared in early April, when the exchange rate was testing the 1,300,000 level, that a reasonable exchange rate for late April would be 1,100,000, although I was careful to stress that this was neither a target nor a policy commitment. This was obviously a risky declaration, and I got criticized by some purists who thought that a minister of economic affairs should not make such declarations under a floating rate regime. But at the end of April the exchange rate was very close to that level (at 1,166,000; see table 5.3), even though the Central Bank had in no way targeted it—adding to my credibility in some quarters.

I believe that our refusal to give in to panic attacks and our effort to talk up the exchange rate helped reduce corporate and financial sector distress in the first half of 2001, preventing what could have become a vicious circle of bankruptcies, further panic triggered by those bankruptcies, bank failures, and further attacks on the currency. The IMF was quite unhappy about the Central Bank interventions because it tended to underestimate markets' vulnerability to panic caused by the open positions of so many actors in the economy and because it was hard for it to argue with its shareholders in favor of substantial new resources for Turkey if it looked like those resources might be used for "futile" attempts at exchange rate stabilization. As a result, particularly during the run-up to an IMF board meeting in May 2001, the Central Bank had quite a few tense exchanges with the Fund.

But the outcome of our IMF negotiations was a compromise that, in hindsight, was probably optimal. The Central Bank started an orderly, preannounced program of small auctions to help supply foreign exchange to the markets, and it rarely intervened in a direct, unannounced manner. Moreover, the situation changed in August 2001, with panic having subsided and the current account beginning to show a surplus. With my full support, the Central Bank began implementing a truly clean float. The foreign exchange market started to function in a more stable way and, except during a few weeks following the September 11 terror attack on the United States, in late August 2001 the Turkish lira began fluctuating around a gently appreciating trend—helping to reduce interest rates and further easing fears about debt dynamics.

These positive developments could have been reversed by the worldwide crisis atmosphere created the September 11 attacks. Turkey was particularly vulnerable because of the economic importance of its tourism sector and its proximity to the Middle East. A quickly negotiated enhancement to our IMF program, with new financing commitments for 2002, allowed us to overcome the fears triggered by September 11 and, from the end of October onward, resume the progress that had started in August. On the whole I maintain a very positive view of the way we changed our exchange rate regime and the transitional period of limited interventions.

That does not mean, however, that I am in favor of a total free float over the medium term. The real danger, starting in 2002, is no longer excessive depreciation but excessive appreciation—or, to put it differently, cycles of excessive appreciation having inevitably to be followed by rapid depreciation as the current account deficit starts widening. I do not believe in the purist view that the freer the market, the less fluctuation there will be. Volatility and massive uncertainty in the foreign exchange market have real costs in terms of growth and employment for medium-size, open economies such as Turkey (where imports plus exports account for more than 40 percent of GDP).

As a first step toward addressing this concern, I believe that a Chilean-type tax on short-term capital inflows would be helpful. Once confidence is restored and inflation has fallen below 20 percent for a sustained period, I believe that an initially wide but gradually narrowing exchange rate band—compatible with a "soft" inflation targeting policy—will become a feasible and desirable alternative to a free float. Hungary implemented such a narrowing band in the 1990s and succeeded in lowering inflation from the high 20s to well below 10 percent by the end of the decade. Such a regime would also lay the groundwork for Turkey eventually adopting the euro, which could become desirable after inflation has declined to eurozone levels, hopefully in five or six years. I am convinced that macroeconomic policy must be fine-tuned to avoid the risks created by excessive volatility.

Debt Sustainability, Fiscal Policy, and the Macroeconomic Framework

The crisis also created an immediate need to revise Turkey's macroeconomic framework. Before that could be done, we had to decide how to handle the large public debt burden. There were essentially three possibilities. The first was to consider some form of nonvoluntary restructuring of domestic, foreign, or both types of debt. The second was to try to monetize the debt and reduce the real burden through inflation. In essence this approach is really just a less explicit form of involuntary restructuring. The third option was to embark on a fully voluntary strategy.

We quickly rejected the first option, although we carefully considered its pros and cons. More than 60 percent of public debt was internal, much of it to the domestic banking system, which was weak and had eroded its capital base—although in the crisis days it was difficult to determine the extent of that erosion. Restructuring that debt in a nonvoluntary way would also have required restructuring banks' liabilities. Such nonvoluntary restructuring of deposits would have led to another massive loss of confidence from which Turkey would have a hard time recovering. In essence, nonvoluntary restructuring of domestic debt would have led to nationalization of the entire banking system, including banks' industrial assets, at least temporarily. This would have imposed a tremendous burden on the government's already strained management capacity.

In terms of Turkey's relationships with the rest of the world, restructuring deposits would have required imposing capital controls. All this would also have led to a restructuring of foreign debt, resulting in a serious and lasting loss of confidence, rendering normal access to international capital markets impossible for at least three years, and imposing an extra cost on any borrowing for much longer. Moreover, it would have been impossible to implement such a strategy in a well-coordinated and decisive way given the state of the ruling coalition, the readiness of government ministers to blame and attack their colleagues, and the impossibility of keeping anything confidential beyond the small team consisting of the most senior treasury and Central Bank officials and the head of the Banking Regulation and Supervision Agency.

The second form of involuntary restructuring, through inflation, would essentially have led to the same kind of catastrophe, given Turkey's circumstances. The average maturity of Turkey's internal debt hardly exceeded one year, with floating rate notes accounting for nearly 40 percent of that debt. So, substantially reducing the real value of that debt would have been possible only through hyperinflation. Moreover, the average maturity of bank deposits was less than three months, so rapid inflationary erosion of the public debt that banks carried on their balance sheets would have led to widespread bank failures, because they would rapidly have lost their deposits. Although real hyperinflation could have reduced the domestic debt, it would have been an expropriation of the banks and the citizens holding deposits—leading to the same kind of political and social breakdown as a debt default.

Having rejected nonvoluntary restructuring as viable or desirable, it was essential to reject it totally and publicly, and to work hard to implement a macroeconomic framework compatible with voluntary refinancing of the debt. After some hesitation in March, I was convinced that this was by far the best strategy for Turkey and that involuntary restructuring would lead to economic, social, and political chaos, imposing a particularly large burden on the poorest and most vulnerable parts of the population. We had to convince markets and the public that there was a feasible macroeconomic framework that would allow us to stabilize and than reduce the ratio of debt to GDP, thereby achieving debt sustainability and restoring market access at reasonable cost.

Basic macroeconomic accounting tells us that when the ratio of debt to GDP is close to 100 percent, as was the case in 2001 for Turkey, the sum of real GDP growth and the ratio of the primary fiscal balance to GNP must exceed the real interest rate on the stock of public debt. The primary fiscal balance is the only variable here that can be considered a policy instrument, so it is natural that it was at the center of the policy debate. But it is important to remember that the three key variables in the debt dynamics equation are not independent of each other. By itself a large primary surplus has a positive impact on debt dynamics. But if it leads to lower output, the net effect becomes ambiguous.

Table 5.4 summarizes the fiscal story. The program that had been agreed with the IMF at the end of 1999 already required a major fiscal effort, with the primary surplus targeted at 3.7 percent of GNP (net of earthquake reconstruction costs) for 2000 and 2001, from a base of −2.0 percent in 1999. In December 2000 this target was revised to 5.0 percent for 2001 (and later, 5.5 percent; see below) after the shock caused by the bank failure in November.

With the currency attack of February 2001 having immediately led to serious debt sustainability questions, it was clear that we needed a macroeconomic framework that would show a convincing path out of the explosive debt dynamics triggered by the crisis. But it was also clear that we were heading for a major contraction of output in 2001 due to the severe disorganization of the payments system and bank credit, and the loss of both foreign and domestic confidence impeding all spending decisions. At the same time, the value of the dollar had doubled, leading to major cost-push inflation. It was truly the worst of all worlds, yet we had to rapidly set our fiscal targets.

In the kind of situation we were in, tightening fiscal policy has at least three important effects. The first is the short–term "Keynesian" effect of directly and immediately reducing domestic demand, which has a contractionary effect on output. This effect should not be ignored and has been a source of criticism of IMF programs, particularly at the start of the East Asian crisis. The second effect, assuming a given monetary target, is to reduce the net supply of government bonds and so reduce interest rates, which has an indirect expansionary effect on domestic demand and output. The third effect is to positively affect expectations about debt dynamics and debt sustainability, which has an expansionary effect.

TABLE 5.4

Actual Fiscal Indicators and IMF Program Targets for Turkey, 1999–2002
(percentage of GNP)

Indicator	1999 actual	2000 original program	2000 actual	2001 original program	2001 revised program	2001 actual	2002 original program	2002 revised program	2002 actual
Primary fiscal balance	−2.0	3.7	3.0	3.7	5.5	5.5	3.7	6.5	4.1
Budget deficit	−10.6		−11.2			−19.9			−15.2
Net public debt	61.0		57.4			94.0			80.0

Source: Central Bank of Turkey, Turkey Undersecretariat of the Treasury, and IMF data.

In spring 2001 we were convinced that the third effect was by far the dominant factor in the immediate aftermath of the crisis. Having rejected bankruptcy as an alternative, we had to convince markets that we would be able to roll over our debt, and we had no choice but to strengthen fiscal policy. But to what extent? The mathematics of debt dynamics provide some broad guidelines, in that one has to be able to project a declining ratio of debt to GNP and credible values for GDP growth, the real exchange rate, and real interest rates. But this accounting cannot provide more than a broad neighborhood for fiscal targets.

In Turkey, right after the February crisis, this neighborhood for the primary surplus was 5–8 percent of GNP for 2001 and 2002. These values were high relative to international experience, reflecting the high debt burden, which at that point included the cost of the banking crisis, the short maturities of this debt, the influence of high past real interest rates on expectations about future rates, and pessimism about the real exchange rate. The determining factor in the primary surplus target for 2001 was the work we did, with IMF staff, on the budget and public sector pricing measures that could get us to the chosen target.

Given that it was already March, it was clear that we could not go much beyond 5.0 percent, because even serious structural reforms could not yield immediate fiscal results. Moreover, we attached enormous importance to setting a reasonable goal, rather than trying to impress the markets with an overly ambitious target that we would not achieve. That is how we arrived at the 5.5 percent of GNP target for 2001. The IMF agreed on this target.

For 2002 IMF senior management asked us to raise the primary surplus target to 6.5 percent—despite the fact that an IMF mission to Turkey in March had tentatively agreed to continue with the 5.5 percent target in 2002. I thought that 6.5 percent was overly ambitious, but we agreed to it as a goal to be revisited in fall 2001 in light of developments at that time. The immediate concern was the fiscal surplus for 2001.

Although there was agreement among our core team and agreement with the IMF, we had a hard time convincing markets, and particularly foreign analysts, that we could achieve the 5.5 percent target in 2001. We also had enormous problems convincing the public, and particularly domestic business circles, that such tough fiscal policy was necessary and desirable. As the recession deepened in the late spring and summer of 2001, the argument for fiscal stimulus rather than fiscal restraint gained momentum. And by late summer the cabinet of 36 ministers, with just 2 or 3 exceptions, was pressuring me—privately and publicly—to relax the fiscal target.

But we held firm, with support from my treasury colleagues and the Central Bank throughout this difficult period, as we relentlessly tried to explain why these policies were necessary and salutary. May had been a good month, in terms of the behavior of interest rates and the exchange rate, because of the IMF board meeting held then and the release of the first tranche of the new standby credit. But as resistance against the pace of structural reforms, the new exchange rate regime, and the tough fiscal policy stance mounted in June and July, the exchange rate continued on a downward trend, and interest rates started returning to unsustainably high levels. Finally in late August the reward came, with the exchange rate stabilizing and interest rates starting to decline.

I firmly believe that this turnaround was due to the fact that we had frontloaded the structural reforms and succeeded in getting them through Parliament quickly. Equally important was the fact that we were successful in implementing our fiscal policy. As monthly and quarterly data became available, markets started to believe that we meant what we said and would be able to roll over our debt as promised.

I am convinced that had we chosen 6.5 percent as the primary surplus target for 2001 and then achieved only 5.5 percent, we would not have reaped the benefits of the more modest but realized 5.5 percent target. My point is that after an exchange rate collapse and a debt crisis, restoring credibility is 80 percent of the task. To restore credibility, you have to show that your word is your bond. Of course, the more you can achieve, the better it is—and the rapid pace of structural reforms certainly helped us. But in terms of macroeconomic indicators it is crucial to choose targets that can be and are met. This is more important than issuing unrealistic projections of more rapidly declining debt ratios.

For the purposes of this lecture that is all the detail I will provide about the fiscal story, though subsequent events presented further challenges. For example, September 11 generated a serious new shock, reversing favorable trends and temporarily threatening a new crisis in September and October. But we were able to overcome this setback thanks to the credibility we had gained and decisive action by the IMF and World Bank. As noted, an enhanced IMF program negotiated by late October provided new financing for 2002. In addition, macroeconomic indicators resumed their favorable trends in November 2001. By early 2002, about one year after the collapse and despite the shock of September 11, the crisis had been overcome and Turkey had resumed growth in a stable macroeconomic environment.

After I resigned from the government in the second half of 2002, fiscal policy weakened significantly—largely because of the elections held in November of that year. But fiscal policy was back on track in 2003, and when this lecture was written it looked as if even the more ambitious 6.5 percent primary surplus target set for 2003 would almost be met. Although the story of what happened after 2001 is beyond the scope of this lecture, I do want to make one important point. In a medium-term perspective the quality of fiscal policy is as important as the aggregate figures. It is especially important to distinguish between current spending levels and the components of spending that are good investments for the future, such as education. I believe that it would create substantial new risks to maintain the 6.5 percent primary surplus target without careful analyzing the structure of revenue and spending. A more realistic target of 5.0 percent of GNP, with the 1.5 percentage point difference strictly allocated to high-quality investments, would be a better fiscal strategy. Indeed, postponing priority public investment is another way of accumulating contingent liabilities.

Wage Policy and Labor Relations

After joining the government, the first meeting I had with outside parties was with labor union leaders on 4 March 2001. In summer 2002, when I explained my polit-

ical decisions—to resign as minister and run for Parliament—I did it at a press conference in the headquarters of the main Turkish labor union. Those decisions came
to me naturally, because all my life I have been a dedicated social democrat. For those
who share that view of the world and those values, the distribution of income, quality of life, preservation of the environment, promotion of social cohesion, and solidarity with the vulnerable are as important as economic growth and competitiveness.
History has taught us that without growth, poor people's income cannot increase in
a durable way. Thus growth must be a central objective of economic policy, even for
social democrats. But it should not be the only objective, and certain qualitative elements in the life of nations cannot be reduced to data on per capita income.

One of my main objectives in spring 2001 was to preserve social peace in a country where output was contracting quickly, unemployment was rising steadily, and limited transparency and privileged relationships between political and business groups
had led to huge rents at the expense of common welfare. The open emergence of
social tension and possible violence in the streets in protest against the crisis would
have greatly increased the probability of a complete Argentine-type collapse due to
further loss of confidence, with all the ensuing costs—not least for the poorest population groups. In such situations, whatever one's political orientation, the success of
crisis management depends on preserving social peace. Yet at the same time, resources
are terribly scarce and there is a need for spending cuts, wage restraint, and public sector restructuring, which usually cannot proceed without layoffs.

Of course, organized labor is not at the bottom of any country's income distribution. In Turkey, as in most middle-income emerging market economies, landless
peasants and the urban unemployed are the poorest, most vulnerable sections of the
population. Still, organized labor retains critical importance for social cohesion and
for the social dynamics of a reform and stabilization program in many emerging
market economies. Accordingly, from my first days of taking office I had sought the
advice and support of organized labor—and labor leaders responded to the great sacrifices we asked of them with enormous responsibility and patriotism.

Labor was not responsible for the huge losses in the banking system or the burdens imposed on the Turkish economy by the lack of transparency in public procurement and the energy sector. Yet it was asked to accept nominal wage contracts
well below expected inflation, amounting to real wage cuts of 15–20 percent. The
only way to convince workers of the necessity of such restraint was to explain that
without it an even worse situation—with even greater declines in living standards
and even more unemployment—would be unavoidable.

Turkey's formal labor market is segmented into the private sector, unionized labor
in the public sector, and civil servants. What is unusual is that the same job (say, that
of driver), is routinely done by both civil servants and unionized public employees,
depending on rather arbitrary circumstances. Civil servants do not have the right to
strike, and their wages are significantly lower than those of comparable unionized
workers. At the same time, civil servant status ensures legal job security.

It was against this background that in spring 2001 we embarked on wage negotiations with public workers for 2001–02. Reducing wages for public workers was

essential to the credibility of the reform program and fiscal policy, because of the role it played in achieving the primary surplus target and underscoring our determination to substantially reduce inflation. Public sector wage agreements also send a signal to the private sector and strongly influence inflation expectations. Still, it was difficult to ask unions to agree to what amounted to significant cuts in their members' real wages. I did not have formal responsibility for negotiating the public sector wage deal; that responsibility was explicitly assigned to another minister. But I was coordinating the economic reform program, and I had to convince the IMF that the deal we negotiated was appropriate. Along with the Central Bank governor, I was also the one who would sign the letter of intent.

Without exaggeration, these were some of the most difficult days of my life. Our fiscal targets required considerable wage restraint. The IMF requested a paragraph in the letter of intent amounting to a commitment to reduce real wages by about 15 percent given expected inflation. It also urged us not to allow backward indexation, which was one of the main reasons it had been so hard to cut inflation in the past. It was mid-April, pressure on the exchange rate and interest rates continued, and the letter of intent had to be finalized well before we could hope to conclude negotiations with the unions. The IMF and the Bank wanted to know what the outcomes would be and wanted explicit language to that effect in the letter of intent.

I was determined not to commit the government to a particular ceiling on the nominal wage increase in the letter of intent before we had negotiated it with the unions. These negotiations were occurring in a democracy where collective bargaining is a constitutional right of organized labor. I believed that committing ourselves to a detailed outcome before the negotiations was unacceptable.

On the other hand, the IMF's team was worried that a fiscally unsustainable deal would emerge after its board meeting—undermining the reform program from the start. In such circumstances IMF practice around the world includes government commitments that are known to its board but not explicitly part of the published letter of intent. Such "secrecy" is sometimes unavoidable when it involves market-sensitive information such as exchange rate policies. Except in such circumstances, I strongly believe that all agreements reached should be made public, there should be no secret economic diplomacy, and the public has the right to know government commitments to international institutions. From the beginning I had dedicated the Turkish government to such transparency and refused to enter into commitments that would not be made public, because I believed that our policies should be openly stated for everyone to see. I remember that for an entire day we did not advance at all on this matter during our discussions with the IMF team.

Finally, under great stress I developed a formula that turned out to be a solution. I could commit to a wage policy that would reduce, over time, the average ratio of the wage of unionized public employees to the wage of civil servants. We agreed to reduce the ratio from 2.6 at the end of 2000 to 2.1 at the end of 2001 and 2.0 at the end of 2002. This formula stressed equity and did not require nominal ceilings as such. It did implicitly commit us to wage restraint because civil servant wage scales were pretty firmly set, but it did leave room for some flexibility. After a bit of further debate the IMF team accepted this approach, which was explicitly included in the publicly released letter of intent, and we finalized everything in a fully transparent manner.

A few days before the IMF board meeting we were engaged in the final, difficult negotiations with the unions. We asked them to agree to nominal wage increases 20 percent below expected inflation for the first year, with no ex post indexation for the first six months—to be partly compensated by a lump sum "catch up" payment to be paid in the second year of the contract period, but with no real increase for the second year. I also asked that at the end of each six-month period, if inflation exceeded expectations, the wage increase for that period not exceed 60 percent of the discrepancy in the second half of the first year and in the second year.

The negotiations took place in a relatively positive atmosphere. Mutual trust had been established during our earlier meetings, when the unions had realized that my sympathies were with them and they could trust me to do the best I could while keeping the reform program on track. Nonetheless, it took us many days and long hours to agree on the nominal increases. We also argued endlessly over the catch-up payment and, in the end, they agreed that it would be a cash payment not built into the wage structure.

The unions would not, however, agree to less than full ex post indexation for the six-month periods after the first, despite my efforts to explain why gradual de-indexation of the economy was so important in the fight against inflation. After several breakdowns in our negotiations, I agreed to move from 60 percent to 80 percent indexation. They fought it tooth and nail—even threatening a general strike—but finally agreed on the condition that there be 100 percent ex post indexation in the second six-month period of the two-year contract. At that point we were all psychologically exhausted, and the union leader, representing the dominant federation in the public sector, simply did not have the background knowledge that I had on the critical and negative role of indexation in disinflation program. Moreover, the unions needed that final victory.

We struck the deal in the presence of the prime minister, and expressed hope that the compromise would help Turkey overcome the crisis. Social peace was preserved, Turkish Airlines brought a record number of tourists to Turkey without any of the threatened industrial actions, and the reform program could be implemented without disruption despite the enormous sacrifices it demanded from almost all segments of society. A year and a half later the union leader with whom I had negotiated so hard joined me in the November 2002 elections, and we became members of Parliament representing the same social democratic party.

The Role of the Bretton Woods Institutions

In conclusion I would like to discuss the role of the Bretton Woods institutions during this critical crisis management period in Turkey, in terms of both financial support and policy advice and conditionality. I have no doubt that without financial support from the Bretton Woods institutions—especially the IMF—Turkey would have had to go through a major debt default in early 2001 (at the latest). IMF and World Bank medium-term financial resources cost, on average, 400–500 basis points (4–5 percentage points) less than the very limited funds Turkey could obtain from international financial markets in the year following the crisis, and even less than domestic debt.

These resources allowed a de facto voluntary refinancing of Turkey's huge short-term domestic debt as well as some expensive medium-term foreign debt, including liabilities that had accumulated in the banking system. Moreover, only after the start of the IMF program did we succeed in lengthening maturities of domestic debt, through a voluntary debt swap conducted with domestic banks in June 2001. Between May 2001 and the end of 2002 net use of IMF credit totaled $17 billion—an IMF record in terms of the percentage of a country's quota, with outstanding credit reaching 1,685 percent of the quota at the end of 2002. But except for a valuable but modest contribution from the World Bank, averaging about $1 billion a year in net disbursements in 2001 and 2002, there was no other multilateral or bilateral (including G-7) financing, in contrast to what had happened for countries such as Mexico in 1994 or the Republic of Korea in 1997.

The net foreign resources that Turkey managed to borrow from official sources over a two-year period was about 14 percent of annual GDP. This financing enabled us to avoid default, keep the lira convertible, avoid expropriating deposit holders, preserve social peace and avoid possible deaths that could have resulted from social unrest, push through deep structural reforms establishing a more efficient and more transparent economy, and resume rapid growth in less than a year after the February 2001 attack on the lira. (The State Institute of Statistics has estimated Turkey's growth in 2002 at 7.8 percent—a remarkable rebound in a year when the world economy was in recession.)

I believe that the reforms undertaken during the crisis also brought us much closer to the European Union in terms of laws and regulations. Unless the new government makes major mistakes in the near future, the financial support from the Bretton Woods institutions will prove to have been justified and a good example of why these institutions exist and why they must have sufficient resources to do their jobs. If their financial support had been half-hearted, it would have been worse than useless. We would not have been able to avoid default and the associated costs, our nonrestructurable debt would have increased—and the Bretton-Woods institutions would have had a failure to explain. The lesson in terms of financial support is that if such institutions believe in a reform program, they should go all the way in financing it. And if they do not believe in it, they should not provide any resources.

Turning to policy advice and conditionality, I believe that the Bretton Woods institutions have a mixed record in Turkey because of the program supported in 2000. Much of the technical work done by the staff of the IMF and the Bank has been of the highest quality, and during my tenure as a minister in 2001–02 we benefited greatly from their technical advice. The IMF has a deep understanding of Turkey's fiscal system, and the Bank has provided exemplary analysis of sectors such as energy and telecommunications.

But in hindsight the program pursued in 2000, based on a quasi currency board, was a mistake given the political coalition in place, structural weaknesses in the banking system, and insufficient margin of safety in fiscal policy. Allowing an upfront devaluation in December 1999 and adding another percentage point to the primary surplus target for 2000 could have provided that margin of safety—provided that the tightening of bank supervision had also started immediately. These were all things that the Bretton Woods institutions had proposed but did not insist on, leading to tremendous costs later. Good conditionality is not just desirable but necessary.

On the other hand, conditionality must be appropriate and reflect what is feasible. I strongly believe that it can emerge only from careful, close interactions between IMF and World Bank staff, who know the world and international experience, and national experts and political figures, who have the kind of knowledge of domestic affairs that not even the best Bretton Woods expert can acquire. The key is mutual confidence. The domestic team must believe that the Bretton Woods team is sincerely trying to find the best solutions, is highly competent, and is trying to maximize financial support. And the Bretton Woods team must believe that the domestic team is not playing games and will do its best to implement what is agreed.

On several occasions in 2001 we had genuine differences with the IMF. It was strongly opposed to Central Bank interventions intended to moderate exchange rate overshooting in the first half of 2001. It was also upset about the outcome of the public sector wage negotiations described above. But in the end I was able to convince the IMF team that this was the best we could achieve and that social peace was an asset we should try very hard to preserve. Such mutual confidence is perhaps the most important ingredient for a successful reform program. Without it, the policies that emerge and form the basis for conditionality are unlikely to be optimal.

Having stressed the importance of mutual confidence between negotiating teams, I will end by referring to the broader issue of confidence in and legitimacy for the Bretton Woods institutions—particularly the IMF—in terms of public opinion. In most emerging market economies a large segment of the public sees these institutions as primarily reflecting the wishes of the United States and, to a lesser degree, the G-7. Though this perception is greatly exaggerated, it is there, and it is not just an unfortunate detail. It undermines country ownership of reforms, makes reforms more reversible, and at times threatens social peace.

For reforms supported by the IMF and World Bank to be more effective and enduring, these institutions must continue their efforts to free themselves from excessive dependence on their main shareholders, and facilitate steps toward more democratic and hence more legitimate forms of global governance. The world must move toward new, stronger global governance that reflects the realities of the 21st century, not the world of 1945. I believe that closer links between the United Nations—which, for all its weaknesses, has a degree of public legitimacy not shared by others—and institutions such as the IMF, Bank, and World Trade Organization could help make economic reform programs backed by international resources more effective and robust. People must feel that they, or at least their representatives, are true participants in and owners of the international system. Such a sense of ownership could help overcome the serious mistrust that undermines many reforms and often derails the efforts of both reformers and Bank and IMF staff.

In recent years a lot of progress has been made in this direction. But much remains to be done. If the large shareholders of the Bretton Woods institutions want the resources they contribute to have a lasting effect, and if they want a more stable world economy, they must support the professionalism and political neutrality of these institutions—while giving a greater say in their governance to the representatives of the billions of people affected by their actions. The common goal must be combining good policies and technical competence with greater democratic legitimacy. As democracy advances in developing countries, it is both more necessary and more feasible to achieve that goal.

Comment

Roque B. Fernández

I GREATLY APPRECIATE THE OPPORTUNITY TO COMMENT ON KEMAL DERVIŞ'S LECTURE. I am deeply interested in Turkey's experiences because Argentina has had similar problems on the political front, on the economic front, and in dealing with international organizations. Derviş has a unique perspective, having worked in academia, in international organizations, and as a practitioner in politics and in the economic administration of his country. Moreover, I believe that he achieved significant results during his short tenure in the Turkish administration.

Assessing—and Reassessing—Crises

Derviş says that Turkey's February 2001 crisis stemmed from the interaction between a weak banking sector, a nominal anchor exchange rate policy, and insufficiently strong fiscal policy. When analyzing the dynamics of a crisis—especially when they are responsible for managing it—policymakers sometimes miss other relevant issues in other parts of the world. The same thing happens in the rest of the world and in multilateral organizations, such as the International Monetary Fund (IMF) and the World Bank, which often miss the day-to-day dynamics observed by those managing a crisis.

During his presentation Derviş noted that, when evaluating the dynamics of a crisis, we cannot "rerun history." That reminded me of Jorge Luis Borges, an Argentine writer who elaborated the concept of "predicting history" to refer to the same phenomenon. This concept captures the contradictory nature of economic policy evaluations when done at different points in time. "Predicting history" will allow me to provide both an economic perspective and a political opinion on what happened in Turkey. I can do so because sometimes when more data becomes available on what happened in a crisis country, one comes up with a completely different interpretation of what seemed to be the facts when policy actions were first defined or evaluated. To support this conclusion and my overall analysis, I will draw on the recent crisis in Argentina and compare its experiences with those of Turkey.

For example, in 2002 the media and some technical reports concluded that the Argentine crisis—which started with the government default on its foreign debt in late 2001—had originated in the 1990s. They determined that the fiscal deficit had appreciated the real exchange rate and increased debt. (Note that this evaluation of Argentina's fiscal and exchange rate policy is similar to Derviş's conclusion that Turkey's crisis partly resulted from its preannounced exchange rate policy and insufficiently strong fiscal policy.) Accordingly, most casual observers have probably been convinced (or at least swayed to believe) that the default was the natural outcome of unsustainable and growing debt. But new data and new analysis indicate that it was not. As a result independent analysts have begun rewriting or "predicting" the history of Argentina's crisis.

In 1991 the federal government had $34 billion in unregistered debt (not including social security debt), a concept similar to what Derviş calls "contingent liabilities." Together, registered and unregistered debt equaled 54 percent of GDP. In 2001 federal debt was the same, 54 percent of GDP, although between 1991 and 2001 states and local governments increased their debt from 5 percent to 10 percent of GDP (including the province of Buenos Aires, which accounts for more than half of Argentina's GDP).

But during the 1990s Argentina also introduced far-reaching social security reforms that sharply reduced contingent liabilities. Unregistered social security debt fell from 158 percent of GDP in 1991 to 73 percent in 2001. Thus total debt, when properly recorded, fell significantly—from 217 percent of GDP in 1991 to 137 percent in 2001. Thus it does not make to much sense to talk about the debt increase in the 1990s.

My political opinion on Turkey is that responsibility for its debt increase should be assigned to those who incurred the debt, not those who registered it. Given that Turkey's debt rose from 70 percent to 100 percent of GDP during its crisis (not including social security but taking into account other contingent liabilities), Derviş was responsible for registering a previously incurred debt. For that he received the support of professional economists and the criticism of opposing politicians, including those who had originated the debt. This is why, whenever possible, politicians avoid debt registration.

Exchange Rates, Capital Outflows, and the Trade Balance

What lessons does Argentina offer for other emerging economies facing volatile capital flows that could jeopardize fundamental structural reforms? After the tequila crisis of 1994–95, Argentina increased the average maturity of its outstanding debt and lowered interest rates. Then, because of the East Asian, Russian, and Brazilian crises in 1997–99, the maturity of Argentine debt was reduced and its cost was raised. These developments illustrate the perverse dynamics of capital outflows, which not only make it harder to service debt but also affect the exchange rate.

Looking at the real exchange rate, the approach that Derviş advocates is correct in that nominal anchors cannot be used to promote long-run real competitiveness.

But in the short run they may have some real effects. This point supports arguments for keeping some freedom in exchange rate policy to allow for better absorption of real shocks, such as sudden capital outflows.

Although I think that Derviş's exchange rate analysis reflects a pragmatic approach, in Argentina very high real exchange rates have coincided with the country's most severe economic downturns—including hyperinflation and peaks in poverty. Thus a high real exchange rate is not necessarily beneficial. Indeed, it often signals widespread capital outflows. Moreover, the real exchange rate should be carefully analyzed relative to the real interest rate. There is ample evidence that higher real interest rates are positively correlated with real exchange rate depreciation, which is why exchange rate crises are often linked to financial crises.

In terms of trade, the more than doubling of Argentina's exchange rate in the first half of 2002 did not cause a sustained increase in exports; there was a short-run increase in the first half of 2002 that reversed in the second half. Imports, however, fell significantly in the second half of 2001 (prior to the devaluation) and remained low in 2002. As a result the trade balance improved.

But the low level of imports reflected a drop in investment, because most of Argentina's capital goods were imported. Thus imports had a lot to do with the replenishment of the capital stock and the future evolution of real GDP. As a result the improvement in the trade balance that originated in the reduction in imports caused a technological regression.

Sudden Stops in Capital Flows

Again, "predicting history" is the work of independent analysts; in this section I draw on research by Calvo, Izquierdo, and Talvi (2002) analyzing economic developments in Latin America in the late 1990s. In the second half of 1998 Russia's crisis produced a sudden stop in capital flows to many countries in the region, including Argentina, Brazil, Chile, Colombia, Mexico, Peru, and Venezuela. All these countries were hit hard by this halt in flows, which forced them to significantly adjust the current account in their balance of payments (by cutting deficits). As noted, in Argentina most of the adjustment had to be made in capital imports, leading to a recession with external origins.

These sudden stops occurred independently of the policy mistakes supposedly made in these countries. It is simply not possible that all these countries were making exactly the same mistakes. Thus there is no doubt that what happened was an external shock—and policymakers must be extremely careful not to let external shocks affect the ongoing struggle for structural reforms.

Ownership of Economic Policy

Another point emphasized by Derviş involves ownership of a country's economic reforms. He rightly points out that political support is crucial. Indeed, I believe that managing a crisis requires finding, at the very beginning, the political support required to define the reform program. Doing so is very difficult, and I think that Derviş did a good job in this regard.

Like most crisis countries, Argentina and Turkey each assigned a group of technocrats to develop a plan for economic recovery and to negotiate with the IMF and other international financial institutions. This is where the problem of ownership begins. Members of parliament in crisis countries will generally argue that the reform plan is not their responsibility. Usually they will also criticize the plan, arguing that the technicians are against the poor, against the general public, against the economy, against the nation. Accordingly, they will often disregard the plan or not accept ownership of it.

Politicians also usually send mixed signals—for example, first by voting for reform, then giving a speech arguing against it. These contradictions will be justified on the grounds that support for structural reform by the national congress was required to get program approval from the IMF and other financial institutions. This pattern has been followed in Argentina, Brazil, Chile, Mexico, and many other countries.

I think that during a crisis it is of utmost importance for policymakers to be able to induce politicians to accept ownership of reform programs. But it is equally important that ownership be achieved in international organizations. In some cases, for example, IMF staff has diagnosed the situation in a crisis country and recommended that the institution either support or not support a recovery program there. Yet in analyzing the same situation, and likely for political reasons, its Board of Governors has reached the opposite conclusion.

In 2001, for example, IMF staff did not believe that Argentina should receive the $6 billion in support that it was requesting. But there was political interference at the board level arguing that the support was necessary; otherwise Brazil and other countries in the region would be affected. As a result the IMF supported a debt refinancing program that did not address Argentina's structural problems, and the program failed.

I completely agree with Derviş that recovery is not just a matter of eliminating small deficits in the next budget or financing the next external payment. It also requires taking a long-term perspective on solving the country's problems. That did not happen in Argentina, and as a result it received an enormous amount of money ($6 billion was a historical record for IMF support to Argentina) for a program that the IMF did not own. The money came in one window and went out another, canceling claims of private creditors anticipating the risk of default. Thus the IMF resources, as well as liquid reserves from pension funds and the Central Bank (whose president was fired when attempting to defend the bank's independence), were used to finance capital outflows. Nevertheless, all those resources were insufficient to reestablish the credibility that would have allowed for government debt refinancing in world capital markets. As a result Argentina ended up with a default crisis in late 2001.

Thus I believe that ownership is a very important issue. But if it does not go both ways—with ownership by the country as well as the IMF—there should not be an IMF program. And if there is one, as Derviş points out, it must be adequately financed to fully ensure credibility and normal access to capital markets.

International Financing and Collective Action Clauses

The issue of financing raises another issue on which I will conclude my comments. In the short run it is difficult for crisis countries to secure sufficient financial resources to support recovery. I do not think that international organizations are ready to significantly increase financing for such operations, which are akin to a lender of last resort in a closed economy. These organizations seem unwilling to even discuss this issue, presumably for political reasons. Such discussions are more common in academia. Thus countries experiencing crises will have to recognize that, as in Argentina and Turkey, liquidity constraints will not be eliminated in the near future.

So, I strongly endorse the analysis behind some of the recent recommendations made in the international community—especially Anne Krueger's (2002) proposal that new debt include collective action clauses. This approach would enable the creditors of a country experiencing severe external shocks to agree on collective action, allowing a qualified majority to make a decision on debt restructuring that could be effectively enforced.

A word of caution is needed here, because sound theoretical analyses argue that collective action clauses might eliminate international lending. But without such clauses, debt restructuring negotiations can drag on and on, aggravating a crisis and affecting the evolution of international lending. These issues merit further research and discussion (see, for example, Fernández and Fernández 2004).

References

Calvo, G., A. Izquierdo, and E. Talvi. 2002. "Sudden Stops, The Real Exchange Rate and Fiscal Sustainability: Argentina's Lessons." Inter-American Development Bank, Research Department, Washington, D.C.

Fernández, K., and R. B. Fernández. 2004. "Willingness to Pay and the Sovereign Debt Contract." Universidad del CEMA. [www.cema.edu.ar/u/rbf/].

Krueger, A. 2002. "A New Approach to Sovereign Debt Restructuring." International Monetary Fund, Washington, D.C.

Comment

Steven Radelet

In the tense, delicate negotiations that occur during severe financial crises, personalities matter. Individuals can make the difference between success and failure. Markets are fragile, and decisions must be made quickly based on incomplete information. For markets to settle and begin to rebound—rather than spiral out of control—mutual confidence between key negotiators is crucial.

In that regard Kemal Derviş made a huge difference in helping to resolve Turkey's 2001 crisis. He worked hard, had good instincts, and bridged the gaps between the rest of the Turkish government, financial markets, and the international community. Few if any other people could have steered the Turkish economy with the skill and effectiveness shown by Derviş in those difficult days. His lecture provides an invaluable perspective on Turkey's crisis and the response to it, giving an insider's account and analysis of the economics and politics driving key decisions.

Causes of the Crisis

Several key ingredients contributed to Turkey's 2001 crisis and to the government's ability to respond to it. As Derviş recounts, the combination of a nominal anchor on the exchange rate, a weak banking system, and lax fiscal policy was at the core of the crisis. In addition, he mentions the buildup of short-term capital inflows—a feature common to all the countries that experienced financial crises in the mid- and late 1990s, including (in order) Mexico, Thailand, Indonesia, the Republic of Korea, Russia, and Argentina.

Turkey's soft peg and high interest rates attracted a large amount of volatile capital inflows. By December 2000 its short-term external debt had reached $31 billion (an increase of about $8 billion over the year before), while foreign exchange reserves had dropped to just over $22 billion. Significant domestic debt—most with very short maturities—made this imbalance much worse. This situation left the Turkish economy extremely vulnerable. Once sentiment began to turn against it in late 2000 (due to the collapse of a major bank), creditors recognized that there were not enough reserves to cover all the short-term debt, and started to flee. After the first attack on the Turkish lira in November 2000, it was only a matter of time before a major crisis. In retrospect, moving to a freely floating exchange rate at that time would have prevented the much greater damage that occurred in February 2001. Even better, as Derviş notes, would have been a different exchange rate system in the International Monetary Fund (IMF) program of December 1999.

Turkey differed from the East Asian crisis countries because of its large fiscal deficit and enormous total debt. None of the East Asian countries began their crises with large fiscal deficits, and only Indonesia had large total debt (though all the Asian countries had high short-term debt). Turkey's large fiscal deficit and total debt made its crisis more like those in Mexico and Russia. Although these features did not directly contribute to the onset of Turkey's crisis, they significantly curtailed the policy options available once it began. For example, Thailand and especially Korea had much more fiscal space and ability to convert short-term debt to longer-term obligations than did Turkey. Thus Turkey faced much harder choices than did Thailand or Korea.

Responses to the Crisis

The Turkish government and the IMF crafted an appropriate recovery program after Turkey's currency collapsed in 2001. The program was much better designed than earlier IMF programs in Thailand, Indonesia, and Korea, as well as the previous Turkish program. It struck an appropriate balance between macroeconomic policies and structural reforms.

The primary fiscal balance was a focus of the program, with a target set at a difficult but achievable 5.5 percent of GDP for 2001. As Derviş points out, it was much more sensible to set such a target and achieve it than to set too high a target (such as 6.5 percent of GDP) and fall short. Achieving the target helped the government gain credibility and provided confidence to both international and domestic capital markets.

The program was also well implemented, though performance could have been better in a few areas. For example, unlike Derviş I believe that a freely floating exchange rate in the immediate aftermath of the crisis would have provided much more confidence and a quicker rebound that did the series of small exchange rate interventions. Moreover, the Central Bank should have moved much more swiftly to lower interest rates, since there was little link between interest rates and inflation at that point, and higher interest rates simply drove up the cost of borrowing and the amount the government had to borrow. But these are relatively minor issues of judgment rather than fundamental issues of program design.

Turkey's policy reforms would not have succeeded without substantial financial support from the international community. The IMF approved standby arrangements of $20.5 billion in 1999 and $16.6 billion in 2002, among its largest programs ever. This magnitude of support was crucial to restoring market confidence and easing Turkey's enormous liquidity squeeze.

Turkey received such financing partly because of the size of its economy and crisis, but also because of its geopolitical importance. The United States and Europe did not want to see a financial meltdown in early 2001 in a predominantly Muslim country so close to the Middle East that hosts a major military base for the North Atlantic Treaty Organization (NATO). U.S. President George W. Bush's administration (in which I served, following my service in Bill Clinton's administration) quickly backed down from its campaign rhetoric of "no big bailouts" when confronted with the stark reality of a major ally facing the harsh choices of debt default (with a bank meltdown), hyperinflation, or a large package of international financing.

But the large amount of IMF financing was a double-edged sword. On the one hand, it was fundamental in supporting the recovery program and restoring economic stability and confidence. As Derviş points out, it had to be large for the program to succeed. But on the other hand, such funds must be paid back—and under the terms of the IMF agreement, paid back relatively quickly (within four or five years). A large portion of the IMF financing was used to repay short-term loans to international creditors, meaning that Turkey's total debt did not decline (it actually increased), although the terms improved significantly. Turkey is scheduled to repay the IMF about $5.5 billion in 2004, $8.9 billion in 2005, and $12.1 billion in 2006. It is nearly impossible to envisage a scenario in which these obligations are fully repaid on schedule. They will almost certainly have to be rolled over, implying that Turkey is likely to continue its long relationship with the IMF for a while longer.

Turkey's financial position has improved significantly since early 2001. Reserves have grown to $33 billion, while short-term debt has dropped to less than $23 billion. The exchange rate system is functioning satisfactorily, and the lira is no longer an easy target for speculators. But total debt remains at 75 percent of GDP, with interest payments accounting for 17 percent of GDP. As a result the government will have to maintain a primary surplus of at least 6 percent of GDP for the foreseeable future. Moreover, the banking system remains fragile, as do other parts of the economy.

Turkey has come a long way since its crisis, and Derviş and his colleagues deserve much of the credit. But the country is far from out of the woods, and will require significant time, strong economic management, good fortune, and continued support to reduce its vulnerabilities and lay the foundations for sustained growth.

Fernando Henrique Cardoso

Former President of Brazil

Fernando Henrique Cardoso has been at the center of Brazilian public life for four decades, most recently as President for two terms spanning 1995–2002. Born in Rio de Janeiro in 1931, Cardoso was trained as a sociologist at the University of São Paulo. In the late 1960s he emerged as an influential figure in the analysis of large-scale social change, international development, dependency, democracy, and state reform. Cardoso held a chaired professorship at the University of São Paulo and was Associate Director of Studies at the École des Hautes Études en Sciences Sociales (in Paris) and Visiting Professor at the Collège de France and University of Paris-Nanterre. He also taught at Cambridge as Simon Bolivar Professor, and at Stanford University and the University of California at Berkeley. His many influential publications include *Dependency and Development in Latin America* (with E. Faletto, 1979) and *Charting a New Course: The Politics of Globalization and Social Transformation* (edited by M. Font, 2001).

Building on his successful intellectual and academic career, Cardoso became deeply involved in Brazil's struggle for democracy. Elected Senator in 1982, he was a Founding Member of the Brazilian Social Democratic Party. He served as Minister of Foreign Affairs in 1992–93 and Minister of Finance in 1993–94. His two terms as President were marked by his success in bringing inflation to low and stable levels, improving social indicators (particularly in the lagging Northeast region), and consolidating a role for civil society in Brazilian democracy.

Cardoso's current positions include Chairman of the Club of Madrid and Co-Chairman of the Inter-American Dialogue. He is also a member of the Board of Trustees of the Rockefeller Foundation and the Institute for Advanced Study (Princeton University). In addition, Cardoso is Professor "at large" at Brown University and holds the "Cultures of the South" chair at the U.S. Library of Congress. He recently presided over the United Nations Panel of Eminent Personalities on the relationship between the U.N. and civil society.

6 Reflections and Lessons from a Decade of Social Reforms in Brazil

Fernando Henrique Cardoso

IT HAS BEEN A WHILE SINCE I HAVE ADDRESSED SUCH A LARGE AUDIENCE, SINCE I NOW live a rather quiet life working in the Library of Congress. But I am happy to be here among friends, especially given their generous views of my accomplishments. And I am very pleased to see that the World Bank continues to recognize the importance of addressing the causes and challenges of development. As I will stress during my presentation, I believe that these issues deserve as much attention today as they did when the Bretton Woods structure was designed more than a half-century ago—though it goes without saying that the idea of development has undergone a dramatic conceptual change since the early days of the World Bank.

Evolving Notions of Development

During the late 1950s and most of the 1960s development was equated with material progress and economic growth. Leading that perspective was Professor W. W. Rostow, with his five-stage theory of development, and everyone was obliged to read his book.

At the time I viewed the development process differently, so I spent some of my early years as a professor at the University of São Paulo criticizing Rostow. Still, he was a pioneer in showing that it is possible for countries to develop. Developing countries were supposed to follow a predetermined, uniform path toward development, based on the historical experiences of rich countries. History was said to show that growth would necessarily lead to higher living standards.

Then dependency theory came up with the variable of politics, and the basic criticism that other analysts—including Raul Prebisch, Celso Furtado, and the Economic Commission for Latin America—and I made of such growth theories was that they were based almost entirely on economic notions and failed to recognize that development entails political factors. We emphasized, for example, that the structural ties between the center and the periphery could vary depending on historical backgrounds, the role of states, so on. Thus there were several types of dependency, and that is what we emphasized during the late 1960s and early 1970s.

At that time even the notion of "multinational" was nonexistent. That notion did not emerge until the 1970s. So, when I wrote a book on dependency and development in 1969, I tried to invent concepts to explain what was happening. But I used the wrong label, and said that what was occurring was an internationalization of internal markets.

The changes, however, were much more profound than that: they involved a global transformation in the system of production. But from my perspective it was just an internationalization of markets. And I was stressing that it was possible, despite that change, to achieve development. That is why I titled one of my books *Dependency and Development*, rather than just *Dependency*.

All my work during that period, in the late 1960s, revisited another perspective that claimed all development depended on the center. I believed the opposite: that development depends on how each country's historical and structural situation relates to the center. My point was that it is possible to have different patterns of development.

Several years later, in the 1970s, I wrote some articles in which I coined a new term: "associated dependent development." The idea was to define a concept acknowledging the linkages between the interests of multinational corporations and local entrepreneurs, and show that it is feasible to pursue a form of development that was to some extent dependent, but to some extent connected with local forces.

So, during that period I argued that depending on how political and social forces were organized—not to mention the role of the state—economic growth could follow different paths, with different effects on domestic structures. And Brazil's authoritarian experience showed that growth could part ways with (and indeed, be completely unrelated to) equity. The country's high growth rates in the early 1970s did not translate into better social indicators. It became clear that unless development policies were geared toward improving welfare, economic growth could fall short of meeting basic social needs.

In the mid-1970s, for example, I did some research on growth and poverty in São Paulo. Because the government was hardly paying any attention to providing the city's huge inflow of migrants with adequate public services, economic progress was not improving the lives of thousands of people. On the contrary, the data were rather disturbing. The percentage of households with sewerage services in metropolitan São Paulo had fallen from 35 percent in 1971 to 12 percent in 1975. Thus it came as no surprise that the infant mortality rate was 45 percent higher in 1973 than in 1960.

So this was quite a clear case. Brazilian economic growth in the 1970s was very impressive, with an average growth rate of about 7 percent. But social development was a disaster. And because of the book I co-wrote on growth and poverty in São Paulo, during the military regime a bomb was thrown into my office. We were accused of being connected with the international communist movement. The idea was that such criticism was basically leftist criticism.

But the fact remains that economic growth is not enough to improve social welfare. In Brazil that was obvious in the 1970s. But as time passed, there emerged many new notions about development. In 1972 the Stockholm conference on the environment introduced the idea of reconciling economic growth with environmental protection. At the time the Brazilian government was oriented toward very rapid, almost Soviet-style economic growth. Though it was opposed to communism, the style was the same.

Indeed, an important minister even claimed that God blesses pollution, because pollution means development, and economic growth, and industrialization. That was the perception of development in the 1970s, and in response researchers came up with the idea of eco-development. Then by the time of the 1992 Rio Earth Summit—and much to the credit of people like Maurice Strong and Ignacy Sachs—it was clear that it was necessary to adopt the more forward-looking concept of sustainable development, which encompassed a political dimension, a social dimension, and an ecological dimension in addition to economic growth.

After the Rio conference perceptions of development changed a lot. Other issues closely related to development followed, such as the Copenhagen conference on social development, the Beijing conference on women's rights, and the Johannesburg conference on sustainable development. At the same time, causes such as women's rights and the struggle against racial discrimination have moved to the top of the international agenda. What seems to lie behind this deconstruction of the concept of development is the growing perception that economic growth proves meaningful only if it is understood as part of a larger process. That entails respecting the environment and promoting human rights and other collective aspirations.

Advances in Human Development

The notion of human development is the latest, most successful attempt to bring the concept of development in line with the multiple expectations of contemporary societies. Amartya Sen stands second to none as the intellectual mentor of this concept.

I need not emphasize how honored I felt to receive a year ago from U.N. Secretary-General Kofi Annan the first-ever Mahbub ul Haq Award for contributions to human development. I took the award not as a personal tribute but as a welcome recognition of the joint efforts of the Brazilian state and people in addressing centuries of negligence with regard to living standards in the country.

Had there not been such an uncompromising collective endeavor, it would not have been possible for Brazil's human development index—measured by the United Nations Development Programme (UNDP)—to rise from 0.70 in 1991 to 0.76 in 2000. The UNDP also deserves recognition in this regard, because the creation of this index was very important. It gives us, as practitioners, an instrument for measuring progress.

It is worth emphasizing that the human development index rose across Brazil as all states and practically all municipalities performed better. Indeed, 99.89 percent of 5,700 municipalities are performing better according to this index. And without that kind of measurement, it is not possible to stimulate people, and it is not possible to judge progress.

In several areas there has been competition to see how much can be done to improve people's welfare, as measured by this kind of index. Less populous municipalities, with populations below 50,000, have done particularly well, with their indexes improving by an average of 15 percent in eight years. And the index of the municipality that had performed the worst in 1991, Euclides da Cunha (in the hinterlands of the state of Bahia), increased by 31 percent.

So, by 2000 just 23 municipalities had a low human development index. Moreover, 574 municipalities have a higher index, with levels comparable to those in developed countries. This is an impressive and important achievement, because it shows progress to the population, and even encourages political leaders to compete for better performance.

Taking apart the index, progress has been achieved in all its components: income, life expectancy at birth, school attendance, and literacy. Between 1991 and 2000 average household income rose from 228 to 297 reals a month—a 30 percent increase. Though average real incomes have fallen over the past three years due to the currency devaluation and falling employment, average monthly earnings between 1994 (after the introduction of the Real Plan) and 2002 were 25 percent higher than in the early 1990s.

At the same time, life expectancy rose from 66 to 68 years between 1991 and 2000. Even more significant, the infant mortality rate (not included in the human development index) dropped from 48 to 28 per 1,000 in this short period. And the country's poorest region, the northeast, achieved the greatest gains, with a reduction of 40 percent, from 72 to 44 per 1,000.

In terms of education, Brazil has nearly achieved the goal of having every child attend school, with attendance around 98 percent. Again, the most significant gains have been in the northeast, as well as among black and low-income populations. Thus practically all Brazilians between 7 and 14 are in school.

And although the national average was 93 percent in 1991, among blacks it was just 75 percent. Today 93 percent of blacks are attending school—a major improvement. Similarly, in the poorest regions, such as the northeast, the attendance rate moved from 79 to 93 percent between 1992 and 1999. Thus access to education has improved dramatically for members of society who have never had access to anything.

In Brazil education also means food, because the vast majority of primary education is provided by public schools, and such schools have feeding programs. In every school, students receive at least one meal a day. And in the poorest communities they receive two meals a day. Moreover, the government is doubling the amount of food provided in the poorest areas, and the program is being decentralized and improved. Thus more universal access to education means better access to food.

Social Spending and Equity

The goal of reducing regional social disparities in Brazil was greatly enhanced by the Alvorada Project, which targeted the poorest of the poor in 2,361 municipalities in 23 states where the human development index was 0.500 or less. So again, we were able to give more focus to our policies, because we had an instrument to measure who were really the poorest. The project's budget reached $3.6 billion and involved 15 government social programs ranging from farm support to water and sanitation services.

Even more far-reaching is the Social Protection Network put in place by the federal government over the past decade. The network encompasses 13 nationwide programs to transfer income to the most vulnerable segments of society, which amounts to 36.7 million people—including low-income families, the elderly, children, disabled people, pregnant and breast-feeding women, and small farmers.

The network is funded by an annual budget of about $8 billion. That amount is equal to the income tax collected every year from individuals and corporations. Thus Brazilians cannot claim that they do not want to pay taxes because they do not know what the government will do with the money. Data on tax spending are available on the Internet, so transparency is very high.

So, all the income tax collected by the federal government goes directly to the poorest part of the population. Thus we are engaged in a direct form of income redistribution: taking money from taxpayers and giving it to those who do not have any. Although critics call this a liberal welfare program, it is much more than that. It is not just providing access to education and food, but also transferring income to the poorest part of the population.

It takes time to see the effects of such efforts, and to evaluate the impact of such broad initiatives on the country's social structure. Some programs—such as the school grant, the food grant, child labor eradication, and even insurance—will produce more tangible results only in the long run. But just the other day I was pleased to read that the leader of the Senate was making a speech celebrating the fact that a survey had found that the number of starving people was decreasing in Brazil. Indeed, the entire government was celebrating. And, I might add, they were celebrating the achievements of my government. But I am sure that in 10 years we will be celebrating even more, because this kind of program—and progress—does not belong to one government alone.

So, although it takes time for social programs to have significant consequences, there are clear signs that Brazil's social picture is improving, in some cases dramatically. Consider the Gini coefficient, which fell from 0.60 in 1993 to 0.57 in 2001. Although that is a small decrease, changes in the Gini usually occur very slowly. And despite various shocks, the distribution of income has become less unjust. During this period the richest 10 percent of the Brazilian population saw its income increase by 13 percent, while the poorest 20 percent saw an increase of 63 percent. Thus the poorest part of the population is seeing much faster improvements than the richest.

But while I think that the Gini coefficient is important, it needs to be used carefully. In Africa, for instance, the Gini is improving in some areas—because everyone has gotten poorer. So it is important to look at what is behind the data. In Brazil the changes in the Gini coefficient are the result of a real process of income redistribution. The gap between rich and poor people is gradually becoming less disturbing, and the number of people living below the poverty line has fallen dramatically.

Between 1994 and 2002 Brazil pursued one of the longest sustainable poverty reduction programs in Western history.

An impressive number of people have benefited from Brazil's stabilization and social programs. Just before the Real Plan was implemented in 1992, 41 percent of Brazilians lived in poverty. By 2002 that share was 33 percent—a decrease of about 20 percent in 10 years. The population below the poverty line is still about 50 million people, which is a huge number, but at least 12 million people are better off now than they were 10 years ago. There has also been steady progress on the minimum wage, which rose 27 percent in real terms between 1994 and 2002, reaching its highest level in 40 years.

I am well aware that the data I have cited are far from ensuring Brazil's social redemption. Still, I am firmly convinced that they are robust enough to show that the country is on the right track. We still have a long way to go. But as my dear friend Vilmar Faria—a brilliant sociologist who recently died—used to say, the glass is half full rather than half empty. And it is becoming fuller. Most important, we have devised ways to finish the job we have started.

Principles for Development

What principles guide development efforts in Brazil? First, there is a virtuous cycle between democracy and human development. The coexistence of economic growth and higher poverty in São Paulo in the mid-1970s is unlikely to occur in a democratic environment. To preserve their legitimacy, elected governments should prove capable of meeting social demands. Governments no longer derive their legitimacy solely from supporting the right causes or engaging in effective combat, but from delivering well what their constituencies expect of them. Today's model is not what to do but how to do it in the most efficient, cost-effective way.

I think that this point is clear. Because of democracy, the social situation in São Paulo was much better in the 1990s than in the mid-1970s. So even though economic growth was disappointing, development outcomes were extremely positive.

Such outcomes largely depend on social and political circumstances, including social pressure. People's demands are very important, and governments can no longer dismiss them. People are more organized than ever, and public opinion—and intellectual public opinion—are agents of real transformation in society. Change no longer depends solely on economic growth.

When I say that what is important is how to do things in the most efficient, cost-effective manner, I am not suggesting that values and ethical considerations no longer matter to public agency. Politics has not been confined to technical optimization of interests, and values are as important to politics as ever. But they are important in a different way. In defining the common good—and the general will—political agents are now expected to engage in deliberative exercises with a multitude of actors.

Rather than a predetermined variable, as in Rousseau, the general will is seen as the outcome of extensive, open-ended deliberations. Hence it is important that the state maintain a republican mindset and have a clear view of the ultimate values that political decisions should promote. Otherwise it risks being held hostage to corporatist interests. As always, virtue is expected to prevail over vice in the conduct of public affairs.

The state is expected to be more enlightened today than in the past. The task of fitting many conflicting demands into public policies can be successfully pursued only if the necessary expertise is available to evaluate and fine-tune inputs. To be meaningful, republicanism must be effective. Public virtues cannot be cultivated in the abstract: they have to be couched in technical competence.

The second principle for effective development is that the state learn how to spend better. I am not denying the importance, when macroeconomic indicators allow it, of increasing social spending. Indeed, despite constant financial constraints, Brazil has steadily increased social spending. In 1994 social spending accounted for about 11 percent of GDP, whereas in 2002 it was more than 14 percent—the highest level ever.

Again, democracy has been fundamental to such developments. The state must pay attention to people; it cannot just not care. But it must also be enlightened— meaning that it has to be capable of attracting talented, effective staff. People want more than just to elect their representatives and confer on them legitimacy to perform: they also want to participate in political deliberations. So, though difficult, the modern state must foster people's participation.

Because of this, democracy means more than it did in the past. The general will, repeating Rousseau, is much more concrete these days. It is not just expressed in vague, abstract terms. It has been transformed into a much more practical process of active, popular participation in decisionmaking. Because of that, in a situation like Brazil's, assuming that the state is much more enlightened than it was before, the result is that we spend more on social issues.

That is why I used to become a bit angry when people said that Brazil had a neoliberal government, because what we did in Brazil was exactly the opposite. We reconstructed the state apparatus in a modern way to cope with new demands and needs. We never proposed shrinking the state apparatus. On the contrary, we expanded it—perhaps too much, not because of social spending, but because of taxes. We may have increased taxes too much. So now we may need to balance that out.

But in any case, our goal was not to dismantle the state apparatus. It was to transform it into something capable of coping with modern times—not just in terms of promoting good social policies and opening the state to broader participation, but also reorganizing its structure so that in areas where it did not invest directly, such as energy and telecommunications, it would have new agencies to ensure that private companies performed well and the public interest was protected. That is why growth in the federal government's social spending since the mid-1990s has been significantly higher than growth in GDP. And what has mattered most is that social spending has been focused on the neediest of the needy, rather than being channeled to special interests.

Guidelines for Social Spending

I have already stressed the extent to which this principle has underpinned key initiatives, such as the Alvorada Project and the Social Protection Network. Of equal importance has been ensuring that government money reaches its intended recipients. Doing so has required breaking with long-standing government vices such as clientelism, waste, and corruption. To that end, Brazil has introduced new practices to improve the quality and productivity of social spending.

First, services and resources have been decentralized using objective criteria. Dramatic improvements in health services testify to the importance of empowering municipalities to act as stewards of the state, as ensured by the Unified Health System.

Second, low-income families have been given direct access to social benefits without having to deal with intermediaries, bureaucracies, or exchanges of favors. This has been made possible by the introduction of magnetically encoded Citizen Cards, which are distributed to mothers for the withdrawal of their families' benefits—an approach that provides an important safeguard against clientelism.

Making women responsible for their families' care has also empowered them. Women receive the cards by mail, giving them direct access to benefit money. I think that this approach is very important, because I believe that a lot of development depends on democratizing society. If a country can do that, other challenges are much easier to address. Thus it is crucial to transform the way that governments and bureaucracies relate to public opinion.

Third, enormous emphasis has been placed on enhancing civil society's participation in the design, implementation, and control of public policies to increase accountability and transparency. In addition, no effort has been spared in promoting social responsibility, which has produced extremely positive results. Initiatives like the Solidarity Community have succeeded only because of the disposition of business groups and society as a whole to share with the state the task of mitigating social problems.

Brazil's HIV/AIDS prevention program is another important example of a close partnership between the state and civil society in the design, implementation, and control of public policies. This program started in 1988, and it was not an initiative supported by one person or one party or one sector of the bureaucracy: it was far more wide-reaching. Brazilian society understood that if nothing was done to control the spread of AIDS, it would be a huge disaster. So we put up a united front, and Brazil became the first developing country to adopt as official policy free, universal access to life-saving drugs against the disease.

The government also decided that it had to inform the public about the risks of certain kinds of sex—but not tell them not to have sex. So we emphasized the importance of safer sex, and used television and other media to teach the population how to use condoms. Doing that is not easy in a Catholic country. There was tremendous debate, and political parties are always afraid of public opinion. But the public is much brighter than the elite believes, and was receptive to good information.

But the fight against HIV/AIDS involved much more than that. The government also had to fight multinational pharmaceutical companies on intellectual property rights—and made some progress in that area during the international trade negotiations in Doha, Qatar, in 2001—to earn the right to produce certain medicines. As a result the costs of AIDS medicines fell considerably in Brazil.

In all these battles, the government has requested and received the cooperation of those infected with HIV/AIDS. Moreover, they have controlled the prevention program through nongovernmental organizations (NGOs). Those NGOs work with the government and in society, and their efforts have allowed for a very positive result: one of the few cases in the world where, though not eliminated, the disease's progression has been stopped.

This is an example of what I mean when I say that development requires a kind of partnership where government is more open to society, including criticism from society. Indeed, when I first became president I found NGOs extremely difficult to deal with. But by the end of my term, I suggested that we change their label from nongovernmental organizations to new governmental organizations.

Lessons from Experience—and Recommendations for the Future

Although the situation in Brazil is not perfect, and much remains to be done, we are making progress on development. And it is possible, and essential, that we make more progress. What is important is that we know how to do it. For that we are indebted to international financial institutions: the Inter-American Development Bank (IDB), the World Bank, and the International Monetary Fund (IMF).

Based on my experiences, the main lesson of Brazil's development is that it is crucial to have effective, comprehensive social policies. Even if the economic situation is not that wonderful, much can be done on the social front. Still, social policies are not enough: strong economic growth is also required, and we must improve our growth rate. Yet as with governments in other developing countries, we have limited room for maneuver, because so much of our progress depends on the global situation. I am not blaming the IMF, World Bank, or IDB. But it is a fact of today's world economy that financial markets are very difficult to deal with because of some aspects of globalization.

It is also true that development partly depends on domestic efforts. Brazil must perform better, and we must modernize their institutions. We have to be more responsible in spending money, and so on. All those things are undoubtedly true. Still, much depends on the international atmosphere. And who knows what will happen in the near future?

Brazil has the potential to grow by 6–7 percent a year. In recent years we have raised our productivity, enabling us to grow faster. But our growth will not depend solely on the actions of the government. Although most people—even presidents— would like to believe that the country can achieve whatever goals it sets, that is not true. Much depends on fortune: on circumstances far beyond the government's decisionmaking capacity and control. In just the past decade recall the cycle of financial crises that started in 1994 in Mexico. I came to power in 1995, suffering the consequences of that crisis. Then in 1997 there was the East Asian crisis, in 1998 the Russian one, and in 1998–99 the Brazilian one, followed by those in Argentina and Turkey as well as the recession in the United States.

Each of these shocks had terrible consequences for Brazil, because they destroyed high expectations and forecasts. I realize that forecasts are partly based on local circumstances, and that there is an interplay between foreign and domestic events. What Brazil and other developing country governments have to do is make society, the state, and markets more resilient to such events.

Still, the Brazilian government and private sector cannot completely dictate the country's growth rates, because growth partly depends on global circumstances. But what it can do—and indeed, must do—is strengthen links with the global economic system, and hopefully improve that system. I believe that some transformations in the global system are crucial not just for Brazil, but for the prospects of all developing countries. Such reforms are being discussed in the United Nations, and the timing is right: changes must be made.

Those changes should include the roles of the Bretton Woods institutions. The first such change involves the IMF, which I do not believe has enough leverage to cope with the threats and challenges facing its member countries. As an example, in 2002 the Brazilian government—after having made enormous efforts to resolve its economic problems—decided to ask the IMF for additional support. It was not difficult to get the support; the IMF reacted very promptly. And to my surprise, it was not difficult to convince my political opponents of the need for this agreement. But when the IMF informed the international markets that Brazil had received an additional $30 billion, the markets hardly paid any attention, because they were more concerned—and uneasy—about the future president and the future administration.

In the past the IMF was so powerful that its support for a country would calm uncertainty in international markets. But that is no longer the case, because international capital flows are so high, and the possibility of turmoil so great, that even the IMF cannot control the situation and show that there is no reason for such anxiety. Thus I think that more power should be given to the IMF.

The second such change involves the World Bank. Over the years I have tried in vain to explain to Brazilians that our country receives considerable support from the Bank. But the fact is that each year the Brazilian National Bank for Development provides about $12 billion in loans—at least half as much as the World Bank gives to the entire world. That is hardly reassuring. Brazilian entrepreneurs are constantly complaining that they do not have enough support, that it is impossible for them to grow, and that they cannot invest more because they do not have access to enough credit. And they have access to at least half the amount of resources as the World Bank provides to cope with the entire world's development needs.

So, something is wrong here. And what I am saying, in conclusion, is not out of demagoguery alone. Granted, I am a politician, and some degree of demagoguery is always present in the speech of a former president. But there is more to it. I make this point because I think that it is time for serious reflection on what must be done to eliminate poverty around the world. This is a challenge that must be solved during this century. And without a more energetic impulse from international institutions, and without a democratization of international agenda setting at the U.N. level— through discussions with the leading powers as well as the fundamental agencies responsible for the global economy—it will be extremely difficult to move forward on this front.

As I have noted, Brazil is making progress. But when that progress is compared with what needs to be done, it is clear that enormous efforts remain. It cannot be only a domestic effort: it has to be an international effort. Without the profound changes in international markets and institutions identified above, Brazil will be doomed to repeat many of its past experiences. So in the name of our interests, it is essential to continue to pursue further transformations at the international level.

Comment

Enrique V. Iglesias

I AM PLEASED TO BE COMMENTING ON THE EXCELLENT LECTURE OF MY GOOD FRIEND, Fernando Henrique Cardoso. I have been privileged to witness the developments he describes, having followed Brazil closely for many years—particularly the years when he was president. Moreover, we have known each other for about 40 years, and I have always respected his vast wisdom.

I am also pleased to be here with Stanley Fischer, with whom I have shared many interesting experiences in our joint work; he at the International Monetary Fund (IMF) and I at the Inter-American Development Bank (IDB). I have immense admiration for Stan because he has a great mind as well as a great heart. Thus I am honored to be here with these two men and with our friends from the World Bank.

Pillars of Recent Brazilian Policies

Cardoso's lecture synthesizes the three basic goals of recent Brazilian policies. The first is consolidating democracy, which has been growing stronger since the mid-1980s—reflecting continuous progress on institutional and policy reforms. I have observed this building and consolidation of democracy, and Cardoso's administration contributed enormously to these achievements.

Second, Brazil has been committed to implementing sound macroeconomic policies despite difficult circumstances. The government has had to stabilize the economy through consistently strong fiscal and monetary policies, while at the same time opening Brazil to the competitive forces of the global economy. The rules of the game of today's global market require countries to become more efficient and more competitive.

Third, Cardoso discusses social programs. It is not easy to address the challenges of society when poverty is widespread, yet Brazil has made impressive advances. Although much remains to be done, the United Nations has wisely recognized Brazil's recent achievements on social policies.

Pursuing these three goals—consolidating democracy, improving macroeconomic policies, and responding to the demands of society—simultaneously is not easy, and I think that Cardoso's administration did an excellent job. And though Brazil's glass remains half empty, it is important to remember how things were when these reforms began. The imperative of sustaining efforts in these three dimensions is really the main message of Cardoso's speech, as well as the reality of Brazil in recent years.

Development Lessons from the Past Half-century

Brazil is a good example of Latin America's evolving approach to and concept of development. In the early 1950s many of the region's current development practitioners drank wisdom and ideas from the same fountains, such as those of the Economic Commission for Latin America and the Caribbean (ECLAC). Back then our concept of development was fairly simple, and we thought that we had a solution for everything.

We have since learned that development is much more complex. Moreover, development cannot be viewed in a vacuum: it must take into account the social, economic, and political conditions that help determine the limits of what can be done and what can be delivered. I am sure that Cardoso has shared these challenges and realizations.

Development work also does not occur in a vacuum of international relations. International conditions are increasingly relevant for everyone, but particularly in developing countries. Again, I think that these lessons have become clear to all of us.

Over the past 50 years Latin America has been home to an extremely interesting range of development experiences and ideologies, from purely monetarist approaches to the planning and socialist approaches of Cuba. Brazil is a good example of the lessons that have accumulated over the years. In the 1960s Brazil—a country that contained the highly developed São Paulo area as well as the northeastern region, which was at the other extreme—became a major focus for development economists in Latin America. The basic approach we advocated was the same as that being pursued by Brazil, including import substitution and a much more activist government.

I think that was the right approach, because in those days people looked to the public sector to take the lead in almost everything. The private sector was hardly discussed. No one was opposed to it; it just did not seem to exist. Thus the government played an active role in development in Brazil and elsewhere in Latin America. And in the 1960s the region experienced considerable social advancement and economic progress.

The 1970s, however, generated less positive lessons for Brazil and the rest of the region. First, too little attention had been paid to economic balances. For example, persistently high inflation led to recognition of the importance of sound macroeconomic policies. This respect for fiscal discipline has endured, as shown by Brazil's current administration. Second, it became clear that import substitution has its limits and that economies should be open to international markets. Again, over the years Brazil has provided a good example of this lesson. And third, the 1970s provided a lesson about social populism. With good intentions, countries had tried to redistribute nominal income—an approach fraught with difficulties. We learned instead that social progress requires strong social policies.

Then in the 1980s Latin America's debt crisis emerged, and again Brazil's experience was extremely informative, setting the stage for the experiences that Cardoso describes. And at the end of the decade the region began applying the policies defined as the Washington consensus—restoring stability, achieving social and fiscal equilibria with monetary policies, opening economies, and so on. The region's economies opened to each other, to the rest of the hemisphere, and to the rest of the world. They also began reforming the role of the state. Throughout all these periods Brazil has provided useful and interesting lessons for the rest of Latin America.

Perspectives on Reform

Although the reforms resulting from the above experiences were sound, they were insufficient. In recent years Brazil has shown that even when many steps have been taken, many more are needed—and certain lessons must be learned. For example, the challenges of managing international financial flows are widely known, yet it is still not clear exactly how Latin American countries should deal with them. The region's countries also need to increase savings and exports, strengthen institutions, and solidify the relationship between the private and public sectors.

One thing that troubles me, given the lessons of history, is why certain debates persist in Latin America. Among these is the relationship between the public and private sectors—an issue that has been resolved in other parts of the world. Again, Brazil is a good example of this being an area where efforts are being made to improve, leave behind old debates, and take a more pragmatic approach.

In sum, I think that Brazil is a good example—being, after all, the biggest country in the region—of learning from experience. And I think that Cardoso's presidency made a brilliant contribution to the country in the three major areas identified above: political, economic, and social. Because of that, I think that we can look to the future with optimism. In today's world we cannot afford to be pessimistic: we need a lot of good news, and the good news comes from what Cardoso told us today.

Comment

Stanley Fischer

IT IS A GREAT PLEASURE TO BE HERE AMONG FRIENDS AND FORMER COLLEAGUES, AND particularly to be sharing the stage with President Fernando Henrique Cardoso and Enrique Iglesias, who have both made such important contributions to development in Latin America. President Cardoso has played a historic role in cementing democracy and implementing a range of forward-thinking policies in Brazil. Even in the face of enormous pressures—such as the difficult economic crises confronting Brazil in the late 1990s—he has always exhibited exemplary grace, calm, and confidence. Those traits undoubtedly contributed a great deal to the fact that despite the crises, during the decade Brazil made enormous progress on the social issues the president describes in his lecture.

As for my friend Enrique Iglesias, I was reminded of him when President Cardoso referred to those who see the glass as half empty or half full. Michael Mussa used to say of Enrique's and my close friend, Michel Camdessus, that he sees the glass as half full even when there is no glass. Enrique is a bit like that, too. When there is a problem in Latin America and people in Washington, D.C. can help solve it, you can be sure that Enrique and the Inter-American Development Bank (IDB) will be there—facing the challenge rather than saying how difficult it is and how rules and procedures make it impossible to do anything. So it is easy to understand why I am happy to be sharing a platform with President Cardoso and Enrique Iglesias.

Features of Brazil's Success

President Cardoso's lecture is both interesting and unusual. As far as I can remember, it is the first I have ever been asked to discuss that contains the word *deconstruction*—and that refers not to the tearing down of a building, but to the interpretation of a text. Similarly, I have never before had the privilege of discussing a presentation in which Rousseau is central to the text.

President Cardoso focuses on the impressive social progress that Brazil achieved in the 1990s. These results were largely due to successful policy interventions, the first being the Real Plan, which ended Brazil's long-standing high inflation. Just as important were a series of microeconomic and structural policies—especially in education—that continued even as Brazil experienced macroeconomic crises and slow growth near the end of the decade. Although these outcomes did not receive much outside attention during the crises, they show that such interventions can work even in an economy that is not growing very quickly.

President Cardoso also outlines some of the principles that helped ensure the success of these programs, including popular participation and the involvement of beneficiaries, particularly women, in their design and implementation. These principles were among those later embodied in the initiatives associated with debt reduction in the poorest countries, such as the Poverty Reduction and Growth Facility developed by the International Monetary Fund (IMF) and World Bank.

It is worth bearing in mind one point about Brazil's successes in implementing social programs in the 1990s—namely, that it is one of the few countries at its level of development that does not suffer from a shortfall in government revenue. Brazil's tax revenues are much higher as a share of GDP than those in other Latin American countries, including Argentina and Mexico. This gives Brazil more room for such interventions. This crucial difference underscores the need to strengthen tax systems in many developing countries. However, we should also recognize that Brazil's tax system needs to be strengthened by being made more efficient—because some taxes are very high and many are very inefficient—and that Brazil's public spending patterns are also far from efficient.

President Cardoso emphasizes another important point: the role of democracy in producing these changes. In some developing countries and among some economists there is a hankering for a strong (read: authoritarian) government, headed by a strong leader who will implement reforms. It was partly on the basis of negotiations with the Brazilian government during my tenure at the IMF that I concluded it was generally better to reach agreement with a democratic government than an authoritarian one. The IMF knew that once the Brazilian government committed to a program, it expected to be able to get congressional agreement on and implement it. And because the government was democratic, the program had a legitimacy that programs under authoritarian governments are unlikely to have.

I have become increasingly less impressed by the argument that authoritarian governments are good for growth. I think that view is an illusion: those making the argument usually refer to Augusto Pinochet, the progress that Chile made in the 1980s, and his successful handover of power after elections in late 1989. But Pinochet's success in the second half of the 1980s was preceded by a major macroeconomic crisis in 1979–82. More important, Pinochet's administration was just one example of successful economic development under a Latin American dictator between the 1970s and 1990s. At least 25 other dictators made a shambles of economic development and ended up, partly because of their failures, having to hand over leadership to democracies to try to solve the problems they had left behind.

Other Issues

I now turn to three other issues raised in President Cardoso's lecture. The first involves the relationship between growth and social indicators, about which I have four points. First, growth is not enough to improve social indicators—a fact that Cardoso makes clear in his presentation. Second, growth is not necessary for short-term improvements in social indicators. For a time, social programs like those implemented in Brazil can improve literacy, health, and possibly the income distribution even in a no-growth economy. Third, growth helps governments that want to improve social conditions.

But fourth, and most important, sustained reductions in poverty are not possible without sustained growth. A government can redistribute for several years, and it may be vital to do so. But reductions in poverty of the magnitude achieved over the past decade in China and increasingly in India are primarily the result of growth, not redistribution policies. This point raises the dilemma of the tradeoffs between growth and distribution, and of what to do in countries like China, where almost everyone's income has risen during the growth process but the income distribution has nonetheless almost certainly worsened.

The second issue relates to the end of President Cardoso's lecture, where he says that the international system should do more to support development. He makes several points. The first is that he is not talking about aid. But we should not ignore the role of aid, particularly for the poorest countries, and targeted assistance to deal with special problems.

He also notes the need for less volatility and fewer crises in the global economic system. I believe that significant progress has been made in this area, particularly with the adoption of flexible exchange rates in most (though not all) emerging market economies. Indeed, if Brazil had had a pegged exchange rate in 2002, it would have experienced a 1990s-style emerging market crisis. Although the economy was put under severe stress, it held together, and it is emerging from that period much better than it would have with a pegged rate. The other changes on the agenda of international financial institutions and the G-20 to reduce the frequency of crises and strengthen the flexibility of economies—including better policies and stronger domestic institutions—also need to be implemented.

President Cardoso says that good fortune helps determine growth, and that is certainly true. But people and countries help determine their fortunes. Recently, for example, I read about research conducted in Britain on supposedly lucky people. Some people believe that they have luck, and some people do not. The researchers designed several experiments to see if they could discern differences among these people. One experiment involved partially concealing cash along the path on the way to the place of the experiment. It turned out that people who thought they were lucky were more likely to find the money. The conclusion was that people who consider themselves lucky are also looking for opportunities.

This is a polite way of saying that Brazil could do a lot more to benefit from the global economy. In one area in particular, trade, Brazil has not done as much as it could have to integrate with the global economy. One can argue—as Brazilian governments have—that it cannot promote trade because its main exports, which are based on agriculture and natural resources, are kept out of industrial countries. That is true, and it is deplorable. Analysts and policymakers need to keep emphasizing the need for better access for developing country products to industrial country markets.

That said, it remains true that Brazil's development would be substantially aided if it were to increase industrial exports in addition to those based on agriculture and natural resources. Although it is beginning to do much better in that regard, Brazilian policy has not been export-oriented to the extent that it could have been, and growth has suffered as a result.

No country has grown at the 6–7 percent rates that Brazil should aspire to—and is capable of—without massively increasing exports. That is a direction in which Brazil should be heading. One way is by reducing its protectionism. As long as Brazilian producers are protected, they will not see any need to enter export markets. Fortunately this situation finally appears to be changing, as Brazilian exports have expanded impressively in the past year.

Finally, in his introduction President Cardoso says that the challenges of development deserve as much attention today as they did when the Bretton Woods structure was designed more than half a century ago. That is correct. And that is why it is appropriate that this discussion has taken place at the World Bank, which has a crucial role to play in meeting the challenges of development—and why it is appropriate that President Cardoso, whose government did so much to address these challenges and to advance Brazil's development, presented his excellent lecture here.

Alejandro Foxley

Senator and Former Minister of Finance, Chile

Born in Chile in 1939, Senator Alejandro Foxley received his Ph.D. in Economics from the University of Wisconsin. He has held a number of academic positions at various universities, including the University of Sussex, Oxford University, Massachusetts Institute of Technology, University of California at Berkeley, University of California at San Diego, and University of Notre Dame. He has also written or edited 12 books on economic development and problems of democracy, among other themes.

In addition to his distinguished academic career, Foxley has had a notable career in public service both in Chile and for international organizations. From 1990–94 he was Chile's Minister of Finance under President Patricio Aylwin, who led the country's first democratic administration after the military regime of Augusto Pinochet. Under Foxley, Chile deepened economic reforms and extended social opportunities to new segments of society. While Finance Minister, Foxley also served on the Board of Governors of the World Bank and Inter-American Development Bank.

In 1994–97 Foxley was President of Chile's Christian Democratic Party. Since 1998 he has been Senator of Chile, including serving as Chairman of the Senate Finance Committee.

7 Lessons from Chile's Development in the 1990s

Alejandro Foxley

IN DECEMBER 1989 PATRICIO AYLWIN WAS ELECTED PRESIDENT OF CHILE IN FREE elections, ending 17 years of military rule by Augusto Pinochet. Aylwin represented a center-left coalition of Christian Democratic and Socialist parties.

Pinochet's regime had forcefully repressed any sign of opposition. During his rule many labor leaders, civil society representatives, and opposition leaders spent time in jail. Some were tortured; others disappeared. As a result many Chileans expected a full reversal of the government policies pursued in 1973–89.

The military government had initiated a deep process of reforms, opening up the economy, eliminating a lot of regulation, and privatizing state companies and social security. Still, the economic record of the Pinochet administration was mixed. Macroeconomic performance was uneven, with economic growth averaging 2.9 percent over the 17-year period (Ffrench-Davis and Laban 1996). Two deep recessions, in 1974–1975 and in 1982–84, account for much of the mediocre performance.

In 1982, after three years of experimenting with a fixed exchange rate, Chile's financial sector collapsed. GNP fell 16 percent and unemployment jumped to 30 percent. As a result half of Chilean households were living in poverty in 1982. The subsequent banking crisis cost the country 30–42 percent of GDP, according to various estimates (Frydl 1999; Held 2001).

The economy recovered in 1985–89, with growth averaging 5.2 percent a year in 1983–89. But the Pinochet administration, trying to win the presidential election for its new candidate in 1989, had greatly expanded government spending and cut taxes. As a result the new democratic government inherited an overheated economy, with inflation reaching 30 percent in 1989. Imports were growing by 30 percent a year, and a huge balance of payment deficit was developing. By the time of Aylwin's inauguration in early 1990, 40 percent of Chileans lived below the poverty line. (For a general discussion of this period, see Pizarro, Raczynski, and Vial 1996 and Ffrench-Davis 1999.)

The popular perception was that Pinochet's economic model had been inherently unfair to the lower and middle classes. Thus deep changes were expected from the new administration. At the same time, the private sector and Pinochet supporters had very negative attitudes toward the new regime. They believed that the new government would enter into the populist cycle so typical of recent Latin American history (Dornbusch and Edwards 1991). These groups expected the new economic team to give in to popular demands for higher public spending and big wage increases, leading to high inflation—followed by social disorder and general strikes. They also expected people whose human rights had been systematically violated during the military rule to try to get even.

Two personal anecdotes reflect the low expectations for the new administration and its economic team, which I headed. On the day I was appointed minister of finance, Rudi Dornbusch—then an economics professor at the Massachusetts Institute of Technology (MIT) and a good friend—sent me a fax saying, "Congratulations; please don't mess it up." A few months earlier the main private sector umbrella organization invited me, as the likely head of the new administration's economic team, to address more than a thousand business executives. I gave what I thought was a reasonable presentation. Then during the question and answer period that followed, someone in the audience raised his hand and said, "I have listened to your remarks very carefully, and I don't believe a word of what you are saying."

The New Economic Approach: Growth with Equity

Thus it was clear that our first challenge was to build trust and credibility in the new administration's ability to govern responsibly and effectively. To achieve that goal, we had to prove that our economic program—based on the notion of growth with equity—was guided by sound policies (Foxley 1993; Perry and Leipziger 1999). Accordingly, we imposed on ourselves a challenging course of action. Two strong commitments were made public at the very beginning. First, we would develop and maintain a significant budget surplus throughout the entire presidential term. This commitment was fulfilled. Under the Aylwin administration (March 1990–March 1994) the budget surplus averaged 1.7 percent of GDP (table 7.1).

The second commitment was to reduce public debt, which had reached 47 percent of GDP by the end of the Pinochet period. We committed ourselves to increasing government savings to 5 percent of GDP and to using some of those savings to prepay public debt. By 1993 public debt had been cut to 29 percent of GDP (table 7.2).

We also had to convince the public that we were serious about redressing the social imbalances inherited from the previous regime. To that end we introduced tax reform to increase the tax burden by 3 percent of GDP. The tax package involved raising the corporate tax rate from 10 to 15 percent, the value added tax (VAT) rate from 16 to 18 percent, and income tax rates for high-income groups, as well as introducing taxation based on effective (not presumed) rents for agricultural and transport activities (see below).

This legislation was controversial, and initially was almost universally opposed. But within three months it had been enacted into law by an almost unanimous vote in

TABLE 7.1
Chile's Economic Performance, 1990–93
(percent; annual average)

Indicator	Average
GDP growth	7.8
Domestic savings/GDP	22.0
Balance of payments deficit/current account	2.5
Investment/GDP (real)	27.8
Productivity growth	4.1
Real wage growth	4.6
Employment growth	3.5
Government savings/GDP	4.3
Budget surplus/GDP	1.7

Source: Banco Central de Chile 2001.

TABLE 7.2
Chile's Annual Economic Indicators, 1990–93
(percent)

Indicator	1990	1991	1992	1993
GDP growth	3.7	8.0	12.3	7.0
Inflation	27.3	18.7	12.7	12.2
Unemployment	7.8	8.2	6.7	6.5
Poverty (percentage of population)	39			28
Extreme poverty (percentage of population)	12.9			7.6
Government savings/GDP	2.6	3.9	5.3	5.3
Budget surplus/GDP	0.8	1.6	2.3	2.0
Public debt/GDP	43.0	37.4	30.9	28.7
Public debt/GDP (net)	36.4	30.1	22.6	18.8

Source: Banco Central de Chile 2001.

both chambers of Congress. The tax reform increased tax revenues by 23 percent in real terms in 1991, by 13 percent in 1992, and by 10 percent in 1993 (Marcel 1999).

The early success with tax reform proved crucial to later developments. The government had said that all of the new tax revenues would be used to reduce poverty, improve health and education, and provide housing for poor people. And that promise was kept. Under the Aylwin administration poverty dropped from 40 percent to 28 percent. Overall public spending on the social sectors rose 32 percent, with spending on health increasing by 54 percent and on education by 40 percent. As people recognized the efforts being made on the social front, the administration's growth with equity concept became concrete and credible—marking a clear departure from the exclusive growth focus of the Pinochet regime's economic strategy (Mideplan 1996).

The other major social reform was the enactment of new labor legislation. The challenge was to restore basic labor rights that had been suppressed by the military government. Most relevant labor leaders had spent long periods in jail, and labor unions had encountered severe restrictions in their attempts to defend worker rights. The new labor legislation sought to strengthen collective bargaining at the firm level but opposed industrywide wage negotiations, as demanded by the national organization of workers. After a few months of tripartite negotiations, labor reform was made into law (Cortazar 1993).

In addition, a permanent tripartite dialogue was established with the private sector and labor organizations, with the government represented by the ministers of finance, economy, and labor. The dialogue was formal yet open, with the press given full access to the proceedings and conclusions. We met twice a year, and it was at those meetings that agreements were reached on income policies, social security issues, and other social policies.

Tripartite consensus building was new in Chile. The notion behind it was that bridges had to be built between labor and business, and that the new government had to catalyze the process. Business leaders had been pinochetistas and were skeptical and suspicious of the democratic government. Meanwhile, labor organizations considered business their enemy.

These changes in social policies were complemented by two other reforms designed to stimulate investment and economic growth. One sought to induce deeper integration of Chile with the world economy. External tariffs were unilaterally cut from 15 percent to 11 percent during the Aylwin administration, and were further cut to 6 percent during Eduardo Frei's administration (1994–2000).

The Aylwin government also decided to initiate a policy of open regionalism, seeking free trade agreements with a number of countries. The first agreement was signed with Mexico in 1991, followed by others with Colombia and Venezuela during the Aylwin administration and then with Canada, the European Union, and the United States during the Frei and Lagos (2000–present) administrations (Rosales 2004; Saez and others 1995; Agosín and Ffrench-Davis 1998; Ffrench-Davis and Muñoz 2002). Once these agreements are fully effective, Chile will have an effective external tariff of less than 2 percent.

The other component was capital market reform, which sought to deepen Chile's capital markets (Eyzaguirre and Lefort 1999). Chile had privatized its pension funds in the early 1980s, and they were accumulating substantial savings. But those savings were not being channeled to new companies or to investment funds, and they were not allowed to be invested abroad. Instead the portfolios of pension funds were heavily concentrated in government bonds. There was an obvious mismatch between firms' need for access to long-term financing and the rigid regulation governing the investments of pension funds and other institutional investors. Capital market reform made this regulation much more flexible. It also introduced better, independent risk assessment mechanisms for the more flexible investment options, and better regulation of conflicts of interest in the financial sector. After this reform was approved by

Congress in 1993, it was followed by further steps in the same direction during the Frei and Lagos administrations.

Results of the New Approach

The growth with equity strategy was generally successful. Under the Aylwin administration the economy grew by an average of 7.8 percent a year. This was made possible by a substantial increase in investment, which rose from 25 percent of GDP in 1991 to 31 percent in 1993 (in real terms). In addition, productivity grew by 4.1 percent in 1990–93, while employment expanded by 3.5 percent a year. Real wages followed the trend in productivity, increasing by 4.6 percent a year (see table 7.1).

The government also met (and exceeded) its target for savings, with the public savings rate rising from 2.6 percent of GDP in 1990 to 5.3 percent in 1992 and 1993. The budget surplus also increased, from 0.8 percent of GDP in 1990 to 2.0 percent in 1993, with an average for the period of 1.7 percent.

As noted, the government also honored its commitment to reduce public debt. The Aylwin administration's prepayment of its obligations reduced public debt from 47 percent of GDP in 1989 to 29 percent in 1993 (in gross terms, and 19 percent in net terms). This policy was continued by the Frei and Lagos administrations, causing public debt to fall to 16 percent of GDP in 2002 (in gross terms, and 11 percent in net terms).

The Aylwin administration's strategy also significantly improved social equity. Between 1990 and 1993 poverty fell from 39 percent to 28 percent, while extreme poverty dropped from 13 percent to 8 percent. And as noted, during this period public social spending rose 32 percent, jumping 54 percent on health and 40 percent on education.

The distribution of income also improved during that time, with the Gini coefficient falling from 55 in 1987 to 53 in 1994. Although that modest improvement was reversed in 1998, the redistributive effects of government programs remain impressive when monetary transfers and social spending in areas such as health, education, and housing are taken into account. In 1998 the richest fifth of the population had 20 times the monetary income of the poorest fifth. But when government social spending is taken into account, that income disparity shrinks from 20 to 11 times. About 60 percent of the reduction in inequality is due to government spending on education, 25 percent to spending on health, and 11 percent to monetary transfers (World Bank 2002).

What explains Chile's strong economic growth in the 1990s? A simplistic view would say that it was the result of economic reforms initiated by the Pinochet government. An equally simplistic view would say that it was the result of the democratic forces that came into power in 1990, awakening creative forces that allowed the economy to grow very quickly from 1990 until 1998.

A key to understanding Chile's good growth performance is reflected in the distinctive phrase developed by the new economic authorities in 1990. We proposed "continuity and change" in economic policies. Continuity was essential to take advantage of the upsurge in entrepreneurship that the reforms of the 1970s and 1980s had unleashed. But growth was not impressive for most of the Pinochet years—only in the last five (1985–89), when earlier reforms were bearing fruit and the economy was benefiting from ample excess capacity as a result of the economic collapse of 1982.

The good results of the 1990s, on the other hand, were based on accumulated social capital shared by all sectors of Chilean society in the early part of the decade. This social capital was fostered by a variety of developments:

- In the 1970s the government anticipated the trend toward globalization and unilaterally opened the economy to foreign competition.

- The private sector responded to this challenge by adapting to the new conditions and becoming more efficient and aggressive in foreign markets.

- A new sense of fairness emerged throughout society, exemplified by the Aylwin government's growth with equity strategy—including its fight against poverty. The consequent perception of stability resulted in spectacular growth in private investment during the early 1990s.

- Well-functioning, transparent, democratic institutions resulted in rational, predictable rules and policies (see Foxley and Claudio 1999).

- An effective state apparatus also played a key role in Chile's success (see Marcel 1999).

- Sound, consistent macroeconomic policies were in place—reflecting a collective learning process that began in the 1970s with many policy mistakes, but that improved through the 1980s and 1990s.

- Reforms were a continuous process, starting with a restructuring of public finances and the labor market in 1990, followed by lowering of external tariffs, deepening of domestic capital markets, and decentralization of decisionmaking from the center to regions and municipalities, and, in later years, ambitious education and judicial reforms.

- Politics were of a high quality, and placed a strong emphasis in building consensus (see the next section).

The Political Economy of Reform

One distinctive feature of Chile's economic policies in the1990s was the high quality of decisionmaking, with efforts guided by the desire to achieve consensus. After years of violent confrontation, the new democracy had to prove its ability to integrate various perspectives in a shared agenda (see Foxley and Claudio 1999; for comparative country experiences, see Haggard and Kaufman 1995).

We viewed our task not only to be producing sound policies, but also building the coalitions needed to support the reforms and policies involved in the growth with equity strategy. Accordingly, we fostered ad hoc coalitions that could develop agreements among conflicting interest groups.

Reform initiatives were packed with various components that would ensure the support of key economic and political actors. At the same time, the policy packages presented to Congress were also intended to weaken opposition to the proposed economic measures (Navia and Velasco 2003).

This approach involved two risks. The first was that the government would be paralyzed by conflicting pressures from different interest groups. The second was that the desire for consensus would result in policies that were watered-down or distorted versions of the original objectives. Preventing these undesirable outcomes required exerting strong but thoughtful leadership—being flexible on secondary objectives and unmovable on the main one. A critical component of this approach involved using the bully pulpit of the media, particularly television, to explain policy goals and make them seem reasonable to a majority of the electorate. Here I illustrate this approach using three critical policy decisions made in the first half of President Aylwin's term. All three are useful for drawing lessons applicable elsewhere.

Spending political capital: tax reform

It is often said that the success or failure of a new administration is decided in its first 100 days. Although that might be an overstatement, it seems to be true that—at least in Latin America, where consensus politics is a scarce commodity—the toughest reforms should be tackled as early as possible, taking full advantage of the brief honeymoon period that accompanies most new governments.

People expect a new president to promote changes, but are often not clear about what sacrifices those changes would imply for them. For any new administration the temptation is to start with reforms that will not encounter much resistance. But reformist governments are often distracted by unexpected events that require rapid responses. In Mexico, for example, President Vicente Fox was forced to shift his focus from his major initial effort, tax reform, to the problem of indigenous peoples' rights in the state of Chiapas. As a result Fox decided that tax reform, a cornerstone of his growth with equity strategy, would be put before Congress only after the Chiapas problem had been dealt with and enough time had passed to build a majority in Congress in favor of reform (Navia and Velasco 2003). But when the tax reform was finally introduced, there was no longer support for it.

In contrast, consider Chile's experience with tax reform in 1990. The reform involved an across the board tax increase, including corporate, personal income, value added, agricultural, and transport taxes. Naturally, the proposal inspired widespread opposition. Every political and population group had an argument against the various components of the tax package.

The government, however, decided to spend all of its prestige and political capital fighting for tax reform. We thought that without a substantial increase in tax revenues, the equity component of the government's strategy would not be feasible. And if that component failed, it would be perceived as a campaign ploy—and the new democratic administration would be rapidly discredited.

We knew that we were indirectly touching on issues that people cared about deeply: social and income inequality. Pinochet's economic policies had been perceived as being unfair to the lower and middle classes. Massive poverty was widely visible, and opinion polls in the last few years of the military government found that poverty and inequality were widespread concerns. In fact, Pinochet lost the national referendum that he called in 1988, among other reasons because of the poverty afflicting large segments of the population. Poverty and inequality were also the reason the candidate he chose lost the presidential election by a wide margin in 1989.

Moreover, we knew that there was high hidden demand for political consensus and cooperation—not confrontation—in Chilean society (Boeninger 1997). Accordingly, the tax increase was popularly sold as the only way to introduce solidarity in economic policy, as a necessary step to legitimize the economic model initiated by the military government, and as an opportunity for Pinochet supporters to prove that they were capable of compromise by supporting, in Congress, a policy package based on social equity.

The government used a carrot and stick approach to build political support. We told the opposition that they would have equal say on how the new tax revenues would be spent on different social programs. At the same time, in the media we denounced the "selfish interest groups and political parties" unable to understand the problem of massive poverty and the need for urgent action. We were on television daily calling for a national agreement to combat poverty.

The strategy worked. In fewer than the critical first 100 days, an agreement was signed with the main opposition party—with the support of business and labor leaders—and Congress approved the tax increase in record time. The vote in the Senate was 30 in favor, 2 against.

The proper selection of the initial key reform, and its successful conclusion, not only strengthened the government's authority, it also increased its legitimacy as representing the general interests of regular people instead of the vested interests of the better off. As a result public support for the government increased dramatically as a direct result of a tax increase that would adversely affect everyone's income!

Responding to unexpected shocks: the Gulf War

In mid-1990 the Aylwin administration was applying a tough stabilization policy. The Central Bank had raised interest rates to about 15 percent, and monetary and fiscal policies were contractionary. Still, the fight against the rising inflation and overheated economy inherited from the Pinochet administration had not yet produced results.

The problem was compounded by the surge in oil prices resulting from the invasion of Kuwait by Iraq in August 2000. Chile imports 85 percent of its oil. Thus the oil price shock endangered the stabilization policy by putting severe cost pressures on Chilean industry.

Chileans were exasperated by the economic slowdown forced by the stabilization package. Populist voices were asking the government to ignore the oil shock and measure an "underlying" rate of inflation that did not take into account the increase in oil prices. At one point it was even suggested that the price of oil be excluded from the consumer price index altogether.

Instead, in October 1990 the government introduced a policy package that required additional sacrifices. Table 7.3 identifies the main components of the package and the constituents supporting specific policies. The package transferred to consumers the entire increase in oil prices. It also created a Petroleum Stabilization Fund, to smooth out future price fluctuations for oil and derivatives. At the same time, it was necessary to compensate for the cost push factor behind the oil shock by cutting costs elsewhere. We decided to take the risk of calling on labor unions and business representatives to agree on a package of shared sacrifices.

We asked the National Workers Organization to accept a wage increase lower than the annual inflation rate. Inflation had been about 30 percent over the past 12 months, and the government offered to increase the salaries of public employees by 25 percent in 1991. This offer was initially rejected. Then the government added that everyone would share the burden, and that government spending would be cut by 5 percent.

The key aspect of this seemingly neutral proposal to labor unions was a significant reduction in military spending. The reason was that Pinochet had imposed, by decree, a guaranteed floor on the military budget. Thus the new administration was legally prohibited from cutting the military budget. We decided to challenge that prohibition, and told the labor unions that we would be willing to make the challenge public—provided they supported the entire policy package, including the wage increase lower than the inflation rate.

It was a risky strategy. But we realized that there are often symbolic elements in a policy package that are not especially substantive, but that can make the difference in whether it is accepted. Because Pinochet had imprisoned labor leaders and been head of the army during his regime, cutting the military budget carried huge symbolic meaning for labor unions. But Pinochet's status as head of the army also meant that military cutbacks could get us into deep trouble.

Before announcing the proposal publicly, I presented it to my good friend, Manuel Bustos, the president of the main labor union organization. Manuel initially said, "No way." But after a couple days he called me one night at 11 p.m. and said,

TABLE 7.3

Chile's Policy Response to the Gulf War and its Oil Price Shock

Policy	Supporters
• Raise domestic oil prices	• Financial markets
• Create Petroleum Stabilization Fund	• Consumers
• Reduce government spending	• Private sector
• Reduce military spending	• Civilian population, labor unions
• Agree with labor unions to lower real wages	• Private sector
• Lower interest rates	• Private sector
• Introduce measures to save energy	• Environmentalists

"Alejandro, we have to talk." He came to my house and said, "Look, what do you have to offer?"

I said, "What about cutting military expenditures?"

He said, "You won't be able to do that. That's impossible. You will get into deep, deep trouble."

"But what if I deliver that, Manuel? Then what would you be able to accept? We cannot increase wages at the rate of inflation. You have to accept a much lower rate." And we started discussing how much lower would that be. The result: a few days later we announced a policy package that included a 5 percent, across the board reduction in wages and a 5 percent reduction in government spending—including the military. With labor on board with this package of broad spending cuts, we were able to win the military's cooperation.

The labor unions accepted our offer not necessarily because it made economic sense, but because of its strong symbolic meaning. They were willing to support the democratic government challenging Pinochet even though it meant a sacrifice in their wages.

Once labor supported the policy package, it was easy to persuade the private sector. The self-imposed cut in government spending showed that the government was committed to fiscal discipline even under adverse circumstances. In addition, good coordination between the minister of finance and the president of the Central Bank led the Central Bank—appreciating the strong austerity signal produced by the public sector—to create more space for private sector expansion by reducing high interest rates, from 13 percent in September 1990 to 9 percent in December.

The package was completed by appealing to citizens—particularly environmental groups, which were seeking energy-saving measures to reduce the high pollution from cars and the public transport system. In Santiago alone, 2,500 highly polluting buses were taken out of circulation. In addition, restrictions were imposed on the circulation of cars. These decisions, marginal to the main objective of the policy package, had symbolic importance for civil society groups with broader social concerns, such as environmental protection.

The policy package was extremely successful. Although monthly inflation had shot up to 5 percent in September 1990 and 4 percent in October, it fell dramatically in subsequent months: to 0.9 percent in November, 0.5 percent in December, and 0.1 percent in February 1991. And as it turned out, labor unions made a good compromise when they accepted a wage increase of 25 percent for 1991 relative to past annual inflation of 30 percent. The apparent loss in real wages was more than compensated by the fact that in 1991 inflation fell sharply, to 19 percent. Thus real wages actually increased. Moreover, after this successful episode, labor unions accepted the use of expected future inflation, not past inflation, in collective bargaining (as well as expected increases in productivity).

Exploiting new opportunities: excessive capital inflows

In the early 1990s Latin America was once again beginning to enjoy a period of massive capital inflows. In Chile this process was reinforced by high interest rates, sound economic policies, and a lack of social disruptions. As a result Chile was being flooded by foreign funds.

As policymakers the problem we faced was how to deal with a persistent, significant appreciation of the exchange rate. Chile's growth strategy was based on exports, and drastic appreciation of the peso was making the export sector less and less competitive. At the same time, aggressive bankers were offering over-the-counter loans in cheap dollars to anyone willing to go into debt—firms and consumers alike. We were worried about a financial bubble being fed by excessive capital inflows.

In response we proposed a unilateral reduction in external tariffs from 15 percent to 11 percent, knowing that higher demand for imports would help sustain a more reasonable exchange rate. Such a policy is usually resisted by domestic industry. So again, we relied on the bully pulpit to weaken the resistance, arguing that the main beneficiaries of trade opening would be the consumers who would be paying less for higher-quality imports. Whetting the appetite of consumers proved extremely effective in reducing resistance from members of Congress.

Exporters supported the decision because it promised an equilibrium exchange rate less biased against exports. And progressive politicians and people on the left, usually suspicious of too much opening to world markets, welcomed our next key decision: imposing, in June 1991, a tax on short-term capital inflows. A 20 percent reserve requirement for one-year loans (later increased to 30 percent) and a 1.2 percent stamp tax on external credit transactions discouraged "hot" money and were highly effective in preventing excessive capital inflows. The maturity of incoming loans shifted to medium and long term, and short-term capital inflows plummeted (Zahler 1998, Velasco and Cabezas 1998).

We knew that this policy would be effective only in the short term, because financial agents would eventually find ways to avoid paying the tax. Indeed, this is the argument often made by analysts looking beyond the short-term impact of such a policy: they conclude that it fails to prevent capital inflows when the market environment is favorable, as it was in Chile. But the tax on short term capital was extremely useful for Chile in the early 1990s. It helped avoid excessive exchange rate appreciation that would have hurt the export sector, Chile's engine of growth.

The restrictions on capital inflows were reinforced by efforts to facilitate outflows. Banks were allowed to operate freely abroad (Zahler 1998). The resulting policy package represented a rather unorthodox mix, with more opening to trade and capital outflows, and restrictions on inflows. But the package worked well: economic growth surged to 8.0 percent in 1991 and 12.3 percent in 1992.

As with the response to the oil shock, diverse interest groups aligned themselves behind these unorthodox policies, each for different reasons. But that was enough to allow us to introduce and pass a law that in just two days (in June 1991) unilaterally reduced external tariffs from 15 percent to 11 percent. This is as good an example as any of the high-quality decisionmaking by the executive and legislative branches that has been a distinguishing factor in Chile's recent development.

Policy Lessons

It is often asked why Chile has been so much more successful than many of its Latin American neighbors. The reasons are not black and white. Although Chile had clear policy successes in the 1990s, it also had failures. But the same is true of countries such as Brazil, Costa Rica, the Dominican Republic, and Mexico. This section discusses some of Chile's strengths, as well as some of its weaknesses.

Capacity to absorb external shocks

A recent evaluation of Latin American economic reforms over the past 20 years shows that external shocks can rapidly undo progress achieved on many macroeconomic fronts (Kuczynski and Williamson 2003). Chile, however, has shown a strong capacity to absorb such shocks. Thus managing crises and learning how to absorb external shocks are key aspects of successful macroeconomic reforms in Latin America.

Capital volatility can have a devastating impact on emerging economies—as learned by Mexico in 1994, East Asian economies in 1997, Russia in 1998, and Turkey and Argentina more recently. The rules of the game for international financial flows are unlikely to change in the foreseeable future: a new financial architecture will not emerge. Thus the only option is for emerging economies to learn how to live with sudden inflows and outflows of capital.

Chile made some well-timed policy decisions to ameliorate the boom-bust cycles associated with volatile external financial flows. One critical decision made in 1990—not particularly popular at the time—was to use government savings accumulated in the good years to retire public debt. This made room for countercyclical fiscal policy in the bad years without endangering the country's payment capacity when the economy slowed down.

Policy continuity is another valuable asset. The debt reduction policy of the Aylwin government was continued by the Frei and Lagos administrations. As a result public debt fell from 47 percent of GDP in 1989 to 12 percent in 2004.

Commitment to a budget surplus has also proven to be a valuable asset. Because Aylwin needed economic credibility in the transition to democracy, his administration was determined to achieve a budget surplus—no matter what the circumstances. After public debt had been drastically reduced, the Lagos administration was able to restate the policy goal as that of achieving a structural budget surplus of 1 percent of GDP. That approach allowed the government to run a deficit during the recent economic downturn, consistent with a surplus to be achieved as soon as the economy recovers.

Inflation targeting is another policy goal designed to improve the economy's capacity to absorb shocks—especially external shocks. Once a persistent low rate of inflation has been achieved and debt and government spending are under control, countercyclical monetary policy can be very helpful in avoiding a recessionary cycle in the economy.

If not handed wisely, however, inflation targeting can have negative spillovers. An example is a 1998 episode involving interest rate policy. The Central Bank had not paid much attention to the consequences for the Chilean economy of the 1997 East Asian financial crisis. Capital inflows had decreased sharply, and a devaluation of the peso followed. The Central Bank, concerned about not meeting its inflation target, increased the interest rate from 6.5 percent in September 1997 to 18.0 percent a year later (Banco Central de Chile 2001). This sharp increase helped trigger a recession in 1999, when economic growth was negative at −2.4 percent. It also contributed to a five-year period when average economic growth fell to less than 3 percent a year, down from nearly 8 percent in the early and mid-1990s.

Thus part of the economic slowdown was caused by an overshoot in interest rate increases by the Central Bank, worried that the government was overspending at a time when inflationary pressures were picking up—a valid concern. In late 1997 the Frei administration, facing strong pressures from political parties unhappy about the results of parliamentary elections, had decided to expand social spending, including a significant increase in pensions. But the timing was wrong, and it gave the Central Bank an excuse to initiate an overly contractionary monetary policy, the effects of which would be felt for several years.

What caused this failure in coordination between the Central Bank and the Ministry of Finance? Essentially, the ministry proved too vulnerable to political pressure, and the bank had a very strong sense of its autonomy and of its mandate to reduce inflation—regardless of the effects on output and employment. Had the Central Bank had a mandate to reduce inflation while also concerning itself with output and employment (as in the United States), the overshoot in interest rate increases might have been avoided. The lesson is that Central Bank autonomy and inflation targeting do not always ensure optimal policy outcomes. Autonomy is not a substitute for technically grounded good judgment. And excessive autonomy may feed excessive rigidity in targeting lower inflation at any cost.

Exchange rate policy is also critical. Not long ago, economists were heatedly arguing in favor of convertibility, fixed exchange rates, and dollarization as a way of advancing economic reforms. But in the early 1980s Chile had experienced the devastating consequences of a lethal mix of a fixed exchange rate, deregulation of the banking sector, and free inflows of cheap dollar loans into the domestic economy. As noted, the financial sector collapsed in 1982, and the economy shrunk 16 percent in one year, with unemployment reaching 30 percent. As noted, the rescue package for financial institutions cost Chilean taxpayers 30–42 percent of GDP. Argentina and Mexico also learned the hard way that those policies do not work. After the bad experience of the 1980s, Chile chose to pursue flexible exchange rates, with a crawling peg at the beginning and a free floating rate since 2000.

This combination of policy decisions has allowed the Chilean economy to avoid financial crisis, a loss of competitiveness, and massive bankruptcies—while other economies in the region have experienced yet more busts in the boom-bust cycle. Brazil, under Fernando Henrique Cardoso, has also avoided crisis by pursuing similar policies.

Although restrictions on short-term capital inflows have been effective in Chile—enforced during booms, when capital inflows rose, and eliminated when

external capital was scarce—we have reluctantly agreed to abolish reserve requirements on capital inflows (except in emergencies) as part of the Free Trade Agreement
between Chile and the United States. The U.S. Treasury proved to be more orthodox
here than the International Monetary Fund (IMF) and other international financial
institutions.

As a counterpoint to the type of policies described above, what would be the
worst possible combination of policies to deal with external shocks? That would
probably be a fixed exchange rate, unrestricted capital inflows, high public debt,
ample access for firms and consumers to cheap dollar-denominated loans, and systematic budget deficits. Such a mix is a recipe for disaster.

Effective institutions

The World Bank recently completed a study comparing institutions and macroeconomic policies in Chile and other countries. It concluded that the quality and standards of Chile's institutions are generally—but not entirely—comparable to those in
OECD countries (World Bank 2003).

Chile's success in such studies is partly explained by its high political stability,
strong rule of law, and low corruption. Moreover, institutional upgrading has been an
explicit objective of public policy since at least 1990. Good rules have been established and respected by all recent governments concerning an autonomous Central
Bank, independent and noncorrupt judiciary, and proper government spending and
debt. In fact, the Chilean Congress cannot increase government expenditures or
impose tax changes: those are exclusive initiatives of the executive branch. Congress
can only reduce public expenditures. And municipalities and regional governments
cannot go into debt unless expressly authorized by the minister of finance.

These rules are strict, rigid, and universally followed. Moreover, Chile ranks
18th—a level equivalent to Germany and the United States—in an index by Transparency International that measures transparency and corruption in public institutions. But that is only part of the story.

Recent mini-scandals in Chile's public sector have revealed two areas where
transparency has not been the norm. One is campaign finance, the other is bonuses
paid under the table to high-level public executives. First, until recently there was no
legislation regulating campaign contributions. As a result candidates depended on a
few large contributors, who then felt free to ask members of Congress for favors or
special interest legislation.

The second problem area involved the inadequate remuneration of top government officials. Nobody dared to confront the powerful public employees union,
which opposed changes in the rigid salary scale in the public sector. That led to private contractors of public works being asked to contribute to a fund to finance extra
pay for top officials—creating scandal, publicly and legally.

These scandals occurred because entire areas of modernization of the state were
unwisely postponed. The lesson of these developments is that modernization of the
public sector, including campaign finance, should be part of the first generation of

reforms, not later. If a country fails to do that, it makes itself vulnerable to nontransparent relationships between the public and private sectors, and such relationships can easily become a source of corruption.

Another area where Chile has lagged behind is in reforming bureaucratic procedures. As an example, consider that registering a new business in Chile requires 10 procedures, 28 business days, and $620. In Canada it takes 2 procedures, 2 days, and $280. Some legislative steps have been taken to address this issue, such as the passing of a law of "administrative silence": if the bureaucracy does not meet a deadline in terms of procedures and permits, the application is assumed to be approved.

The more general point is that reform of the state has no clear constituency supporting it (Navia and Velasco 1993). In fact, it usually encounters opposition from teachers, public sector unions, doctors, health care workers, and the like. The temptation for politicians is not to confront these special interests, and to postpone the necessary reform. This issue has not been settled in Chile, and it could increasingly be an obstacle to further productivity growth in the Chilean economy.

Third Generation Reforms—and Shortfalls in Innovation

The question has often been raised: Why was Chile able to grow by nearly 8 percent a year for much of the 1990s, but has not been able to grow by more than 3 percent since the East Asian crisis? Obviously part of the answer lies in adverse external conditions. Terms of trade have deteriorated sharply for the Chilean economy, and current export growth of 5 percent (in volume) is half of what it was a decade ago.

But a more significant explanation lies in a slowdown in increases in productivity. Whereas productivity growth was more than 4 percent a year in the first part of the 1990s, it was less than 1 percent in 2002 and 2003. Indeed, in a recent study on the Chilean economy the World Bank (2003) concludes that faster growth is unlikely to resume unless a coordinated effort is made to increase productivity.

The Bank study finds that in terms of innovation, Chile is an underperformer relative to other countries with similar income levels. Chilean firms are good at doing more of the same—meaning, exporting traditional raw materials with little value added. But they underinvest in research and development and are not closely connected to the latest technological changes introduced by competitor nations—and thus are not a source of new and powerful ideas from which the country could develop new comparative advantages. It is indicative of this reality that venture capital funds in Chile do not find enough fundable projects. Innovation is simply not there.

At the same time, the government is inhibited by what can be called the "industrial policies trauma." Although the import substitution strategy prevailing throughout Latin America in 1950–80 produced high growth rates in the first two decades, it ended up hiding inefficiencies that became an obstacle to growth. Accordingly, conventional wisdom among economists has come to see industrial support policies as wrong and inefficient. Because of that, Chile's public sector is legally forbidden from supplying capital to new businesses and is hesitant to provide incentives or matching grants to startups—unlike what the governments of Finland, Singapore, and other economies do generously and without ideological or political constraints.

As a result the Chilean Development Agency handles a large number of tiny programs that support small business, technological innovation, and research and development. But to give an idea of the limits, the maximum share of matching grants for innovative projects is 6 percent, whereas in Finland the public sector contribution can reach 70 percent of the resources needed to introduce an innovation or startup (Castells and Himanen 2002). For the same reasons the Chilean government is also reluctant to engage in strategic discussions by sector in order to identify new opportunities or competitive advantages, as Finland does so successfully.

The World Bank study poses many key questions that Chilean policymakers do not know how to answer: How do you induce changes in the strategies of traditional firms? How do you attract foreign direct investment in high-technology sectors—what incentives are required, and at what cost? How do you trigger innovation in a more systemic way? Is it a random trial and error process, as Hausmann and Rodrik (2002) suggest? How do you promote clusters? And which incentives work—and which do not?

The World Bank study (2003, vol. 1, p. 239) concludes that "there is a price to be paid for complacency and a premium to be gained by being a first mover. A more aggressive industrial policy stance has risks if poorly managed, but Chile's track record in economic policy is superb. Failure to reach out and become a new leader in the knowledge-based economy risks condemning the country to suboptimal growth performance and unfulfilled social expectations."

This warning is valid for other emerging economies. The recent successes of Hungary, India, Ireland, Singapore, and others are the result of specific local conditions and policies. Such outcomes suggest that the awakening of a society's creative forces is a process about which we know very little. Yet it should be at the core of the new third generation reforms that countries like Chile—and many others at similar levels of development—need to undertake.

Development Lessons of the 1990s

For Latin American policymakers and politicians, the basic fact of life in the 1990s was the ongoing existence of external shocks. When about to leave office at the end of his second term, President Cardoso of Brazil remarked that when he was first elected (in 1993), he never imagined that he would have to deal with continuous external shocks that sidetracked the country's economy and distracted attention from the program he had offered the Brazilian people during his campaign. Mexico's tequila crisis of 1994 was followed by the East Asian and Russian crises, by the crisis suffered by Brazil itself, and by the crises in Turkey and Argentina in later years—each of which has a severe impact on the Brazilian economy. It speaks highly of Cardoso's leadership that despite such negative circumstances, his government was generally successful in modernizing the Brazilian economy and improving living conditions for poor Brazilians.

In many emerging economies the volatility of capital flows has ended up being the most significant determinant of policy outcomes. Countries that have succeeded in absorbing external shocks have been those that learned the hard way from previous financial crises, that economic policy in the 1990s had to be designed for worst-case scenarios.

A few rules of thumb help maximize shock absorption:

- Put a high priority on increasing public savings up front.
- Commit the government to a structural budget surplus.
- Reduce debt significantly.
- Use flexible exchange rates and inflation targeting to guide monetary policy.
- Establish clear, rigid rules restricting local and regional government spending and debt.
- Do not allow the legislature to increase public spending or tamper with the tax structure when the national budget is presented to parliament.

Prudent use of these rules provides insurance against potentially catastrophic external shocks, although it does not guarantee that the economy will move in the trajectory of its growth potential. In fact, some slack in demand and underused capacity might prevail. But that is better than the boom-bust cycle familiar to most Latin American countries.

On the other hand, credibility has proven critical for sustained efforts at economic and institutional reforms. Unpopular policy decisions should be made at the beginning, and a new administration should build trust by demonstrating that it can govern even under adverse circumstances. Recent experiences with President Luiz Inacio Lula da Silva's policies in Brazil and the strong, positive market response are clear examples. Self-imposed difficult decisions create respect and authority for a new leader.

A key strategic decision in the reform process is which reforms should come first. From Chile it seems clear that spending political capital wisely is fundamental. It usually involves choosing one very difficult reform first, and spending political capital there. If successful, the government will have more room and authority for other reforms. If the issue selected is not the most important and difficult, when the more pressing issue is later tackled it might be too late. President Fox's experience with postponing tax reform in Mexico is telling. A legislature will likely not pass at a later stage what it might feel obliged to approve during the first 100 days of a new administration.

A growth objective, as stressed in the original Washington consensus, may not be enough to rally support for comprehensive reforms. Alternatively, a growth with equity strategy generates much broader political support and thus enhances capacity to move ahead with needed changes. An active social policy, effective in substantially reducing poverty, is at the heart of a growth with equity development strategy.

Institutional change is particularly difficult. Because it has no particular constituency supporting it, and a lot of vested interests opposing it, the tendency is to postpone it—making it a second generation reform. But by then it might be too late.

A country subject to the tensions involved in managing capital volatility, external shocks, and economic instability needs strong, predictable, transparent institutions to process the ever-changing external environment in an open economy. That is why a strong argument can be made to make institutional reform one of the high-priority changes needed at the start for economic reforms to succeed. Latin America's recent failures with economic reforms are more related to weak, unreliable, or corrupt institutions than to the nature of the reforms.

Moreover, responses to institutional crises can provide a springboard for reforms that might otherwise not have been feasible. Chile faced a deep institutional crisis as it transitioned to democracy, and such a crisis often results in a failed state. But it also provides an opportunity to get to the root of a country's problems—and for me one of the lessons of this experience was not to resent those who came before you. Moreover, exhibiting that attitude every day builds credibility for reforms.

Even after democracy had progressed, Chile's corruption scandals in 2002 awakened politicians in the government and the opposition to a reality that put at risk everything Chile had achieved in the previous two decades. As a result all political parties agreed on an ambitious program to modernize the public sector, including 49 initiatives that go well beyond solving corruption problems and, in fact, seek to establish a professional, apolitical civil service, regulate campaign finance, introduce incentives and flexibility for better performance in public services, and so on. This was an unintended consequence of political scandal and crisis.

The surprising agreement was possible for two reasons. The political stability and clear rules of the game on political competition, plus the perception of political fatigue in the coalition government after 12 years in power, made the opposition believe that it might win the next election. Taking charge in a country with a strong economy and low social conflict seemed to be in its interest. On the other hand, the persistence with which the Aylwin, Frei, and Lagos administrations invested in consensus building with the opposition over the prior 12 years seemed to pay off in times of crisis. The sunk social capital was there, and the opposition made it possible to move smoothly from a serious political crisis to a phase of new innovative reforms that had previously seemed nonviable.

This lesson is interesting. A good countercyclical fiscal policy involves saving in good times in order to be able to spend during bad. In democratic politics it is possible to think of a countercyclical consensus building strategy: Offer attractive agreements to the opposition when the government is at a peak of political support. Invest in goodwill in good years. Call on the opposition for certain reciprocity at times of crisis. This recipe makes for high-quality fiscal policy as well as high-quality politics.

The art of packaging policy innovations is not a common talent in the economics profession. Successful experiences in the 1990s show that there is a delicate, subtle way to handle contradictory pressures from conflicting interest groups in order to build support for complex policy proposals with rationales not obvious to noneconomists. This is not a sufficiently recognized essential ingredient for successful reform. But as long as the policy package includes the government's main policy goal, the rest can be tailored to suit real or symbolic preferences of key social and political actors. Several concrete examples of this have been provided.

Beyond these rather obvious lessons, the relevant question is how to make use of the full potential embedded in the reforms of the 1990s. The unfinished agenda necessarily implies going back to basics. The main challenge seems to e achieving continued, endogenous increases in productivity.

This is an area where there is less consensus. How do you trigger innovations in economies where governments are often forced to focus on crisis management and where the entrepreneurial culture is in its infancy? This is the main deficit in Latin American economies. History does not teach us how to awaken the creative forces of society, making this perhaps the most difficult challenge in the years ahead.

References

Agosín, M., and R. Ffrench-Davis. 1998. "La inversión externa de Chile." In R. Cortazar, ed., *Construyendo opciones*. Santiago, Chile: Ediciones Dolmen.

Banco Central de Chile. 2001. "Indic adores economics y socials de Chile 1960–2000." Santiago, Chile.

Boeninger, E. 1997. *Democracies en Chile: lections para la gobernabilidad*. Santiago, Chile: Editorial Andrés Bello.

Castells, M., and P. Himanen. 2002. *The Information Society and the Welfare State: the Finnish Model*. New York: Oxford University Press.

Cortazar, R. 1993. *Política laboral en Chile democrático*. Santiago, Chile: Ediciones Dolmen.

Dornsbusch, R., and S. Edwards. 1991. *The Macroeconomics of Populism in Latin America*. Chicago, Ill.: University of Chicago Press.

Eyzaguirre, N. 2002. *Estado de la hacienda pública*. Santiago: Gobierno de Chile.

Eyzaguirre, N., and F. Lefort. 1999. "Capital Markets in Chile, 1985–97: A Case of Successful International Financial Integration." In G. Perry and D. Leipziger, eds., *Chile: Recent Policy Lessons and Emerging Challenges*. World Bank Development Studies. Washington, D.C.: World Bank.

Ffrench-Davis, R. 1999. *Entre el neoliberalismo y el crecimiento con equidad*. Santiago, Chile: Ediciones Dolmen.

Ffrench-Davis, R., and R. Laban. 1996. "Macroeconomic Performance in Chile." In C. Pizarro, D. Raczynski, and J. Vial, eds., *Social and Economic Policies in Chile's Transition to Democracy*. Santiago, Chile: United Nations Children's Fund and Economic Research Corporation for Latin America.

Ffrench- Davis, R., and O. Muñoz. 2002. "Las políticas económicas y sus efectos." In O. Muñoz and others, eds., *El período del Presidente Frei Ruiz Tagle*. Santiago, Chile: Editorial Universitaria.

Foxley, A. 1993. *Economía política de la transición.* Santiago, Chile: Ediciones Dolmen.

Foxley, A., and C. Sapelli. 1999. "Chile's Political Economy in the 1990s: Some Governance Issues." In G. Perry and D. Leipziger, eds., *Chile: Recent Policy Lessons and Emerging Challenges.* World Bank Development Studies. Washington, D.C.: World Bank.

Frydl, E. J. 1999. "The Length and Cost of Banking Crisis." IMF Working Paper 99/30. International Monetary Fund, Washington, D.C.

Haggard, S., and R. Kaufman. 1995. *The Political Economy of Democratic Transitions.* Princeton, N.J.: Princeton University Press.

Hausmann, R., and D. Rodrik. 2002. "Economic Development as Self-Discovery." Working paper. Harvard University, Kennedy School, Cambridge, Mass.

Held, G. 2001. "The Chilean Banking Crisis of the 1980s." Asia-Pacific Economic Cooperation Policy Dialogue on Bank Failure Management Paper.

Kuczynski, P., and J. Williamson, eds. 2003. *After the Washington Consensus.* Washington, D.C.: Institute of International Economics.

Laban, R., and F. Larrain. 1994. "The Chilean Experience with Capital Mobility." In B. Bosworth, R. Dornbusch, and R. Laban, eds., *The Chilean Economy, Policy Lessons and Challenges.* Washington, D.C.: Brookings Institution.

Marcel, M. 1999. "Effectiveness of the State and Development Lessons from the Chilean Experience." In G. Perry and D. Leipziger, eds., *Chile: Recent Policy Lessons and Emerging Challenges.* World Bank Development Studies. Washington, D.C.: World Bank.

Mideplan. 1996. *Balance de seis años de las políticas sociales 1990–1996.* Santiago, Chile: Ediciones Mideplan.

Navia, P, and A Velasco. 2003. "The Politics of Second Generation Reforms." In P. Kuczynski and J. Williamson, eds., *After the Washington Consensus.* Washington, D.C.: Institute of International Economics.

Perry, G., and D. Leipziger, eds. 1999. *Chile: Recent Policy Lessons and Emerging Challenges.* World Bank Development Studies. Washington, D.C.: World Bank.

Pizarro, C., D. Raczynski, and J. Vial, eds. 1996. *Social and Economic Policies in Chile's Transition to Democracy.* Santiago, Chile: United Nations Children's Fund and Economic Research Corporation for Latin America.

Pizarro, C. 1996. "The First Tax Reform during the Transition Government." In C. Pizarro, D. Raczynski, and J. Vial, eds., *Social and Economic Policies in Chile's Transition to Democracy.* Santiago, Chile: United Nations Children's Fund and Economic Research Corporation for Latin America.

Rosales, O. 2004. "Chile's Multidimensional Trade Policy." In V. Aggarwal, R. Espach, and J. Tulchin, eds., *The Strategic Dynamics of Latin American Trade.* Palo Alto, Calif.: Stanford University Press.

Saez, S., and others. 1995. "Antecedentes y resultados de la estrategia comercial del gobierno de Aylwin." Estudios CIEPLAN 41. Economic Research Corporation for Latin America, Santiago, Chile

UNICEF (United Nations Children's Fund) and CIEPLAN (Economic Research Corporation for Latin America). 1996. *Social and Economic Policies in Chile's Transition to Democracy.* Santiago, Chile.

Velasco, A., and P. Cabezas. 1998. "Alternative Responses to Capital Inflows: A Tale of Two Countries." In M. Kahler, ed., *Capital Flows and Financial Crisis.* New York: Council on Foreign Relations.

World Bank. 2002. *Chile's High Growth Economy, Poverty and Income Distribution 1987–1998.* Washington, D.C.

————. 2003. *Chile New Economy Study.* Washington, D.C.

Zahler, R. 1998. "El Banco Central y la política macroeconómica de Chile en los años noventa." Revista de la CEPAL 64. Economic Commission for Latin America and the Caribbean, Santiago, Chile.

Comment

Nancy Birdsall

LET ME START BY CONGRATULATING THE WORLD BANK FOR SPONSORING THIS SERIES of lectures by development practitioners. We are extremely fortunate to have started the series with Alejandro Foxley's insights on Chile's success in the 1990s. Indeed, if Foxley's rich insights and ideas are any indication, this series will generate enormous benefits for the development community. Here I will focus on how Foxley's presentation contributes to the current debate on the shortcomings of the Washington consensus, then suggest areas where his discussion is incomplete—or at least insufficiently explicit—in terms of assessing the context for reforms in Chile and the resulting lessons for other developing countries.

After the Washington Consensus: Fairness, Political Legitimacy, and the State

In the 1990s, when we thought there was consensus on fundamental economic reforms, the emphasis in Latin America was on how to implement those reforms politically, as opposed to what the reforms should be. Foxley's lecture makes the simple point that the what and the how of reforms are inextricably linked, and that notions of how to implement reforms are bound to influence ideas about what reforms should be. Most of Foxley's examples of successful political implementation of difficult economic reforms rest on one of two pillars: the reforms were sold as fair and just, or they built on and reinforced the concept of legitimate, democratic government.

The Washington consensus was not concerned about fairness. Indeed, in his article defining the term, John Williamson (1990) noted that issues of equity and income distribution were not on the agenda at the time. In contrast, in describing the early 1990s (when the Washington consensus was at its height in Latin America) Foxley argues that voters approved the tax increase introduced by Patricio Aylwin's new administration because it was explicitly sold as being—and indeed was—fair and just.

The idea of fairness, broadly conceived, was also at the heart of labor's willingness to accept a wage cut (when rapid fiscal adjustment was required in response to an external shock), because the government linked the cut to a sacrifice elsewhere: namely, a reduction in the military budget. Indeed, almost all of Foxley's examples of success in introducing tough policies involve creating a sense of balance and fairness for different groups such as consumers, exporters, bankers, environmentalists, and unions.

The Washington consensus also failed to identify mechanisms for handling the volatility that external and other shocks imposed on emerging markets in the 1990s. (Kuczynski and Williamson 2003 discuss volatility as one of four issues not foreseen in the original list.) Foxley makes two post–Washington consensus points in describing Chile's success in dealing with such volatility. One is the much discussed, sensible approach of limiting volatile capital inflows. Less discussed is the need, in responding to shocks, to build on and reinforce with citizens the legitimacy of a democratic government. A legitimate government can lead as well as follow popular (voter) opinion, and can shape citizens' views as well as be shaped by them.

Put another way, a government that advertises the "fairness" of its policies need not be populist. Fairness and legitimacy can reinforce each other. It is in this context that Foxley's emphasis on the need to exploit the initial honeymoon of a new, legitimate government is best seen. His argument for moving quickly with reforms is not the traditional one—of a big bang to undo the counterattack of interest groups—but a new one, of exploiting and reinforcing the government's legitimate leadership.

Argentina provides a counterexample. Its reforms in the 1990s were undermined by the absence of any sense of fairness and by a failure to build political legitimacy, eventually leading to the collapse of political comity in the face of multiple pressures. There is a lesson here for Brazil's newly elected government, led by Luis Inacio Lula da Silva (Lula), which has a narrow window of opportunity to reinforce its legitimacy by pushing through critical but fair and sensible reforms.

Finally, Foxley identifies industrial policy as a route to innovation. That is surely a sign that we have entered an era that is, literally, "after" the Washington consensus. The taboo on active industrial policy is gone. Jeffrey Sachs and Joseph Stiglitz have said that it is time for the state to be more activist in its approach to industrial policy. In his comments on Foxley's lecture, Ricardo Hausmann (in this volume) also mentions this issue. Foxley, however, is careful. His proposal that Chile consider industrial policy is made in a specific and limited context: of an already legitimate state that has created and maintained a level playing field (fairness in the market), now exploring a new step to support innovation.

The Missing Context

Only in retrospect is it evident that Chile entered the 1990s better able to exploit the benefits of global growth during the decade than did most other emerging market economies. The good policies of Chile's newly democratic government helped, of course, and it would have been easy for the country to veer off course. But other factors were also at work. For example, Argentina and Brazil entered the 1990s with high internal debt and hidden pension and other liabilities, and those countries and Turkey had recently experienced high inflation (and fears of devaluation). By contrast, at the time of its political transition Chile had relatively low debt, a banking system that had already undergone crisis and reform, and a decade of fiscal discipline under its belt. These conditions did not make policymaking easy—just easier than it would have been otherwise.

It is an unpleasant but clear fact that Chile's prior authoritarian government paved the way for some of the democratic government's critical reforms. Increases in social spending under the Aylwin government are one example. Without the social sector reforms introduced by Augusto Pinochet's government, those increases could not have been introduced so quickly, because they simply would have created more inefficiency and waste (as is too often the case elsewhere in Latin America). The prior reforms made the politically popular (and fair) increases in social spending economically sensible and efficient. For example, fee increases at public universities had reduced entitlements that had earlier been largely captured by the urban rich and middle class. Similarly, reduced spending on teachers and health workers—made possible because the authoritarian government had weakened public employee unions— had opened the door to much better targeting of social spending on poor Chileans.

The same was true for labor market reforms. The Pinochet government imposed labor market "flexibility" that made it politically possible, as well as eminently just, for the Aylwin government to introduce collective bargaining at the firm level (something no other Latin American government has been able to do), implement minimum wage legislation, and create fully funded (by employers and employees) unemployment and other social insurance programs. Chile's democratic government was not saddled with undoing costly protection of jobs and wages—a task its neighbors could not manage politically. As a result Chile's labor reforms in the 1990s could be guided by economically sound thinking about the need to emphasize job creation and job mobility. Apparently it is politically easier to legislate change from the left— providing new worker protections where there were virtually none, while avoiding populist inefficiencies—than from the right.

Finally, Chile entered the 1990s with a middle class under political duress but economically intact. A simple, useful indicator of the economic presence of the middle-income group in a society is the ratio of income per capita of those in the top income (or expenditure) quintile to those in the fourth and third quintiles. That ratio is 3.5 in Chile, compared with 4.3 in Guatemala and 5.0 in Brazil—and just 1.9 in Taiwan, China (Birdsall, Graham, and Pettinato 2000). Similarly, in 1990 adults in Chile had an average of about seven years of education, compared with four years in Brazil (Barro and Lee 2000). To the extent that a strong middle class provides the ballast for sustaining sound economic policy in a stormy global economy, Foxley and his colleagues faced a somewhat easier task.

Their policies, as Foxley describes, were not just economically sound. They were also politically wise, reflecting a sense of fairness and an eagerness to exploit and rebuild a democratic government's legitimacy. Other developing countries may not have as "easy" a context—economic or political—from which to start reforms. But that is not to say they cannot, thanks to Alejandro Foxley's vivid description, extract important lessons from Chile's experience.

References

Barro, Robert J., and Jong-Wha Lee. Barro. 2000. "International Data on Educational Attainment: Updates and Implications." CID Working Paper 42. Center for International Development, Cambridge, Mass.

Birdsall, Nancy, Carol Graham, and Stefano Pettinato. 2000. "Stuck in the Tunnel: Is Globalization Muddling the Middle Class?" CSED Working Paper 14. Center on Social and Economic Dynamics, Washington, D.C.

Kuczynski, Pedro-Pablo, and John Williamson, eds. 2003. *After the Washington Consensus.* Washington, D.C.: Institute for International Economics.

Williamson, John. 1990. "What Washington Means by Policy Reform." In J. Williamson, ed., *Latin American Adjustment: How Much Has Happened?* Washington, D.C.: Institute for International Economics.

Comment

Eliana Cardoso

ECONOMISTS HAVE FOUND MUCH TO AGREE ON IN ANALYZING CHILE'S SUCCESS DUR-
ing the 1990s. Alejandro Foxley's lecture explores the origins of this success and
makes a first-rate contribution to discussions of politics and economic policy in
developing countries. It also offers timely advice, particularly for Brazil and its current dilemmas.

My comments focus on three topics. First, in reviewing the lessons identified by
Foxley, I stress two that are important for Brazil today. Second, I ask which countries
could replicate Chile's experience with capital controls and point out that such controls are not useful exactly where they are most needed. Finally, I compare Chile's
achievements with experiences elsewhere.

Lessons for Brazil

Foxley observes that when Patricio Aylwin was elected in late 1989, the general public considered the prevailing economic model (which had opened the economy and
privatized and reformed social security) unfair and expected radical changes from the
new center-left government. At the same time, businesspeople feared that the new
government would lead Chile back to the vicious populist cycle that has long reigned
in most of Latin America.

Such fears proved unfounded. Aylwin and his team knew that their first challenge
was to build confidence in the government's ability to govern responsibly. Thus they
announced the goal of achieving a fiscal budget surplus throughout Aylwin's presidency. The administration also understood that policy announcements were not
enough, and so dedicated itself to building alliances that would appease various interest groups while guaranteeing support and approval for key goals.

When these comments were written (in June 2003), Brazilian President Luis Inacio Lula da Silva (Lula) seemed to be trying to do the same things. He began his
administration by showing that he can govern responsibly. He promised fiscal auster-

ity and social security reform while building support in congress for approval of needed legislation. It remains to be seen whether he will have the same success as Aylwin or whether the radical members of his party will spoil the game, as radicals in Chile did during Salvador Allende's administration three decades ago. But times have changed in Latin America, and there is deeper understanding of the importance of balanced fiscal policies than there was 30 years ago. Accordingly, there is a good chance that Lula will end up looking more like Aylwin than like Allende.

Another important lesson for Brazil from Chile involves disinflation. Rather than being overly ambitious, Chile disinflated gradually—without killing growth and without overstretching the appreciation of the peso that had occurred in response to capital inflows. Such a balanced approach is rare. Most finance ministers cannot resist the temptation to use capital inflows and an appreciating real exchange rate to disinflate too quickly, only to see their efforts create a balance of payments crisis.

Capital Controls

Overvalued exchange rates and balance of payments crises lead to my second set of comments, on capital controls. It has become a cliché to advise developing countries to open their capital accounts slowly and use Chilean-type taxation of capital flows to avoid the volatility induced by sudden changes in financial market sentiment. Yet until the debt crisis of the 1980s, Latin American countries (particularly Brazil) had all sorts of capital controls. Nonetheless, large sums of money flowed in and out of the region.

Today all 25 emerging market economies have opened their capital accounts. Reversing this policy would be ineffective because investors and bankers have learned how to evade capital controls. Thus it seems pointless to recommend such controls to other developing countries, many of which are in Africa, where capital does not flow in for reasons having little to do with controls. Moreover, the evidence from Chile, as Foxley notes, is that controls remain effective only in the short run. That is why Chile removed them in the late 1990s.

In the first half of 2003 short-run capital flows returned to Latin America and contributed to an appreciation of exchange rates, notably in Brazil. Policymakers know that these inflows result from excess liquidity in global financial markets, increased investor appetite for risk, and a search for attractive interest rate spreads. They are also aware that market sentiment can easily reverse. Still, it would be difficult to argue that introducing capital controls would do Brazil any good. The country still needs to roll over significant external debt this year, and scaring away capital would not be the best strategy for achieving that goal. Perhaps Brazil will be able to lower interest rates in the near future, thereby reducing capital inflows and exchange rate appreciation—even if doing so contributes to higher inflation than the targets set for 2003 and 2004.

Sustainable Long-term Growth

In recent decades Brazil, Chile, and other Latin American countries have experienced some long-lasting periods of growth, with expansions lasting up to 12 years in a few cases. But such growth has not been sustainable. For example, between 1968 and 1980 strong growth caused Brazil's per capita income to jump from 67 percent to 118 percent of Chile's. But within a few years the situation had reversed, and between 1985 and 1997 Chile's per capita income increased from 86 percent to 153 percent of Brazil's. Then between 1997 and 2000 per capita income in Chile (measured in terms of purchasing power parity) fell relative to that in the United States (Loyaza, Fajnzylber, and Calderón 2002). The big question facing Chile now is whether it can turn things around and grow as fast as it did in the 1990s.

Sustaining growth over many decades makes a huge difference to a country's economy. In 1960 the Republic of Korea's per capita income was slightly more than one-third of Chile's. In 2000 it was nearly 1.5 times as high—an impressive change (Loyaza, Fajnzylber, and Calderón 2002).

The World Bank has emphasized the role of institutions in explaining different growth rates across countries. It would be interesting to know the institutional differences between Chile and Korea that would explain such enormous differences in their long-term growth rates. One of the most striking differences between the two countries over the past 40 years has been the changes in their real exchange rates. Between 1960 and 2000 Korea's real exchange rate was fairly stable relative to Chile's, and very competitive throughout the period. By contrast, Chile's exchange rate was overvalued between 1960 and 1972 and volatile between 1972 and 1984. Since 1985 it has been very competitive and fairly stable, despite some real appreciation starting in 1995 (Loyaza, Fajnzylber, and Calderón 2002). I believe that exchange rate behavior explains the variations in Chile's growth performance over the past four decades.

So, what lessons does Chile offer other countries? An important question is how to achieve competitive, stable real exchange rates given that most economists believe central banks should not target exchange rates but instead should pursue inflation targets under floating exchange rate regimes. The answer (as Foxley suggests) may be to pursue fiscal austerity. Having small public debt relative to GDP and maintaining fiscal balance enable governments to pursue countercyclical policies when times turn tough. Countries with large debt relative to GDP, such as Brazil, have a long period ahead during which they will have to focus on reducing the debt. After correcting past overspending, as Chile did in the early 1990s, Brazil would then be able to implement a more balanced, countercyclical fiscal policy.

Reference

Loyaza, Norman, Pablo Fajnzylber, and César Calderón. 2002. "Economic Growth in Latin America and the Caribbean." World Bank, Washington, D.C.

Comment

Ricardo Hausmann

IT IS AN HONOR AND A PLEASURE TO COMMENT ON ALEJANDRO FOXLEY'S INTERESTING and insightful lecture. I have known Alejandro for about 20 years, since he was in the opposition under Augusto Pinochet's dictatorship, heading the Center for Economic Research on Latin America (CIEPLAN)—Chile's most prestigious think tank. I was in especially close contact with him during his tenure as Chile's minister of finance, which overlapped with my tenure as Venezuela's minister of planning. At his suggestion, I succeeded him as chairman of the World Bank–International Monetary Fund Development Committee. He gave me sound advice and even took time during a trip to Caracas to speak to the opposition COPEI party—his Christian Democrat brethren—to convince them to behave in a constructive, responsible manner toward the administration of which I was part. That is just one example of Alejandro's long-term commitment to building consensus and promoting responsible political behavior.

Alejandro should get a lot of credit for Chile's economic success during its difficult transition to democracy. With a business community highly distrustful of the new government and with ample political reasons to make a radical departure from public policies broadly seen as unfair, it would have been easy to confuse the baby and the bathwater. But Alejandro made the right choices in strengthening the market, expanding social policy, ensuring fiscal sustainability, and taking a cautious approach to irrational (market) exuberance (before that term had been invented).

As a result Chile became a model for the rest of Latin America. Trade liberalization had been implemented and seemed to be paying off. Fiscal discipline seemed consistent with high growth. Financial reform appeared to be generating benefits. Privatization looked promising. Social security reform seemed very interesting. And it all came packaged in remarkable macroeconomic results. In the 1980s Chile was the only Latin American country where per capita income grew in line with that in the United States. Among the region's other nine largest countries, the income gap with the United States grew by more than 10 percent in Colombia, more than 20 percent in Uruguay, Brazil, Ecuador, and Panama, more than 30 percent in Mexico,

Venezuela, and Argentina, and more than 40 percent in Peru. Thus copying Chile made sense.

Other Latin American countries did better after adopting Chilean-style policies in the early 1990s. Between 1990 and 1970 Peru, Uruguay, Panama, Argentina, and Colombia grew faster than the United States but still lagged behind Chile. During this period it was clear that countries that pursued Chilean-style reforms grew faster. It appeared as if not only were Chile's policies good for Chile, but they seemed to travel well. One puzzle appeared during this time: if Chile maintained its market-oriented policies while other countries improved theirs, shouldn't they have grown faster? Could it be that something else was behind Chile's high growth?

But then came the Russian crisis and the collapse in capital flows to developing countries. In 1998–2002 per capita income growth in the 10 largest Latin American countries, including Chile, fell behind that in the United States—although Chile was the best performer. Brazil, Panama, and Peru saw their relative incomes fall by more than 5 percent, Ecuador and Colombia by more than 10 percent, and Venezuela, Uruguay, and Argentina by more than 20 percent.

It took less than seven years for the main countries involved in World War I and II to return to their prewar income levels. One would have expected that after seven years of reform, Latin American countries would have been able to undo much of the damage of the debt crisis. Between 1980 and 2002 Chile saw its per capita income relative to that in the United States rise by more than 30 percent—while Uruguay, Mexico, Brazil, and Ecuador fell by more than 30 percent and Venezuela and Argentina fell by more than 40 percent. Why has the Chilean experience been so difficult to copy?

In this respect I believe that Alejandro's advice is wise. His emphasis on the ability to absorb external shocks may have allowed Chile, after 1998, to weather the sudden stop in capital flows with less domestic damage than elsewhere. The advice to target a structural fiscal surplus in order to build credibility and create fiscal space to adopt countercyclical policies paid off during this period. His bet on exchange rate flexibility and his gradual move toward inflation targeting was prescient and gave Chile the flexibility to navigate through the treacherous waters that sunk Argentina, Brazil, and Uruguay. The emphasis on policy continuity and consensus building allowed Chile to go through this period without a Venezuelan crisis or a Mexican gridlock.

These are wise and profound lessons, and should be taken seriously both by governments and by individual policymakers. But do they explain Chile's exceptional growth performance? Let me express my doubts. Fiscal discipline is much easier to maintain when an economy is growing and tax revenues are more abundant every year. Sustaining a fiscal surplus in this context is easier than in a stagnant economy. In addition, credibility is easier to establish when outcomes are good, because it is presumed that policies and institutions will be left in place if they are not considered faulty. Bad outcomes create a large constituency in favor of change and hence lower the expected durability of the rules of the game. When an economy delivers growth and jobs, there is a demand to leave in place the policies underpinning it. This reverse causality from outcomes to policy credibility and institutional durability seems to be part of the Chilean story, especially after Alejandro's tenure in the Ministry of Finance. This was the message that Rudi Dornbusch sent to Alejandro: "Don't mess it up"—and he did not.

Compare this with a star reformer such as El Salvador. Policy credibility there is limited by the fact that the opposition party (FMLN) may yet gain power, just as the left did in Chile. But it is unclear to investors whether it would choose a finance minister with the policies and values of Alejandro Foxley. Moreover, because growth has not been as impressive, there is less of a sense that there is something valuable to preserve. That is also probably why the markets were so concerned with the potential electoral success of Lula in Brazil. With lackluster growth and a currency crisis as a legacy, would Lula behave like Foxley? So far he has, and may reap the benefits—but markets had more reasons to doubt this outcome.

So, maybe there is an alternative explanation for Chile's rapid growth. Perhaps rapid growth made society want to stick to its policy choices—an explanation that accounts for the difficulties in copying Chile's experience elsewhere. For a long time Chile's macroeconomic imbalances and political strife did not provide an adequate environment to implement the investment ideas that the society was generating. Mining opportunities and Chile's geographic similarity to the West Coast of the United States have been the two most important sources of investment ideas behind Chilean exports. Exploiting them did not require trade liberalization, financial reform, or social security reform.

Instead, the mining privatization of 1980 allowed for a boom in copper exports. The bulk of the Chilean export miracle was due to changes in the property regime in agriculture (after the agrarian reform and counter-reform of the early and mid-1970s), investments in specific know-how through the University of California at Davis, and experiments by Fundación Chile. Certainly, macroeconomic stability and good finance helped. But the converse is not true: good finance would not have created a salmon industry or a fiscal surplus the fruit industry. It is these investment ideas that have been missing elsewhere.

I can provide some circumstantial evidence in favor of this view. For example, between 1920 and 1980 Chile was one of the world's worst growth performers. At 1.4 percent annual growth in per capita income, it ranked 26 out of the 30 countries in Angus Maddison's dataset. The growth miracle since 1984 has essentially brought Chile's per capita income, relative to that of the United States, back to 1950s levels. Seen in this way, it looks like a long-term recovery: not a cyclical recovery, where a depressed country returns to its installed capacity, but in a more long-term sense, where it returns to its "equilibrium path of ideas." It looks impressive relative to the performance of a more recent star reformer—El Salvador—but modest relative to that of the Republic of Korea, a country that was significantly poorer than both until the late 1970s.

This alternative view has several implications. First, unless a country has a stock of unused ideas, improving macroeconomic stability and market conditions may not have as big an effect on growth. El Salvador's problem may not be insufficient trade liberalization or fiscal consolidation. It may be a lack of unused investment ideas:

unresolved problems in agriculture and world prices have destroyed the ideas of coffee, cotton, and sugar, but alternatives are hard to find.

Beyond adopting Washington consensus policies, what makes Chile's experience hard to replicate is that it was a country with a large pool of unused investment ideas that experienced a drop in political risk once it became clear that the left was market friendly. El Salvador lacks the ideas and the political transition, while Brazil still lacks the macroeconomic stability

But Chile may be running out of ideas. Recent growth has been lackluster. True, the international environment has been inhospitable, but that has not stopped China or Korea from growing. As Alejandro points out, Chile's innovation indicators are unimpressive. This outcome is not unrelated to the fact that the reigning policy paradigm has a dangerous allergy to anything resembling "industrial policy." This paradigm argues that a visible government hand does more harm than good in addressing market failures because it inevitably falls victim to rent seeking, corruption, and capture.

Yet innovation is an area full of market failures. Finding out whether Chile can become an exporter of peaches or apples costs a lot of money (in fact, the answer is peaches, but not apples), but such findings are easily exploited by new investors. Such investors cannot adequately appropriate the social benefits of innovation and so tend to underprovide them. Not addressing such market failures through government action may keep a country honest—but poor. That may be the message from the comparison with Korea.

Finding ways to adequately stimulate the appearance of new investment ideas without falling into even worse government failures is probably the binding constraint in maintaining Chile's high growth and in achieving it in other countries. We are fortunate to have Alejandro Foxley, who with his wisdom may help us think through this next challenge, just as he has guided us before through so many others.

Mario I. Blejer

Former Governor, Central Bank of Argentina

Mario I. Blejer was born in Córdoba, Argentina, in 1948, and received a Ph.D. in Economics from the University of Chicago in 1975. He was on the faculties of the Hebrew University of Jerusalem and Boston University before joining the International Monetary Fund (IMF) in 1980. Blejer had a distinguished career in the IMF, working in the Asian, European, Monetary and Exchange, Fiscal, and Research Departments over a more than 20-year career. Along the way he served brief stints as Associate Professor of Economics and International Business at New York University's Graduate School of Business (1983–84), Senior Adviser to the World Bank's Europe and Central Asia Region (1992–93), and Walter Rathenau Professor of Economics at the Hebrew University (1996–97). He has also held various visiting professorships and written numerous books and articles on monetary policy, including for noted journals such as *American Economic Review* and *Journal of Economic Literature*.

Blejer enjoyed a brief but exciting time in public service as Deputy Governor of the Central Bank of Argentina in 2001 and Governor of the Central Bank in 2002, at the apex of the most severe financial crisis in the country's history. During that time he defused a banking crisis and managed the peso's transition from convertibility with the U.S. dollar to a floating currency. By the time he left the Central Bank in mid-2002, the worst of the crisis had passed and hyperinflation had been avoided. Blejer is now Director of the Center for Central Banking Studies and Adviser to the Governor of the Bank of England.

8 Managing Argentina's 2002 Financial Crisis

Mario I. Blejer

I AM GRATEFUL TO HAVE BEEN ASKED TO PARTICIPATE IN THIS INTERESTING EVENT. I understand that I was invited to share some lessons from my recent public sector experience, particularly what one can learn from financial crisis and the resulting transition.

Although my public service lasted only a year, it occurred at a complex time and provided a wealth of experiences. That year, 2002, saw what was probably the worst financial crisis in Argentine history. As is often stated, reality is always more complicated than theory, and one of the most important things I learned that year is that there are major differences between how one thinks and operates in normal times and in times of crisis. Thus there is policymaking for normal times—and policymaking for crises. There are many ways to define the differences between the two, but four basic elements characterize the approach required when dealing with extreme circumstances:

- One has to rapidly understand the nature and causes of the crisis, and define well the tradeoffs involved in resolving a systemic breakdown.

- It is crucial to quickly devise an operational strategy—thinking boldly and not necessarily adhering to standard prescriptions. Crisis management differs from standard economic policy, and one has to be willing to implement decisive and occasionally risky measures.

- Policymakers must persevere when implementing the strategy. Although it is important to learn from mistakes, changing course too often during a crisis could be extremely detrimental.

- Once the crisis has abated, it is time to learn lessons, both to adapt the strategy in order to fully stabilize the situation and, more important, to avoid the resurgence of the same problems that created the crisis originally.

Although I follow this basic script in recounting the Argentine crisis, I also tell the story from my own perspective—or, more specifically, that of the Central Bank. Thus this account is not the complete story of the event, but a reflection of my experience.

The Nature of the Crisis

The Argentine crisis resulted from extremely large macroeconomic imbalances, two significant components of which were a currency collapse and a bank run. Though both aspects are interrelated, they were caused by a number and a combination of different factors.

Following a bout of hyperinflation in the late 1980s, in 1991 Argentina introduced a quasi currency board system that set the exchange rate of the peso on par with the U.S. dollar.[1] This system was largely successful in restoring price stability and, in conjunction with broad structural reforms—including privatization, pension reforms, and trade and financial liberalization—led to accelerated economic growth for much of the decade. The system survived contagion from Mexico's "tequila crisis" in 1994–95 but came under pressure from the deepening recession and increasing unemployment that started in late 1998 (following the Russian and Brazilian crises). Then an attack on the peso developed and become increasingly intense, peaking in January 2002—when the system collapsed and the currency was first devalued and then floated.

Thus the Argentine currency crisis is usually analyzed in the context of these events. The main questions are, what were the weaknesses of the currency board regime, and what were the main causes of its demise? Among the many interpretations advanced, three elements have been emphasized:

- The reduced competitiveness of the Argentine economy, caused by an overvaluation of the peso under the fixed exchange rate.
- Inconsistent macroeconomic policies, particularly persistent fiscal imbalances and growing debt.
- A sudden reduction in foreign capital flows, as in other emerging markets.

Any explanation for the collapse of the currency board should combine these elements. Macroeconomic policies were inconsistent with the rigidities of the system—particularly the fixed exchange rate—and the economy was highly vulnerable to reversals in capital flows. The fiscal situation began deteriorating in 1996, causing public debt eventually to balloon and country risk to increase. In terms of the exchange rate regime, the Argentine crisis does not prove that a currency board is always wrong or unsustainable. It only proves the need for consistent policies. Macroeconomic policies should be consistent with the growth rate produced by the saving and investment balance. Argentina's fiscal situation was not consistent, and so given the inflexibility of the currency board the system was unsustainable. This also caused part of the country's banking problems.

Although exchange rate uncertainty created problems in the banking sector, the banking sector was highly dollarized, so there was not really an exchange risk—certainly not one that could have caused the banking sector to collapse. The collapse was caused largely by sovereign risk, arising mainly from the government's abuse of the banking sector following its inability to adjust the budget. Argentina was not the only Latin American country to experience capital flight during this time, but the size of its capital flow reversal combined with its fiscal and currency problems to result in crisis.

The bank run lasted 16 months, with private sector deposits falling from the equivalent of $80 billion in March 2001 to about $15 billion in July 2002 (figure 8.1). Deposits began falling soon after the president changed the country's economic team. The drop in deposits led to restrictions on withdrawals (the *corralito*, discussed below) and the imposition of interest rate ceilings. Although devaluation and "pesification" in early 2002 implied that deposits were redenominated into pesos, they continued to fall.

Causes

Although deposits fell for several reasons, the main one was growing government abuse. First the government interfered with the Central Bank's autonomy, then changed its authorities, then changed the composition and level of reserve requirements to finance the debt that was hardest to sell. Depositors feared that these and other government policies would make banks insolvent and lead to the confiscation of deposits.

Such fears were rational, because ultimately something similar happened. Pressure on banks to finance the fiscal deficit caused public assets to displace private assets on banks' balance sheets, and banks eventually became highly exposed to public debt. In 2001, for example, public assets jumped from about 20 percent to 60 percent of private assets (figure 8.2). With public assets accounting for a rising share of bank portfolios, private deposits dropped and country risk increased. Moreover, these two

FIGURE 8.1

Private Sector Deposits Began Falling in Argentina in Early 2001

Billions of Argentine pesos

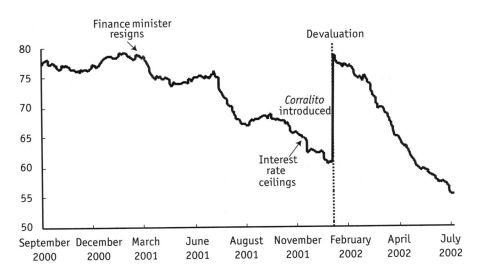

Source: Central Bank of Argentina data.

FIGURE 8.2

As the Crisis Worsened, Public Assets Displaced Private Ones on Bank Balance Sheets

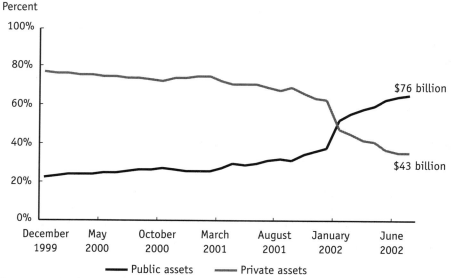

Percent

$76 billion

$43 billion

Public assets   Private assets

Source: Central Bank of Argentina data.

latter developments were mutually reinforcing. As country risk increased, people withdrew their money from banks—and as deposits fell, country risk increased.

In November 2001 the accelerating bank run and growing possibility of a banking system collapse led the government to impose the corralito—comprehensive foreign exchange controls and limits on bank withdrawals. Together these restrictions effectively ended the convertibility regime. They also enraged Argentine citizens, who saw the measures as a prelude to confiscation of their assets. In December 2001 public demonstrations and riots resulted in the fall of President Fernando de la Rua's government. An interim administration (in office for just one week) followed, and it declared a default on Argentina's public debt. Later, when managing the crisis, we had to take into consideration the public's anger over the corralito: the riots that forced the government out of power were serious and violent.

In January 2002 Eduardo Duhalde was installed as president. During the first two weeks of his administration a number of emergency measures were implemented. The currency board was abandoned, and the peso was first devalued by 40 percent and a few weeks later floated. Then, in a drastic move, the economy was pesified—that is, most contracts originally denominated in U.S. dollars were redenominated in pesos. Of particular significance was the treatment of the banking sector, which was pesified asymmetrically—meaning that dollar deposits were redenominated at 1.4 pesos per dollar, while dollar assets were converted at 1 peso per dollar. The resulting huge losses in bank balance sheets were to be compensated by the government.

Responses and tradeoffs—and the dilemma for the Central Bank

Given the impossibility of withdrawing money and with deposits being changed from dollars to pesos at an artificial rate, confidence in the currency and the government plummeted. Meanwhile, the bank run continued, and a run on the peso started. Depositors continued to withdraw money from banks up to the allowed limits, then appealed to the judicial system to let them get the rest. After 10 years, convertibility had become something of a social contract in Argentina, and breaking with it was understandably traumatic. Many analysts claim that Argentina should have abandoned the convertibility regime during the good times in the mid-1990s. But that is not a useful operational perspective, because it is equivalent to saying that a married couple should get divorced when the relationship is going well. I do not think that there was any scenario in which Argentina could have given up convertibility without causing trauma.

From the Central Bank's point of view, the most serious problem was the lack of money market and debt instruments to conduct open market operations (or any other active monetary policies). That was because the government had defaulted on its bonds, there were no Central Bank instruments due to the rules of the currency board, and corporate bonds were unavailable.

It was then—at the end of January 2002, after the devaluation and the asymmetric pesification had been implemented—that I was appointed governor of the Central Bank. At that point the Central Bank faced an extremely difficult choice. It could either finance the bank run, risking hyperinflation, or do nothing, risking a collapse of the banking sector. This dilemma arose because, having regained its function as lender of last resort after the currency board was abandoned, the Central Bank could provide the liquidity needed to finance the bank run. But given the lack of money market and debt instruments needed to sterilize this injection of liquidity, such a move risked fueling a run on the peso, leading to rapid devaluation and almost certainly hyperinflation.

Alternatively, the Central Bank could have tried to control the money supply by limiting the rediscount facility and letting banks deal with the deposit run on their own. But this approach could have resulted in widespread bank failures and, through contagion and domino effects, a collapse of the banking sector. Thus the tradeoff was clear—and clearly unpleasant. The Central Bank could either allow hyperinflation and avoid a bank collapse, or pursue stability and run the risk of one.

The Strategy Adopted

The only possible stopgap approach was to try to slow the bank run while developing a sterilization instrument to avoid inflationary pressures. The Central Bank had to provide money to finance the bank run, but the inflationary impact could be eased if much of that money was reabsorbed with some instrument—one attractive enough to compete with the dollar. An intermediate strategy along these lines was implemented, consisting of three elements.

First, the Central Bank sought to stretch the limits of liquidity assistance, in an effort to slow the pace of the bank run by preventing massive bank closures, which could have further fueled the panic. The rediscount facility was used to provide liquidity to banks under attack. But such support was made contingent on stringent conditions, including liquidity contributions from bank shareholders. Eventually two foreign banks closed because foreign shareholders refused to accept those conditions.

Second, the Central Bank developed sterilization instruments to absorb at least some of the liquidity issued. In this context it was crucial to stress the difference, increasingly perceived by the market, between an autonomous Central Bank and a defaulted sovereign. It was also necessary to sustain high real interest rates to compete with the U.S. dollar. The Central Bank reasoned that if it could offer high returns on its paper, banks could buy them and offer high returns to their clients— leading people to leave at least some money in banks.

Finally, the Central Bank intervened in the foreign exchange market to prevent disorderly behavior and fight the belief (widespread in early 2002) that the dollar was bound to spiral up. If the exchange rate had skyrocketed, it would have been impossible to sell domestic assets—and at the time it was deemed possible for the exchange rate to jump from 1:1 (pesos to dollars) to something like 7:1. So, to prevent rapid, chaotic devaluation, the Central Bank decided to actively intervene in the foreign exchange market despite pressure from the International Monetary Fund (IMF) not to do so. The IMF argued that the banks might be insolvent, so providing liquidity was foolish; and that intervening in the foreign exchange market would merely draw down reserves and send a bad signal to markets. It preferred that we allow for an overshooting.

I was well aware that there would be an overshooting if we did not intervene. In fact, I thought that it would go on continually, and be an "ever-shooting"! So we had a major clash with the IMF on these issues. Our strategy at the Central Bank was based on the view that, given the lack of reference for the correct exchange rate, exchange rate expectations had to be stabilized for the bank to develop a market for its sterilization instruments. Otherwise, the interest rate needed to induce significant demand for the new instruments would reach unreasonable levels. In other words, an interest rate defense and active foreign exchange market intervention were complementary rather than substitute policies.

These three policies were popularly characterized as a Central Bank attempt to increase demand for domestic assets—and in this way stop the bank run and the currency run—by inducing greed to overcome panic. The bank's main consideration was that greed (interest rate policy) cannot overcome panic unless panic is also reduced by controlling chaotic conditions in the foreign exchange market through active intervention.

Implementation Issues

The Central Bank began implementing its strategy in early 2002.[2] It provided substantive rediscount liquidity to illiquid banks, financing about one-third of the drop in private deposits (figure 8.3). The rest was financed by a contraction in bank loans and shareholder resources (reserves). Almost all banks complied with our requirement to provide resources, and we closed the one bank that did not. An active market was developed for Central Bank bills (called LEBACs), initially with maturities of 7 days and then 14 and 28 days, in pesos and dollars. Interest rates reached 140 percent in the program's early stages. The Central Bank also repaid more than $1 billion in foreign debt resulting from a repo operation in the 1990s. The bank had acquired this debt in a failed effort to protect the banking system, and had to repay it to prevent its own default and provide credibility to the LEBACs.

To prevent the exchange rate from overshooting, foreign exchange reserves were used to intervene in the foreign exchange market. Although this intervention was active, it did not peg the rate, which devalued from 1.0 to 3.6 pesos per dollar. In the first five months intervention costs totaled about $2 billion. As noted, these efforts ran counter to IMF advice. But the Central Bank believed that such advice was unreasonable, because Brazil was allowed to intervene in the foreign exchange market under its IMF program. Yet Argentina was told not to draw on its reserves, and to let the peso fall against the dollar uncontrolled.

I believe that we were right to oppose the IMF's advice. Given the nature of Argentina's crisis, foreign exchange intervention was crucial. Conventional IMF advice for dealing with a currency run—by raising interest rates—might be appropriate under normal circumstances. But when there is a major crisis of confidence in the financial system, no one will buy domestically denominated assets.

As noted, during crises high interest rates and foreign exchange interventions can complement each other. Moreover, it was critical to remain consistent on this point.

FIGURE 8.3

Central Bank Liquidity Assistance Financed about a Third of the Drop in Private Deposits

Billions of Argentine pesos

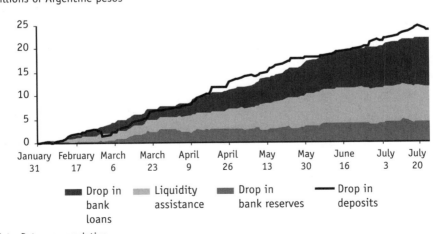

Note: Data are cumulative.
Source: Central Bank of Argentina data.

A central bank cannot simply intervene in foreign exchange markets one day, then not the next. Its actions must show that the return on domestic assets will be high and the return on foreign assets will be low. By intervening it can get people to return to domestic assets—not because they love them, but because the difference in returns is so high.

The initial results of Central Bank intervention were not encouraging because the run on deposits persisted despite the high deposit rates offered by banks. But in mid-July 2002 private deposits stopped falling and soon started to recover (figure 8.4). At that point the Central Bank stopped providing liquidity assistance. In July the exchange rate stabilized and began appreciating, so the Central Bank stopped selling and started buying dollars to rebuild its reserves (figure 8.5). By December 2002 the bank had regained more than the stock lost through its interventions.

The demand for LEBACs grew strongly. Maturities have been extended—recently reaching up to 18 months—and interest rates have fallen to 3–24 percent, depending on the maturity. In addition, stabilization of the exchange rate has caused a sharp drop in inflation. After reaching 10 percent in April 2002, inflation fell to less than 1 percent a month by the end of the year.

By September 2002 the worst of the crisis had passed. And more important, the most feared developments did not occur: there was no hyperinflation and the financial system did not collapse. But the situation remains highly complex and, as of autumn 2003, had not been fully resolved.

Still, in the midst of one of the most severe financial crises in Argentine history, Central Bank policy was appropriate in terms of monetary management. It would have been impossible without the fiscal adjustment that occurred, although that adjustment was due to some distortionary taxes. After I left the Central Bank, my

FIGURE 8.4

In Mid-2002 Private Deposits Started to Recover
Billions of Argentine pesos

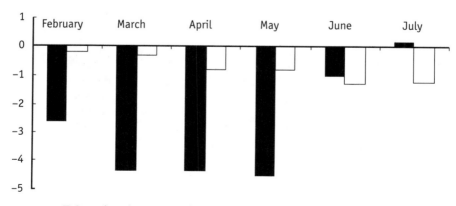

Source: Central Bank of Argentina data.

FIGURE 8.5

By Late 2002 Central Bank Had Recovered its Intervention Costs, and the Exchange Rate Was Improving

Billions of U.S. dollars and Argentine pesos/U.S. dollar

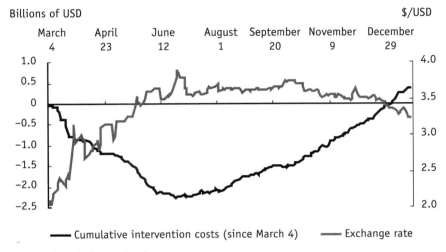

Source: Central Bank of Argentina data.

successor did a good job of perfecting and deepening the bank's approach. The main challenge was to restore confidence in monetary and financial institutions, and that was indeed achieved.

If Argentina's recent crisis were a movie, it would be a thriller—not a comedy, but also not a horror movie. At the height of the crisis, the sense that another hyperinflationary episode could trigger civil war was quite real given the anger being vented on the streets. Some academics were claiming that hyperinflation was both unavoidable and in fact desirable, because it would wipe out the financial system and allow it to start fresh. Though that may have been true from some theoretical standpoint, it was extremely dangerous from a sociopolitical perspective. Fortunately neither hyperinflation nor the worst scenarios of social unrest occurred. And although we do not know how the story will ultimately turn out, the outlook has improved dramatically, at least from a monetary point of view. If other variables can be controlled as well, the problems leading to and resulting from the crisis can be solved. An important lesson is that while the Central Bank has considerable power to reverse certain situations, it cannot solve a full-blown crisis by itself. Doing so requires nearly every instrument that a country has at its disposal.

Main Lessons

The most important lesson from the crisis is that, if properly managed, greed always has more power than panic—but efforts must be made to address both issues. In addition, beyond the minutiae of the Argentine crisis, the experience offers some more general lessons—five of which are briefly described below.

The potential fragility of financial institutions

The crisis shows that the strength, solvency, and stability of financial systems cannot be taken for granted based on static measures. Indeed, financial structures can deteriorate very quickly. Weak macroeconomic policies, inappropriate market interventions, and other poorly chosen policies may swiftly condemn a system with good regulation, supervision, and capitalization. Indeed, if governments choose to exploit rather than protect a properly developed financial market, the system's robustness is no guarantee of its survival. Financial crises are not necessarily caused by weak financial systems, but by damaging policies and adverse macroeconomic environments.

Public financing and crowding out

A significant issue, related to the above point, involves the public sector resorting—forcefully and excessively—to private financial markets (particularly banks and other voluntary savings schemes, such as pension and money funds) to fund its excessive financing needs. In addition to the distortions and reduced efficiency that such actions could cause by misallocating credit away from the private sector, the accumulation of government liabilities on the balance sheets of financial institutions could be highly destabilizing if perceptions of public sector default become widespread. Thus the preservation of a healthy financial sector makes it imperative for the government to resist the temptation to use financial system resources to avoid needed fiscal adjustments, in terms of both flows (financing current budget imbalances) and stocks (unsustainable rolling over of outstanding debt).

The functions of foreign banks

Opening financial markets to foreign institutions can accelerate the development of local markets—through better technology, enhanced access to international finance, closer integration of payment systems, and so on. Incorporation of foreign institutions may also increase the credibility of local systems, domestically and internationally. But Argentina's experience also shows that a more internationalized financial system does not guarantee stability or make the domestic system immune to external and domestic shocks.

This is because the deficiencies of a weak, unstable legal and institutional framework cannot be solved, or ignored, by importing external institutions. Moreover, inappropriate policies and severe external shocks will eventually have a similar impact on various system components. Though it sometimes seems reasonable, it is not plausible to expect foreign institutions to be willing (even if they were more able) to absorb external or domestic shocks in a completely different way from their domestic counterparts.

The importance of liquidity

The availability of liquidity is crucial to the development of the financial system and to the prevention and management of financial crises. The growth of financial intermediation and the healthy development of financial structures require temporary liquidity assistance to survive unexpected developments—without creating perverse expectations. A well-established, credible, and nondistorting lender of last resort is a crucial component of financial expansion.

Again, Argentina's experience is illustrative in this context. The currency board system prevented the Central Bank from acting as a lender of last resort. Although substitutes were sought—foreign banks were seen as providing their own mechanisms for securing liquidity if they needed it, and the Central Bank tried to develop a creative repo facility—neither element managed to prevent the serious banking crisis. But once the Central Bank recovered its ability to act as a lender of last resort, after the currency board was abandoned, its aggressive rediscount policy prevented the total collapse of the banking sector and contributed to its recuperation.

The role of capital controls

It was once believed that opening capital markets to free international movements of capital enhances financial market development. But the crises of the past decade have revived debates about the role of capital controls. Although it is not really possible to reach definitive conclusions, the issue has at least three dimensions.

In the long run, capital market integration (openness) is desirable because it boosts efficiency and improves the allocation of financial resources. But there are questions about how to make the transition. Capital account liberalization requires preconditions and proper sequencing because abrupt changes can have disruptive consequences. A gradual approach involves fewer risks and is more conducive to the proper integration of country characteristics.

But a third dimension should be taken into account: the use—hopefully temporary—of capital controls as a crisis management instrument. As recent crises show, a country's ability to regain some control is crucial in dealing with emergencies. The authorities' capacity to limit the free flow of capital could be vital in containing a crisis and restoring confidence. As in many other areas, dealing with crises enhances the ability to value the importance of pragmatism over textbook solutions.

Notes

1. The Argentine system—known as *convertibility*—was not an orthodox currency board because it allowed for less than full foreign exchange coverage of the monetary base. Up to one-third of the coverage could take the form of Argentine government bonds as long as they were fully traded in international markets.

2. The strategy was strongly supported by the improved fiscal outlook that started to emerge in the second quarter of 2002. Largely because of an export tax and the effects of inflation on nominal revenues, as well as constant nominal wages, the cash fiscal position turned positive, and for the most part no monetary support was required from the monetary authority.

Comment

Agustín Carstens

It is a pleasure to have been invited to participate in this series, and particularly to have been asked to comment on Mario Blejer's excellent presentation. My comments will focus on the lessons from Argentina's recent crisis, first addressing those drawn by Mario and then those drawn by the International Monetary Fund (IMF), including from its own operations. At the outset I want to acknowledge that I found convincing Mario's brilliant exposition on the abuse of the banking sector by the Argentine authorities. Thus I will not touch on that issue here.

Blejer's Lessons

Being the outstanding economist that he is, Mario first identifies the causes for the collapse of Argentina's currency board. He concludes that any plausible explanation should combine three elements: the loss of competitiveness, the macroeconomic policy inconsistencies, and the sudden stop argument.

I would add two ingredients to this cocktail. First, the regime's setup invited an involuntary cover-up of its flaws. International surveillance fell victim to concerns about undermining confidence in existing policies, and it is likely due to this fact that a more active, timely discussion about an exit strategy did not occur.

Second, throughout the 1990s the authorities actively promoted dollarization to enhance, in the short term, the currency board's declining credibility. Eventually the high degree of dollarization in the financial system expedited the regime's collapse. Starting in the late 1990s, the public wanted to be sure that their dollar and peso deposits in the Argentine banking system were effectively the same as dollar deposits in Miami. When they realized that the equivalence promised by the currency board was a fiction, a currency and bank run ensued—giving rise to twin and inseparable currency and banking crises. I raise this issue because it has policy implications. Promoting dollarization to defend an exchange rate regime is, most of the time, a dangerous approach.

Mario spends a good portion of his presentation describing the ingenious strategy that he, as Central Bank governor, developed to stabilize the main nominal prices in the economy and, at the same time, stem a huge hemorrhage from the banking system. The key to his strategy, in his words, was that an interest rate defense and active foreign market intervention were complementary rather than substitute policies.

I believe that this conclusion should be appropriately conditioned. It is valid subject to, first, one's willingness to risk the faith of the banking system and, second, one's readiness to impose massive capital controls and incur wide-ranging defaults. Mario acknowledges that the jury is still out on this approach.

At best, I would say that the by no means small victory Mario achieved provided Argentina with a window of opportunity to address other pressing issues: fiscal imbalances, unsustainable debt, the banking crisis, and the default in domestic and foreign capital markets. It is still too early to tell if Mario's window of opportunity has been appropriately used by the Argentine authorities.

Finally, I think that Mario is too hard on the IMF's position on foreign exchange intervention. This difference of opinion probably lies in the fact that the IMF was not negotiating only with the Central Bank but with the country as a whole, and when one considers what was happening on the fiscal side—with the debt facing the financial system—the IMF's position is understandable. It is also relevant to recall that the IMF's rules oblige it to look at a program country's capacity to repay.

The IMF's Lessons

Argentina's crisis has led the IMF to draw at least seven lessons for crisis prevention and management. First, considerable work remains to be done on crisis anticipation and prevention. Argentina is a reminder that severe vulnerabilities can build up even in countries widely considered star performers. It is extremely disconcerting that most of the usual indicators of impending difficulties did not appear alarming until Argentina's situation had deteriorated to the point where there was no good exit.

Second, a careful and critical assessment is needed of the links between structural reforms and growth. Growth projections were a central element in the failure of many interested parties to identify the vulnerabilities building up in Argentina during the boom years of the 1990s. During that time Argentina's growth projections were based on what was, in hindsight, an overly favorable reading of the benefits of the structural reforms that had occurred and of prospects that further reforms would be implemented.

Third, a new focus is needed on sovereign debt and debt dynamics, in terms of both preventing and resolving credit crises. It is striking that, when Argentina's debt started on the path of no return, its level (as share of GDP) was in a range not previously considered alarming. This experience clearly calls for a more cautious assessment of debt levels given the scope for adjustment in the event of adverse circumstances.

Fourth, with regard to crisis resolution, the Argentine crisis indicates the importance of timely debt restructuring in cases where debt dynamics have become irreversible. Once debt restructuring has become unavoidable, measures to delay it are likely to raise the costs of a crisis and further complicate its resolution.

Fifth, as Mario points out, the Argentine crisis illustrates the pervasive effects of a default on the financial system and macroeconomic policies. A default can make the exchange rate regime unviable and compromise an otherwise healthy financial system. This experience suggests that it would be desirable to find a more orderly approach to debt restructuring.

Sixth, an exchange rate regime needs to fit a country's economic and political realities. I would not conclude that Argentina's currency board was a mistake from the start. On the contrary, the currency board was critical in taming hyperinflation where many other approaches had failed, as Mario explains. But relative to other regimes a currency board puts much more stringent demands on fiscal and financial policies as well as on the flexibility of trade and the labor market. An earlier exit would have been preferable—and while it would not have been painless, it likely would have been less painful than what occurred.

Finally, there are limits to the ability of an exchange rate arrangement to discipline other aspects of economic policy in a way that ensures stability. Argentina's experience is also a reminder that hard pegs are not as hard as is often supposed. In extreme cases a government can unwind a currency board, albeit at considerable cost to the country. The forced redenomination from U.S. dollars to pesos of bank assets and liabilities also serves as a reminder that there are limits to the extent to which durable hardening can occur through formal dollarization.

Argentina's crisis also provided lessons specific to the IMF's operations. The occurrence and severity of the crisis were extremely disturbing for the IMF given its extensive engagement in Argentina for many years beforehand. There is little doubt that this experience calls for some fresh thinking about the IMF's role, both in normal times and in the context of crisis.

Among the important lessons the IMF has learned are, first, there are shortcomings in its surveillance in identifying key vulnerabilities early and bringing about needed changes once those vulnerabilities become apparent. Argentina's experience highlights the risk that, in a program country where attention is focused on implementation of the program, it is easy to lose sight of the need for a fresh and critical assessment of the overall direction of policies.

A second lesson is in an area where the Argentine experience has had an important impact—the decision to commit IMF resources. Argentina's crisis raises difficult questions about how the IMF can strike the right balance between supporting a member country experiencing difficulties without financing and implicitly perpetuating policies doomed to failure. After the collapse of Argentina's currency board, the IMF took a more cautious approach by waiting for the authorities to assemble a viable policy package rather than rushing to provide new financing.

The third lesson is that the Argentine experience raises more general questions about the IMF's use of its seal of approval. Attempts to make strategic use of the seal of approval ultimately devalue that signal and compromise the IMF's credibility more generally. Limits to the IMF's involvement should be based on the underlying quality of policies, not on the perceived cost of withdrawing support. That said, IMF decisions to continue or withdraw its support to member countries are always made under uncertainty, and it is more likely than not that the IMF will continue to make occasional errors in judgment and decisions that prove wrong ex post.

The fourth and final lesson is that the IMF should not provide financing in situations where debt dynamics are clearly unsustainable. To the extent that such financing helps stave off needed debt restructuring, it only compounds the ultimate cost of such restructuring. This consideration has led the IMF to search for better ways of facilitating debt restructuring in cases where it is a necessary part of the policy package.

Almost certainly, these are not the only lessons from Argentina's crisis. But we at the IMF are continuing to draw and learn from such lessons, particularly for our operations. That such a severe crisis occurred in a country that had performed reasonably well in a succession of IMF-supported programs makes it all the more important that we continue to do so.

Comment

Vijay Kelkar

I AM PLEASED TO HAVE BEEN INVITED TO PARTICIPATE IN THIS IMPORTANT LECTURE series, and I congratulate my good friend Mario for his illuminating discussion of Argentina's recent crisis. He has provided an important perspective—that of an insider—and identified valuable lessons for policymaking during crises.

Argentina's crisis has been widely studied and debated, and important papers on the topic have been written by Michael Mussa, Ricardo Hausmann, and Sebastian Edwards. To these I have little to add; I am not an expert on Argentina. Indeed, I asked the organizers of this lecture why, with Murilo Portugal and Agustin Carstens as participants, they were inviting me. They said that I would bring a perspective from another part of the world, helping to understand why countries respond to crises differently.

Thus my main goal is to provide a political economy perspective of crisis management, taking into account the determinants of why crises occur. My comments first focus on Argentina and India, analyzing their similarities and differences. I then discuss the role of the International Monetary Fund (IMF) in crisis countries, particularly Argentina.

Comparing India and Argentina—Features and Outcomes

Argentina and India share a few similar problems. Both have experienced persistent fiscal deficits. Like Argentina, India has been unable to increase taxes as a share of GDP, and it has a fiscal problem at the provincial level. Both countries have a framework of labor laws that stifles the labor market. And both are less open than some other emerging economies.

Some people have argued that in the late 1990s and early 2000s Argentina experienced a "perfect storm" and, consequently, had a unique kind of crisis. But during the same period India also faced many major shocks, both internal and external. These started with the East Asian crisis, followed by international sanctions imposed in 1998 (in response to nuclear testing). In addition, India experienced several natural disasters that had a big impact on the economy. India also had oil shocks that, because it is a net importer of oil (unlike Argentina), resulted in terms of trade losses of as much as 2 percent of GDP. Finally, there were financial sector problems, including a major run on UTI—India's largest mutual fund, which is owned by the government and accounts for almost 4 percent of GDP.

Despite these many shocks, India has had better economic outcomes than Argentina. Although there was a balance of payments crisis in 1991, it was resolved quickly, and since then India's economy has grown continuously and at high rates. Indeed, India's growth rate has been higher and more stable than Argentina's for the past 30 years. Given the two countries' many similarities in terms of structural conditions and numerous shocks, what explains these different outcomes?

First, although India had a large fiscal deficit, it was entirely domestically financed. Foreign borrowing is not required to finance the deficit because household savings are high and have grown over the past decade. Thus the deficit could be entirely financed through domestic savings. And although state governments have fiscal deficits, India's constitution does not allow them to borrow from abroad. Even for domestic borrowing they must get permission from the central government.

Second, perhaps contrary to many people's perceptions, India's restrictive labor laws apply only to the organized sector, which accounts for just 10 percent of the workforce. Thus 90 percent of the workforce essentially faces flexible labor market conditions, which means that India is probably as flexible as many OECD countries. This is one of the main reasons India adjusts to shocks much faster than do many other emerging market economies.

Third, over the past 20 years India has had low inflation—averaging less than 7 percent a year—resulting in a thriving government bond market. Inflation has been kept low because it is extremely expensive politically. Hence investors have faith in the government's anti-inflation policies, fostering the growing market in government securities. In fact, India can now issue government securities with maturities of up to 25 years.

Finally, exchange rate policy has been flexible, with the rate determined by the market. India's approach has been described as being in the middle of the two extremes, following what can be called a managed float. Although no targets are set, there is still flexibility.

One of the most useful ways of understanding these differences is through a model developed by Dani Rodrik. The model argues that the response to shocks in an economy—that is, the change in growth rates—is a function of latent social conflicts and the institutional framework for managing them. I believe that this explains India's sustained growth despite repeated shocks.

The most important institutional element for managing shocks is India's vibrant democracy. Democracy is usually underappreciated in terms of how it allows a country to absorb shocks (because of the associated political institutions) and enhances its ability to adjust. Moreover, with India's strong social institutions, democracy provides a better way of sharing pain. This is important because a shock requires adjustment, and if the cost of adjustment is not shared equitably there will be problems. In 1966, for example, India had a major domestic shock because of output losses due to drought, and in 1974–75 and 1979–80 it faced major oil crises. In all these cases the system ensured that the pain of adjustment was borne equitably.

I believe that this approach is what enables the economic system to manage conflicts while sustaining reforms and fostering growth with adjustment. Democratic institutions have made it possible for India to absorb even large shocks and still maintain its healthy growth rate.

IMF Responses to Crises

Argentina has been under the IMF's watch for the past 10 years, first through a precautionary program and then through a full-blown one. Despite this oversight the country became mired in crisis, raising questions about the IMF's accountability. In the two years after the crisis began in mid-2001, Argentina lost more than $100 billion in income. In addition, poverty rose by nearly 60 percent, with more than 5 million people pushed below the poverty line. Rural poverty exceeds 70 percent. Thus Argentina has paid enormous social costs, and there should be accountability for these outcomes—not only among policymakers but also the international community, including the IMF.

One lesson I have learned from reading the literature is that had the IMF approved a much larger program at an earlier stage, Argentina probably would not have borne these heavy costs. One reason for resistance to a large program was that the IMF uses quotas to determine country programs, and a large program would have exceeded Argentina's quota. But this argument is a bit unconvincing, because the real issue is that the IMF's total available funding is too small. Its funding has not kept pace with growth in global trade, GDP, or capital flows.

Thus the IMF's size was a major problem. Had its size increased in line with changes in the global economy, the IMF would have been able to give Argentina the support it required. As Mario indicated in his presentation, the country's economy has started to recover in a very short period. Still, it has had to pay extremely high social costs. Had the IMF provided more support earlier on, there could have been a softer landing for the Argentine economy.

Arguments against such support usually invoke the threat of moral hazard. But I have examined the IMF's analyses, and there is little evidence of moral hazard on the borrower's side. Papers by Michael Mussa and even the IMF indicate, however, that there may have been evidence of moral hazard on the part of lenders.

Even before Argentina's crisis there were interesting proposals on how to address its emerging problems. For example, Mezele offered a proposal on how to intervene in a market-friendly way to achieve a debt workout and thus make options available to Argentina so that it would not be denied access to capital markets. So, had the IMF provided more resources at an earlier stage or attempted innovative initiatives, it could have avoided a major dislocation in the economy. And again, one of the main reasons that did not happen is that the IMF's size did not keep pace with developments in the global economy.

Another problem, in my view, is that large IMF programs are too brief. When attempting major structural changes, an IMF program should have a much longer duration. Argentina's IMF program should be converted to something like an Extended Fund Facility with a longer time profile, rather than the kind of program now in place.

In advanced countries reform programs are seldom frontloaded in the way that the IMF proposes to emerging market economies. Thus I think that IMF programs should be much better designed. The IMF does not give adequate attention to the political economy of reforms or to the fact that different countries have different institutional capacities for managing social conflict. These issues require program designs different from the straightjacket facility that the Fund tries to impose. Thus in crisis situations the IMF should look beyond macroeconomics, and take into account the deeper determinants or the political economy of adjustment.

Montek S. Ahluwalia

Former Secretary, Department of Economic Affairs, India

Born in India in 1943, Montek S. Ahluwalia received a B.A. Hons in Economics from Delhi University and an M.A. and M.Phil in Economics from Oxford University, where he was a Rhodes Scholar. He spent his early career as an economist at the World Bank, where he worked in the Public Finance and Income Distribution Divisions. He left the Bank in 1979 to begin a long career of public service in the Indian government, first as Economic Adviser in the Ministry of Finance, a position he held until 1985. From 1985–90 he was Additional Secretary and later Special Secretary to the Prime Minister, and from 1990–91 was Commerce Secretary. He rejoined the Ministry of Finance in 1991, where he was Finance Secretary from 1993–98. From 1998–2001 he was Member of both the Planning Commission and the Economic Advisory Council to the Prime Minister. Throughout the 1990s Ahluwalia played a major role in designing and implementing groundbreaking economic reforms, helping to place India on the high-growth trajectory it enjoys today.

Ahluwalia left the Indian government in 2001 to become the first Director of the Independent Evaluation Office at the International Monetary Fund (IMF). There he oversaw the IMF's self-evaluation of its role in Argentina's financial crisis. When he left the position in 2004, the IMF Executive Board commended him by saying, "Mr. Ahluwalia has successfully established independent evaluation as an essential element for the effective functioning of the Fund with respect to its surveillance, program, and technical assistance activities in support of its members." In mid-2004 he began a Cabinet-level position as Deputy Chairman of India's Planning Commission. Ahluwalia cowrote (with Hollis Chenery and others) *Redistribution with Growth: An Approach to Policy* (Oxford University Press, 1975). He has also written extensively for professional journals on India's economic reforms and global financial architecture.

9 Lessons from India's Economic Reforms

Montek S. Ahluwalia

IT IS A GREAT HONOR TO HAVE BEEN ASKED TO GIVE THIS LECTURE, JOINING A SERIES of extremely distinguished practitioners in development policy. It is also a pleasure to be doing so at the World Bank, where I had my first job after graduating from university. I have many pleasant memories of my days at the Bank and especially the many friendships I formed at the time.

The lecturers in this series have been asked to provide personal reflections rather than deep analyses—to draw lessons from their experiences and discuss what they would have done differently had they known then what they know now. That seems simple enough, but of course it is not. In my current position, which involves conducting ex post evaluations of International Monetary Fund (IMF) programs, I am very conscious that it is extremely difficult to determine what constitutes a valid lesson. A lesson necessarily implies some kind of statement about counterfactuals—that if things had been done differently, outcomes would have differed as well—and establishing sound counterfactuals is extremely difficult. Having genuflected before this qualification, I propose to get into the spirit of these lectures by skirting analyses and simply asserting my perceptions, leaving it to scholars to test whether these perceptions, and the lessons drawn from them, are valid.

India's Economic Performance and Reforms since the 1970s

Before attempting to draw lessons, let me first summarize India's economic performance over the past three decades. When I returned to India in 1979, after a decade at the Bank, the country was generally regarded as a growth laggard. In the 1970s its GDP growth averaged just 3.2 percent a year—lower than in Sub-Saharan Africa, East Asia, Latin America, and the global average for developing countries (table 9.1). India also fared poorly relative to other large developing countries, ranking 17 in a sample of 20 (table 9.2). Its growth performance improved considerably in the 1980s, rising to an annual average of 5.7 percent and causing its rank to rise to 7 among the sample of 20 countries. Growth rates improved further in the first half of the 1990s.

The acceleration of growth in the 1980s was associated with a process of policy rethinking and (very partial) reforms. This rethinking was spurred partly by mainstream thinking about development policy but mainly by the example of the superior performance of many East Asian countries. The World Bank is the principal source of data on comparative economic performance among developing countries, and it should be a source of satisfaction to those who collate and publish these data that the picture they present has an impact on policymaking.

The main lesson that Indian policymakers learned from this comparison was that India's economic system needed to be redesigned. The system was characterized by extensive government controls over private sector activity in the form of investment licensing and price controls, high levels of tariff protection combined with quantitative restrictions on imports, restrictive controls on foreign investment, and so on. This system came to be regarded as dysfunctional and in need of change.

Nevertheless, the control system was not fundamentally altered in the 1980s. It remained in place, but was operated more liberally. Controls were relaxed in marginal ways by removing some industries from licensing controls, allowing some automatic expansion in licensed capacity, and removing some imports from controls. More important, the controls in place were generally operated more permissively, in the sense that there was less suspicion of private sector activity and permissions needed were more freely given.

As this process of incremental liberalization proceeded and produced good results in the 1980s, many technocrats were convinced that deeper, more systemic changes were needed. Several committees were appointed to review various aspects of the economic management system, and these committees recommended further liberalization. Many of these recommendations were implemented in the 1990s.

The reforms of the 1990s were triggered by the fact that India experienced a severe balance of payments crisis in 1991. The new administration, headed by Prime Minister Narasimha Rao, appointed a technocrat and economist, Manmohan Singh,

TABLE 9.1

Average Annual GDP Growth in India, China, and Developing Regions, 1971–2003

Country/region	1971–80	1981–90	1992–97	1998–2003
India	3.2	5.7	6.7	5.7
China	6.3	9.3	11.5	7.7
Sub-Saharan Africa	3.3	2.2	2.3	3.0
Developing Asia excl. China and India	5.8	5.0	6.2	2.7
Middle East and North Africa	6.3	2.4	3.3	4.3
Latin America and Caribbean	6.1	1.5	3.9	1.3
All developing countries	5.5	4.1	6.3	4.5

Source: IMF, World Economic Outlook.

TABLE 9.2
Average Annual GDP Growth in 20 Large Emerging Economies, 1971–2003

Region/country	1971–80	1981–90	1992–97	1998–2003
South Asia				
India	3.2	5.7	6.7	5.7
Bangladesh	1.8	3.7	4.8	5.2
Pakistan	4.8	6.0	3.6	3.8
East Asia				
China	6.3	9.3	11.5	7.7
Indonesia	7.8	5.4	7.1	0.5
Korea, Rep. of	7.7	8.7	6.6	4.3
Malaysia	8.0	6.1	9.2	2.7
Philippines	6.0	1.8	3.8	3.4
Thailand	6.9	7.9	6.5	1.8
Vietnam	3.9	5.9	8.8	5.0
Middle East and North Africa				
Egypt	5.8	5.2	3.0	4.0
Turkey	5.5	5.2	5.1	1.9
Sub-Saharan Africa				
Nigeria	4.4	2.2	2.7	2.7
South Africa	3.5	1.5	2.1	2.4
Tanzania	3.7	3.3	2.5	5.2
Latin America				
Argentina	2.9	−1.1	5.5	−1.7
Brazil	8.6	1.6	3.4	1.6
Chile	2.8	3.3	8.3	2.5
Mexico	6.9	1.9	2.6	2.9
Venezuela	4.1	1.0	2.4	−4.2

Source: IMF, *World Economic Outlook.*

as minister of finance. Singh (who is now prime minister) unveiled a comprehensive program of economic reforms, including:

- Abandoning the earlier predisposition in favor of a dominant role for the public sector and recognizing the importance of the private sector as a leading engine of growth.

- Placing much greater reliance on market forces and competition as the primary means of increasing efficiency.

- Opening the economy to international trade, foreign investment, and foreign technology.

Because reforms were implemented at a time of crisis, when the economy also had to resort to IMF financing and a structural adjustment loan from the World Bank, they were criticized as being driven by the IMF and World Bank. But the fact is that the package of reforms was the outcome of considerable internal thinking. Although the reforms were broadly in line with what was considered sensible policy by international institutions, this was more a reflection of a genuine convergence of views on development policy than of pressure exerted by the IMF and the Bank. One indication of the extent to which the design of the package was homegrown is that in many areas— especially privatization and the pace of external liberalization—India's reforms differed significantly from those in typical IMF–Bank programs. Another indication is that the reforms were continued even though the crisis was overcome relatively quickly.

The initial response to the reforms was an impressive acceleration in annual GDP growth, which averaged 6.7 percent in the first half of the reform period (1992–97). This acceleration was widely viewed as vindicating the government's approach. But in the second half of the reform period (1998–2003) the growth rate decelerated to an average of about 5.7 percent. Not surprisingly, there has been a great deal of concern in India about this deceleration.

The deceleration can be explained by two factors. First, global economic growth slowed in the wake of the East Asian crisis and the collapse of the technology boom in the United States. Among the 20 comparator countries mentioned earlier, India's rank in 1992–97, when growth accelerated, was 6 out of 20. But in 1998–2003, when India's growth decelerated, its rank rose to 2 (see table 9.2). Second, there was a weakening in the pace of reforms. I will touch on this issue and its implications at various points in this lecture.

Lessons from India's Experience

The above description suggests that India's reforms may not have been as successful as we would have liked. Still, India's growth was higher than that of many comparator countries in recent decades. What can be drawn from this experience? Six lessons seem to me to be of special relevance.

The first lesson relates to the importance of a homegrown approach for reforms to take hold. The second relates to the inevitability of gradual implementation in a pluralist, highly participatory democracy. The third is that implementation of complex reforms involves a process of learning and discovery, which means that there will inevitably be some false starts and midcourse adjustments in the implementation process. The fourth is that when dealing with multiple reforms on several fronts, careful attention must be paid to sequencing. The fifth relates to India's federal political structure and the increased importance of policy action at the subnational level in an environment where the central government is liberalizing controls. Finally, India's experience yields important lessons about poverty alleviation.

A homegrown approach

The broad direction of India's reforms was by no means unique. I have already mentioned that the reforms implemented in the 1980s, and especially in the 1990s, reflected the emerging consensus on development policy in the international community. The difference from many other countries that took the same path is that India's reforms were not dictated from the outside. Although the reforms were supported by financial assistance from the IMF and the Bank—which implies that they met with the approval of these institutions—they were not an externally designed blueprint thrust on an unwilling government.

On the contrary, the broad direction of reforms had been extensively discussed internally, and there was fairly wide domestic consensus that changes along these lines were needed. This is not to say that the reforms were universally accepted, but democracies are not given to encouraging universal acceptance. Indeed, they put a significant premium on adversarial debate. The point is that the reforms had substantial homegrown support.

Several committees had recommended reforms well before they were introduced. I recall a discussion with the prime minister in 1989 on why and how so many East Asian countries were doing so well, and why India was lagging behind. I argued that the main reason was that India's economic policies were not conducive to rapid growth and needed wide-ranging reforms. I was asked to write a paper on the subject, which I did and which was discussed internally in the government. I mention this incident only to illustrate that we were not operating in completely virgin territory: the intellectual foundation for the reforms was already in place. Had that not been the case, it would have been extremely difficult to make many of the changes that were made in 1991 because resistance would have been too strong, and it would have looked like they had been imposed by technocrats cut off from the mainstream.

A gradual approach

The second lesson that emerges from India's experience is that the pace of reforms is dictated by economic and political forces, and it is difficult to force that pace beyond a certain point. In India, with its highly pluralist and participatory democracy, this meant that reforms were gradualist. The more impatient of my friends often argued that it was more like glacialism, because you could barely see the movements taking place. The process was often compared unfavorably with Latin America, where similar reforms were adopted much more vigorously and with much greater speed.

There were two somewhat different reasons why India's reforms were implemented in a gradualist fashion. First, there were areas of reforms where there was broad technocratic and political consensus on what needed to be done, based on established theoretical and empirical work. But implementation was deliberately stretched out due to a desire to avoid sudden changes and spread the costs of adjustment over a longer period. Second, in certain areas gradualism arose because there was consensus that change was needed, but no consensus on how far it should go. In such cases some steps were taken but it was never clear whether further steps would be taken.

An example of the first type of gradualism is the conduct of reforms involving external liberalization. In the late 1970s India suffered from a grossly overvalued exchange rate as a result of tight import controls as well as a varied, but generally very high, tariff structure. There was considerable agreement in technocratic circles that quantitative restrictions on imports were dysfunctional and should be phased out. In addition, tariffs had to be reduced over time and the exchange rate had to be devalued to provide incentives for domestic production as tariffs were cut.

The 1980s saw some partial steps to address this problem. The exchange rate was managed in a way that achieved a steady depreciation in real terms, eroding the impact of quantitative restrictions. There was also some limited relaxation in quantitative restrictions, but little progress on tariffs. In fact, where quantitative import licensing was reduced, tariffs were actually raised as a way of shifting from quantitative restrictions to tariffs.

The reforms of the 1990s envisaged a systemic change on all three fronts but at a graduated pace. In 1991 the fixed exchange rate was devalued by 25 percent (in two successive steps) to a more reasonable level. Since import controls were to be liberalized, it was logical to shift to a system that allowed greater exchange rate flexibility. This was done in two stages. In 1992 a dual exchange rate was introduced, with one fixed rate at which exporters were expected to surrender 30 percent of export earnings (which were then used to finance essential imports such as petroleum and to meet government debt servicing obligations) and a floating rate at which all other transactions took place based on the demand and supply of foreign exchange. There was no indication at the time on how long the dual exchange rate system would be kept, but the government clearly intended it to be a transitional measure, and internally we were clear that if the market exchange rate did not get pushed to unreasonable levels, the two rates would quickly be unified. In 1993 the dual exchange rate was replaced by a single exchange rate that was effectively market-determined.

Gradualism was also evident in phasing out import licensing. Licensing was phased out fairly quickly for all nonconsumer goods (intermediate goods and capital goods), but it remained in place for consumer goods until as late as 2002. Throughout this period a steady effort was made to cut tariffs, and the weighted average import tariff fell from more than 80 percent in 1991 to about 30 percent in 1997. There was a reversal in 1997, partly because Indian industry began to feel the pressure of competition after the East Asian crisis, but the process of reducing tariffs resumed in 2000. India's weighted average tariff is now about 24 percent. Though definitely an improvement relative to 1991, it is three times as high as that in East Asia, and that is despite the fact that for the past five years a declared objective of government policy has been to approximate East Asian tariffs.

Looking back, I have no doubt that we were too cautious and we should—and probably could—have moved faster. The case for gradualism was that a slower pace would evoke less opposition, and this was probably true. But there are two somewhat obvious disadvantages to this type of gradualist approach. First, although it minimizes pain in the short run, it also postpones benefits and to that extent does not build a strong enough constituency for reforms. For example, the export response normally associated with trade reform was slow to materialize in India. It has emerged in the past four or five years, but it would have occurred much earlier if we had been bolder on this front. A second disadvantage is that gradualism gives more time for opponents of reform to mobilize, and all the more so because the benefits of reform are necessarily muted. The reversal of tariff cuts in 1997 was to some extent a concession to growing protectionist pressures from industry.

The second type of gradualism refers to situations where there was consensus on the need for policy change, but no consensus on how far to go. That was the case with privatization. Unlike in Eastern Europe, where privatization was politically attractive because it was part of a structural change that was generally supported, in India there was little public support for privatization. The pressure for change came from the technocracy, which recognized that too many loss-making public enterprises imposed a drain on the budget. But even among this group there was no conviction about the need for wholesale privatization as an ideology. Rather, there was a desire to privatize all loss-making units, in the belief that private entrepreneurs would do a better job, and to privatize units in sectors where no strategic interests were being served and private ownership was clearly more appropriate (hotels and simple consumer goods were the most obvious candidates in this category).

Even this limited approach had little support outside the technocracy when reforms began in the early 1990s. The process was driven primarily by the need to raise resources for the budget and was limited to selling minority shares in public enterprises (described as "disinvestment" rather than privatization). While the primary motivation was to raise revenue, there was also a belief that by bringing in private shareholders, management of public enterprises would take on a more commercial orientation.

The Congress government, which began the process of disinvestment, was succeeded after the 1996 elections by a left of center government that was not expected to favor privatization. It is an interesting example of the way gradualism helped build consensus that the new government did not reverse policy. Instead it focused on process issues, criticizing the earlier process as one in which the choice of which public enterprises would be privatized was arbitrary and nontransparent.

To remedy this problem, the government created a Disinvestment Commission to examine the issue, hold hearings, talk to all stakeholders, and then make recommendations. The government did not endorse any particular policy; it simply established a commission to make recommendations on which units should be privatized and to what extent or in what manner. The commission held consultations and submitted reports recommending different courses of action for different public sector units, including full privatization in some cases.

Since the government was in office less than two years, it collapsed before it had to make any decisions on these recommendations. Following the elections of 1997, it was succeeded by a right of center coalition led by the Bharatiya Janata Party (BJP). The new government decided to accept the recommendations on privatization, and in 1998 announced that it would transfer management control of all nonstrategic public enterprises. A new Ministry of Disinvestment was created to push the process more vigorously.

The first two privatizations involving a change in management occurred in 1999 and 2000 and created tremendous controversy. Company workers took the matter to court, saying that privatization was illegal. Numerous nongovernmental organizations (NGOs) also opposed the government's efforts, as did a variety of other individuals and institutions, with many filing petitions accusing it of doing something wrong. The Supreme Court considered the matter and pronounced that the government was perfectly within its rights to sell public enterprises. But while the principle was established and some units were privatized, the government was unable to overcome internal resistance to privatizing some of the most attractive public units in the petroleum sector, despite its declared intention to do so.

Relative to Latin America, where privatization was pushed enthusiastically, India looked uncertain about its intentions and slow in its decisionmaking. Indeed, investment bankers often commented that India's approach was difficult to understand and that it looked as if we did not know what we were doing. But the fact is that privatization did not command sufficient public support. The government took a series of partial steps and encouraged active public debate, giving many voices a chance to be heard. This approach was aimed at building sufficient consensus before moving forward. In general, changes were made opportunistically, with the government moving forward when it sensed an opportunity—but being just as willing to hold back when there was opposition.[1]

India's experience with privatization shows that ensuring debate on a policy does not guarantee that consensus will emerge. The essence of democracy is that it is adversarial, and parties participating in a democratic process do not have a compulsion to reach an agreement. On the contrary, opponents will remain opposed even after an issue has been extensively debated, at least until public opinion changes very broadly.

This point is important in the context of the push by the IMF and World Bank for various types of participatory processes in formulating Poverty Reduction Strategy Papers (PRSPs). There is often an unstated assumption that if all stakeholders are involved in such discussions, it will be possible to reach agreement. But that is by no means certain. Debate is an essential part of the political process, and while it helps ensure participation, it does not guarantee convergence. Indeed, it can sometimes even sharpen conflicts that might have remained muted in the absence of debate. In short, public debate does not eliminate the need for political leaders to make decisions in areas where full support may not be forthcoming. In the end, politicians still have to take risks—and if they fail, their opponents will obviously try to capitalize on those failures.

Complex reforms

The third lesson relates to the special challenges posed when attempting second generation reforms, which are much more complex. This was evident in India's experience with reforms aimed at introducing private participation in infrastructure sectors such as electricity generation and distribution, telecommunications, and roads. It was evident in the early 1990s that India had huge infrastructure gaps and that the gaps could not be filled through a strategy based purely on public investment. Infrastructure services had traditionally been delivered by government-owned suppliers that charged very low user fees and so did not generate adequate resources within the system. The government's fiscal situation did not allow it to cover the resources shortfall, making the system inherently unsustainable. Thus a change in policy was essential.

One way of solving these problems was to end the public sector monopoly and open these sectors to private investment. This approach was readily accepted, but the complexity of the reforms needed to achieve it was not recognized. There was a tendency to think that if only private entry were allowed, India would be flooded with new investors setting up infrastructure projects. The technocracy was aware that enabling reforms would be needed, but in retrospect I do not think that we appreciated the extent and complexity of the preconditions needed to attract private investment in infrastructure.

Let me illustrate by describing what happened in the case of electricity. Initially, the policy aimed at attracting private investors into the generation of electricity without addressing the lack of financial viability of the distribution segment. Distribution, which was a public sector monopoly, suffered from an unviable tariff structure that charged some consumers far less than the cost of power. Public distribution companies also suffered from large-scale undercollection due to a combination of operational inefficiency and corruption in the form of deliberate underbilling. The effort to attract private investors to sell power to financially bankrupt monopoly buyers could succeed only if the government guaranteed power purchases, and there was a flood of applicants seeking to set up plants backed by such guarantees.

Although state governments were willing to provide guarantees, their weak financial positions typically made investors seek counter-guarantees from the central government, which initially resisted giving them. In the end some limited guarantees were given, but many of these plants ran into other problems.

The World Bank Group—especially the International Finance Corporation (IFC)—was actively involved in this process, and it pushed for the structural changes needed to allow private players to operate in the power sector. But I think it is fair to say that the Bank Group also underestimated the complexity of such reforms. For example, I remember being told on many occasions that India was insufficiently sensitive to the needs of private actors in the power sector, and Pakistan's Hub River Project was frequently cited as a model of effective private participation. Yet that project has since become an example of everything that can go wrong with project design.

Even when the focus shifted to privatizing electricity distribution under the supervision of a statutory regulator, there were unexpected problems. In Delhi, for example, when a regulator was finally put in place, it laid down regulations for determining power tariffs on the basis of a cost-based tariff structure. Although such structures are not perfect, they are quite common. But the initial regulations did not generate confidence among private sector players. The regulations listed the various factors to be taken into account in determining costs—but they also stated that in exceptional circumstances, regulators could depart from any of them. Such omnibus clauses giving governments a great deal of power are readily accepted in a public sector framework, since public utilities can appeal to the government to take a reasonable view. But when a private utility is expected to provide $1 billion in investment—$800 million of which is going to be borrowed—tariff regulations containing such large potential for arbitrariness are unlikely to be acceptable.

India also had problems introducing private participation in telecommunications, but with somewhat different results. Again, the initial policies for attracting private investment did not take adequate account of the complexities involved. In telecommunications, low tariffs were much less important than in electric power because long-distance telephone charges were too high to start with, and private investors were quite willing to enter the market because they knew that consumers would be willing to pay for their services.

But there were other problems. First, investors wanted a regulatory environment that would ensure interconnection with the incumbent service provider on reasonable terms. A regulator was established, but it did not have sufficient powers to enforce a level playing field for private investors relative to the incumbent. Second, investors initially bid unrealistically high fees for telecommunications licenses and soon complained that revenue streams would not support such high payments. This led to demands to renegotiate the license fees, because otherwise the new system would not be sustainable. Not surprisingly, there was severe criticism that changes were being made in response to lobbying by the private sector—which they were. But the government felt that enforcing the original conditions was impractical, because it would lead to prolonged legal wrangles as well as service interruptions for many consumers.

In the end the problem was resolved by restructuring the regulatory authority, increasing its powers and converting the payments to be made by licensees into a share of revenues instead of fixed license fees. The evolution of policy in this area can be described as a kind of learning by doing, adjusting policies that were not quite right in a series of steps. This was obviously not ideal, but unlike with electric power, private participation in telecommunications succeeded. Capacity expanded considerably, and there were visible improvements in the quality and supply of services, as well as a reduction in their cost.

To summarize, reforms in infrastructure development were generally much more complex than we had expected, and the results therefore varied across sectors. In some sectors, such as electric power, we faced problems from the very beginning that continue even today. In others, such as telecommunications, there was a process of periodic adjustments in policy that were controversial at the time but appear to have worked in the end. It is tempting to think that by anticipating sufficiently, one could ensure a policy design that would avoid problems subsequently. In practice however, it is difficult to hold back initiatives because their design is imperfect—especially if many participants are keen on making progress. Some learning by doing is therefore unavoidable, and it is important to retain flexibility in policy to allow for such improvements.

The importance of sequencing

Because reforms in some areas are essential to success in others, broadly based reforms require that careful attention be paid to sequencing. This becomes even more important when a gradual approach is used, because gradualism inevitably reduces the effectiveness of other reforms. If gradualism means fitful progress, as was the case in India in many areas, then correct sequencing is that much harder to achieve because reforms in some areas may be held up by unexpected opposition. In hindsight, Indian policy toward sequencing got it right in some cases and wrong in others.

An interesting example of sequencing problems relates to the need to remove domestic distortions before, or at least at the same time as, lowering external barriers. India got this sequencing right in one sense, because domestic industrial liberalization was implemented much earlier than external liberalization. However, there were important exceptions. The policy of reserving certain items for production by small-scale industries was a domestic distortion that should have been eliminated well before external liberalization. But doing so proved politically difficult, and all that could be achieved was a progressive reduction in the list of reserved industries. Over 10 years the reserved list was cut from about 800 to 500.

A faster pace would have been more logical and would have helped these industries adjust sooner to the new, more competitive environment. To realize the competitive potential of exports such as garments, toys, and leather goods—areas where China has done incredibly well—Indian producers should have been allowed to produce on larger, more credible scales. Technocrats recommended such changes in the mid-1990s, but political constraints prevented the government from making them. Indeed, only in 2002 were significant adjustments made in this area.

An area where India got sequencing right was liberalization of the capital account. Many countries have liberalized capital flows before developing a strong financial sector, and suffered as a result. India avoided this problem. It had traditionally followed restrictive policies toward external debt. The government never borrowed abroad, and commercial organizations could not incur external debt without government permission—and the government was very restrictive in granting such permission. It also did not allow commercial organizations to take on short-term loans, only long-term, and even those were subject to a global limit determined by the minister of finance.

In the mid-1990s, when there was ample liquidity in world markets, there was a lot of pressure from domestic businesses to liberalize policies on capital flows. That is pretty much what happened in East Asia, and a lot of the instability that arose there in 1997 was the result of huge amounts of short-term external debt having been incurred. India avoided that problem because its decision to liberalize the capital account remained essentially cautious.

This caution did not stem from a desire to avoid change. Indeed, in late 1996 the government appointed an expert committee, headed by a former deputy governor of the Reserve Bank of India, to examine how the capital account should be liberalized. The committee's report, submitted before the East Asian crisis, recommended that India liberalize the capital account in a gradual manner, with appropriate sequencing. The sequence proposed was to first liberalize foreign direct investment, because it is the least volatile, and portfolio investment, because such investment is a little more self-regulating. Investors are less likely to make sharp reversals in portfolio equity flows because stock markets are likely to collapse if they do. The report was emphatic that short-term flows should not be liberalized until the fiscal deficit was brought under control and the banking system was made much stronger. This was good advice that was followed by the government.

Liberalization and state governments

The next lesson involves the extent to which the role of subnational governments becomes more important in a liberalized environment. Earlier, the central government's control over private investment decisions enabled it to spread resources thinly across Indian states. But in a liberalized environment, resources will flow to states where conditions are considered most favorable for private investment.

This tendency was heightened by the fact that state governments responded very differently to liberalization. More enlightened states aggressively adopted investor-friendly policies, trying to attract both domestic and foreign investors. Less enlightened states were laggards in this respect. Some of the poorest states, which have the largest populations, grew slower in the 1990s than in the 1980s. So, while India as a whole experienced faster growth, many important states saw a deceleration. This was not because the central government followed a discriminatory policy. Unlike in China, India's liberalization was not geographically selective. But states responded differently, causing an increase in inequality between states.

This outcome had predictable consequences. It generated pressure on the central government to adopt a more proactive approach to ensure more egalitarian growth processes. Although this objective was widely supported, it was not entirely clear what the central government should do. It could provide more money to slower-growing states, but its resources were limited. Another question was whether additional resources provided to poorly performing states should be unconditional transfers, on equity grounds, or whether they should be linked to efforts that would improve performance. Implicit in the latter approach is the notion that additional transfers to poorly performing states should be linked to greater conditionality. This is a controversial issue, and hard decisions of this type cannot be avoided indefinitely.

The key lesson in this area was that economic liberalization implies that unless state governments actively engage in reforms, the potential benefits of liberalization may not materialize—and that state governments that do not change their approach will actually see a deterioration in economic performance, because of the competitive environment created by reforms. This simple fact took time to sink in, though I am happy to say that it is now much more widely recognized.

Implications for poverty reduction

Finally, India's experience provides some useful lessons on poverty alleviation. It shows that growth is good for poverty alleviation. Poverty did not decline in India in the 1970s, when growth was weak, but it did decline in the 1980s and 1990s, when growth was strong. India is blessed with a wealth of survey data on consumption levels—and an even larger endowment of people willing to analyze it! As a result there is a rich, diverse literature from which you can probably prove whatever you want if you choose your data and analyst appropriately.

That said, a general consensus has emerged. Most experts who have thoroughly examined the issue—including independent international experts such as Angus Deaton—have concluded that not only did poverty decline in India in the 1980s and 1990s, but also that the decline was greater in the 1990s. Poverty did not decline as much as was targeted, but growth also did not reach the levels associated with those targets.

An important issue in the Indian debate is how much reliance should be placed on poverty reduction induced by growth as opposed to poverty reduction resulting from targeted antipoverty programs. India has used both strategies. It has relied heavily on growth and, furthermore, on growth of a particular quality, with an explicit emphasis on the need to accelerate income generation in agriculture. This is not to say that it has achieved this goal. In fact, one of the disturbing facts about India's recent economic performance is that the momentum of agricultural growth was lost in the second half of the 1990s, and this slowdown is part of the reason why there has been dissatisfaction with the equity aspect of recent reforms. However, while this surfaces as an equity issue, it is as much a failure of the growth component of the strategy.

India has also relied on a wide variety of targeted antipoverty programs. These programs are limited in scale but play an important supporting role—because there can be little doubt that the bulk of the reduction in poverty has occurred because the benefits of growth have spilled over sufficiently to poor people.

The main lesson I draw from this experience is that growth helps poverty alleviation and should be as pro-poor as possible. In India, where a large portion of poor people are in rural areas, this means paying special attention to policies that stimulate agricultural growth and nonagricultural economic activity in rural areas. The poverty reduction strategy has not been very effective in this respect in recent years given that agricultural growth slowed in the mid-1990s.

Although it is beyond the scope of this lecture to provide answers on why this has happened, there is growing consensus on many issues relevant in this context. India's approach to agriculture has depended on a combination of subsidies and public investment. Over time, subsidies have expanded while public investment has fallen. This approach should be reversed, with fewer subsidies and more public investment, especially in irrigation and rural roads. In addition, policies should encourage agricultural diversification and agroprocessing. I am not sure that we have all the answers yet. Careful analysis is needed to devise a workable package of reforms, some the responsibility of the central government but many requiring action by state governments.

While on the subject of poverty, I would like to comment on some aspects of poverty reduction as a policy objective where there are interesting differences of perception between policymakers in developing countries and international institutions such as the World Bank and other multilateral development banks. The international institutions focus on poverty alleviation as the overriding objective of policy and are often inclined to view all policy choices from the perspective of what they do for poverty alleviation. This is understandable because the mandates of these institutions, as defined by the development community in industrial countries, define poverty alleviation as the principle international public good that the institutions are meant to promote. Allocation of public resources to these institutions is justified largely on this basis. But policymakers in developing countries necessarily have multiple objectives. Poverty alleviation is clearly one of the most important in low-income countries, but other objectives—such as economic development and achievement of middle-income and ultimately industrial country status—are also important. And these go beyond poverty alleviation, narrowly defined.

This has a number of interesting consequences. First, an exclusive focus on poverty alleviation can lead to a bias in favor of interventions that directly affect poor groups in the short run in a measurable manner, compared with other interventions that have either an indirect (and so not easily measured) impact or a positive impact but over a long time horizon. Since resources are scarce, it is important to recognize the opportunity costs of direct interventions. In India, for example, investments in land development, irrigation, and rural road connectivity may not appear to affect poverty directly because their benefits accrue to the rural population generally. But the net results in terms of impact on poor people may be substantial. It is important that broader infrastructure investments not be shortchanged by an excessive concern with targeting.

Another area of difference between multilateral development banks and practical policymakers is that distributional concerns cannot be limited to the issue of the impact on poverty. Multilateral development banks tend to treat this issue as the only relevant distributional concern. But this does not reflect the compulsions of practical politics: policymakers have to be concerned with broader distributional concerns. It is perfectly possible to envisage a growth process that reduces poverty but increases relative inequality, or the urban-rural divide, or regional inequality. Any of these could become a political problem and would need to be addressed.

Consider a situation where a policy change has no impact on poor people, or is even marginally favorable, but has a churning effect on the distribution above the poverty line—with some groups that were higher up in the distribution pushed down and some lower down pushed up. This may leave the distribution statistically unchanged, but the "impoverishment" of some groups above the poverty line would entail a political price.

All this suggests that politicians have to work with complex objective functions. Ideally, a politician would like to claim that policy reforms have helped poor people, and indeed that every group and region has also benefited.

These are some of the lessons uppermost in my mind as I reflect on India's experience over the past two decades. Some are certainly relevant for policymaking in India in the years ahead.

Note

1. The change of government in 2004 has brought a further modification. The new government has indicated that it will not privatize profit-making public enterprises. But privatization of loss-making enterprises remains an option, as does the sale of minority holdings in profit-making enterprises.

Comment

J. Bradford DeLong

LET ME START BY COMPLIMENTING MONTEK AHLUWALIA ON HIS LECTURE, WHICH provides an admirable overview of the remarkably good news about development that has been coming out of India for nearly two decades. Ahluwalia raises the kinds of questions that this lecture series should address, such as: How much of the remarkable increase in India's growth was due to its (relatively gradualist) reform program? To what extent were the seeds of the past two decades' rapid growth sown by previous investments in social capital and infrastructure (as Dani Rodrik argues in his attempt to create space for social democracy in a neoliberal world)? Were reforms properly sequenced and properly paced? And what remains to be done, in politics and economic policy, to build on the successes of the past two decades? Ahluwalia shows that he is a perfect choice to speak in this series, both because of his skills as an economic analyst and his skills and experience as a policymaker.

I could talk for more than an hour on many of the issues raised in Ahluwalia's lecture, many of which he mentions only in passing. These include:

- His reflections on technocrats' ability to push the limits of the politically possible during the economic reform process.

- The importance of political debate in generating legitimacy for privatization and other reforms.

- The importance of an open reform process (and here provide a sideways look at privatization by decree in Latin America, where a sudden and top-down process can generate backlash because privatization is viewed—sometimes fairly and sometimes unfairly—as another channel that a country's corrupt elites can use to exploit its people).

- The role of political democracy as a meta-institution for building good institutions.

- Sequencing, and how proper sequencing can build support for reform to the extent that the most clearly win-win reforms can be implemented first.

- The danger of slow sequencing and overly gradual reform dissipating political energy.

- How India shows that a reform program can maintain momentum despite major changes in the political climate.

- Liberalization of the capital account.

- How India has dragged its feet on reforming preferences for small-scale enterprises.

- Problems of reform in a federal system where some state governments are not seizing opportunities, whether reform can be sustained under these conditions, and if as a result the people of Uttar Pradesh, Bihar, and elsewhere are seeing income gains flowing to the south and the east but not to them.

But because my time is limited, I think that my remarks will be most valuable if I focus on one of the few topics Ahluwalia did not raise: what must happen in the rich postindustrial core of the world economy for global development to be rapid and successful over the next two generations.

Making Development Progress

The goal of development is clear: to achieve a truly human—or at least more human, and more humane—world, one where the number of people living lives far too close to those of our preindustrial ancestors is numbered at a hundred million rather than in the billions. India's development successes suggest a good way to move forward. Its best development path leads through terrain where computers and telecommunications, fiber optic cables and microprocessor switches, and satellites and packet-switched networks make international trade in many white-collar services (whether reading x-rays, supporting customers, or reconciling bills) as cheap and feasible as iron-hulled ocean-going steamships made trade in agricultural and industrial commodities in the late 19th century.

The gains from such services trade, for both emerging markets and rich postindustrial countries, are and will be immense. But markets function under the aegis of politics. Will rich countries have the political will to encourage rather than slow the growth of this trade?

In Germany in the late 19th century, political interference slowed trade. When the army officer-landlords of Prussia and Pomerania in eastern Germany recognized that the proletarians of Hamburg wanted cheap bread made using wheat imported from the U.S. state of Illinois rather than more costly bread made from Baltic shore-grown rye, they struck an alliance with the steelmasters of the Ruhr. The alliance resulted in tariffs on U.S. grain and British manufactures as well as more authoritarian rule to ensure that the government kept its thumb on the scales—elevating agricultural rents and industrial profits while depressing real wages. In Alexander Gerschenkron's view, as expressed in his *Bread and Democracy in Germany*, this was when German politics began to go horribly wrong.

I do not think there is any chance that the United States will repeat the foreign policy trajectory that Germany followed a hundred years ago and that made the first half of the 20th century in Europe so interesting. Still, somewhere within three blocks of where we are right now, the chair of the U.S. Council of Economic Advisers, N. Gregory Mankiw, is hiding from the many members of Congress denouncing his claim that outsourcing could be a source of strength and prosperity—rather than weakness and penury—for the U.S. economy.

These fears about outsourcing and trade in white-collar services will pass. They do not reflect the magnitude of this trade, but rather economic problems rooted in low aggregate demand. As the U.S. output gap closes, such fears will diminish. But they will return over the next generation, because the shifts in global employment resulting from comparative advantages in tradable services may be very large indeed.

Lessons for Rich Countries

Thus it is crucial that our reflections on development generate lessons not just for poor emerging market economies but also for rich postindustrial ones. Many of the development successes of the past generation would have been severely attenuated had rich countries, especially the United States, not been open to imports—the United States being the importer of last resort, as it were. And so it will be in the future.

So, to complement the lessons that Ahluwalia identifies for the future of India and for other developing countries that want to follow the path it has taken over the past two decades, I propose two lessons for rich countries. The first needs to be taught by all countries that export to the United States. They need to teach U.S. journalists, politicians, voters, and workers about the U.S. jobs that would not exist without those exports and about the benefits that flow from them—both directly from buyers and users and indirectly from the derived demand for U.S. exports that emerges as long as the Federal Reserve does its job and makes Say's Law hold in practice (even though it does not hold in theory). To make a truly human and humane world over the next two generations, rich country fears that expanding trade will destroy jobs and disrupt the economy need to be replaced by fears that reducing trade, or even failing to expand it, will lead to those same outcomes.

The second lesson is one that those of us voting in rich countries need to teach, and it is about national security. The 21st century will see civilization constantly at war against different forms of terrorism. An important part of that war will involve building a durable alliance among foes of terrorism, and increased world trade can be an important part of that process.

Moreover, I want my U.S. great-grandchildren to grow up in a world where children in India, China, and elsewhere are taught that the United States and other rich countries did a lot to boost economic growth and development around the world early in the 21st century. I do not want them to grow up in a world where children elsewhere are taught that the United States and other rich countries sought to keep them as poor as possible for as long as possible.

Comment

Nurul Islam

MONTEK AHLUWALIA, ONE OF INDIA'S LEADING DEVELOPMENT PRACTITIONERS, PRO-
vides an insightful analysis of his country's recent economic reforms. Because outsiders, especially in neighboring countries, are eager to draw lessons from this history,
my remarks will be colored by Bangladesh's experience.

Drivers of Reform

Successful policy reforms elsewhere in the world have depended on consensus,
commitment, and competence among policymakers and implementers. How and to
what extent did India achieve these features for the reforms undertaken in the 1990s?
According to Ahluwalia, after vigorous debates and discussions among and between
technocrats and policymakers in the 1980s, consensus emerged on the need for market liberalization. But it appears that it was not until the late 1980s that serious debate
on significant policy reforms reached India's inner policy circles and that conclusions
and consensus started to emerge within the government. And it was not until the
early 1990s that policy reforms were initiated.

   Moreover, several Indian analysts have suggested that two additional factors drove
the rethinking of Indian policy during the 1990s. The first was the collapse of the
Soviet Union—and with it, the retreat from socialism and communism in transition
economies. The second was careful analysis of the experiences of the East Asian "miracle" economies, which in many circles had become models for successful growth
and poverty reduction through private enterprise and free market policies. Thus
there was a significant time lag involved in policy debates leading to consensus on
reforms within the Indian government. This carries an important lesson for other
developing countries and their development partners.

   Implementation of India's policy reforms was triggered by its balance of payments
crisis of 1990–91. There is nothing like an economic crisis to focus the minds of policymakers, making it relatively easy to reach consensus and neutralize opposition to

reforms. Ahluwalia asserts that the reform package was homegrown and not imposed by donors.

But there was an intermediate situation between reforms being imposed by donors and being totally homegrown. It was this process of negotiation in the intermediate situation—which only insiders know—that could provide valuable lessons for other developing countries. Thus it would be useful to know whether India presented a program to the International Monetary Fund (IMF) and the IMF looked at it, liked it, and offered the needed assistance without any comments, suggestions, or changes. If the IMF (or other donors) had suggestions or recommendations, did India reject them outright, or did it accept some and reject others—and if so, why? There is also the question of whether there was any deviation from or shortfall in implementation of the agreed program—and if there was, was there any reaction from the IMF (or other donors)? The answers to these kinds of questions would be of enormous interest to development practitioners elsewhere.

To cite a different example of a neighboring country, many reforms in Bangladesh, in both crisis and noncrisis situations, have been driven by donors. This is because Bangladesh is much more dependent on foreign aid than India is or was. Two other factors also contribute to the dominant role that donors play in Bangladesh's policy reforms: the country's limited capacity to formulate, analyze, and negotiate policies and programs, and its small size, economic strength, and political and strategic importance. India, like China, is much better positioned in these two aspects and so commands considerable leverage and bargaining power relative to donors. I would have liked for Ahluwalia to indicate how much leverage India has in such negotiations.

Reforms occur under both crisis and noncrisis conditions. To reach consensus in noncrisis situations, policymakers have to engage in much more bargaining with various interest groups than they do in crisis situations, when opposition is naturally muted. Building consensus in a democracy is an untidy, arduous, time-consuming process involving negotiations within the party in power, between politicians and technocrats (or bureaucrats), and between political parties that may have very different approaches—especially when the opposition party seeks to make it difficult for the ruling party to govern, and not necessarily because it has a different view on policy.

Approaches to Reform

In recent decades India has implemented the same reforms as many other developing countries, including privatization, decontrol, deregulation, and trade liberalization. But the pace and sequence of reforms have differed across countries. Bangladesh introduced trade liberalization earlier and pursued it more quickly and extensively until the mid-1990s. Still, even in the early 2000s Bangladesh's average customs duty was less than India's, though India's tariff structure was more uniform.

Moreover, Bangladesh virtually eliminated quantitative restrictions in the 1980s—while India maintained them, especially on consumer goods, until 2001, based on a balance of payments waiver provided by the World Trade Organization (WTO). India eliminated quantitative restrictions only when a WTO panel, in response to a complaint from the European Union and the United States, ruled against it. This is an example of reform that was not homegrown, but imposed by the WTO.

Similarly, regulations on foreign direct investment (FDI) were only haltingly or partially relaxed in India during the 1990s, whereas Bangladesh and other neighboring countries went quite far in liberalizing such investment during the 1980s. Why was liberalization slower in India than in neighboring countries? Was it because import-competing sectors were more politically powerful in India and able to obstruct the scope and speed of liberalization?

India's reforms slowed in the late 1990s. Was this slowdown the result of a conscious policy of gradualism, or of negotiations with interest groups that slowed the liberalization process? Making matters worse, as India liberalized tariffs, it resorted to extensive use of antidumping duties and soon became the second most prolific user of antidumping duties (after the United States, as reported by the WTO). Was this because there was a breakdown of consensus among technocrats (or bureaucrats) or between them and politicians? Was it due to a lingering desire among policymakers for the old strategy of import substitution and self-sufficiency? Or was it the result of intense opposition by producer groups facing import competition?

Ahluwalia is right to emphasize that liberalization requires a roadmap with clearly defined goals, and that in a democracy it is not feasible to undertake shock therapy or rapid liberalization. He does not mention the importance of mobilizing public opinion. Politicians seeking public support can go over the heads of interest groups—and nothing succeeds like success. India's recent international success in the information technology, biochemical, and pharmaceutical industries creates confidence in its ability to compete in global markets, and may persuade policymakers that risks involved in further liberalization are well worth taking.

As elsewhere, it appears that in India crisis-driven macroeconomic reforms are easier than sector reforms in industry, labor markets, and infrastructure such as energy, transportation, and communications. Sector reforms take longer to implement and produce results, and often involve institutional reforms and restructuring—sometimes including changes in the legal framework. Interest groups adversely affected by sector reforms are better organized and put up more powerful opposition.

Agriculture remains the Achilles' heel of India's reform saga. In addition to high import protection, the sector receives generous input subsidies—such as for electricity, water, and fertilizer—equal to about 9 percent of agricultural value added. Landed interests in heavily agricultural states may be powerful enough in national and local politics to prevent reforms in the sector.

In Bangladesh agriculture is an example of successful policy reforms. Reforms followed a long period of public debates, workshops, and conferences based on considerable empirical analysis and research encouraged and supported by donors. Policymakers and civil servants were continuously exposed to these findings, and used them to guide discussions within the government and with donors. Reforms were implemented gradually but consistently and persistently. Trade and domestic market reforms occurred in fits and starts, with bursts of reforms alternating with slow or no reforms, starting in the early 1980s and continuing through the late 1990s.

Liberalization of imports and deregulation of domestic markets for inputs, combined with their abundant supply, contributed to increased food production in Bangladesh. These changes were followed by liberalization of output markets. The impact of higher, market-determined food prices on poor people was cushioned by targeted distribution through various safety net measures. Efforts were made to maintain adequate food stocks, supported by imports and food aid, though there were occasional price hikes in agricultural inputs and outputs. The success of each reform encouraged the next steps, and the impacts of early reforms were monitored—mitigating policymakers' apprehensions and uncertainties about the possible adverse effects of policy reforms.

One of the mysteries of Indian financial policy, at least to outsiders, is the combination of large budget deficits (the combined deficits of central and state governments are estimated to equal about 10 percent of GDP) and falling interest rates. Falling interest rates are considered an important reason for growing private investment. But what about the conventional wisdom that large and growing deficits lead to rising interest rates, crowding out private investment? Does that assumption not hold because the deficits are domestically financed, through large private savings and borrowing from a compliant banking system dominated by state-owned banks? And if so, is there a limit to the continuation of this policy?

Privatization and deregulation, combined with competing and divergent fiscal and financial incentives provided by India's state governments to attract private investment, have led to growing regional disparities in investment and income. Ahluwalia suggests that India should rely on market forces to generate high average growth across the country, claiming that although this approach would not mitigate regional or personal income disparities, it would reduce poverty. He apparently believes that the dampening effect of higher income inequality on the impact of income growth on poverty reduction is not a matter of great concern—and that in any case, not much can be done about it except aim for accelerated income growth. But what about the possibility that rising interpersonal income inequality and the growing gap between urban and rural incomes will increase sociopolitical tensions, with adverse consequences on growth itself?

Would the large-scale movement of workers from slow-growing to fast-growing states ease regional disparities? Is there a room for policy incentives to facilitate such a process? Would long-awaited labor market reforms help or hinder it? These questions remain unanswered. Ahluwalia asks, with some skepticism, whether it is possible to quantify the contribution that India's poverty alleviation measures (as distinguished from income growth) have made to poverty reduction. Experiences from other countries indicate that these measures, in combination with growth-promoting policies, reduce poverty. The relevant objective is to improve the cost-effectiveness and the targeting of such measures. Cost-effectiveness is equally important for growth-promoting measures.

Ahluwalia does not discuss the relevance of governance—that is, the quality and integrity of institutions (including civil administration), the rule of law, contract and property rights, and so on—and its impact on economic policymaking, implementation, and performance. Are not interstate differences in economic performance largely due, at least in some cases, to differences in the quality of governance? Alternatively, could it be that governance issues have little impact on India's economic policies and performance; and that in recent years the development community has placed undue emphasis on governance? Or is the quality of governance the result, rather than the cause, of superior economic performance and development? Under that process good policies and technology would generate growth momentum, starting the process of improvements in governance that would, in turn, reinforce growth momentum.

Outstanding Issues

Two aspects of India's policy reforms and their impacts on growth remain controversial. Ahluwalia discusses one, which relates to how much import controls and other policies in place until the 1970s and 1980s provided the foundation on which growth was built in the 1990s, facilitated by policy reforms. He does not rule out the possibility that past policies contributed to the development of managerial talents and entrepreneurial abilities. During the 1980s individuals with those skills responded to the incentives offered for the expansion of capacity and to the liberal availability of intermediate inputs administered by a refocused import control and investment licensing regime. As private entrepreneurs gained strength and confidence, they responded vigorously to the opportunities created by market liberalization in the 1990s. Although Ahluwalia recognizes that there is no rigorous way to establish a counterfactual either way, he believes that the growth of the 1980s was not sustainable for long given the severe macroeconomic imbalances fed by large foreign borrowing and that the reforms of the 1990s were essential for growth to be sustained.

A second issue is the extent to which the policies of the 1960s and 1970s for building a highly skilled labor force (through large investments in scientific, technological, managerial, and business education), combined with generous support for public sector research and development, provided a strong basis for subsequent growth in response to changes in incentives and market opening. For example, India's widely acclaimed and successful pharmaceutical and information technology industries owe much to these policies. At the time these policies were highly controversial, and criticized as a sign of distorted priorities and elitist bias in favor of higher education at the expense of literacy and primary education—in a country where a vast share of the population lacked literacy skills and primary education. Critics argue that the low priority given to productivity-enhancing primary education sacrificed long-run gains in income growth greater than the current and future gains from the elitist education policies.

What is the appropriate balance between primary, secondary, and tertiary education in the process of growth? Quantifying the productivity gains from primary education, including the externalities generated by it, remains a challenging and unsettled task. After all, is not primary education a basic human right and therefore an end in itself? This controversy is relevant for other developing countries as they set priorities for education. I hope that researchers, analysts, and policymakers like Ahluwalia throw light on this important component of development strategy.

Comment

Richard Eckaus

I AM PLEASED TO BE PARTICIPATING IN THIS SYMPOSIUM, AND AM GRATEFUL TO THE organizers for inviting me—particularly because I see so many old friends in the audience. In the interests of full disclosure, I should mention that I consider myself a friend of Montek Ahluwalia and of his influential wife, Isher Judge Ahluwalia, who is also a prominent economist.

Mistakes Made on the Road to Reforms

Montek was and is an excellent civil servant. As an irresponsible academic, I can say bluntly and emphatically what his lecture acknowledges only infrequently and diplomatically about India's recent economic reforms and how they were developed: there were big mistakes. The biggest mistakes occurred before Montek arrived on the scene, and he should not be held responsible for those that followed. Though he may be larger than life, he is not larger than the Indian government.

It is not surprising that mistakes were made. Everyone makes mistakes—even irresponsible academics. Yet in India enormous mistakes in economic policy were allowed to persist throughout the 1970s and 1980s. According to Montek, it was not until the second half of the 1980s that the need for bolder economic policies was widely discussed, and even then it took a long time for reforms to start being implemented. Why did it take two decades of disappointing economic performance to generate extensive discussions about the need for change?

Economics provides only part of the answer to this question. Ideology was crucial, both in political parties and among economists and civil servants. In addition, private sector interests opposed to change put pressure on policymakers. Finally, some blame must be assigned to the economists who specialized in these matters, for maintaining beliefs and supporting policies that so clearly were not producing growth or equity. I would give much less weight to the problem of complexity than does Montek.

There were smaller mistakes as well as bigger ones. As an example of a smaller one, consider the mistake India made when trying to attract private investment in the electric power sector. Montek says it was originally believed that attracting private investment would require nothing more than granting necessary permits and signing power purchase agreements. How could anyone have thought that? It was well-known that low, irrational energy prices and faults in the distribution system made it impossible to cover generation and transmission costs. Thus prices would have to be corrected and the distribution system drastically changed to make private investment feasible. Every nongovernmental economist I talked to in India knew that; I cannot believe that the government was not aware of it. But again, for reasons that are not purely economic and that Montek does not explain, this mistake was not recognized.

Why Gradualism?

Montek argues, quite correctly, that India's gradual approach to economic reform was more successful than rapid, comprehensive change would have been. To my mind, the rationale for a big bang approach to economic reform was never much more than an inapt metaphor. A market system involves an extraordinarily complex set of institutions, and to think that they could all be developed at once has always struck me as a basic error—an error that has had enormous costs in many countries.

Still, many questions have been raised about the origins of and support for India's policy of gradualism. Was it an intellectual decision, or were there other sources? Comparing gradualism in China and India, I have the impression that in China gradualism has been a calculated and intentional approach to reform. I do not think that the Chinese authorities have always known exactly what they want in the final pattern of their economy, but they have resolved to move forward step by step, testing as they go. And though gradualism has to some extent been the product of internal party and government disputes, China has always given the impression that it is firmly committed to moving to a market economy.

Montek gives three reasons for gradualism in India: a conscious choice, or intellectual decision, to stretch out reforms; a lack of consensus within government, either within or between technocrats and politicians; and an inadequate appreciation of the complexity of the policy changes needed. I believe that his second reason, a lack of consensus on reform, carries the greatest weight. As indirect evidence, consider the slow growth of foreign private investment in India. The impression given to potential foreign investors was, and to some extent still is, that market reforms in India are uncertain in many dimensions. That impression reflects a lack of consensus that, in turn, suggests to foreign investors that the reforms could be at least partially reversed.

When I first visited China in the mid-1980s, I asked myself why any private investor would want to risk investing there rather than in India. China's market system was more limited, there were more price and allocation controls, there was no legal system with clear protection for property rights, state-owned enterprises dominated many important sectors, and government decisionmaking was opaque at best. Thus the investment climate in India seemed much more favorable.

Despite all that, for many years China has attracted much more foreign investment than India. Why? I think it is because of India's lack of consensus on reforms and, as a result, external uncertainty about India's commitment to them. In India openness to conflicting opinions is an essential part of its democracy, and those conflicting opinions are never voiced silently; they are voiced loudly and emphatically. For example, Montek hints at disagreements within the bureaucracy, which I think were intense— and may have made proponents of reform too bashful in making their case.

I think that Montek overlooks another cause of gradualism in India: official corruption. This can be a delicate subject, but everyone knows it exists—in India, in China, and in most other nations. The general view seems to be that the Indian and Chinese bureaucracies were born in a state of innocence that they subsequently lost.

After independence, India's bureaucracy was recognized as being upright and competent. Before economic reforms, China's bureaucracy had special privileges, but those seemed to be largely institutional rather than personal. The subsequent corruption of the Indian and Chinese bureaucracies resulted from quite different economic forces.

India's bureaucracy was corrupted by its extensive regulations and controls. This system created rents and potential gains for businesses that could exploit it, and made enterprises more than willing to corrupt bureaucrats to obtain privileges. China's bureaucracy, on the other hand, was corrupted by the process of reform, which also offered gains for enterprises. But in China the gains came from the granting of privileges to exploit potential markets.

Thus the corruption of the Indian bureaucracy was in favor of the status quo, while the corruption of the Chinese bureaucracy was in favor of reform. This difference must have affected the character and speed of reforms. The corruption of China's bureaucracy increased the pace of enterprise investment and marketization of the economy. The corruption of India's bureaucracy, on the other hand, contributed to the gradualism of reforms.

Economic and Political Challenges in India

Some of India's most difficult economic and political issues involve the relationships between the central and state governments and the varying economic and social conditions among states. Montek says, quite rightly, that these issues have been exacerbated by the increasing importance of state governments and political parties. Central government responsibilities for state government deficits and central government standards for state government activities are among the country's most contentious political and economic issues.

But these issues are not only economic. The growing strength of state political parties has sharply reduced the central government's leverage in dealing with states. Moreover, there have been significant failures to improve economic and social conditions in the agriculture sector. Short-term changes in the overall prosperity of the Indian economy remain largely driven by monsoon cycles. Good monsoons mean increased prosperity and faster growth, while bad monsoons mean that everything slows down.

Monsoons are acts of God. But their consequences depend, to a considerable extent, on the acts of humans. The antidotes to bad monsoons are well-known: more irrigation and more efficient use of irrigation. Although India has made large increases in irrigated land, further large increases are needed. They will be expensive, but the consequences of not having them are also expensive.

Mitigating the effects of monsoon cycles on agricultural production would help even out economic cycles throughout India's economy. It would also help raise incomes in rural areas, where India's poverty is concentrated. But as Montek points out, other measures are needed to bring rural populations the benefits of economic reform and progress.

More efficient agricultural production is impeded by misplaced subsidies for fertilizer, electricity, and irrigation water and by misplaced support prices for agricultural outputs. Economic reforms have, as yet, done little to reduce these, and here again the obstacles are often due to the political power of state political parties. Yet conditions are desperate in rural areas.

Assessing India's Reforms

How should India's economic reforms be judged overall? It is too early to conduct a final assessment, and will be for some time. But a progress report can be made, and must praise the reforms for shaking up the old system. That system, heavy with regulations and controls, tried to shape India's future as one where no one would go hungry—yet hunger persisted in part because of economic policy mistakes, which often originated in ideology.

The old system also meant that Indians would share to only a limited extent in the extraordinary advances in welfare and individual development that modern life makes possible. Though there are things to criticize in the extent and manners of the reforms, there is much for which credit must be given. And a substantial amount of that credit should go to Montek Ahluwalia, who was a major force in shaping the reforms.

Finally, let me assume my old role as a teacher. I see many young faces in this audience, generously listening to the older people speaking before you. What should young people learn from India's reform experience? Certainly, more understanding about what has happened there. But there is also a general lesson: mistakes are inevitable, but they can be reduced by continued skeptical examination of policies and ideas—including one's own.

Zhou Xiaochuan

Governor, People's Bank of China

Born in 1948, Zhou Xiaochuan graduated from the Beijing Chemical Engineering Institute in 1975. He received his Ph.D. in economic-systems engineering from Qinghua University in 1985. In 1986, he became a member in the Economic System Reform Steering Group of the State Council (a post he held until 1987), the same year he became deputy director of the Institute of Chinese Economic System Reform and Research and a member of the National Committee on Economic System Reform. He also served as assistant minister of foreign trade from 1986 to 1989.

Dr. Zhou's direct affiliation with the banking sector began with his joining the board of the Bank of China (BOC) as an executive director in 1991. He ascended to BOC vice president in 1995, the same year that he also became head of the State Administration of Foreign Exchange (SAFE). In November 1996, while retaining the SAFE post, he moved on to the vice governorship of the People's Bank of China (PBC), a position he held for a little over a year. In February 1998, he was appointed president of the China Construction Bank (CCB), and in April that year he relinquished his SAFE post. Dr. Zhou held the position of CCB president until 2000, when he became Chairman of the China Securities Regulatory Commission (CSRC). In January 2003, he was appointed Governor of PBC and became the chairman of the China Monetary Policy Committee.

In addition, Dr. Zhou is an honorary president and professor in the business school of the University of Science and Technology of China, a professor at the graduate school of the PBC, and a professor at the Qinghua University School of Management. He has published over 10 books and over 100 academic articles in Chinese and international journals. Moreover, he won more than once the Sun Yefang Economic Science Dissertation Prize, the highest prize in Chinese economic studies. In 1986, collaborating with others, Dr. Zhou carried out a research project on General Quantitative Analysis and Policy Simulation and won the first prize for China Technological Advancement.

10 China's Recent Reforms

Zhou Xiaochuan

IN THE LATE 1970S CHINA BEGAN IMPLEMENTING WIDE-RANGING ECONOMIC reforms, shifting to a socialist market economy. In the early 1990s many other countries embarked on economic transitions, moving from centrally planned to market economies. These processes shared similar objectives and mechanisms—but there were also important differences.

This essay first considers the foundations of planned and market economies, and analyzes the possible approaches to shifting from one system to the other. It then discusses China's experiences, including its reforms in trade practices, banking systems, capital markets, and state-owned enterprises. Finally, the essay addresses the key question raised by this lecture series: what would China have done differently in the 1990s had it known then what it knows now?

Reforms in Centrally Planned Economies

Centrally planned and market economies have very different theoretical starting points. Market economies generally achieve general equilibrium, with partial equilibrium in each economic sector, and markets clear based on market prices and production functions in each sector. There are no cross-sector subsidies; any redistribution is the result of fiscal policy designed to support a specific development strategy and income redistribution goal.

Centrally planned economies are completely different. Historically, their top priority was to promote industrialization, an approach financed by highly distorted prices. Thus in some centrally planned economies, such as China, the industrialization strategy resulted in agriculture subsidizing industry, because prices for agricultural goods were set artificially low to provide affordable inputs for industry. Similarly, the consumer goods industry subsidized heavy industry. In addition, exporters subsidized importers—especially heavy industry importers, enabling them to buy equipment and raw materials very cheaply. Centrally planned economies also maintained other obstacles to the free movement of resources, capital, and labor to protect heavy industry and advance industrialization.

One approach to market-oriented reform is to quickly and radically correct all these types of distortions. But that approach is likely to make inefficient enterprises and sectors become insolvent or cease operations, resulting in higher unemployment and lower per capita income and savings.

Rapid restructuring can also have other undesirable outcomes. In the banking sector, for example, if prudential standards are implemented overnight and firms are assessed according to their creditworthiness, there will be few qualified borrowers. As a result banking activities may shrink. Thus a lot of redistribution is needed in the transition from centrally planned to market economies—but such redistribution may cause social and economic instability.

Another approach to market reform is to implement change gradually. Under this approach the first step is to reduce policy biases against agriculture, the consumer goods industry, and exporters. But subsidies for heavy industry are not eliminated immediately, so sufficient room and time are needed for this type of restructuring.

When countries began moving away from central planning, no one knew whether rapid or gradual restructuring was more likely to achieve desired goals. But for China and many other transition economies, gradual restructuring seemed to be the better choice. It was clear that such reforms would require additional resources, especially financial resources. So, despite operating in a confusing environment during the reform period, banks had to be active intermediaries.

Because market-oriented reform requires enormous changes in trade systems, one of the most pressing issues for a transition economy is how to adjust its approach to foreign trade. Established market economies rely on the General Agreement on Tariffs and Trade (GATT) to regulate their trade activities. In formerly socialist countries—such as those in Eastern Europe and the former Soviet Union—the equivalent organization was the Council for Mutual Economic Assistance (CMEA), which was dissolved in 1991.

The CMEA was based on some of the same principles as GATT, the main ones being that different countries have different comparative advantages and that trade can benefit all the member countries of the organization. But GATT is based on market rules, while the CMEA was based on central planning and involved more country-specific negotiations among members.

The CMEA provoked negative sentiment among many of its members because the Soviet Union—as an economic giant and global superpower—often treated smaller member countries unfairly. Still, abandoning the CMEA was not really an option for such countries, because doing so would have meant giving up the trade benefits it provided.

After the CMEA was abolished, its former members began looking for new trade partners, particularly in Western Europe. But many transition economies could not make the swift changes in production quality and worker skills required for trade with more advanced economies. Because reduced trade with other transition economies was not compensated by increased trade elsewhere, there was a sharp drop in foreign trade—causing a decline in overall production.

Although consumers in transition economies wanted to buy the higher-quality goods produced in Western countries, they did not have enough money to do so. Per capita incomes were low, and foreign exchange reserves were small. Moreover, product standards—like living standards—differ across countries at different levels of development, and often change slowly. Given the financial difficulties facing transition economies, it may have been unreasonable for their consumers to suddenly expect to have higher-quality goods from more advanced economies. Indeed, if former Soviet Union countries, Eastern European countries, and China had been more realistic, they could have maintained a trade system like the CMEA, which probably would have been beneficial. Instead, in the early 1990s trade and production plummeted in transition economies, causing a sharp increase in unemployment.

China's Experiences

How do China's experiences compare with those of other transition economies? One of the biggest differences is that China introduced economic reforms and openness much earlier, in the late 1970s. Still, like other transition economies—and partly in response to the developments there—it underwent significant changes in the 1990s.

China's reform philosophy aims to provide immediate benefits, because if reforms caused suffering the population might not support them. By contrast, if the government can show the benefits of reforms, it will be more likely to win support and maintain momentum for them.

Trade

By the early 1990s China had already achieved relatively strong, diversified trade performance. Thus it was not overly concerned about its trade with other transition economies, because such activity accounted for a small share of its total trade.

Still, at the time China had solid trade relationships with its neighbors—Kazakhstan, the Kyrgyz Republic, Mongolia, Myanmar, Russia, Tajikistan, Vietnam—mainly involving low-quality goods and barter or counter trade, as well as some "normal" trade in goods (such as oil or natural gas) paid for with hard currency. But then Russia decided to pursue a new approach, and sought instead to trade only in high-quality goods, cease barter and counter trade, and rely solely on payments in hard currency.

As in other transition economies, however, few Russian consumers could afford such imports. The country had limited foreign exchange, and its banks were incapable of handling trade settlement and finance. Customs performance was also weak, with a lot of so-called agreed inspections, agreed tariffs, and corruption.

In the early 1990s trade performance was especially strong in two parts of China. Shenzhen City, which is close to Hong Kong, grew quickly because of its convenient and efficient trade facilities, while Heilongjiang, a northeastern province near Russia, was a rising star because of fast-growing border and counter trade. But after Russia changed its approach, Heilongjiang and its Russian trade partners experienced declining production.

Today Heilongjiang is one of China's most economically challenged provinces, which also hurts Russia. The same outcomes have occurred in Kazakhstan and Mongolia, because these countries have also abandoned traditional (barter and counter) trade with China. At the same time, China's trade with Myanmar, Vietnam, and other neighbors has developed quite smoothly, because these countries accept renminbi in trade transactions.

Fiscal resources and the financial sector

As noted, the gradual approach to market reform and restructuring requires additional resources, particularly in the financial sector. In China the first major reform was to liberalize agricultural prices, which required finding other resources to subsidize industrialization. In addition, although the exchange rate was raised to reduce subsidies for importers, new sources were found to maintain import subsidies. Similarly, heavy industry was no longer subsidized by the consumer goods industry, but it too found new sources of support.

Such changes, introduced in the 1980s, continue today. Thus China's gradual approach to reform has meant continued reliance on cross-sector subsidies. Though not economically optimal, such reallocations seem unavoidable. At the same time, steps have been taken to achieve Pareto improvements—strengthening the economy, providing widespread benefits, achieving reform momentum—with reforms reflecting financial results and constraints.

Reflecting the textbook concept of reform needs, fiscal support was required to achieve these outcomes. Yet during the 1980s there was a drop in fiscal resources because subsidies—including tax breaks—were increasing, especially for weak sectors. Moreover, financial discipline and accounting standards were weak, tax reform was proceeding slowly, and tax collectors were often corrupt. As a result tax revenue fell. Thus China realized that it would have to rely on other resources and that it would have to be selective in pursuing needed reforms.

In 1979 China's tax collections were 28 percent of GDP. But by 2003 they were only about 10 percent—the lowest level among developing countries. In addition to the widespread tax cuts and other weaknesses, fiscal resources have fallen because of government policy toward commercial banks. For example, the government has encouraged banks to lend to new companies that have no capital, allowing them to borrow at 100 percent leverage in an effort to create new enterprises. This approach has generated enormous nonperforming loans for banks.

The government has also encouraged banks to support state-owned enterprises in order to sustain their production, maintain employment, import equipment, promote new technology, and train workers in new skills. In addition, banks have sometimes supported social restructuring and welfare programs, and until 1995 they occasionally financed government deficit spending. Though such efforts may be considered crucial to economic transition, they have absorbed a massive amount of bank resources and worsened the problem of nonperforming loans.

Over time, however, the role of banks has changed. Accounting, borrowing, and other standards have improved, and some insolvent banks have been closed. And with fewer customers qualified as borrowers, banking activity has shrunk and banks have played a smaller role in financing reforms. Moreover, as with other changes, bank reforms have been more gradual in China than in other transition economies.

Still, China has experienced some of the banking problems that have plagued other transition economies. It also suffered damage from the East Asian financial crisis in 1997–98. Accordingly, many analysts have questioned whether China can resolve the high level of nonperforming loans and address other bank weaknesses.

But the East Asian crisis also provided China with valuable lessons, leading it to change its lending culture and end government intervention in the market for bank credit. As a result, since 1998 the proportion of nonperforming loans has been cut in half, and industrial restructuring and policy loans have been almost entirely phased out. Thus many bank issues have been addressed, either through regulation or legislation. Moreover, China recently began restructuring state-owned banks—including improving their capital adequacy, establishing good corporate governance systems, and listing them in the stock market to strengthen market discipline. The Central Bank of China is confident that it can overcome remaining difficulties.

Because of these improvements, fiscal resources have become much stronger in recent years. In addition, foreign exchange reserves and gold reserves are high, as are broad money and the savings rate. The recovery of the banking system has also been aided by the global economy, which has enabled a reasonable interest rate spread and encouraged foreign investment.

Stock market development

In an effort to provide alternatives to fiscal resources, China began developing a stock market in the early 1990s. But this move was fraught with challenges, including shortcomings related to the market's mentality, legitimacy, and training. For example, at that time there were very low standards for accounting, disclosure, initial public offerings (IPOs), and secondary offerings, and China did not have a company law or a securities law.

If international standards had been used, not many companies would have been of high enough quality to be listed. Though efforts were made to choose good companies, by international standards the listed companies were weak. Many were undercapitalized, so they desperately needed equity financing. These companies also issued corporate bonds—and there have been many defaults.

The stock market absorbs excess liquidity in the economy to reduce inflationary pressures, making it easier for the government to achieve stability while pursuing reforms. Until the East Asian financial crisis the market was also used to support state-owned enterprises, but that approach has been abandoned.

From the outset China has sought to implement good market rules. Emphasis has been placed on strengthening standards for accounting, disclosure, and corporate governance. In addition, the government has recognized the importance of supervision and professionalism, to fight fraud and price manipulations. Efforts have also been made to attract and educate institutional investors—because when the market was formed, there were none.

To support capital market services, China needed good accounting firms, law firms, rating agencies, and evaluation agencies. Thus it has allowed foreign service providers to enter the Chinese market—while working hard to develop domestic ones, which usually take a long time to mature.

The stock market has also required new legislation. In the mid-1990s a company law was introduced, and in 1998 a securities law. The bankruptcy law is being revised, and collective investment laws are being developed. In addition, the government is considering whether to compensate some investors who lost money on companies that were listed improperly, though it is not clear where those resources would come from.

These efforts have dramatically improved corporate governance in China. Because rules for capital markets are completely different from those for domestic enterprises, there has been widespread reform of state enterprises. Thus the higher standards that have resulted from developing the stock exchange have provided benefits beyond its direct economic effects.

China's stock market has a market capitalization equal to 40–50 percent of GDP—a decent size. More than 1,300 companies are listed, and the average daily trade volume is $2.5 billion. In addition, overseas listings of Chinese companies have market capitalization of 20–30 percent of GDP.[1]

Many issues remain to be addressed in the development of China's capital markets. For instance, the stock market has created nonperforming loans for banks, because some companies have (illegally) used bank loans to speculate in the stock market. With the recent market downturn, these investments became bad loans.

Moreover, it is an enormous task to build discipline and investor confidence in capital markets. But doing so is crucial to raising productivity and creating new wealth, as China did in the 1990s. High economic growth was maintained, exports were strong, and employment and worker income levels improved considerably. In addition, the savings rate rose from 32 percent in 1990 to 38 percent in the late 1990s—and recently reached 40 percent, which is probably too high.

State-owned enterprises

Although most Western economists do not believe that failing state-owned enterprises can be revived, China has managed to do so. In many cases the financial situation of these firms was not especially dire, and to date one-third have been successfully restructured. They have undergone partial privatizations, forming joint ventures with private or foreign investors, and then gone public—increasing government resources.

Another third of state enterprises have failed, and have been closed or soon will be, creating nonperforming loans and pension liabilities. For the other third the outcome remains to be seen. They are struggling. Perhaps parts of them will succeed, and parts will fail. Most are still producing low-quality products, and some have high pension burdens.

Labor market rigidity and low labor mobility have inhibited faster changes in weak state enterprises. And indeed, the change in state-owned activity has been slow, with state enterprises accounting for 50 percent of GDP in 1994 and 48 percent in 2002. The reason is that even though one-third of state enterprises—including large ones—have been successfully reformed, state control exceeds 51 percent in many that have become joint ventures.

In response, the government has begun promoting foreign-funded enterprises, leading to rapid growth in such firms. The government has decided that mixed ownership is the most effective approach, where the state owns part of enterprises but is not in a controlling position. This approach has contributed to rising exports and savings rates. In addition, broad money (M2) has shown constant growth, reaching 180 percent of GDP in 2002—compared with 30–40 percent in most transition economies. Thus resources are being generated to support further development and reforms, and to address the challenges identified above.

Remaining challenges

From the outset, the Chinese government has been able to maintain momentum for needed reforms. Despite occasional opposition from interest groups and bureaucrats, there has always been tremendous public support.

Still, several challenges remain, the most important being nonperforming loans and capital market distortions. The government recognizes that weak standards in these areas create tensions with investors. Moreover, because World Trade Organization (WTO) commitments do not pay much attention to capital markets, openness in China's capital markets has proceeded slowly—especially relative to the banking sector, the insurance sector, and trade in industry and services.

Conclusion

In summary, during the 1990s China took a gradual approach to reforms, and made efforts to diversify sources of financing for them. The government also did its best to achieve Pareto improvements—as well as resolve any problems remaining or created during the decade. In addition, clear targets were set for the final stages of the economic transition.

The question posed by this lecture series is, what would Chinese policymakers have done differently had they known in 1990 what they know now? And the answer is, the approach probably would not have differed much. China's path in the 1990s was determined half by design and half by compromise. At the time few economies had addressed the issues surrounding the transition from state to market, and many Chinese people—including government officials—disliked the shock therapy approach. They underestimated the importance of financial sector problems, and they retained a strong belief in state enterprises. Such beliefs strongly influenced decisionmaking.

One possible area of improvement would have involved introducing better, earlier tax reform; tax collections are still a huge problem in China. In addition, it would have been helpful if steps had been taken sooner to address intergovernmental fiscal issues—the relationship between the central government and local and municipal governments.

In addition, despite the banking reform inspired by the East Asian crisis, China moved slower than it could have. Moreover, China could have had more effective negotiations with other transition economies, including members of the Commonwealth of Independent States and Central and Eastern European countries, to avoid declining trade and production.

The final area of potential improvement involves the pension liabilities of China's state-owned enterprises. During the 1990s the World Bank and International Monetary Fund (IMF) constantly urged China to address two of its biggest economic problems: nonperforming loans and pension liabilities. As noted, nonperforming loans have been reduced as part of banking reform. Net pension liabilities remain a serious problem—and an implicit fiscal liability. It is unclear whether the government will have enough resources to cover this liability, which is much larger than that created by nonperforming loans. Thus a huge task remains in addressing the sustainability of the country's pay as you go pension system.

Note

1. Other transition economies also introduced stock exchanges in the early 1990s. Some started earlier, partly because of voucher privatization, which sometimes provided a strong initial boost to capital market development. Still, market capitalization in many transition economies, such as the Czech Republic and Poland, is only 10–20 percent of GDP. In the best performer, Slovenia, it is more than 40 percent. But in others—Bulgaria, Romania, Ukraine, some Central Asian economies—capitalization is less than 5 percent of GDP. Recently, however, there have been some positive developments; for instance, Kazakhstan developed corporate bond markets quite smoothly.

Comment

C. Fred Bergsten

Zhou Xiaochuan provides an incredibly rich panorama of China's development story, including how it compares with other transition economies and where things stand today. He emphasizes the importance of trade for China's development strategy, including the need for major changes in the country's trade system. I will make a few remarks on that issue and then relate it to two of the biggest threats to China's continued rapid growth and development—and how those might best be resolved.

Of all the impressive elements of China's development strategy, the one that has long stood out in my mind is its dramatic trade opening—particularly its use of trade opening, integration with the world economy, participation in international institutions, and globalization more broadly, including in the financial domain (as Zhou stresses), to promote domestic economic reforms. That point was made most clearly and dramatically to a small meeting I attended with former President Jiang Zemin just after he had negotiated China's World Trade Organization (WTO) entry with the United States in the late 1990s. He said, in perfect English, that he considered China's entry to the WTO to be closely related to his country's "deep sleep" during its feudal period while the West was advancing smartly after the Reformation.

I took that to refer to the famous episode when the British ambassador visited the Chinese emperor in 1793 and said that Britain was ready to trade—and the emperor dismissed him, saying Britain had nothing that China needed. Thus China consciously rejected the first era of globalization in the 19th century. As a result it wound up a failed state, with one of the world's poorest economies and a polity carved up by the world's colonial powers more than a hundred years ago. China's current leadership has devoted itself to avoiding that mistake.

In recent decades China has globalized and opened to the world economy at one of the fastest rates of any country, with trade (exports plus imports) now accounting for more than half of its GDP—four times the level of 30 years ago. Similarly, the United States has tripled its opening to the world economy over the past 30–40 years. Together these two locomotives of the world economy provide clear evidence of the general results that many researchers have found on the close correlation and, indeed, causal relationship between increased globalization and economic development.

Moreover, as noted, China has used its participation in the international economic system—especially the WTO—and its adherence to the system's rules to help overcome opposition to domestic economic reforms. International agreements have often provided a basis for proceeding with the needed changes in internal policies identified by Zhou. Recently, for example, Vice Premier Wu Yi was in Washington, D.C. to negotiate changes in China's intellectual property rules and technical standards that will further promote the reform, liberalization, opening, and success of the Chinese economy.

Thus I think it would be tragic if China were to be hit by protectionist trade measures imposed by the United States or other countries—which is a serious risk. In recent months the United States has dramatically tightened its quotas for textile and apparel imports, brought cases against Chinese furniture and television exporters, and been pressured to file Section 301 petitions against China's undervalued exchange rate and system of labor standards. These developments reflect growing U.S. concerns about trade, globalization, and the country's so-called jobless recovery, concerns that have taken on greater political importance given the pending U.S. elections. Such developments seriously threaten China's continued economic success.

As economists we know that China is not to blame for any significant part of U.S. unemployment or decline in manufacturing jobs. We also know that the huge U.S. bilateral trade deficit with China is overstated in U.S. statistics and that in any case we should not pay attention to bilateral deficits, particularly since most U.S. imports from China previously came from other countries rather than from domestic production.

But we also know that there are serious problems in the international trade and financial regime. Moreover, political realities pose severe challenges that must be addressed. It would be a tragedy if negative external reactions were to undermine China's wise and subtle strategy of integrating with the world economy to promote domestic reforms.

A particular problem facing China is the overheating of its economy, which has been growing very rapidly in recent years. As a result inflationary pressures have resurfaced, and a rapid jump in lending to support the country's unsustainable growth rate risks increasing the level of nonperforming loans that eventually will have to be worked out of the financial system. Thus there is a serious need to restrain domestic growth. The authorities, perhaps a bit belatedly, have recently recognized and started to address this issue. In this regard I congratulate Zhou, because he has clearly been concerned about this issue for some time and working to deal with it.

Enormous capital inflows explain an important part of China's overheating problem. Indeed, one of the most stunning of the many stunning recent statistics about China is that in 2003 its increase in foreign exchange reserves exceeded its growth in GDP. So, despite efforts to sterilize capital inflows, they have added substantially to domestic overheating, inflation pressures, and the like.

China must therefore cope with two important challenges to its continued strong growth: the risk that foreign protectionism will undermine its trade integration strategy and the containment of domestic overheating. Fortunately, one instrument—exchange rate policy—can deal with both.

On the financial side, a large portion of capital inflows are driven by speculation on revaluation of the renminbi. The history of currency changes in fixed rate systems shows that a substantial appreciation would not only choke off inflows but probably also turn them around and support capital outflows. Such outflows would ease the overheating, reduce the buildup of base money, and mitigate inflationary pressures. (A small appreciation would probably be counterproductive because it might accelerate capital inflows, since many investors would think that a small move was insufficient to restore equilibrium and so further moves were likely.)

Similarly, studies of U.S trade policy show that the most potent source of U.S. protectionism is not the unemployment rate but rather the exchange rate of the dollar. Substantial dollar overvaluation leads to huge trade deficits and sharply changes the political economy of trade policy, and so promotes the kind of protectionist policies (especially against China) we are now seeing.

The overvaluation of the U.S. dollar is a global problem and needs to be dealt with on a global basis. But since early 2002 the U.S. dollar's value has fallen by 40–50 percent against the euro and come down substantially against the Canadian dollar, Australian dollar, and other floating currencies. What is needed to complete the dollar adjustment process, which still has far to go, is a movement against a number of other Asian currencies. That suggests a pivotal role for China, because other Asian countries are unwilling to appreciate much against the U.S. dollar since doing so would also mean appreciating against the renminbi and hurting their competitive positions relative to China. Thus most Asian countries (including, to a large extent, Japan) have not yet played much of a role in the necessary global adjustment process, without which there will not be any effective reduction in pressures for protectionist trade policies in the United States. Given the risks facing China's development and its increasingly central role in the world economy, it would thus be prudent for the country to consider changes in its exchange rate policy to help maintain the breathtaking economic success that Zhou describes in his lecture.

Comment

Montek S. Ahluwalia

IT IS AN HONOR TO COMMENT ON ZHOU XIAOCHUAN'S FASCINATING PRESENTATION. We in India have observed China's recent reforms with great admiration, so it is a privilege to hear about them from someone at the highest level of government, speaking from personal experience. Because time is limited, I will focus on just a few points.

Zhou compares China with transition economies, which is one way of assessing its reform experiences. Another is to view it as a low-income country that has achieved rapid growth—which is how we in India have seen it. Do these different perspectives lead to different lessons?

When China is compared with transition economies, the main issue is whether reforms should be based on gradualism or shock therapy. Zhou's lecture identifies some of the reasons—particularly the political environment and political compulsions—transition was pushed so rapidly in Eastern European countries.

Meanwhile China, despite being a low-income country, has achieved stunning growth for more than two decades. Accordingly, when considering economic reforms in India, we never viewed China as an example of gradualism. We always though that China was determined and clear about its goals, and began pursuing them early. Indeed, China initiated its reforms 10 years before India did.

Phenomenally high investment—about 40 percent of GDP—is one of the main factors (if not the main factor) behind China's high growth. Thus other countries aiming for higher growth must achieve much higher investment rates.

But achieving 40 percent investment rates (and corresponding savings rates) is not easy. So, it is crucial that efficiency and other factors be taken into account. And that raises two questions. The first relates to how China is managing financial sector reform. India has similar problems in its financial sector, with high nonperforming loans and the like, and wants to resolve them. Thus we are greatly interested in China's approach.

Indeed, some of Zhou's concerns about financial sector reform are widely shared. As countries globalize—which they must if they want to prosper—they must move their financial sectors toward international standards in terms of openness, prudential norms, and supervisory structures. But rapid changes will not achieve the underlying transformation required to make financial systems more efficient. Though it is easy to introduce a lot of prudential and supervisory norms, by themselves they will only result in much lower lending.

Thus the usual recommendation is for countries to also open up their financial sectors, allowing entry by new private and foreign banks. Doing so, it is claimed, will make the system more efficient. But experiences in many countries suggest that often does not happen. Allowing foreign banks to enter the market does not automatically lead to dramatic growth in banking.

Given these considerations, at what pace should financial sector reform proceed? In international discussions it is almost invariably claimed that a banking system must be privatized if it is to become more efficient. Nearly three-quarters of India's banking system is publicly owned, and in China that share is probably higher; both countries are outliers. Thus I would like to know if China plans to achieve a fast transition in its financial sector, rapidly shrinking the banking system by closing public banks? Or is its strategy to strengthen public banks through the many reforms discussed?

The second question follows on some of the challenges that Fred Bergsten mentions in his comment: that is, the appropriate macroeconomic response in a country experiencing large capital inflows and exchange rate pressures. An obvious move is to liberalize capital outflows. This subject is highly controversial—especially in Asia, where there is a perception that overly rapid liberalization can contribute to financial instability.

But in the framework of a gradual transformation, there must be a role for liberalizing capital inflows. And in any economy where capital outflows are controlled much more carefully, the question arises: how much of the pressure from inflows do you want to ease by liberalizing outflows, as opposed to easing the pressure by letting it reflect itself in the exchange rate? I would be interested to hear Zhou's views on that issue, and thank him again for his interesting and educational presentation.

Leszek Balcerowicz

Former Deputy Prime Minister and Minister of Finance, Poland

Leszek Balcerowicz was born in Lipno, Poland, in 1947. Before earning a Ph.D. in Economics from the Central School of Planning and Statistics (now the Warsaw School of Economics) in 1975, he gained exposure to market economies by earning a Master's of Business Administration (MBA) from St. John's University in New York. Among his academic distinctions are visiting fellowships at the University of Sussex (1985) and Marburg University (1988). Since 1992 Balcerowicz has been Professor at the Warsaw School of Economics, and since 1993 he has been Director, Chair of International Comparative Studies there. From 1992–2000 he was Chairman of the Center for Social and Economic Research (CASE), based in Warsaw.

In 1989 Balcerowicz became Deputy Prime Minister and Minister of Finance in Poland's first noncommunist government since World War II. He was also President of the Economic Committee of the Council of Ministers. During this vital period in Poland's transition he designed and executed radical stabilization and transformation of the economy, holding his positions in government until late 1991. From 1995–2000 Balcerowicz was President of the Freedom Union, a Polish political party. During 1997–2000 he again served as Deputy Prime Minister, Minister of Finance, and President of the Economic Committee of the Council of Ministers. In 2001 he was appointed to his current position as President of the National Bank of Poland. Balcerowicz has written more than 100 publications on economic issues in Poland and abroad, and has received numerous honors from universities and other organizations worldwide.

11 Postcommunist Transition in Comparative Perspective

Leszek Balcerowicz

ANALYSES OF THE TRANSITION FROM COMMUNIST TO MARKET ECONOMIES TRY TO explain the outcomes that have emerged from initial conditions. These outcomes have been the result of internal conditions and policies as well as external developments, and explaining the links between these is the job of economists.

Explaining policies and reforms sometimes requires speculation, which I try to avoid. My goal here is simply to offer observations about the transition experience. Although I will try not to be too Poland-centric in my analysis, I believe that my experiences in guiding Poland's economic policies are useful in answering questions and advancing the discussion. Still, I will try to provide a broader analytical framework.

In this presentation I start by describing initial conditions, just before the collapse of communism. After that I analyze the huge differences in outcomes, economic and noneconomic, among transition economies. I then offer some observations on fiscal developments, financial sector evolution, and privatization. I conclude with a few personal recollections about Poland's reforms.

Initial Conditions and Capacity for Change

Communist countries tended to share several features:

- *Extensive controls* on individual liberty, economic and noneconomic. Private entrepreneurship was banned. State-owned enterprises were subject to central planning, including output commands, rationing of inputs and foreign exchange, price controls, and directed foreign trade. The range of financial assets available to enterprises and individuals was extremely limited. The creation and activities of noneconomic organizations were heavily controlled—that is, civil society was suppressed and political opposition was banned. Foreign travel was restricted. And the media was subject to formal censorship, direct party controls, and personnel policies, and so was largely a tool of communist

propaganda. These controls banned both the market and democracy. In other
words, communism was a form of antimarket dictatorship.

- *A bloated welfare state*, including relatively large in-kind transfers for education
and health care, social protection delivered by state-owned enterprises, and
artificially low prices for food, energy, and housing. The social safety net typical of some market economies did not exist because the need for it was sharply
limited through the curtailment of individuals' opportunities and risks. This
welfare state reflected the wasteful economic system. For example, overem-
ployment provided job security but contributed to low productivity.

- *A peculiar set of public goods*. For example, defense spending was excessive and
shaped by the imperial aspiration of Soviet elites. Law and order were maintained, but at the cost of practices typical of a police state. Moreover, the legal
framework and judicial system were ill suited to the market economy, rule of
law, and free society.

The inherent weaknesses of communist economies worsened over time relative to
market economies. Whereas in 1950 Poland and Spain had about the same per capita
income, by 1990 Poland's was 40 percent of Spain's. Similar gaps emerged between East
and West Germany, Hungary and Austria, and North and South Korea. Such outcomes
were the price of a system that deprived people of liberty, especially economic liberty.
That system derived from Marxism, which claims that the market—in other words,
economic liberty—is the source of underdevelopment. Unfortunately, for many years
such thinking was quite influential in certain branches of development economics.

Such indicators also show the inefficiency of the communist system, and indicate
how much waste there was in transition economies. For example, in the early 1990s
industrial productivity was much lower in transition economies than in other middle-income countries such as Chile, the Republic of Korea, and Mexico. One reason
was that officially there was no unemployment, because all unemployment was dis-
guised. Another reason was that skilled people were not used productively.

Being wasteful economically, communist economies were also wasteful ecologically, because economic efficiency is essential for ecological efficiency. An economically inefficient system uses a lot of energy and raw materials, which is ecologically
wasteful. Communist economies used a lot more energy to produce a unit of GDP
(or, put another way, produced fewer units of GDP per unit of energy) than did
countries like Chile, Korea, Mexico, and Thailand. They also generated more carbon
dioxide emissions per unit of GDP. That is why market-friendly reforms are essential—though insufficient—for environmental improvement when making the transition from communism.

The pervasive state controls and lack of market institutions under communism
called for institutional and structural reforms on two fronts. The first was liberalization,
to reverse constraints on economic freedom and thus release private entrepreneurship
and market forces. The second was institutional development and restructuring, such as
creating new institutions (stock exchanges, bank supervisors) and transforming inherited ones (privatizing state enterprises, reforming court systems). The institutional

reforms had to be accompanied by macroeconomic stabilization, the urgency of which depended on inherited macroeconomic imbalances (see below).

Although all these efforts could be started at about the same time, it takes longer to create efficient, market-friendly institutions than to liberalize and stabilize the economy. But that was not a reason to delay liberalization and stabilization until institution building bore fruit. Quite the contrary: under such a strategy economic disarray could only grow while the precious time of "extraordinary politics" was wasted, putting at serious risk each of these efforts (see Balcerowicz 1995).

Differences in inherited conditions and structures—policies and institutions— had important effects across all transition economies. For example, although all communist countries depended on other communist countries for trade (because they were isolated from the West), there were differences in this trade dependence reflecting countries' size, political status, and other factors. The Baltic states, for example, being much smaller, were much more dependent on exports to other members of the Council for Mutual Economic Assistance, with such exports accounting for 41 percent of GDP in Lithuania, 37 percent in Latvia, and 30 percent in Estonia—compared with 6 percent in the former Czechoslovakia and 4 percent in Romania. These variations had strong implications for GDP dynamics after the transition began.

Another important aspect of initial conditions involved human capital. In-kind public transfers, such as for education, were fairly large in all communist systems. As a result school enrollments were high. But the quality of education varied considerably. It was weak in the social sciences, but pretty strong in science and mathematics. Public health systems were also strong (except in Central Asia), with good health indicators relative to countries like Chile, Korea, Mexico, and Thailand.

Thus human capital was fairly well developed in all transition economies. The problem is that this is a mobile factor: it can move. And how it moves depends on policies, what prospects a country creates with its policies, and whether educated people remain in a country after it has been opened.

So even though education systems were much better than economic systems in transition economies, and produced a "surplus" of educated people, this was sort of a waste. This surplus human capital was largely untapped during the professional lives of educated individuals. However, the stock of human capital represented one of the few assets at the start of the transition, positively distinguishing postcommunist countries from most other emerging economies. But human capital is mobile, and—with the newly introduced freedom of emigration—the challenge has been to retain it domestically. It is here that good policies turned out to be doubly important: by shaping the economic situation and its prospects, they not only determined the current welfare but also influenced the propensity of educated people to continue working in their countries—thus affecting long-term developments.

There were also big differences in macroeconomic imbalances at the start of the transition, as measured by repressed inflation and black market premiums. Macroeconomic stabilization was a far more urgent, demanding task for Bulgaria, Poland, Romania, and countries of the former Soviet Union than for Hungary and the former Czechoslovakia.

Given subsequent developments in transition economies, it appears that how bad inherited conditions are is less important than how quickly they can be improved—given proper policies. With the right policies, certain initial conditions can generate rapid economic growth. Examples include an economic structure with a large share of repressed but easily privatized sectors, a large pool of educated workers, or a favorable location. But some initial conditions hamper economic growth, at least in the short run. The main examples are large trade dependence on collapsing markets, a large share of declining sectors, or difficult access to large and dynamic markets.

Initial conditions varied considerably at the start of the transition. Small former Soviet republics were much more dependent on exports to other members of the Council for Mutual Economic Assistance than were Czechoslovakia, Hungary, or Poland. Armenia and the Kyrgyz Republic, both small and landlocked, have a much less favorable location than do the Baltic countries (Estonia, Latvia, Lithuania) or Moldova.

But far more important differences in initial conditions prevailed in most former Soviet countries, including Russia, in the early 1990s, and in China at the start of its reforms in the late 1970s. Russia, being much more developed, had a much larger share of industry and much smaller share of easily privatized agriculture. In China 69 percent of the labor force was employed in agriculture in 1980, compared with 14 percent in Russia in 1990. China also displayed much smaller macroeconomic imbalances than did most former Soviet countries. These differences in initial conditions explain much of China's better transition performance. Radical external opening—foreign trade, foreign direct investment—also played an important role in China's development.

Outcomes and Performance Indicators

Perhaps the most striking feature of outcomes since the collapse of communism is their enormous variation: transition economies that have done well have done much better than those that have fared poorly. In other words, the situation in communist societies was much more similar some 15 years ago than it is today. These variations are evident in a wide range of areas.

Differences

Consider GDP, where there have been enormous differences relative to initial levels. In Poland GDP was 30 percent higher in 2002 than in 1989—while in Ukraine it was 54 percent lower. These are official data, so if informal sectors were added the differences would be smaller, though still huge. Moreover, a number of factors have overstated the GDP decline in transition economies. For example, GDP levels under communism were largely inflated due to wasteful investments, excessive stocks, large military expenditures, and value-diminishing activities, all of which were counted as positive contributions to GDP (Åslund 2001). Corrections for these inflated figures have been recorded as declines in GDP (and often interpreted as declines in welfare). But these and other factors do not fundamentally change the relative picture.

All transition economies have made considerable progress in lowering inflation. But countries that have achieved better results on growth have also achieved better results on inflation. So, disinflation is good for growth.

Between 1992 and 2001 changes in industrial labor productivity also varied enormously across transition economies—ranging from 2 percent in Moldova to 146 percent in Hungary. Some of these differences were due to the varying extent of enterprise restructuring. Countries with smaller increases in labor productivity tended to sustain more labor hoarding and subsequently display less statistical unemployment than did countries with higher increases in labor productivity.

Massive differences are also apparent in inflows of foreign direct investment. Such investment usually follows economic success and strengthens subsequent economic growth, especially through technology transfers. Thus differences in foreign direct investment are one of the clearest indicators of the quality of a country's economic environment, as well as a determinant of future growth. During 1989–2002 the Czech Republic was the leader among transition economies in per capita terms, receiving $3,413—more than Chile, the star performer in emerging economies, which got $2,472. In Poland per capita foreign direct investment was $997, about the same as in Greece and Mexico. By contrast, Ukraine attracted $99 per capita, Moldova $84, and Russia $50.

As with economic dimensions, noneconomic outcomes have also varied considerably across transition economies—with countries that have performed better on the first tending to do better on the second. Take the environment. Being highly wasteful, the Soviet-type economy was also very damaging to the environment. One of the main reasons was a low ratio of GDP to energy consumption (low energy efficiency). Transition economies have differed in the evolution of this measure. Since 1989 Central and Eastern European countries have considerably increased the energy efficiency of their economies, achieving levels comparable to or better than those in the Republic of Korea. Kazakhstan and the Kyrgyz Republic have also made great progress. In contrast, energy efficiency in Russia and Ukraine has remained at low levels.

Another measure of an economy's environmental impact involves carbon dioxide emissions per unit of GDP. Since 1989 this measure has fallen considerably in Central and Eastern Europe as well as in Kazakhstan and the Kyrgyz Republic—while it has increased in Ukraine and stayed high in Russia. In 1999 the transition economies with the lowest carbon dioxide emissions per unit of GDP (Armenia, Czech Republic, Hungary, Latvia) were similar in this respect to Chile, Greece, Korea, Mexico, and Thailand.

In terms of life expectancy at birth, the best performers—Armenia, the Czech Republic, Poland, the Slovak Republic, and Lithuania—have achieved levels similar to those of Korea and Mexico and better than Thailand. Life expectancy has increased in Central and Eastern Europe but fallen in Kazakhstan, the Kyrgyz Republic, Russia, and Ukraine. A similar differentiation is apparent in infant mortality rates. Central and Eastern European countries have recorded substantial declines relative to Chile, Mexico, and Thailand, while Russia and Ukraine have registered no improvements.

Although an optimal distribution of income cannot be established in a non-subjective way, sharply increased (or high) income inequality is often considered a negative phenomenon. A popular cliché is that faster growth goes hand in hand with higher income inequality, as measured by the Gini coefficient, across transition economies. Yet the fastest increases and highest levels of income inequality have been recorded by Russia and Ukraine, countries with poor relative growth records over 1987–98. Better growth performers during this period (the Czech Republic, Hungary, Poland) displayed, on average, smaller increases and lower levels of the Gini coefficient.

Explanations

The enormous differences in outcomes after the collapse of communism obviously pose questions about their causes. There is already a large empirical literature that focuses on relative growth performance and tries to disentangle the role of initial conditions, external factors (such the impact of Russia's 1998 crisis on other transition economies), and policies.

As noted, initial conditions in post-Soviet economies were generally less conducive to quick economic improvement than those in China in the late 1970s. But they also varied considerably. Small former Soviet republics—Armenia, Estonia, Georgia, the Kyrgyz Republic, Latvia, Lithuania, Moldova—heavily dependent on exports to Russia suffered huge external shocks as a result of the collapse of the Soviet Union and the Soviet trading system. Some were constrained in reorienting their foreign trade due to their distance from the West (Armenia, the Kyrgyz Republic). Being less dependent on the Soviet trading system, Central and Eastern European countries suffered smaller shocks to their GDP. Russia was in the most favorable situation because its size made it less dependent on exports to other socialist economies. As a large exporter of oil and gas to its former satellites, it was able to obtain large terms of trade gains thanks to changes in world prices of these goods. Thus Russia's profound decline in official GDP cannot be explained by unfavorable external shocks.[1]

However large the differences in initial conditions, they explain only part of the relative growth performance—and only in the early phase after the collapse of communism. Differences in longer-run growth are mostly due to different policies—that is, the different extent of market-oriented reforms.

Figure 11.1 compares GDP developments in the Kyrgyz Republic and Moldova. It shows that more extensive market-oriented reforms—as measured by the share of the private sector in GDP—can overcome the effects of an unfavorable location. Thus the Kyrgyz Republic has achieved more favorable GDP dynamics than Moldova.

The strong link between market-oriented reforms and growth has been also been found in many empirical studies. Table 11.1 summarizes the main findings of these studies. At the same time, I do not know of a single empirical that shows less reforms were better for economic growth, under comparable conditions, than more reforms.

It should be stressed that the picture of relative economic growth among transition economies is not static. In recent years some members of the Commonwealth of Independent States (CIS) started to grow much faster than the average for Cen-

FIGURE 11.1

GDP and Private Sector Participation in the Kyrgyz Republic and Moldova, 1989–2001

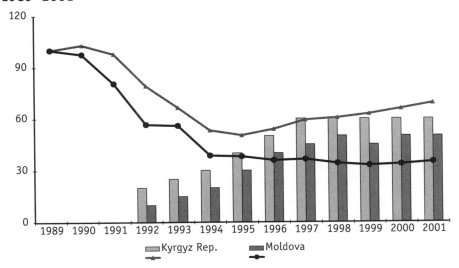

Note: GDP: 1989 = 100 (lines); Private sector share of GDP: percent (bars)
Source: *EBRD Transition Report 2002.*

TABLE 11.1

Empirical Studies Reviewing Experiences of Transition Economies

Berg and others (1999)	*"The role of initial conditions in explaining cross-sectional variation in growth is surprisingly minor; in particular, the difference in performance between the CEE and the Baltics, Russia, and other countries of the former Soviet Union is mostly explained by differences in structural reforms (even at the beginning of transition), rather than initial conditions."*
Fischer and Sahay (2000)	*"The experience accumulated in the past decade, whether viewed informally or with the help of data, charts, and regressions, provides support for the view that the most successful transition economies are those that have both stabilised and undertaken comprehensive reforms, and that more and faster reform is better than less and slower reform."*
Havrylyshyn and van Rooden (2000)	*"(...) progress in achieving macroeconomic stabilization and implementing broad-based economic reforms remain the key determinants of growth in transition countries."*
Havrylyshyn and others (2000)	*"Unfavourable initial conditions should not become an excuse for inaction.(...) First, their negative effects decline over time. Second, the empirical studies clearly suggest that these effects can be compensated by modestly faster progress on reforms. Third, perhaps the main fact is indirect; that is, unfavourable initial conditions result in less political will and capacity for reform, and less reform means less growth."*

tral and Eastern European countries. A good case in point is Armenia, where better growth performance cannot be linked to favorable external developments. Instead one must look to an improved economic system: a low ratio of taxes to GDP, fiscal discipline, and considerably enlarged economic freedom.

There has been a tendency for noneconomic outcomes (such as health and environmental indicators) to improve in line with economic outcomes. Why? This issue has not been investigated as much as relative growth performance. But it can be shown that some crucial factors conducive to economic outcomes are also conducive to noneconomic ones. Market-oriented reforms increase economic efficiency, including the production and consumption of energy and raw materials, and that contributes to a reduction in environmental pollution. In addition, the separation of enterprises from the state—through privatization and introduction of the rule of law—has helped the enforcement of ecological regulations. And both privatization and the rule of law are fundamental determinants of long-run growth.

Different health developments can also be linked to economic reforms. For example, economic liberalization changes the availability and relative prices of foodstuffs, and at the same time this liberalization is crucial for economic growth (Balcerowicz 1998).

Additional Observations

Though there have been many interesting developments related to the collapse of communism, I have time to deal with just a few.

Fiscal developments

Transition economies started with a high (though varied) level of general government spending relative to GDP—much higher than was typical of the East Asian tigers, as exemplified by Korea. Subsequent fiscal developments differed enormously. Most Central and Eastern European countries lowered such spending, but to levels still much higher than is typical for countries with their per capita income. This raises the question of whether such a fiscal stance is compatible with a rapid and sustained real convergence. Few countries have managed to lower their spending to GDP ratios in an orderly manner and to levels typical of fast growers elsewhere; exceptions include Kazakhstan, the Kyrgyz Republic, and Lithuania. The challenge for these countries is to maintain these levels in the interests of future growth.

Financial sector

Financial sectors in transition economies, as measured by shares of domestic credit to the private sector and market capitalization of listed companies relative to GDP, are underdeveloped relative to those in Chile, Greece, Korea, and Thailand (figure 11.2). Still, they tend to be much healthier than China's huge financial sector, which is burdened with a high share of nonperforming loans. Given their current positions, transition economies can expect a lot of financial deepening, if they are able to grow over the long run.

FIGURE 11.2

Domestic Credit to Private Sector and Market Capitalization of Listed Companies, 2001

(percentage of GDP)

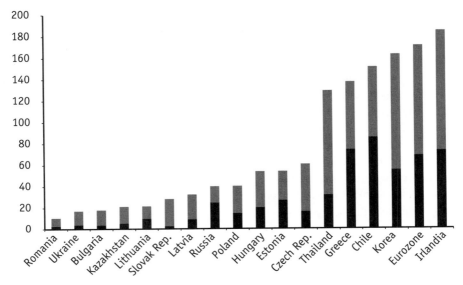

■Stock market capitalization   ■Domestic credit to private sector

Source: World Bank, *World Development Indicators 2003.*

It is striking that most of these economies achieved extensive external and internal liberalization of their financial sectors in a relatively short period and, for the most part, without major disturbances. Those outcomes cast doubt on the claim that financial liberalization was a major reason for growth failures in the postsocialist world. The reasons lay elsewhere; as noted, a lack of market-oriented reforms blocked the growth of transition economies.

Privatization

Privatization of a state-dominated economy takes longer than its liberalization and stabilization. In the short run a radical change in the environment facing state enterprises—thanks to decisive liberalization and stabilization—can improve the behavior of these firms (Pinto, Belka, and Krajewski 1992, 1993). But in the long run there is no substitute for their privatization, and to my knowledge there is no empirical case—of a successful economy dominated by state enterprises—that proves the contrary.

Moreover, a delay in privatization typically does not lend value to a state enterprise; indeed, it subtracts it. In assessing privatization, countries should avoid a "nirvana" approach—that is, comparing it with an ideal but most likely unachievable yardstick. Instead, comparisons should be made with feasible options. Such an approach would make people think twice before condemning, say, privatization in Russia.

Personal Recollections

This lecture series asks for my recollections and lessons that go with them. Here are some (see also Balcerowicz 1995, pp. 341–48).

Two of the basic questions I was interested in as a student of economic reforms was, first, why economic reforms in socialist countries had been partly or wholly reversed and, second, why they had failed to significantly increase overall efficiency. My general response to these questions was that economic reforms had failed because they were not radical enough. They did not reach a certain threshold of necessary changes rapidly; in other words, a "critical mass" of such changes was not achieved. So I entered the government with a strong antigradualist attitude toward economic reform. This belief was based not only on the experiences of previous reforms, but also on conclusions I drew form social psychology, especially Leon Festinger's theory of cognitive dissonance. One of the findings of this theory is that people are more likely to change their attitudes and behaviors if they are faced with radical changes in their environment that they consider irreversible, as opposed to changes that are only gradual.

With respect to stabilization, I knew that regardless of institutional differences, a radical approach was needed to put the brakes on hyperinflation. The institutional differences had, I felt, two consequences. First, given the asymmetry of the labor market, because of the absence of private owners in what was still a socialist economy, there was a need for extraordinarily tough wage controls to rein in the tendency toward runaway inflation. Second, because the tough program of stabilization had to be introduced in a basically nonprivate economy, its supply response was more uncertain and could be even worse than that seen in Latin American economies. But the alternative strategies had, I believed, much less chance of success.

With respect to eliminating shortages, I believed the problems were caused by price controls and supply rigidities, not the soft budget constraints of enterprises. The latter, in my opinion, was one of the main factors responsible for enterprises' low efficiency, as it implied the absence of competition.

Another important lesson involved the absence of competition. Import substitution and heavy regulation of the economy are sufficient to cause low efficiency and widespread rent seeking; formally, private property cannot remedy this situation. These were the negative conclusions I drew from the experiences of many Latin American countries and India, and from the economic literature, especially from the writings of Bella Balassa and Anne Krueger.

In the spring of 1989 I wrote a paper about which reforms should be introduced in Poland if it were free. I had no idea that a few months later I would be in charge of the country's economic stabilization and transformation. The proposed steps included rapid liberalization of prices, tough macroeconomic policy, convertibility of the Polish zloty, liberalization of the foreign trade regime, and the quickest possible privatization.

I had a clear perception from the very beginning that because of the inherited hyperinflation, we had to choose between an almost hopeless strategy and a risky one. There was no option without risk. An almost hopeless strategy would have involved neglecting the stabilization part of the program, and focusing instead on the transformation part.

It was my view that a strategy of tolerating hyperinflation would make stabilization more difficult over time, and the related chaos of hyperinflation would make rapid transformation, including privatization, scarcely possible. So that strategy, "privatization first, stabilization later," would probably have resulted in neither privatization nor stabilization.

It was thus reasonable to choose a strategy that was as risky but not hopeless: starting stabilization and transformation at about the same time. Stabilization measures and the liberalization part of the program of transformation could be implemented more rapidly than privatization and other institutional reforms. The radical strategy consisted, therefore, of the rapid introduction of a stabilization and liberalization package while at the same time undertaking more time-consuming institutional reforms. This implied, given the differences in possible speed, that radical stabilization and liberalization had to be introduced in the economy before it was fundamentally transformed. The risk in this strategy was that the supply response of such an economy was weaker and could be more uncertain than in a free market economy. But I always compared these risks with those of delaying stabilization or liberalization (or implementing them gradually). It was obvious to me that the latter strategies are almost hopeless. I viewed the economic reforms as a radical but comprehensive package, the elements of which complemented one another.

Within liberalization, the freeing of prices was crucial, necessary to rapidly eliminate shortages and obtain better price information. Radical price liberalization required, in my view, a decisive liberalization of foreign trade, which in turn included the unification of exchange rates and currency convertibility. These moves were also indispensable for obtaining better relative prices. In addition, the fixing of the newly unified exchange rate played an important role in the stabilization program, and the introduction of convertibility signaled a decisive break with past partial and unsuccessful reforms.

Liberalization also included eliminating remaining restrictions on the creation and growth of private firms. This was an important part of the legal framework for economic activity, as it introduced free entry and enabled spontaneous growth of the private sector. Privatization of enterprises was for me the key part of the institutional restructuring. I viewed privatization as the most important type of enterprise reform and the most important condition for enterprise restructuring. Expanding private enterprise was, to my mind, crucial for solving the main structural problem facing Poland (and all postcommunist economies, for that matter): low and decreasing efficiency.

I also remembered that the potential inherent in the private sector can be fully released only if there is competition and an outward orientation of the economy. That is why a liberal foreign trade regime was for me an important complement to privatization and an important condition for increasing the overall efficiency of the economy. I also believed that some increase in that efficiency might be achieved through foreign trade liberalization, preceding the full privatization of state enterprises. However, to obtain the maximum possible increase in efficiency, privatization and other changes must be combined.

While I was reasonably sure about the general features of the target model and the related broad lines of policies, there were a number of specific issues where I felt that economics supplied little advice and thus I perceived a substantial uncertainty—which I tried to reduce with additional analytical work, if possible. Practically all the important economic variables were subject to great uncertainty. For example, there were conflicting hypotheses about how fast the initial large price increases would spread across the economy; in other words, what the inflation path would look like. I did not know how long we would be able to keep the exchange rate at its initial level. We were uncertain when and on what scale the bankruptcies of enterprises would occur. In fact, they started later than expected and on a smaller scale. We forecasted moderate growth of exports in 1990. In fact, they exploded, growing by 43 percent.

However, I was reasonably certain about the general directions of change—that is, the general relationships between the policy measures and the changes in economic variables, the time lags between the two, and the magnitude of the reaction. Thus I was sure that the stabilization and liberalization package, if maintained, would stop hyperinflation and eliminate shortages. I was also sure that sooner or later, privatization of the economy, competition, and export-oriented growth would greatly enhance efficiency and so solve the perennial problem that plagued the former socialist economy.

There were many questions about the methods of enterprise privatization. Should we privatize using only the classical methods, or should we adopt mass privatization schemes? As it turned out, though we were ready to pursue mass privatization, we encountered political obstacles. Thus it is not true that Poland opted for slower privatization than, for example, the Czech Republic: we were blocked. Our economic performance probably would have been better if we had privatized more quickly, including through mass privatization.

Conclusion

Countries that inherited communist economies had to implement two basic kinds of institutional reforms: a comprehensive liberalization and a vast program of building or restructuring institutions conducive to or required by a free society and a stable and dynamic market economy. These postcommunist reforms have been a spectacular case of a broader tendency to reduce the excesses of statism and to move toward the free markets present in Western countries and in many developing countries as well. The experiences of transition economies strongly suggest that the greater were the extent of market-oriented reforms, the better were both economic and noneconomic outcomes.

The postcommunist transition has produced several policy innovations, such as mass privatization, pension reform, and flat taxes. It also confirmed that a successful transition toward a limited state and its counterpart—the market—is crucial to long-run development.

Note

1. The decline in Russia's recorded GDP may be largely due to a large share of military expenditures previously counted as part of GDP. For more on this and other reasons for this decline, see Aslund (2001) and Shleifer and Treisman (2003).

References

Aslund, Anders. 2001. *Building Capitalism. The Transformation of the Former Soviet Bloc.* Cambridge: Cambridge University Press.

Balcerowicz, Leszek. 1995. *Socialism, Capitalism, Transformation.* Central European University Press.

———. 1998. "Economic Forces and Health." In *Dialogue and Universalism.*

Berg, Andrew, E. Borensztein, R. Sahay, and J. Zettelmeyer. 1999. "The Evolution of Output in Transition Economies." International Monetary Fund, Washington, D.C.

EBRD (European Bank for Reconstruction and Development). 2002. *Transition Report 2002.* London.

Fischer, Stanley, and R. Sahay. 2000. "The Transition Economies after Ten Years." International Monetary Fund, Washington, D.C.

Havrylyshyn, Oleh, and R. van Rooden. 2000. "Institutions Matter in Transition, But So Do Policies." International Monetary Fund, Washington, D.C.

Havrylyshyn, Oleh, T. Wolf, J. Berengaut, M. Castello-Branco, R. van Rooden, and V. Mercer-Blackman. 2000. "Growth Experience in Transition Countries, 1990–98." International Monetary Fund, Washington, D.C.

Pinto, Brian, M. Belka, and S. Krajewski. 1992. "Microeconomics and Transformation in Poland: A Survey of State Enterprise Responses." World Bank, Washington, D.C.

———. 1993. "Transforming State Enterprises in Poland: Microeconomic Evidence on Adjustment." World Bank, Washington, D.C.

Shleifer, Andrei, and D. Treisman. 2003. "A Normal Country." National Bureau of Economic Research, Cambridge, Mass.

Comment

D. Mario Nuti

IT IS A PLEASURE TO BE HERE, AND I AM GRATEFUL FOR THE OPPORTUNITY TO COM-
ment on Leszek Balcerowicz's lecture. I have known Balcerowicz for more than 20
years and have interacted with him in various capacities: as a European Commission
official visiting Poland's Ministry of Finance at the inception of the Balcerowicz
plan, as an adviser to another Polish minister of finance dealing with the National
Bank of Poland, and as a fellow academic before and since the transition. Thus we
have met on both friendly and somewhat adversarial occasions, and it is good to be
on neutral ground in this forum.

Contrasting Views of Transition

Balcerowicz presents an exceptionally idealized vision of the transition. His picture of
Poland's pretransition system is a caricature of the Stalinist version of 1950: it ignores
more than 40 years of economic reforms and is not the system he inherited in 1989 as
minister of finance. He compares income and health data for 1989 and 2002 and so
ignores the depth—and for many countries, the very existence—of a transition recession and health crisis in the intervening years, thus avoiding a discussion of the extent
and causes of those developments. Balcerowicz claims that transition economies simply
have to adopt the right policies and good results will follow; that the faster and deeper
are liberalization, stabilization, and privatization, the faster will be recovery and growth.

Balcerowicz says little about his role in the transition and the associated recession
in Poland, and nothing about monetary policy, central banking, interest rates, and
coordination of monetary and fiscal policy. Does he believe that monetary policy
does not matter? Or does he believe that there were no policy choices in this area
and that all central banks in transition economies, equally independent, have invariably followed the one correct policy—and that this had had the same effect throughout? Neither belief is justified. Finally, I do not see in Balcerowicz's lecture the
"reality check" and critique of his experiences that were among the goals of this lec-

ture series, so that we can learn from failures. Thus in these comments I will qualify and supplement Balcerowicz's analysis, examining the reality of transition in contrast to the official, idealized version he presents.

The Legacy of the Old System

The old system described by Balcerowicz has little in common with the system he inherited. To some extent the old system was worse than he portrays: in the dependence of state enterprises on sector ministries, in the segmentation of monetary circulation into cash and noncash circuits, and in symbolic nominal interest rates and overvalued, inconsistent, multiple exchange rates. Above all, endemic excess demand was much deeper and larger than Balcerowicz seems to realize (Nuti 1986), though he is correct that shortages had nothing to do with Janos Kornai's explanation in terms of soft budget constraints.

Still, in the 1970s and 1980s many Central and Eastern European countries made serious attempts to reform the Soviet-style economic system. In Poland these efforts mushroomed in 1980–81, when at least seven reform programs were publicly debated—including one authored by Balcerowicz and his team at the Higher School of Planning and Statistics (Szkola Glowna Planowania I Statystyki, or SGPiS) calling for greater reliance on markets and enterprise autonomy.

Under the system that Balcerowicz took over in September 1989, Poland's private sector accounted for about a quarter of GDP, not only in agriculture and services but also in manufacturing. The two circuits of monetary circulation had been unified and there was an independent central bank surrounded by commercial banks (with state, private domestic, and mixed foreign ownership). Exporters could retain export earnings, use them freely for imports, or transfer them to other firms. The central bank auctioned significant amounts of foreign currency to the highest bidders, and there was no longer a black market for foreign exchange. Previous governments had raised prices significantly, especially in 1989, and by August 1989 market-validated prices prevailed in half of consumption transactions.

Although these features did not add up to a new system, they immensely facilitated Poland's transition. Reforms cannot work in an environment of endemic shortages, and it was this collateral feature of the centrally planned economy that ultimately caused its collapse. Still, even if reforms failed to construct an alternative viable system of "market socialism," they achieved significant partial changes that greatly aided the subsequent transition to a market economy. Indeed, transition performance has depended much more on the extent of previous reforms than on variables often used as alternatives, such as a country's distance from Brussels or length of time it spent under a socialist regime.

The Depth of the Transition Recession

Throughout Central and Eastern Europe, the transition was accompanied by a deep and protracted recession. By looking at GDP levels in 1989 and 2002, Balcerowicz loses sight of this intervening recession. He misses all of it in countries that by 2002 had overtaken initial levels (Albania, Poland, Slovak Republic, Slovenia, Uzbekistan) and most of it in all the other countries, where by 2002 recovery was well under way. Yet recession was an essential aspect of the transition and should not be overlooked. Although data on the transition recession underestimate large qualitative improvements in output and living standards, they also neglect adverse distributional trends. Quantitatively, the achievements of the 10–12 years of transition are not as impressive as one might have expected.

To some extent the transition recession could be a statistical delusion. The old system exaggerated output, underestimated deflators, and included every productive unit. The new system tends to underestimate achievements (to avoid taxes), applies more reliable deflators, uses samples, and does not include much of the informal economy. Moreover, consumers are now better off because there are no shortages and they have more choices.

But many old informal activities have surfaced since being legalized, boosting instead of depressing transition achievements. Consumer surplus is not part of national income accounting, and there are other indicators of falling living standards. According to Mundell (1997), the transition recession was greater than that of the Great Depression in 1929. Indeed, it was worse than that caused in the 14th century by the Black Death—which at least reduced population as well as income, thus preserving living standards.

Was the recession expected? Although Fischer and Sahay (2000) argue that it was, in his book *800 Days* Balcerowicz (1992) acknowledges that he had not anticipated its large scale and long duration. What were the causes?

The recession is often blamed on too much shock therapy or, on the contrary, too much gradualism. But both perspectives are too narrow, and there has been a great deal of misunderstanding—because the recession involved several shocks, and only some could be avoided.

The shock of raising prices to market-clearing levels in one stroke was essential and long overdue. No system, market or planned, can function normally in the face of permanent excess demand. Shortages sometimes occur in market economies, but only for a small range of necessities, for relatively short periods, and in exceptional circumstances, usually signaling an inadequate distribution network. Administered prices consistently below equilibrium, and the associated shortages, were never part of the original socialist design and were a tragic misunderstanding that ultimately brought down the Soviet-type system.

During transition a number of other things should also be done immediately and simultaneously, including legalizing private ownership and enterprise, opening access to foreign trade for all economic agents without bureaucratic obstacles such as licenses and registration, eliminating quantitative trade restrictions, unifying the exchange rate, and establishing current account convertibility for residents. All these changes can be done by decree, literally from one day to the next, and there is no point in waiting.

Conversely, some adjustments take time and should be given all the time they need: introducing legislation, establishing jurisprudence, and building institutions, financial markets, regulatory frameworks, and reputation and trust. It is counterproductive to pretend otherwise. The choice between shock therapy and gradualism, with intermediate gradations, exists in only a handful of areas: trade liberalization, elimination of subsidies, privatization, capital account convertibility, and (especially) disinflation. There seems to be a widespread presupposition, shared by Balcerowicz, that whenever there is a choice between gradual and rapid change, as in these five areas, rapid change is preferable. I strongly disagree. In these areas the merits of shock and gradualism cannot be discussed a priori because they depend on the tradeoffs between policy targets that such a choice generates at a particular time and place, and on the preferences of government decisionmakers about such policy targets.

The transition recession was caused not so much by the necessary shock of price liberalization but by unnecessary shocks in such areas—not least premature (unilateral) trade liberalization, later reversed. The recession was also caused by the disintegration of trade and currency areas, as well as the disorganization that resulted from the lag between the disappearance of old institutions and the appearance of new ones, and between the dissolution of old interenterprise linkages and the establishment of new ones (Blanchard 1994). Above all, the recession was due to policy errors: the wrong instruments, the wrong dosage of instruments, or both, and particularly overshooting (Nuti and Portes 1993).

The Quality of Policies and the Problem of Overshooting

Differences in comparative transition performance largely depend on the quality of policies. When Balcerowicz talks about the quality of policies, he invariably means whether a country has liberalized, stabilized, and privatized according to some quantitative assessment embodied in arbitrary but reasonable indexes produced by international institutions and experts. This approach neglects two major factors in explaining comparative performance (in transition economies as elsewhere): namely, the choice of instruments and their quantitative strength. This approach is equivalent to judging the healthiness of a person's eating habits by looking at whether he or she diets or does not, instead of looking at the kind of diet and the level of intake within it.

Poor policies are exemplified by overshooting, as occurred in both of Balcerowicz's terms as minister of finance. There is no doubt that in 1990–91 the Balcerowicz plan overshot; indeed, I have it on his authority. In February 1990 I visited Warsaw on a mission for the EC Directorate General for Economic and Monetary Affairs. I met Balcerowicz, and he asked what I thought of his stabilization program, which was to become the prototype for almost all transition economies. I told him that he had overshot, because he was running an unintended budget surplus, a much tighter monetary policy than announced, and a current account surplus due to excessive devaluation, with accumulating foreign reserves that had to be expensively sterilized. Balcerowicz recognized all this but said there was nothing he could do, because if he did anything everyone would think he was abandoning the plan and there would be no stabilization.

Balcerowicz and his team faced daunting tasks at the beginning of transition and stabilization. Still, it was clear that the original program would overshoot. At the start of 1990 the exchange rate was fixed at the former rate prevailing in the free segment of the dual free and administered market. That rate was obviously higher than the equilibrium rate in a unified free market for foreign exchange, and the excess devaluation was inflationary—with a feedback effect on recession through the use of monetary targets fixed in nominal terms and embodying an underestimated prospective inflation. This led to an unintended credit crunch. Real wages, being indexed to prices with extremely low elasticities, took the brunt of macroeconomic adjustment; they collapsed and so depressed demand. Investment was out of the question. Disorganization was rampant, and recession set in. Excess devaluation also led to a current account surplus and to the unexpected and unwanted accumulation of foreign reserves, which were expensive to sterilize because the central bank had to borrow back liquidity from the public at an interest rate lower than it obtained on its foreign reserves.

Thus I would like Balcerowicz to reconsider whether he would really do the same things all over again—with the benefit not so much of hindsight but of common sense. Imagine an alternative scenario in which prices were still freed to find their market-clearing levels, but wages were also freed, or a lower and affordable real wage was indexed at 100 percent instead of the entire current level being indexed at just 10 percent of the inflation rate. In this alternative scenario money targets would not have been fixed in nominal terms but kept constant in real terms, the exchange rate would have been floated (and thus devalued significantly less than it was in January 1990), and money interest rates would have been adjusted more frequently, rising and falling with inflation but at a rate lower than inflation, without targeting intermittently a positive real rate. Under such policies, overshooting, if any, would have been less severe. Other poor policies during the transition recession included excessively high interest rates, unsustainably overvalued exchange rates, and limits on government budget deficits fixed in terms of cash instead of accruals.

Comparing National Governments

Comparative transition analysis should include policies implemented by different governments over time in the same country. During Balcerowicz's first term as minister of finance and under Poland's first postcommunist legislature—a period sometimes called "shock without therapy"—unemployment rose from a negligible level to a peak of 17 percent in 1994. Then over the next few years, under Grzegorz Kolodko's "Strategy for Poland," unemployment fell to about 10 percent and GDP rose by 28 percent (corresponding to almost the entire 29 percent increase that occurred in 1989–2001; see Kolodko and Nuti 1997). During the 1997 electoral campaign Balcerowicz criticized the government for its supposedly low growth rate and promised to double GDP over the next 10 years. (Though in fact, the growth rate was 7.5 percent in the second quarter of 1997, higher than the 7.2 percent needed to double GDP in 10 years.)

Once back in office, Balcerowicz adopted a policy of cooling—indeed, overcooling—the economy to 3 percent growth by the second quarter of 2000 (though the budget deficit increased with his acquiescence), when he stepped down as minister of finance. Growth deceleration continued under the high interest rates and strong exchange rates adopted by Balcerowicz as governor of the National Bank of Poland (a position he has held since 2001), overfulfilling the target for reducing inflation and raising unemployment to more than 17 percent. Income growth resumed when Kolodko took over again as finance minister (2002–03), reflecting his policies of financial restructuring and debt reduction of enterprises, institutional development, more active public policy (especially in investment), and public finance reform. This significantly different performance under different governments was likely the direct result of varying policy quality.

Conclusion

In 1992 U.S. President George Bush said of the transition (after Yogi Berra) that "no one said that it was going to be easy, and no one was right." But some people were more right than others. There were different ways of navigating the uncharted waters of the transition, and some were—or would have been—better than others. We knew or should have known that then, and we certainly should know it now. I look forward to the contribution that Balcerowicz can undoubtedly make to our understanding of these issues.

Note

The author is grateful to R.W. Davies, Hubert Gabrish, Roberto Nzagha, and Oleksiy Shvets for valuable comments.

References

Balcerowicz, Leszek. 1992. *800 Dni* [800 Days]. Warsaw: BGW.

Blanchard, Olivier. 1994. *The Economics of Post-communist Transition*. Oxford: Blackwell.

Fischer, Stanley, and Ratna Sahay. 2000. "The Transition Economies after Ten Years." IMF Working Paper WP/00/30. International Monetary Fund, Washington, D.C.

Kolodko, Gregorz W., and Domenico Mario Nuti. 1997. "The Polish Alternative: Old Myths, Hard Facts and New Strategies in the Successful Transformation of the Polish Economy." Working Paper 33. United Nations–World Institute for Development Economics Research (WIDER), Helsinki.

Mundell, Robert W. 1997. "The Great Contraction in Transition Economies." In Mario I. Blejer and Marko Skreb, eds., *Macroeconomic Stabilisation in Transition Economies*. Cambridge: Cambridge University Press.

Nuti, Domenico Mario. 1986. "Hidden and Repressed Inflation in Soviet-type Economies: Definitions, Measurements and Stabilisation." *Contributions to Political*

Economy 5: 37–82. Reprinted in C. Davis and W. Charemza, eds. 1989. *Models of Disequilibrium and Shortage in Centrally Planned Economies*. London: Chapam and Hall.

Nuti, Domenico Mario, and Richard Portes. 1993. "Central Europe: The Way Forward." In R. Portes, ed., *Economic Transformation in Central Europe: A Progress Report*. London: Centre for Economic Policy Research and Brussels: EC Official Publications.

Comment

Jan Svejnar

I AM PLEASED TO BE HERE, AND PARTICULARLY TO BE DISCUSSING THE PRESENTATION by Leszek Balcerowicz. The organizers of this lecture series could hardly have chosen a better practitioner to teach lessons about the development experiences of the 1990s. In addition to his strong academic credentials, Leszek was the original architect of economic recovery at the start of the transition. Leszek and his collaborators also founded and run one of the best think tanks in Central and Eastern Europe: the CASE Foundation, which has produced numerous studies and valuable insights on the transition.

Leszek's lecture provides a crisp, refreshing comparative analysis—one that is valuable in looking back and trying to figure out what has happened during the transition. Because I find little to disagree with in the lecture, I will offer some comments that relate to and extend the discussion.

Balcerowicz's Analysis

Leszek provides many analytical insights. His lecture starts with a theoretical and conceptual framework that analyzes the communist system and stresses similarities across communist countries—such as extensive controls and strong welfare and police states—but also important differences—such as varying health indicators, levels of infrastructure development, dependence on the Council for Mutual Economic Assistance (COMECON), and so on. These phenomena should be kept in mind as one analyzes transition economies. Although their initial conditions differed considerably at the start of the transition, their historical economic performance, especially during the final years of communism, was generally dismal. Communist regimes were fairly successful in their early years, especially after World War II, but did much worse in the 1970s and 1980s.

Performance during the transition has been well documented. After universal initial declines in output, countries have exhibited enormous variation in performance indicators such as economic growth rates (which have been relatively high in Central Europe and much lower to the east). In contrast, there has been almost universal success in controlling inflation. Thus some indicators show substantial variation in the performance of transition economies, while others indicate more consistency.

Leszek also describes how policies have influenced outcomes, sometimes unintentionally. The income inequality results he presents are inherently tied to social transfer mechanisms (social security systems) in these countries. In Central Europe social transfers have contained the sharp increases in inequality that would have been generated by the introduction of the market system. In countries like Russia, by contrast, transfer mechanisms have been regressive—exacerbating the inequalities generated by the market system and making income distribution more unequal. These were largely unintended consequences of existing tax and transfer systems.

Leszek then considers some of the reasons for these different outcomes, offering a useful comparative analysis. Transition has been a unique, major, systemic experiment, not just a minor set of reforms. And as noted, across countries there have been wildly diverse initial conditions, policy responses, and outcomes. I largely agree with Leszek's analysis, and would reach a similar conclusion if asked what had happened during the transition. But some important methodological issues need to be addressed, and one's support for the results of this type of analysis hinge on these issues.

Methodological Issues

The main methodological issue is the extent to which policy variables related to performance indicators are truly exogenous—meaning, the extent to which policies affect outcomes but are not influenced by them and the extent to which policymakers are not influenced by economic developments when setting and (especially) implementing policies. This issue has led to an intense empirical search for good instrumental variables—variables correlated with policy variables but not outcome variables. Some of the studies that Leszek cites to support his arguments try to do just that. Still, opinions vary widely on how much progress has been made in this area and on whether the results are sufficiently credible.

On a related note, other variables—such as fixed differences across countries related to geography or other factors—may proxy for policy variables. For instance, since the early 1990s the fastest-growing transition economies (in terms of real GDP) have been clustered to the west, while the slower-growing ones have been to the east. Thus it seems like advocates of geography (or something closely correlated with it) rather than policies as an explanation for performance could have a field day here. Important exceptions, however, suggest that policies matter. The westernmost transition economy, the Czech Republic, had rising GDP until about 1996, but then entered a recession. So geography does not explain everything.

Results may also vary with different performance indicators, a possibility raised by Leszek. I would add that using indexes to measure performance can be treacherous, because indexes are based on subjective weights. Even if the weights are equal across an index's various components, different movements in the individual components can produce the same overall movement in the index.

Other Issues and Questions

A few other issues are worth considering to more fully understand what has happened during the transition. The role of policies is especially crucial, especially at the micro level—using data on firms, individuals, and institutions and analyzing how these agents interact. There has been a lot of research in this area, and it would be useful to integrate it with the macro story that Leszek presents. Major issues include the determinants and effects on country performance of different:

- Forms and sequencing of privatization.
- Types of ownership and corporate governance.
- Approaches to and enforcement of foreign and domestic investment laws.
- Institutional developments in labor and capital markets.

Privatization and ownership structures are extremely important. There have been many studies, but as with macro analyses, many of the findings may not be as credible as they are claimed to be. A lot of studies treat the selection of firms for privatization as a random choice or control for it inadequately. There are also related policy questions, such as: What determines the speed, form, and sequencing of privatization? Have governments tried to optimize their approaches? If so, relative to what? What have governments really intended to achieve? How have they proceeded? What has influenced them? Some studies have addressed these issues, but not many.

A related question is, do some forms of privatization and ownership result in more effective corporate governance and better economic performance than others? There is growing evidence that concentrated foreign ownership has a more positive effect on performance than, say, domestic or dispersed ownership. This point is vital to the design and implementation of privatization and postprivatization policies.

Finally, the potential indirect effects of privatization are not well understood. Does privatization, for instance, contribute to economic growth and development by spurring the development of market institutions such as capital markets?

Issues related to foreign direct investment in transition economies are also critical, including what determines it and how it affects country performance. Inflows of such investment have been uneven across transition economies and over time. Central European and Baltic countries have recently been major recipients of foreign direct investment, and there is enough variation in such investment among transition economies to precisely identify its effects.

Although issues related to the emergence and performance of entrepreneurs and startup firms are generally acknowledged to be significant, again there is surprisingly little solid information. There is a feeling that such firms are a major engine of growth during the transition, but more clear evidence is needed. Recent studies indicate that the shift of workers to these firms from traditional firms has been much larger and occurred much faster than previously imagined. That raises some interesting policy questions: Should efforts focus on new private firms rather than privatized state enterprises? Are new firms going to be more important in the medium and long run? And what are the main constraints to their development? Access to capital? Institutional and legal barriers? Corruption? This area deserves additional attention.

The functioning of labor markets and the effects of unemployment in transition economies remain a huge puzzle. Some countries, such as Poland and the Slovak Republic, have done quite well in terms of economic growth and institutional development, yet their unemployment rates are twice as high as in some of the region's slower-growing economies. To what extent is this related to labor market regulation or other features of these economies?

Of equal importance is the role played by banks during the transition. Many banks provided credit to poorly performing (usually large) firms while rationing it to small firms. But this problem was not always evident unless one was inside the bank. Even then, what amazed me when I examined the banking sector in transition economies in the mid-1990s was that even international bank auditors often could not predict a banking crisis in the making. As a result policymakers often realized that there was a huge problem only after it was too late—the banks involved were too large to fail, and rescue operations had significant budget implications.

Speaking of budget issues, a particularly vexing problem is that the most advanced transition economies (except Slovenia) have suddenly accumulated large budget deficits. A situation that seemed to be under control a few years ago is suddenly out of control, and the problem has arisen in this late phase of the transition, as these countries are about to join the European Union. Understanding how and why this has happened in several countries simultaneously is of considerable interest.

Returning to the banking sector, an intriguing feature from both a policy and an intellectual standpoint is the fact that advanced transition economies have decided to sell all or most of their banks to Western banks. Placing the banking industry in foreign hands seems to have been the only way to put an end to the practice of soft budget constraints in some of these economies. The question that arises is how an industry composed of competing Western banks is going to behave. There are growing indications that these banks are beginning to lend to consumers and to small and medium-size enterprises—retail banking seems to be going very strong, especially in the more advanced economies.

By contrast, stock exchange activity has been quite disappointing. Exchanges rose quickly, set high expectations, and then (except in Poland) stagnated or shrank. The only thing that might save stock markets is pension funds, which may step in and generate demand.

Future Concerns

Looking ahead, a key issue is the extent to which other transition economies will follow the Central European example and rely almost exclusively on foreign banks. Moreover, will a financial sector composed of foreign banks be perceived as providing adequate services? Many developing countries have government-sponsored development banks precisely because governments felt that existing banks were not providing adequate capital and services for development. If foreign banks are not considered adequate, there may be a return to government financing through special banks.

Moreover, what types of firms will become dominant in transition economies? Given that foreign firms and startup firms are doing particularly well, what will happen when these economies really open up, as some have done and others will do? Will there be domestically owned firms on a large scale, or will economies be composed mostly of foreign and newly created domestic firms? Finally, for countries entering the European Union, will the combination of foreign direct investment, local entrepreneurial talent, and *acquis communautaire* result in fast, sustained growth?

Kwesi Botchwey

Former Minister of Finance, Ghana

Born in Ghana, Kwesi Botchwey earned a master of laws (LLM) degree at Yale in 1968 and a doctor of juridical science (SJD) degree at the University of Michigan in 1972. He spent his early career in academia, teaching at the University of Zambia, the University of Dar-Es-Salaam, and the University of Ghana during the period 1970–1982. In 1982, Mr. Botchwey became Ghana's minister of finance, a position he held until 1995. As minister of finance, he was key to the implementation of one of the most far-reaching economic reform programs in Sub-Saharan Africa, earning respect as one of the region's most dedicated reformers.

After leaving the government of Ghana, Mr. Botchwey served as development advisor at the Harvard Institute for International Development from 1996 to 1997, and as director for Africa programs and research and lecturer in public policy at Harvard's Kennedy School of Government from 1998 to 2002. Since 2003, he has served as executive chairman of the African Development Policy Ownership Initiative (ADPOI).

As a tireless advocate for African reform and development, Mr. Botchwey contributes his efforts to a number of organizations. He served as chairman of the Economic Committee of the Global Coalition for Africa from 1991 to 2002; chairman of the African Population Advisory Committee from 1996 to 1998; member of the Board of the Overseas Development Council from 1996 to 2000; and chairman of the Executive Board of the African Capacity Building Foundation from 1998 to 2003. Currently, he is a member of the United Nations Panel of High-Level Personalities on African Development, member of the African Economic Research Consortium Board, founding member of the Carnegie Economic Research Network, and member of the Center for Global Development. Mr. Botchwey has also conducted many consultancy projects and assignments for major international organizations, including the World Bank, the U.N. Development Program, and the European Center for Development Policy and Management.

12 Changing Views and Approaches to Africa's Development

Kwesi Botchwey

I AM DEEPLY HONORED TO HAVE BEEN ASKED TO SPEAK IN THIS DISTINGUISHED LEC-
ture series, and am sincerely grateful to the World Bank for giving me the privilege. I
have decided to share some reflections on the theory and practice of African development over the past two decades, especially the 1990s. I apologize if this topic sounds
dense or even ungainly; I had a hard time deciding what to address here at the Bank,
a citadel of cutting-age knowledge on just about everything under the sun. In the end
I concluded that discussing such a broad topic would give me a convenient pretext for
ruminating on Africa's development experience, on how its development challenges
have come to be understood, and on the efficacy of the current framework for development policy, with its emphasis on reducing poverty and increasing participation.

Recent Ideas and Initiatives

We live in a time of tremendous opportunity for human development and prosperity. But as with many historical conjunctions, it is also a time of great challenge, and
one that harbors potential for enormous tragedy—especially in Sub-Saharan Africa,
where the challenges of development are most daunting.

The onset of the new millennium focused the international community on the
poverty and degradation afflicting much of the developing world, especially South
Asia and Sub-Saharan Africa. It also underscored widespread disappointment with
the painfully slow progress that many countries in these regions have made in reducing poverty despite two decades of policy reforms and, in Africa, a torrent of international initiatives. These include the first United Nations program for a specific
region, the U.N. Program of Action for African Economic Recovery and Development (adopted by the General Assembly in 1986), and its successor, the U.N. New
Agenda for the Development of Africa in the Nineties (adopted in 1991).

The latter initiative was billed as a compact of mutual undertakings under which
Sub-Saharan countries committed to reforms for better economic and political gov-

ernance (including improvements in human rights) and industrial countries committed to, among other things, "innovative and bold" measures to reduce Africa's crippling debt and raise global development assistance to the longstanding target of 0.7 percent of donor country GNP. The idea of a mutual compact or partnership, under which African countries "fulfill their end of the bargain" while industrial countries "reward" them for good performance, continues to permeate G-8 initiatives for African support. Indeed, international development institutions—including the World Bank and Global Coalition for Africa—have recently sold it as a new idea. Yet this approach is partly responsible for the somewhat recriminatory tone of the discourse on solutions to Africa's obdurate development challenges.

In an even more instructive parallel with current international initiatives, the 1991 U.N. initiative also targeted 6 percent annual growth in Sub-Saharan Africa's GDP in the 1990s and a $30 billion increase in official development assistance (ODA) in the program's first year (1992), with 4 percent annual increases thereafter. Yet ODA fell by as much as 43 percent in the 1990s, while GDP growth averaged just 3 percent a year.

Thus it was against a background of many failed regional and international initiatives that the international community signaled a renewed commitment to promoting development by adopting the Millennium Declaration in 2000. Development was also the professed goal of the Doha agenda launched by the World Trade Organization in 2001, and of the U.N. Conference on Financing for Development in Monterrey, Mexico, and World Summit on Sustainable Development in Johannesburg, South Africa, in 2002. All these new declarations and initiatives have acknowledged the serious development challenges facing Sub-Saharan Africa. For instance, the G-8 summit following the Monterrey conference agreed that up to half of the additional aid pledged at the conference would go to Africa.

The renewed international focus on development at the dawn of the millennium was partly influenced by new thinking on development theory and practice. Since the early 1990s economists, development practitioners, and civil society activists have vigorously debated the merits and weaknesses of the neoliberal policy agenda underpinning the Washington consensus. Reviews of Africa's development and reform experiences have been very much part of this debate.

Indeed, for Africa it seems that there is no end to diagnostic studies and the quest for solutions. For example, British Prime Minister Tony Blair recently created yet another commission to examine issues related to Africa's economy, governance, environment, conflict resolution mechanisms, health and education systems, and responses to HIV/AIDS. Blair pointed out that Africa is the only continent to have grown poorer over the past 25 years and risks being left further behind, and directed the commission to issue a comprehensive assessment based on a fresh analysis of Africa's past, present, and future. I am certain that the commission will have a lot to say about the role of the World Bank and allied development and financial institutions in addressing Africa's development challenges.

It is not my intention to provide a lengthy discourse on development theory. I will leave that to better-qualified pundits who, I should add, have achieved a fair bit of consensus on broad development strategies, but continue to contradict one another on many important details. Nor is it my intention to reopen the never-ending debate on what structural adjustment programs have or have not achieved in Africa. Instead I will take some elements of emerging thinking on development generally and on African development in particular, and share some reflections based on my experiences making and managing policy reforms in Ghana in the 1980s and 1990s.

The Washington Consensus and Similar Reforms

John Williamson (in this volume) has said that he did not intend for the policy prescriptions he called the Washington consensus to become a definitive, exhaustive framework to be applied in all developing countries. But quick fixes have a universal appeal, and brilliant summaries and intuition tend to be turned into broader formulas—often over the protests of their inventors.

To take a notorious example, many people still consider Karl Marx's famous rendition of historical materialism to be a universal theory of how social formations emerge and evolve. This is despite Marx's vehement protests that he did not intend it to be a prescription for the path that all countries are destined to follow, regardless of their circumstances. And so it was that in Sub-Saharan Africa, as elsewhere in the developing world—Latin America, South Asia—development strategies in the 1980s and 1990s were defined by structural adjustment programs based on the policies that came to be known as the Washington consensus.

Development policies in the region had been driven by so-called statist and non-market import substitution strategies that were in vogue in the period immediately after independence, and that had produced promising results in some countries through the 1960s. But by the late 1970s and early 1980s these strategies had begun to falter, in part because the region failed to adjust to international hikes in oil prices and interest rates.

By the turn of the millennium, most Sub-Saharan countries had gone through years of economic reforms based on the policy stance of the Washington consensus. According to Williamson, the main changes in development thinking underlying the consensus were recognition of the importance of macroeconomic discipline, trade liberalization rather than import substitution, and industrialization and development of a market economy rather than reliance on the state.

To be sure, in some ways structural adjustment programs entailed a broader agenda for policy reforms than had typical standby arrangements. When we started our reform efforts in Ghana in the early 1980s, our discussions with the International Monetary Fund (IMF) focused almost entirely on the extent of fuel price increases and quarterly exchange rate adjustments. At the time the Bank avoided discussions of macroeconomic issues, taking its cues from IMF-determined macroeconomic frameworks (and their implied resource envelopes) for the programming of investment spending. In those days hapless African finance ministers would leave the austere ambiance of the IMF building, having accepted a tight financial program under protest, then walk across the street only to confront an indignant Bank team, concerned that the program left too little space for development spending!

To some extent the almost exclusive focus on monetary and fiscal discipline in the early stages of Ghana's program was dictated by the prevailing macroeconomic situation. The exchange rate was grossly overvalued, large budget deficits were being financed almost entirely by borrowing from the banking system, and inflation was about 120 percent. But that focus was more a reflection of the development ideology of the time. When the expanded agenda of structural adjustment programs was launched in Ghana in the mid-1980s, it came in an uncontrolled avalanche that strained local capacity, undermined the cohesion of government decisionmaking, and eroded national ownership of the reform program, as different Bank departments competed in launching multiple reforms entailing broadly based deregulation and privatization.

Although there have been quibbles about the role of interruptions and weak implementation in explaining these programs' disappointing outcomes (especially in internal IMF reviews of programs supported by its Enhanced Structural Adjustment Facility in Africa and other regions), there is now general agreement that the programs had major inherent weaknesses. Indeed, Williamson has admitted to major errors in the programs, including their narrow focus on restoring growth—a focus that, in his words, never really faced up to the need to expand employment in particular and opportunities in general, to give poor people a chance to contribute their talents.

Some critics have argued that rapid import liberalization in Sub-Saharan countries undergoing adjustment has tended to have a negative effect on employment and wages, at least in the short to medium term. Others have found that liberalization in Africa and Latin America has increased unemployment because consumers have switched from nontraded goods to imports after the lowering of tariffs and nontariff barriers. In addition, the U.N. Conference on Trade and Development has found that in many cases rapid liberalization in Sub-Saharan Africa has led to wage inequality, raising questions about the timing and sequencing of reforms.

New Concepts of African Development

But recent changes have been much more far-reaching than even these admissions suggest. Indeed, the very concept of African development has changed. Within the Bank and among economists and practitioners generally, African development has come to be seen as a more comprehensive process of transformation than merely raising incomes. The overriding goal of development is now to reduce poverty in a broader sense, including by empowering poor people and ensuring their participation in decisions that affect their lives.

We have come to understand (or at least say) that policy reforms cannot be forced on a country or people from the outside, and that national ownership is crucial to sustained and effective implementation of a reform agenda. We have also realized that the state's role in promoting popular participation and creating a sound investment environment is larger than the somewhat minimalist role assigned to it by the Washington consensus. Finally, we better understand and acknowledge that successful transformation requires an external environment that facilities access to international markets and complements outwardly oriented domestic policy reforms.

Thus we have come a long way in many respects. The extent of the change is reflected in the growing diversity of the Bank's operational instruments, the increasing coverage of its lending programs, and the expanding focus of its research and analytical work. We now march into the discourse on African development intoning a new incantation focused on poverty reduction, governance and institutions, empowerment, and national ownership. The challenge is to ensure that these terms actually signal change and are not designed, like most incantations, to save us from the difficult task of thinking through the difficult processes of change.

Poverty reduction

The focus on poverty reduction as a key objective is the most important feature of new strategies for African development. It is the result of concerns about rising poverty levels in the region despite two decades of adjustment, and of the realization that while growth through better macroeconomic policies is a necessary condition for poverty reduction, it does not always benefit poor people. Accordingly, there has been renewed emphasis on poverty-reducing policies, including improving poor people's access to education and health care and providing safety nets for poor and vulnerable groups when macroeconomic stabilization measures become necessary to address monetary and fiscal crises.

All this is welcome, and World Bank–IMF Poverty Reduction Strategy Papers (PRSPs) have greatly improved in form and content, leading to more informative and transparent budget presentation—while the PRSP process has raised public interest in economic policymaking. But we must guard against the danger of these new processes and their goal of poverty reduction becoming a way of deflecting criticism of the previous neoliberal paradigm. Unless the central problem of resource inadequacy is satisfactorily addressed on the multiple fronts of domestic resource mobilization and foreign trade and debt, African policymakers will continue to face tradeoffs between capital investment and poverty-reducing social spending that simply cannot be resolved. Moreover, this dilemma cannot be obviated merely by encouraging countries to prepare "alternative" macroeconomic scenarios, when the only real alternative is a baseline scenario that IMF staff certify as feasible based on historical trends in domestic and external (especially donor) resource flows.

From a theoretical and analytical perspective, another type of danger is no less significant. The discourse on structural adjustment experiences included vigorous debate on issues of equity, distribution, and contestation. Under the new approach there is a danger that this debate will be squelched by the convenient moral sanction of the poverty reduction label, supported by a parade of pro-poor spending indicators that are nothing more than accounting fiddles, replacing honest debate on development strategy. So, while Poverty Reduction Strategy Papers and the development theory underpinning them have brought us closer to understanding which policies have the potential to produce faster growth with poverty reduction, we do not, at least in Africa—and I suspect in other regions as well—yet understand the workings of the political and political economy processes that would bring about this outcome. Indeed, it seems to me that a number of tendencies threaten to set us back. Two especially worrisome tendencies are common to analyses of Africa's economic performance under the new development strategies.

The cult of quantification

The first of these is what I would call the cult of quantification, especially among economists—that is, a tendency to reduce everything to general statistical categories (what John Hicks called "statistical uniformity") and, worse, to behave as if regressions yield conclusions that are "inevitable" and more or less unaffected by human and social interventions, conclusions that then enable us to determine precisely when particular policy interventions must be made. At a meeting on governance that I attended in Accra a few years ago, one donor representative referred to a study, based on cross-country regressions, that she claimed established precise entry points for effective donor assistance in postconflict situations—two years into the postconflict period! Indeed, even in the domain of the "political economy of development," which should provide a meeting point for economists, political scientists, sociologists, and other social scientists, this cult of quantification and models based on brilliant intuition (at best) have begun to take hold.

We now quantify and grade—often on the basis of opinion surveys that purport to endow these studies with empiricism that surely must be delusive—everything from ethnic tensions to government stability, democratic accountability, law and order, corruption, and quality of bureaucracy. I have difficulty understanding what a score of 4 (on a scale of 1–10) on corruption or quality of bureaucracy really conveys for the entire region of Sub-Saharan Africa relative to a 5 for, say, South Asia.

This subject obviously goes beyond the scope of my lecture. I merely wish to note that it is impossible to make real progress in appreciating the complex political economy processes that influence successful outcomes in development policy in different environments while this cult prevails. The calculus and models often hinder debate by endowing analysis with a veneer of technical neutrality, when in fact it is the product of ideological or political positions that are at the very least contestable. Our method of inquiry, as opposed to our method of presentation, is always anchored in some social theory, whether we admit it or are even conscious of it.

The baggage of recrimination and hubris

A second tendency in the debate on African development is that for recrimination and hubris, which lead to subjective analyses of African development issues. A truly astonishing example of this tendency recently appeared in the *New York Times*. In an article titled "Africa Earned Its Debt," Robert Guest, Africa editor of *The Economist*, claims that "Nigeria, like *most of Africa* [throughout, the emphasis is mine], ought to be rich but is miserably poor. The main reason is that rather than striving to create an environment in which people can freely seek prosperity and happiness, *most* African governments have chosen instead to rob them." Guest also claims that "the main reason Zambia is bankrupt is that it has been ruled with startling incompetence and venality." His evidence? "Its previous president…is *facing* multiple charges of embezzlement." He concludes: "That in a nutshell is why Africans are poor: their leaders keep them that way."

That such views are held by the Africa editor of a respectable journal and published in an equally respectable newspaper speaks volumes about the state of informed debate on the causes of Africa's development challenges. I cite it here not only because it is such an excellent, if outrageous, example of recriminatory and hubristic tendencies in the debate on African development, but also because it espouses a particularly simple theory that explains all development in terms of the role of individual leaders—a sort of latter-day manifestation of what the British historian E. H. Carr called the "Bad King John" theory of history. It is the unspoken social theory that underpins much of the discussion on governance and corruption in Africa.

So, while there has been a shift toward greater depth and breadth in development thinking, some rather atavistic strains remain. The purveyors of the new thinking are to some extent right in pointing out that it differs from the Washington consensus in its emphasis on empowerment and participation, governance and institutions, and national ownership, and in its greater sensitivity to the social costs of adjustment, among others. But the depth and extent of the change can be exaggerated, and analytical and intellectual elements of the emerging paradigm require further probing, refinement, and demystification.

Governance and institutions

Beyond the new emphasis on poverty reduction, the most fundamental shift in development theory on Africa has been the renewed focus on governance and institutions. This renewed focus was, initially at least, probably overdone, and gave the impression of generalized corruption without sufficient analytical work on the varied manifestations of bad governance and the political conditions in which they thrive. By reducing the problems to mere matters of sui generis corruption and predatory behavior by politicians and other public sector actors, it diverted attention from the real causes of market failure and of what was needed to improve the efficiency of nonmarket institutional agreements, and to rein in the influence of informal layers of power (vested interests) in the private sector.

Over time there has been commendable progress in analytical work on governance, especially in the World Bank, the Economic Commission for Africa, and academic writing generally. For example, an Economic Commission for Africa project on governance has begun to do helpful analytical work on governance, broadly defined to include both state and nonstate sectors in the economic and political spheres, and started monitoring performance using indicators and data collection methodologies that capture factual information as well as opinions of expert groups and the general public.

Such developments are extremely encouraging. But again, from a theoretical and analytical point of view, it is important to point out that while such studies have been enormously helpful for understanding the role of governance and institutions in

Africa's development, they have also tended to cloud the debate somewhat. They create the impression that the issues at stake are merely "technical" and "scientific"—that they simply require distilling best practices through cross-country research or, worse, that the new governance and institutions credo is, again, an apolitical substitute for a development strategy, when in fact it is deeply political and ideological.

A central part of the discourse on governance, for instance, revolves around the role of the state. Although the post–Washington consensus worldview sees a larger role for the state in development than the consensus assigned, it sees the role of the state essentially as one of creating a congenial environment for market forces to operate efficiently. It steps beyond this core role only to correct for market failure. In Africa there is a pronounced sentiment that the state is so easily susceptible to capture for rent-seeking purposes that an expanded role for it merely creates space for corruption. This is an ideological position that cannot be validated by econometric demonstration. In the same way, the new focus on judicial reform and the rule of law is in the end based on formalist and functionalist arguments that lawyers know are infinitely more complex than economists tend to think. The institutionalizing and safeguarding of the rule of law and an independent judiciary—widely considered part of an investment-promoting policy framework—rest on assumptions about the merits of formalism and faith in judicial discretion.

My point is simply that the discussion on governance and institutions in Africa often misses the dynamics of the contest for power that lies at the heart of all democratic systems. Democratic governments must win elections, and political parties and electoral campaigns must be funded. The pressures that these dynamics exert on the integrity of economic and especially fiscal management are often the primary motive for rent seeking—as when an incumbent government breaks spending limits to gain political advantage or manipulates the contract award system for financial and political advantage (as happens in even the most advanced democracies). Moreover, there are rents even in liberalized economies; projects funded by export credits are a notorious source. Rents are also often the primary motivation for influencing the shape of institutions and the rules that govern them.

We must rein in our appetite for easy generalizations and convenient categories. It is also important to acknowledge progress made in Africa in improving the capacity of public institutions to fulfill their economic management functions—in making and implementing economic policy, delivering services, and ensuring accountability in the use of public resources—and in internalizing commitments to good governance at the national and regional levels, as evidenced by the New Partnership for Africa's Economic Development (NEPAD) and its peer review mechanism.

Finally, it is important to appreciate that institutions take time to build and must be allowed to evolve, mainly as a result of internal prodding. In this connection it was not particularly helpful for the G-8 countries to rest the entire credibility of the NEPAD initiative on the willingness and action of African leaders in condemning Zimbabwe's President Robert Mugabe, even before the procedures and mechanisms of the peer review process had been established and its members chosen.

Empowerment

I see a few pitfalls in discussions of empowerment. The emphasis on empowerment in the new development thinking is clearly valid, especially in its focus on education and health care. But when it comes to participation the case has been formulated rather carelessly in some of the debate, without proper understanding of its full operational and political implications. That is especially the case when it comes to the legitimacy and mandates of democratic institutions at both the national level (such as parliaments and other oversight bodies) and the local (decentralized) level.

The point of empowerment is not to romanticize poverty or poor people or to create an ultrademocratic environment where all policy is debated and approved by all stakeholders. A recent study by the U.N. Conference on Trade and Development frames the matter well when it notes that replacing conventional institutions of representative democracy with ad hoc mechanisms involving segments of civil society could undermine the fledgling democratic institutions taking root in African societies.

Much confusion and frustration surrounds poor people's participation in the Poverty Reduction Strategy Paper process. What does it mean to have poor people's aspirations reflected in the papers? A 1999 World Bank study of 24 countries, including 8 African countries, showed that in a number of areas—agriculture, labor markets, income distribution, macroeconomic policies, private sector policies—poor people's views and perceptions diverged dramatically from those of governments and international financial institutions.

Such findings are hardly surprising. The challenge is to improve poor people's access to knowledge and information and to establish institutional mechanisms that enable them to canvass support for measures and policies that promote their interests through their elected representatives in national and local legislative bodies. At the local level it is also necessary to set up accountability institutions, without which poor people's aspirations and interests can be subverted by the rural bourgeoisie in many cynical ways.

National ownership

Much has been said and written about local and national ownership of the reform agenda and its implementation, with many analysts calling ownership—along with greatly reduced and simplified conditionality—the most important condition for successful reform. This is most of all what is said to set the new thinking apart from the Washington consensus.

The World Bank and IMF have gone to great lengths to define and circumscribe the role and participation of their staff in preparing and implementing poverty reduction programs. Beyond the broad framework for thematic coverage formulated to guide the preparation of Poverty Reduction Strategy Papers and ensure their compatibility with the requirements of both institutions, their staff are forbidden from playing any but a purely supporting role in these processes.

Yet there are concerns, following recent reviews of select African Poverty Reduction Strategy Papers—including some prepared by national authorities before the

thematic framework and mechanisms of the joint staff assessments were devised—
that the papers' major policy directions are remarkably similar to those pursued
under the structural adjustment programs of the 1980s and 1990s, raising the possibility that perceptions of what donors and international financial institutions would
accept predominate over those of national ownership. Moreover, some nongovernmental organizations continue to argue that the Poverty Reduction Strategy Papers
have simply adopted the policy framework of structural adjustment programs. These
concerns are probably exaggerated. I believe that there has been a change.

But I also believe that ownership remains largely ephemeral in concept and rather
elusive in practice. The metaphors involved, such as the idea of "putting countries in
the driver's seat," betray some of this elusiveness. Part of the problem is that we have
not sufficiently recognized the full implications of the asymmetric power relations
between low-income African countries and the world of donors and international
financial institutions. It is still not clear what scope the countries have for policy
choice and sequencing.

The matter is not helped by the absence of systematic independent review (let
alone adjudication) of differences between African countries and international financial institutions. Low-income countries that have the leverage of market size or
strategic value tend to fare better. In addition, in most countries a culture of aid
dependency and the administrative encumbrances associated with aid flows continue
to divert policymakers' attention from a search for truly national solutions.

Conclusion

There have been important changes in the ways we conceive and theorize about
African development—indeed, all development. I have pointed out that the extent
and depth of the changes are exaggerated in some respects, and that our thinking and
understanding in a number important areas of the emerging paradigm would benefit from further research, analysis, and refinement. Given the pressures on aid flows,
the halting politics of international action on Africa's external debt, and the political
cloud over the successful conclusion of the Doha round, greater rigor in development theory and investment by the Bank—especially in knowledge creation and dissemination—would serve Africa best. But African countries must assume the
responsibility of leadership in this regard.

Comment

Jeffrey Herbst

IT IS A PLEASURE TO BE HERE, AND BOTH AN HONOR AND A CHALLENGE TO FOLLOW Kwesi Botchwey. As a political scientist, I greatly enjoyed Botchwey's lecture. Instead of delivering the usual warnings that the world is about to abandon Africa—which we have heard constantly for the past 20 years—he describes a relationship that it is much more complex and fraught with difficulty.

According to Botchwey, the world loves Africa both too much and too little. Too much because Africa is engaged in an endless, almost frenetic policy dialogue with industrial countries and international financial institutions offering increasingly complicated suggestions about what it should do and how and when it should do it. But too little because the international community does not provide Africa with sufficient resources to pursue a more complex development agenda.

Africa, Aid, and the International Community

One of Botchwey's main criticisms involves how aid is provided. He describes how at various points over the past 20 years, donors have tried to take ownership of economic policy away from African governments in favor of international, domestic, and civil society groups—leading to resentment and distrust on both sides. What caused this strained international relationship with Africa? Three reasons come to mind.

The first is the overall context of development failure. Africa's policies would have been considered much more successful if growth rates had been higher, if wars had not broken out, if resource prices had been higher, if many things had gone differently. But things did not work out that way, partly because of flawed policies but also because of structural conditions in Africa.

Second, perhaps the most important trend in Africa over the past 20 years is the continent's growing heterogeneity. In some African countries (Botswana, Ghana, Mauritius, and a few others) development and integration with the international economy are achievable and on everyone's agenda. But in many, institutional survival is the primary agenda, and development is a distant dream to be considered only when the state is restored. Most African states fall somewhere in between. As a result it has become more difficult—for donors and for Africans—to develop a policy agenda that can be applied across Africa, and for the continent to speak with one voice.

Third, the political dynamics surrounding economic discussions in Africa have been disappointing. Although Botchwey raises concerns about ownership, I have a different complaint: economic policy is hardly debated in most of the many multi-party election campaigns occurring across Africa. Thus, seemingly the main issue facing these countries—how are they going to begin to develop—is pushed to the side. More than anything, that unfortunate oversight reflects a basic failure among African leaders. Too often, not only international financial institutions and Western governments but also African leaders are more comfortable discussing economic policy in Washington, D.C., than in African capitals.

Related to this weakness is a lack, in Africa, of champions of economic policy. Part of the problem is that Africa's big countries (whether by population or land mass)—the Democratic Republic of Congo, Ethiopia, Nigeria, Sudan (South Africa is a partial exception)—have performed extremely poorly, while many of the countries that have done especially well—Botswana and Mauritius, each of which contains just 2 million or so people, along with Ghana, Uganda, and a few others—cannot lead by example. Because of their small sizes, these success stories have had little effect on the economic policies of their neighbors. If one of Africa's big countries had done well, the continent's economic agenda would be much clearer. But as long as the big countries continue to falter, the debate on economic policy will remain inchoate.

Adapting the Development Agenda

Botchwey suggests that the development agenda has become so complex that it is hard for African governments to manage. To the issues he identifies, I would add security. In the 1990s security became perhaps the main obstacle to development in many African countries—creating increasingly tough challenges that make complex policy measures more attractive but more difficult to implement.

What I take away from Botchwey's lecture most of all is that the development agenda has to become more modular and to some extent simpler to adopt, because no developing country—much less poor countries with weak administrative cadres and institutional structures—can do all the things that are required and that the international community thinks are a good idea. Prioritizing and simplifying those goals is difficult, and Botchwey assigns that responsibility to African governments, with international financial institutions and Western governments asked to pay due respect.

Comment

Michael Chege

WHETHER IN THE CONSTRUCTION OF PHYSICAL INFRASTRUCTURE OR THE RECON-
struction of national economies, project design and implementation are at best an art
based on science, and require considerable human imagination. This is the dominant
lesson from Kwesi Botchwey's fascinating account of his experience as Ghana's
finance minister during that country's protracted reform program (1983–94), which
followed two decades of economic regress.

A development practitioner's world differs from that of an economist as much as the
world of an engineer differs from that of a physical scientist. In a widely praised book
on what engineers do, Walter G. Vincenti (1990) quotes a well-regarded British aero-
nautics engineer who says that, like other modern wonders of construction, "aero-
planes are not designed by science but by art, in spite of some pretense and humbug to
the contrary." The engineer immediately adds that although he's not suggesting that
engineering can do without science—since it is grounded in scientific theories—it is
not the same as applied sciences and is separated from physical sciences by a wide gap.

As Vincenti explains, engineers break their main designs into parts, test for compatibility among those, redesign them, and experiment with alternative designs before choosing the product demonstrating the highest functional capability in accordance with user
demands. It is a process of learning by doing, constant adjustment, intuition, and imagination. In *The Strategy of Decision*, David Braybrooke and Charles Lindblom (1965) define
the making and implementation of public policy in roughly the same terms. This is in
contrast to the principles on generating hypotheses and empirically testing them, with
the aim of increasing causal knowledge, that govern the scientific enterprise.

Developments in Ghana's Development

Ghana was the first Sub-Saharan colonial state to achieve independence, in 1957, and
in 1960 boasted a per capita income higher than that of most developing countries—
inspiring confidence in the rest of Africa and beyond. But beset by mismanagement

at all levels, the economy began weakening in the mid-1960s. Until macroeconomic conditions stabilized in 1984, Ghana experienced intermittent negative growth starting in 1966. Growth problems became severe after the country's failure to adjust to the 1974 oil crisis, and chronic under military rule between 1979 and 1983. Obtaining basic daily goods became increasingly difficult due to falling productivity, foreign exchange shortages, high inflation, and (in theory) state-imposed price controls.

Botchwey describes the spirited efforts to change course made by Jerry Rawlings's putatively revolutionary government. Initial efforts involved strict application of socialist, command economics and, when that failed, economic liberalization that saw Ghana emerge as an archetypal case of economic recovery underpinned by macroeconomic stability, donor assistance, and market-led growth.

As with engineering and policymaking processes, these efforts started with trial and error. When the Ghanaian government turned to the International Monetary Fund (IMF) and the World Bank in 1983, it thought of this move not as a betrayal of the socialist goals that brought it to power but as an alternative route to the same end. As a result, by the mid-1980s one school of Marxist political economists in Africa had reconciled itself to the perspective, eloquently endorsed by Karl Marx and Friedrich Engels in *The Communist Manifesto*, that expanding the "bourgeois mode of production" to colonial territories was a positive development relative to existing economic and social conditions. This about-turn was best demonstrated by the endorsement in 1984 of the market-oriented "Berg Report," issued by the World Bank in 1981, by two distinguished Marxist economists from Africa, John Sender and Sheila Smith (1984, 1987), among others.

Among development practitioners, too, the fact that economic growth under state control and ownership had failed was acknowledged by then-President Julius Nyerere (1977) in his 10-year evaluation of Tanzania's socialist blueprint, *The Arusha Declaration*, and by Mozambique's then-President Samora Machel, who in 1980 (based on his experience with radical state intervention) admonished the incoming government of independent Zimbabwe not to nationalize private property or take any action that would lead to an exodus of skilled whites (Meredith 2003). By changing direction in 1983, Ghana was again ahead of the curve among African socialist states. The lesson from this experience is that policy reform was a response to failure—as it often is—rather than a product of inspiration by brilliant new ideas offered to Africa. The critical factor determining success is how soon and determinedly a state reacts to disaster. By turning to the IMF and World Bank, Ghana was fast on its feet relative to its peers, and that made all the difference.

But as Botchwey indicates, changing direction was the easy part. Implementing macroeconomic and sector reforms (as later defined by the Washington consensus) was the hard part. Donors' insistence on measurable targets—for fiscal goals, privatization, and the like—led to counterproductive results. It ignored qualitative factors, varying political difficulties across economic sectors, and the fact that desperate governments seeking aid could produce the statistics that donors wanted, and vice versa. As we now move into the era of mandatory indicators on the Millennium Development Goals and poverty reduction, this is a lesson worth bearing in mind. As explained by Vincenti and by Braybrooke and Lindblom, the best results come from avoiding errors, dividing problems into parts, and subjecting new policies to stringent testing—and rejecting them if they are found deficient.

In Botchwey's experience, rigid adherence to macroeconomic targets was a hindrance to rather than a catalyst for change. Like the approaches implemented around the world in the name of the Washington consensus (see Williamson 2003 and in this volume), it was too doctrinaire. But though many doubts have been raised about this approach, the goals of the Washington consensus—macroeconomic stability, fiscal discipline, low inflation, a carefully targeted money supply—should not be taken lightly. Reckless disregard for these issues was what led to Africa's economic disaster in the first place, as in Ghana until 1983.

Weaknesses in Development Strategies, Data, and Analyses

With the winding down of the economic reform rhetoric of the Washington consensus, the role of well-functioning institutions as a leading determinant of growth has sprung to the fore. In that connection it is worth reiterating Botchwey's methodological criticism of excess quantification in assessing institutional capability and sources of economic growth—as has recently been done far too often for African growth. Like Botchwey, most people with a deep, well-rounded knowledge of the region are profoundly skeptical of this approach.

But the problem is not so much quantification (an unavoidable research tool) as it is careless attribution of causal relationships based on spurious statistical relationships between growth and climate, geography, institutions, culture, violence, ethno-linguistic diversity, and the like. In 1996 Dierdre McCloskey and Stephen Ziliak found that 70 percent of the articles published in the *American Economic Review* in the 1980s failed to distinguish economic from statistical significance, and figures from social realities. In 2004 the authors revisited the situation and found that it had actually worsened: 80 percent of the articles published in the journal in the 1990s committed the same errors and so failed to provide a causal analysis of the practical world of economics (cited in *The Economist*, 31 January 2004). I have seen no rebuttal of these findings.

Enormous damage can arise from actions based on such analyses. For example, a 1999 article in the *Lancet*, Britain's leading medical journal, reported a strong relationship between autism and childhood vaccinations for measles, mumps, and rubella. The scare provoked by the article led to a 10 percent reduction in childhood vaccinations for these diseases—and over the next few years hospitals observed a resurgence in them. By the time authors reversed their findings, the damage had already been done (*The Guardian*, 21 February 2004).

With few exceptions, economic data for Africa are weak. And if such developments can occur in Britain, and in medicine, it calls for careful circumspection in arriving at interpretations and conclusions drawn from the mass of aggregate data on African social and economic conditions. This places an especially onerous responsibility on the World Bank and the IMF, given the influence their research has on African development policy. Since the onset of economic recovery in Ghana, many of its citizens have been dubious about gains from growth. Some of this cynicism is clearly remiss: since 1983 the economy has expanded by more than a third. But there is a distinct possibility that aggregate data miss qualitative and other realities, making it hard to sell reforms to the public.

As a development practitioner, Botchwey is concerned about the current emphasis on popular participation in decisionmaking and its impact on institutional capacity to follow through. Today's development policymakers must meet ever-growing yet contradictory criteria. In addition to participation and rapid growth, attention must be paid to local culture, environmental effects, good governance, a pro-poor stance, empowerment of disadvantaged groups, and gender concerns.

But participation, to take one example, inevitably sharpens political differences. Upstream and downstream water users have different concerns, and pastoralists and neighboring farmers have conflicting land use priorities. Similarly, when asked to name their poverty reduction priorities, poor people (like everyone else) generate long project lists that the national budget cannot handle without incurring unwanted deficits. Accordingly, painful decisions must be made across groups and sectors. To the extent that such problems can be resolved, it is through discordant compromises by free political agents, sequencing expenditures and drawing on conventional notions of equity—that is, through the democratic process that Braybrooke and Lindblom say is the least defective mode of making and implementing policy.

Botchwey's lecture makes clear the dangers of monolithic, straight-arrow, quasi-scientific solutions to Africa's development challenges. To return to Vincenti and to Braybrooke and Lindblom, the construction of physical and social projects is an art grounded in science—a world where one successful step leads to the next. Creativity is crucial. As in the old Napoleonic maxim, "On s'engage et puis on voit." The sooner we recognize that, the better off we will all be.

References

Braybrooke, David, and Charles Lindblom. 1965. *The Strategy of Decision.* New York: Free Press.

McCloskey, Deirdre, and Stephen T. Ziliak. 1996. "The Standard Error of Regressions." *Journal of Economic Literature* 34: 97–114.

Meredith, Martin. 2003. *Robert Mugabe.* London: Public Affairs.

Nyerere, Julius. 1977. *The Arusha Declaration after Ten Years.* Dar es Salaam, Tanzania: Government Printer.

Sender, John, and Sheila Smith. 1984. "What Is Right with the Berg Report and What Is Left of Its Critics." University of Sussex, Institute for Development Studies.

———. 1987. *The Development of Capitalism in Africa.* London: Methuen.

Vincenti, Walter G. 1990. *What Engineers Know and How They Know It.* Baltimore, Md.: The Johns Hopkins University Press.

Williamson, John. 2003. "From Agenda to Damaged Brand Name." *Finance and Development* (September).

Rima Khalaf Hunaidi

Assistant Secretary General, United Nations Development Programme; Former Minister of Planning, Jordan

Born in Kuwait in 1953 and a citizen of Jordan, Rima Khalaf Hunaidi is a graduate of the American University of Beirut (economics) and of Portland State University (M.A. in economics and Ph.D. in system science). She started her professional career in 1979 as a lecturer in the Business School and Department of Economics at Portland State University in Oregon. In 1985, she was appointed director of the Planning and Research Department, Ministry of Planning, in Amman. Between 1990 and 1993 she occupied successively the posts of director-general, Jordan Export Development and Commercial Centers Corporation, and director-general for the Investment Promotion Department in Amman.

She has held high-ranking positions in Jordan, including Minister of Industry and Trade (1993–1995), Minister of Planning (1995–1998), and most recently deputy Prime Minster and Minister of Planning (1999–2000). During her tenure as head of the ministerial economic team, Ms. Hunaidi succeeded in pushing forward the drive for economic reform while simultaneously spearheading the effort for poverty alleviation and strengthening the social safety net.

From November 1997 through September 2000, Ms. Hunaidi served as a Senator in the Upper House of the Jordanian Parliament. Simultaneously, she served as a member of the Economic Consultative Council, a public-private sector initiative established and directly supervised by King Abdullah to promote economic reform and modernization in Jordan. Ms. Hunaidi is holder of the Grand Codon of the Order of Al-Kawkab Al-Urduni ("The Star of Jordan"), bestowed upon her in 1995 by King Hussein bin Talal.

In 2000, Ms. Hunaidi was appointed assistant secretary-general and director, Regional Bureau for Arab States (RBAS), at the United Nations Development Programme.

13 Reform in Hindsight
Promises and Illusions in Jordan

Rima Khalaf Hunaidi

IT GIVES ME GREAT PLEASURE TO BE SPEAKING HERE AMONG FRIENDS AND COL-
leagues. For most of the past two decades I have had the privilege of working with
development partners and specialists on a wide range of issues related to Jordan's
development and, more recently, on broader—and critical—questions about human
development in the Arab world.

In the summer of 2004, Jordan announced the conclusion of its final reform program with the International Monetary Fund (IMF) and World Bank and the start of
a new era of domestically designed economic and structural reforms. Thus this is an
excellent time to reflect on what Jordan has achieved—and what it might have
achieved—since it began pursuing donor-supported reform programs.

My remarks will focus on the origins of Jordan's first major economic crisis and
consequent reforms, the economics of war and peace there, the reforms that have
actually occurred, the lessons from participating in the formulation and implementation of reforms and stabilization policies in turbulent times, and finally the emergence of the Arab *Human Development Reports*.

Jordan's Economy—Booms and Busts

As a non–oil producer in a region floating on oil, Jordan had few economic advantages in the early 1970s. Its production structures were weak, its industrial base was
thin, and its economic institutions were feeble. Exports consisted mainly of phos-
phates and agricultural products. Moreover, the country's economy had been trau-
matized by the 1967 Arab-Israeli War, during which Israel occupied Jordan's West
Bank, imposing severe hardships on its people and economy. Jordan's only advantage
was its educated, relatively skilled workforce.

Then, suddenly and unexpectedly, Jordan had its first encounter with ostensible
prosperity. The 1973 oil boom brought swift riches to Jordan's oil-producing Gulf
neighbors, creating unprecedented opportunities for Jordanians. Hundreds of thou-

sands flocked to Gulf countries to work in relatively high-paying jobs, and sent home remittances that bloated disposable incomes and enabled record levels of consumption. During 1976–85 real income growth averaged 7.2 percent a year—and between 1973 and 1979 it was 11.1 percent.

In addition to remittances, growth was buoyed by foreign aid—particularly from Gulf states, which attached few or no conditions to it—and by increased agricultural exports to regional markets. As a result Jordan was able to invest heavily in infrastructure and social services, particularly education, despite its meager domestic revenues and high military expenditures imposed by Israel's accupation of the West Bank. But the generous assistance from Gulf countries also led to unchecked spending, including a bloated bureaucracy.

By the mid-1980s Jordan was spending more than it earned and consuming more than it produced, with annual consumption averaging 113 percent of GDP in 1980–85. During this time television antennas sprouted on even the tiniest shacks, while better-off Jordanians began engaging in conspicuous consumption of costly goods, clothing, and other imports. But there was no way to sustain this prosperity. It, along with the national budget and balance of payments, depended on the generosity of other countries—which was destined to end.

Economic crisis

Jordan's reversal of fortune started in the mid-1980s, when its oil-producing neighbors entered a prolonged economic downturn due to a rapid drop in oil prices. As the Gulf job market shrank, Jordanians began returning home and oil-based remittances fell. Domestic growth, which was largely dependent on neighboring oil economies, also started to weaken. Consequently there was growing demand for the Jordanian government to fill the gap by sponsoring infrastructure and capital investment.

Although drastic policy changes were needed, the government's newly acquired spending habits proved difficult to change. Instead of introducing fiscal discipline, in the second half of the 1980s the government began taking on short-term foreign debt and other foreign commercial loans, leading to growing budget deficits. Foreign debt shot from $2.9 billion in 1985 to $8.0 billion in 1988. With record fiscal deficits and balance of payment difficulties, foreign reserves dwindled and could cover no more than two weeks of imports.

In 1988 a crash in the foreign exchange market heralded the impending crisis. The exchange rate fell by 50 percent, causing prices to jump and real GDP to plummet. In 1989 the cost of living index rose 26 percent, real GDP fell 16 percent, and per capita income dropped to $1,317—about one-fifth less than in 1985. Moreover, financial instability reduced foreign inflows and increased capital flight and bank difficulties.

Despite the many warning signs in early 1988, few government officials saw them—not because of analytical or institutional weaknesses, but because of inadequate democratic institutions to ensure proper disclosure and accountability by the executive authority. Few planners, decisionmakers, or cabinet members were aware of the volume or nature of commercial and near-commercial borrowing in the second half of the 1980s. There was no parliament to pose questions or demand answers, and no independent media to probe officials. As a result the crisis continued to build.

Economic reform—and political crisis

In late 1988, in response to the worsening economic situation, the government introduced a reform plan. But the plan, though well developed, was too little too late. Jordan could not service its growing debt service obligations, nor could it secure fresh credit. The country needed to restructure and reschedule its debt, and realized that an independent national adjustment program would not succeed. Thus the government asked the IMF and the World Bank for loans and other support to help solve its economic predicament.

In 1989 the government introduced adjustment and stabilization policies based on its agreements with the IMF and the Bank (and other creditors). One of the earliest reforms involved cutting public subsidies for oil products. Though much needed, this measure was introduced in haste—in the absence of democratic institutions to consult with and without thorough assessment of its effects on other sectors.

For example, at the time the transportation sector was highly regulated, with the government setting fees for public transportation, including buses and taxis. The sudden increase in the prices of oil products substantially raised transportation costs, and no steps were taken to adjust transportation tariffs. The increase led to rioting among taxi drivers, and the violence spread to major Jordanian cities, escalating into what became known as the April Insurrection.

The first Jordanian government to introduce macroeconomic reform became the first victim of that reform. But as that government walked out in April 1989, something else much more important walked in—democracy. Moreover, many lessons were learned from the early reform. Some related to the importance of proper sequencing and coordination of reforms, others to the attention that should be paid to their complementarities. But the most important lesson was that no country could succeed in confronting crises, political or economic, without the protection and strength that comes by ensuring the public's participation in decisionmaking.

A new government was installed in April 1989, and plans for parliamentary elections started immediately. By the end of 1989 Jordan had its first elected parliament since the 1967 war, and economic reforms resumed.

War—and peace

But it was not long before crisis hit again. This time it was caused by Iraq's invasion of Kuwait in August 1990. Jordan did not join the international coalition assembled to liberate Kuwait; instead it advocated an Arab solution to drive out Iraq. Jordan's policymakers feared that the presence of some 500,000 foreign soldiers on Arab lands could trigger a radicalization process that would be extremely difficult to reverse. Such fears were justified, as events in the region and abroad (such as the September

11, 2001, attacks in the United States and other terrorist events in Morocco, Saudi Arabia, and Spain) continue to indicate.

The war and Jordan's political position inflicted a heavy toll on the economy. The basic assumptions of the reform program were shattered. Iraq had been the biggest market for Jordan's manufactured exports. But that market was lost as a result of the sanctions imposed on Iraq in 1990, after its invasion of Kuwait. Exacerbating the problem, other Gulf markets—traditionally major destinations for Jordanian agricultural exports—became closed as members of the coalition retaliated against Jordan's position on the war. Furthermore, Jordanians working in Gulf countries began facing various forms of discouragement and started to return to Jordan—some voluntarily, but many not.

The repatriation of over 300,000 Jordanians initially had a positive impact on the economy. More than $1.5 billion in repatriated capital boosted investment, particularly in real estate and housing. Increased consumption boosted demand and hence production. But shortly after, the burden of this sudden 10 percent increase in the population started to be felt, straining the country's infrastructure and markets. Children needed schools, cars needed roads, and Amman did not have enough drinking water. Unemployment soared, and the percentage of the population living in poverty jumped from 3.0 percent in 1986 to 14.4 percent in 1992.

Jordan's prospects brightened with the signing of a peace treaty with Israel in 1994. Peace was expected to invigorate the economy through enhanced exports, increased tourism and investment, reduced military spending, and technology transfers. But these hopes were dashed when Prime Minister Yitzhak Rabin, the architect of peace on the Israeli side, was assassinated by a Jewish extremist in 1995—leading Israel to adopt conservative policies that retracted the promises of peace. The region reverted to instability, severely undermining growth and development.

Jordan's Reforms in the 1990s

Throughout the 1990s the regional environment continued to wreak havoc on Jordan's economy, society, and reform efforts. Still, reforms continued in cooperation with the IMF and the World Bank. Adjustment efforts were supported by successive debt rescheduling programs through the Paris Club, a debt and debt service reduction operation through the London Club, a debt buyback arrangement with Russia (on debt owed to the former Soviet Union), and bilateral debt reductions by France, Germany, the United Kingdom, and the United States worth $800 million.

Jordan's reform program—started in 1989, interrupted by the Gulf War in 1990, and resumed in 1992—did not depart much from the Washington consensus prototype (see Williamson in this volume). It included a stabilization component aimed at achieving macroeconomic stability and a structural adjustment component aimed at enhancing competitiveness. The program also sought to achieve fiscal discipline, redirect spending from indiscriminate subsidies to targeted services, lower marginal tax rates and broaden the tax base, liberalize interest rates, introduce a competitive exchange rate regime, liberalize trade and foreign direct investment, privatize state holdings, abolish entry and exit barriers for foreign and domestic firms, and establish a new growth paradigm based on export-led growth instead of import substitution.

Reforms have generally spread through all sectors and all levels, with varying success, encouraging more efficiency and better resource use. Moreover, poor people have not been neglected: the social safety net has been restructured, made more efficient, and strengthened through a productivity enhancement program that continues today.

Monetary policy

The Central Bank of Jordan maintained a stable expansion of the money supply commensurate with macroeconomic demands while switching from direct to indirect monetary controls by introducing certificates of deposit in 1993. Reserve requirements, initially kept high to boost faith in the dinar, were reduced, and restraints on capital and profit transfers were removed. In 1995 the dinar was pegged to the U.S. dollar. By establishing a clear benchmark, this move gradually led to lower inflation and interest rates and higher foreign reserves.

Trade

As Jordan liberalized its economy, it scaled back protectionism. The weighted average tariff was reduced from 17.5 percent in 1994 to 13.5 percent in mid-2000. Trade liberalization efforts culminated in Jordan's accession to the World Trade Organization, which it officially joined in 2000.

Jordan also joined several economic integration schemes both within and beyond the region. In 1997 it signed the Greater Arab Free Trade Agreement and an association agreement with the European Union. The EU agreement calls for cooperation on economic, social, and political issues and for the establishment, over 12 years, of a free trade area between Jordan and the European Union.

In addition, since 1997 Jordanian goods that comply with certain production conditions have had quota- and duty-free access to U.S. markets. This arrangement has caused Jordan's exports to the United States—mainly textiles and clothing—to shoot from $7 million in 1997 to $581 million in 2003. In addition, in 2000 Jordan signed a free trade agreement with the United States.

Regulation and legislation

During the 1990s Jordan introduced legislative and regulatory reforms to create a more competitive, transparent environment for business and the private sector. Efforts focused on income and sales taxes, investment promotion, securities, insurance, secured financing and leasing, customs, trust, safeguard measures, companies, and intellectual property rights. In 1999–2000 most legislative adjustments involved the legal changes required for WTO membership.

Privatization

With the exception of health and education, privatization has touched almost every sector in Jordan—from industry to water to energy—and the list continues to grow. An Executive Privatization Unit was created in 1996 to develop a comprehensive plan and oversee implementation of the privatization program. In addition, several important laws were introduced or modified to deal with foreseeable legal bottlenecks.

Reform Outcomes—A Mixed Bag

Jordan's reform program achieved many of its objectives. The stabilization program has reduced foreign debt, contained the fiscal deficit, and restored a healthy balance of payments. In 2003 Jordan's total debt (domestic and external) stood at 7.1 billion dinars, or 101 percent of GDP—quite a drop from the 189 percent in 1990. Similarly, the budget deficit fell from 18.0 percent of GDP in 1989 to 11.6 percent in 2003. (The official budget deficit in 2003 was 2.3 percent of GDP, but that was based on a different formula for calculating the deficit than was used in 1989.) And in 2003 foreign reserves reached $4.7 billion (enough to cover 9.5 months of imports), up from $110 million in 1987.

The structural adjustment program was also successful, though more in terms of fulfilling the government's plans than achieving its objectives. (For example, although laws on foreign investment were made more investor friendly, they failed to attract higher levels of foreign direct investment.) Still, Jordan now has one of the region's best legal environments for business. It has also been, by far, the region's most successful privatizer, with several firsts to its credit. These include privatizing the fixed line telephone operator, which used to be wholly owned by the government, and establishing a telecommunications regulatory commission.

But if the ultimate goal of reform was to improve the lives of Jordanians by reinvigorating the economy, another picture emerges. In 2003 per capita income was $1,800—a dismal increase from the precrisis level, representing average annual growth of less than 1 percent over 20 years. So, despite a seemingly revived economy and prospects of continued growth, citizens have yet to feel many improvements in income and perceived welfare. Unemployment was 15.5 percent in 2003, up from 8.3 percent in 1987, and poverty was recently estimated at 14.2 percent, compared with 3.0 percent in 1987. Of course, things could have turned out even worse without the reforms. And such rates might have been better had the reform program addressed these areas specifically.

Personal Observations

During my 15 years as a development practitioner in Jordan, and during a decade-long dialogue with our development partners, I have experienced the joy of seeing results achieved—as well as the pressure of dealing with unforeseeable challenges that bombarded us from both within and beyond our borders. These endeavors taught me two fundamental lessons. First, even the most appropriate, timely, well-conceived development strategies can succeed only with the participation of all stakeholders.

Second, policies, processes, and procedures must be flexible enough to be applied not only top down, but also bottom up, in coordinated stages, with smaller groups, and in many other ways responsive to the needs of society.

But many other lessons were learned. The five most important are described below.

Democracy may delay reforms—but its absence can destroy them

Many of Jordan's reforms required extensive negotiations with parliament. This was not limited to enacting new laws or amending existing ones—which, according to the constitution, is the mandate of parliament—but extended to discussing policies, formulation of which is a constitutional provision of the executive authority. Such negotiations usually resulted in significant changes to the laws or policies agreed between the government and the IMF or World Bank. In addition to being extensive, such negotiations were also time-consuming, prompting some observers to conclude that democracy delays reform. That may be true, but Jordan's experience demonstrates that the absence of democracy is much more damaging because it can blow reforms apart.

Comparing two recent Jordanian experiences with riots provides perhaps the clearest example of this point. In 1996 the country experienced what became known as the bread riots, because they came in response to the higher price of bread that resulted from the removal of government subsidies. Though these riots were cited in many parts of the world as an example of how the policies of international financial institutions incite unrest in the developing world, they were not as severe as the 1989 fuel riots mentioned earlier. The anomaly of people putting fuel before bread can best be explained by the absence of democracy in the 1989 incident and the presence of a well-functioning, representative parliament in the second.

During the fuel riots the government was seen as acting alone in lifting subsidies on oil products. People rebelled against what they considered a misguided unilateral directive from on high, with no popular representation. Sound as it may have been, the policy was rejected by people as an imposition. Seeking to be heard in the absence of a parliament or other peaceful channel to communicate with the government, they marched into the streets to show their anger at not being consulted when the policy was formulated.

In the case of the bread riots the people were represented and their voices were heard. In 1996 a representative, elected parliament was active and fully engaged in the reform process. Though the government was not legally obligated to obtain parliament's approval for the lifting of bread subsidies, it engaged in extensive discussions with parliament's financial committee. After some debate and ensuing significant changes in the policy, the committee endorsed in principle the removal of the subsidies—though it suggested different implementation mechanisms.

Although the elimination of subsidies caused bread prices to triple, the general response was one of informed acceptance. The riots, albeit important and costly, were a localized incident in Jordan's poorest region. Significantly, the main political opposition party—which controlled about one-fifth of the seats in parliament—not only stayed out of the riots but also helped keep them under control.

Jordan's privatization experience provides another example of how democratic processes and institutions protect reforms from being undermined by special interest groups and the personal agendas of decisionmakers. As a country seeks strategic partners to endow its privatization process with high-end managerial and technical skills, it experiences significant pressure from various special interests. These include the donor community, with each contributing country vying to secure deals for its companies. In the absence of an independent and empowered parliament, openly discussing the terms of each sale to ensure that special interests—foreign or domestic—are not involved, external pressure is harder to resist, and can derail or corrupt the process. Jordan's parliament has acted as both arbiter and buffer. Its support for privatization has been sought at every stage, warding off tainted processes and outcomes.

Building a broad constituency for reform is half the battle

Reform brings changes, sometimes painful and controversial. Reform also threatens benefits accruing to special interest groups. When Jordan adjusted bread prices and converted the subsidies into cash transfers, it reduced benefits for the livestock industry (which depended on subsidized bread to feed herds) and for smugglers who sold flour in neighboring countries (who earned huge profits from the difference in prices). Enacting a competition law threatened the interests of business cartels. And implementing privatization and civil service reform antagonized government employees, particularly the less efficient.

None of these groups was large enough to derail the reform program. Each opposed only one element of the package and was rather indifferent to the many others. Yet all gained strength when they formed alliances and lobbied together against the entire reform process. The only way the government could have countered such alliances would have been by building a broad constituency in support of reform and in defense of the public interest. That would have required mobilizing the silent majority that stood to benefit from reform but sat on the fence in the absence of a dynamic public campaign advocating change. In hindsight, the absence of such a campaign posed serious threats to reform. For example, passage of the Competition Law—which protects the interests of the vast majority of consumers—was delayed several times by a small oligarchic minority because popular support was not mobilized. Had it been, the government would not have stood almost alone in the face of opposition. Only when popular discontent with the country's powerful steel cartel peaked did it became possible to pass a law curtailing special interests (in 2002).

Privatization provides another example. It was only in the late 1990s that raising public awareness of the goals and benefits of privatization became a major reform item. And by then it was almost too late. Negative impressions spread by special interest groups had already swayed public opinion, forcing the government to combat, somewhat belatedly, campaigns that at times threatened to undermine the privatization process.

The privatization of telecommunications is a good example. The public telecom corporation was run inefficiently, and ordinary citizens had to wait at least two years to be connected to the service—while influential people could jump the queue, opening the door to corruption. Thus the majority of people stood to benefit from privatization. Yet this majority initially did not support it, because its opponents played up the issue as one of selling national assets to foreigners. Enlisting broad popular support should have been a priority even before privatization began. Having the legislative and executive branches on board is not enough to advance a reform agenda; the people have to be equally informed.

Internal dissent can pose the biggest threat to reform

The Achilles' heel of any reform is dissent within the government on its scope and direction. All cabinet ministers have to be reform minded and support the reform drive, because reform in one sector will eventually touch most others. Reform also requires a change in mindsets, because it involves a new philosophy for managing the economy and advocates freer, more investment-friendly markets. What may initially be seen as a limited fiscal reform will soon affect the workings of every ministry, as when water or electricity tariffs are adjusted or when public enterprises are commercialized or privatized.

But not all reforms are implemented simultaneously. Hence there is always a risk that some within the cabinet, whose turn at reform has not yet come, will distance themselves from the reforms implemented by others, in an effort to appease certain constituencies or curry favor with certain interest groups. When Jordan's government proposed eliminating bread subsidies, for example, some ministers distanced themselves from the measure in front of their constituencies and covertly lobbied members of parliament to introduce amendments to the suggested scheme. At one point this lack of unity threatened the entire process.

This and similar experiences during my tenure offer a clear lesson for reforming governments: build internal consensus and solidify the internal front. Everyone must be on board. If one ministry or another does not support a reform policy, the breach may be extremely harmful. Cracks in the government's consensus discredit the hard medicines of reform and those prescribing them, and invite dissenters to reach out to parliament and others to destroy democratic support and popular consensus.

International financial institutions and national governments may have different priorities

Donor conditionalities are often not entirely consistent with a country's vision for its development. International financial institutions tend to act like credit assessors, and must assure creditors that a debtor nation can repay its debts. Hence the overriding objectives of international financial institutions are macroeconomic stability and movement toward an open economy, with liberalized financial transactions and flows of goods. By achieving these goals, it is argued, countries will accelerate growth and so raise the living standards of their populations. On the other hand, the overriding concern of national policymakers is to improve people's lives by expanding their economic choices. Fiscal discipline and macroeconomic stability are only some of the tools to achieve this, and are not seen as ends in themselves.

Thus while the goals of international financial institutions may overlap significantly with a country's vision—which is essential for cooperation—they are sometimes incongruent with national efforts that have much broader aspirations. This may result in technical disagreements, and creates two challenges for the government. First, how to devise a model program that is both acceptable and achievable. Second, how to supplement that program with what it considers priorities given domestic and regional constraints.

Jordan's vision has entailed the pursuit of development in general and human development in particular. By concentrating on choices and on widening human capabilities, the human development concept implies that people must influence and participate in decisionmaking that shapes their lives. They must be able to take part in the implementation of these decisions and have access to structures that facilitate their monitoring, adjustment, and improvement of the outcomes of these decisions. In other words, to achieve human development, people must have the ability and opportunity to participate in decisionmaking. Hence achieving human development requires three simultaneous endeavors: building human capabilities through education and knowledge dissemination systems, employing those capabilities in productive activities through robust economic growth, and liberating those capabilities through systems of good governance based on the full respect of human freedoms and rights.

International financial institutions tend to focus on the second of these endeavors, economic growth, and ascribe less importance to the other two. As reforms progressed, the biggest challenge for Jordan's government was how to pursue the other two—particularly building human capabilities—without the support of international financial institutions, under budget constraints, and amid calls for cost recovery and user fees that threatened universal access to education and health services. Within such constraints Jordan tried to ensure that spending was effective in raising productivity and achieving sustainable economic growth. It was believed that these policies, if effective and not undercut by regional shocks, would later close the deficit spending gap.

Hence the government focused on prudent spending in vital areas. These included, in addition to supporting education, targeting spending to raise productivity (especially in poor governorates and districts where education and health expenditures were badly needed), reducing the cost of obtaining technology, creating an environment conducive to the production of knowledge goods and services, enhancing the competitiveness of industry, and attracting foreign direct investment. Spending cuts in these areas would have reduced the endowments vital to the development of future generations.

International financial institutions advocate an incomplete reform model

The model of stabilization and structural adjustment discussed above is not meant to advance human development: it is designed to achieve economic growth. Yet the model is insufficient for achieving that goal. Thus governments must exert additional efforts to achieve growth.

For example, the model focuses on budget and balance of payments deficits. But many other deficits and disequilibria can undermine growth or its ability to create jobs. Chief among those is a labor market disequilibrium. Because of this disequilibrium, a substantial percentage of the jobs initially created in Jordan's newly designated industrial zones went to non-Jordanians. To reverse this trend, the government had to introduce new regulations and cash subsidies for training.

Another example of the model's shortcomings is its focus on macroeconomic rather than microeconomic reform. No one can dispute that Jordan succeeded in stabilizing its economy or that macroeconomic reform was consistent with agreements negotiated with the IMF. But microeconomic reform is just as important in enhancing economic competitiveness.

For example, microeconomic reform becomes essential when a country aggressively pursues trade liberalization. Countries are bound to lose if they open their economies to foreign goods and services without simultaneously ensuring that they have done everything possible to enhance the competitiveness of domestic industries. This does not mean that trade liberalization should be delayed. It means that it should be complemented by active government policies that support the competitiveness of domestic industries. Such policies should provide an institutional framework and funding for research and development, offer banks incentives to expand their operations and diversify their instruments to support industrial innovation, allocate grants to provide technical assistance and support to productive sectors, and—most important—adjust education policies to enhance quality at all levels. In Jordan work is under way to upgrade industry and enhance economic competitiveness, by providing an enabling environment to compete worldwide.

Another weakness of the model is that it gives little weight to regional (and global) factors and their potential impact on growth. IMF and World Bank technical assessments tend to exclude risk analysis of regional factors, yet such factors affect reform options and outcomes. Earlier I described how regional factors have wrought havoc on Jordan's economy. One cannot discount the instability caused by the Israeli occupation or by other regional wars, which have brought sudden influxes of refugees into the country, straining resources and infrastructure and diverting development plans. Although no model can forecast such regional events, reforms should be designed in a way that allows flexibility in dealing with exigencies when they emerge.

Finally, the benefits of reform—particularly those linked to trade liberalization—depend as much on what other countries do as on what a reforming country does. Reducing tariffs and removing nontariff barriers undoubtedly benefit a reforming country in principle. But those benefits can easily be eroded if that country's trade partners continue to protect their markets. Jordan has experienced such restrictions in its trade with some of its neighbors—notably Israel, where Jordanian goods, particularly agricultural products, face punishing nontariff barriers, and where Jordan was initially expected to open its markets in a manner disadvantageous to itself.

The fact that the model has shortcomings does not mean that it is fundamentally impaired. On the contrary, it continues to serve as a guide to achieving certain essential elements in reforms that could bring about eventual prosperity. But if the model advocated by international financial institutions is to continue focusing on economic growth, it should be more flexible and conducive to delivering that growth. Governments using the model, on the other hand, should compensate for its limitations through broader development strategies guided by national priorities and aspirations.

Arab *Human Development Reports*: Contributing to a New Development Paradigm for the Region

As discussed, among the most important lessons I have learned is that economic problems cannot be attributed solely to the economic domain. Instead, they are often rooted in political and social structures. Hence they cannot be resolved exclusively through economic policies; they require coordinated, holistic strategies. Since joining the United Nations Development Programme (UNDP), I have had the opportunity to help integrate the implications of this and other lessons in a new regional framework—the Arab *Human Development Reports*. The reports, produced by teams of Arab scholars, have made a groundbreaking contribution to the region's development by introducing a development paradigm that expands the concept of human development and offers important complements to the standard model offered by international financial institutions.

The reports provide the region with a neutral forum for initiating dialogue and debate to build a reform agenda from within. They offer new tools and indexes to measure progress and shortfalls beyond basic needs, as well as solid and independent analyses that can contribute to people-centered development and the mobilization of Arab human capital. Perhaps the most unconventional characteristic of the series is that it links human development to politics, institutional reforms, and good governance.

Analysis and findings

The findings of the first Arab *Human Development Report*, published in 2002, were telling, and showed where policy attention should focus. The report found that over the past decade the Arab region's achievements on the human development index (HDI) remained lower than the world average. At the same time, relative to other regions the Arab world did better on income indicators. Thus the report found that despite the Arab region's material wealth, it is hobbled by a different kind of poverty—a poverty of capabilities and opportunities. This human poverty was traced to three deficits: of freedom, knowledge, and women's empowerment.

Addressing budget and current account deficits while ignoring these other three will not lead to true prosperity. And growth alone will neither bridge these gaps nor put the region on the road to sustainable development. This is a critical lesson from my experiences with reform at the national and regional levels. Addressing these gaps involves tackling human capabilities, building knowledge societies, and promoting systems of good governance based on expanding choices, opportunities, and freedoms.

It is helpful to reflect on some of the examples and data from the 2002 report to substantiate its findings and recommendations. Arab countries spend a larger percentage of GDP on education than any other developing region. By 1995 more than 90 percent of boys and 75 percent of girls were enrolled in primary school, and nearly 60 percent and 50 percent in secondary school. But the enrollment rate for higher education was just 13 percent. Though higher than the average for developing countries (9 percent), this rate is far lower than in industrial countries (60 percent). More vulnerable social groups, such as women and poor people—especially in rural areas—suffer more deprivation of education, especially at higher levels.

Inflation, the introduction of school fees (to recover costs), and pressures on governments pursuing economic reforms and structural adjustment programs have all had negative impacts on the accumulation of human capital in the region, again with especially detrimental effects on women and poor people. There is evidence that the quality of education has deteriorated, with a decline in knowledge acquisition and analytical and creative skills. A mismatch between the labor market and the level of development on one hand, and the education system on the other, has resulted in low labor productivity, wage structure imbalances, high unemployment, and a decline in real wages for most workers.

Successful stabilization in the 1990s led to low inflation and budget deficits, and governments have provided a lot of growth-supporting physical infrastructure. Yet growth rates remain stagnant and overly vulnerable to fluctuations in oil prices. Arab countries have the lowest level of dire poverty among developing regions, as well as low inequality. Yet the impoverishment of capabilities is more pronounced as a result of high illiteracy and inadequate access to quality education. In 1995 at least 12 million people—15 percent of the labor force—were unemployed in the Arab region. If current rates continue, that number is expected to rise to 25 million by 2010.

The report links this situation with institutional impediments to job creation. Labor markets in Arab countries are traditional, severely segmented, and dysfunctional. Moreover, structural adjustment packages have not paid enough attention to reforms that build competitive, efficient labor markets, an essential requirement for growth.

The report shows that when it comes to freedom and political participation, the Arab region scores the lowest in the world. The region also has the world's lowest average score for voice and accountability, based on such key aspects of the political process as civil liberties, political rights, and media independence. In addition, civil society actors continue to face constraints in playing their role, and bureaucratic control of civic associations by public authorities presents serious problems. This indicates that policymaking and decisionmaking are rather exclusive processes, with marginal influence from Arab citizens.

The report acknowledges the destructive impact of conflicts on high and sustained growth and relates future prospects to resolving the region's political crisis through a just and comprehensive peace that respects the rights of all the region's people.

The way forward

To address these deficits and gaps, the 2002 Arab *Human Development Report* identifies three investment priorities: building Arab capabilities and knowledge, using human capabilities by reinvigorating growth and productivity, and promoting good governance. Human development is seen as integral to the region's success in reinvigorating economic growth. A basic policy priority in Arab countries, the report argues, is to create a virtuous cycle whereby economic growth promotes human development and human development in turn promotes economic growth.

The report emphasizes the importance of mobilizing the private sector within an enabling policy and regulatory environment and engaging it with governments and academia in human-intensive rather than capital-intensive research and development. It argues that governments should disengage from productive activities while strengthening their regulatory role to ensure openness and competitiveness.

The report points out that the region's domestic markets are too small to provide the basis for sustainable growth based on manufacturing and services. Hence the most viable response to globalization is openness and constructive engagement, in which Arab countries both contribute to and benefit from globalization. Arab cooperation and enhanced social cohesion will not only yield large economic dividends but also build resilience in the face of the increased economic shocks associated with globalization. Enhancing social cohesion will require improving political rights and political, social, and economic participation.

The report concludes that higher levels of human development cannot be achieved without empowering women and ending their marginalization, improving key governance systems and institutions, and activating the voices of the Arab people. Full respect for human rights and freedoms are the cornerstones of good governance that can unleash creativity and serve empowerment and participation—leading to human development.

Let me close my remarks by saying that, for me, the past 20 years of development practice and reflection have been absorbing, energizing, and immensely fulfilling. In all the gains and breakthroughs, under all the setbacks and frustrations, and against whatever odds and through whatever openings, I am deeply grateful to have been placed to try to make development—the right kind of development—work in my country and my region. The lessons have often been inspiring, occasionally sobering, and always instructive. But the greatest dividends from those lessons accrue, of course, from applying them.

Comment

Samir Radwan

ONE OF THE CHALLENGES OF WRITING OR LECTURING ABOUT THE MIDDLE EAST AND North Africa is how to be candid yet still be accepted in the region. And I think that Rima Khalaf Hunaidi has elegantly managed to strike that balance. Indeed, what you read between the lines is as important as what you read on the lines. And that is really the value of her presentation.

Dealing with difficult issues—such as creating a development paradigm or model, or designing a reform package—requires much more than just knowing your economics well. It demands combining disciplines and having a certain sensitivity to the subject matter, so that at the end of the day you remain relevant. Rima offers a practitioner's reflections on two experiences: the story of Jordan and the issue of reform in the region as a whole.

One of the themes of Rima's presentation is that reform is no easy task. A long-term perspective is required, and reformers will not be able to satisfy their clients by throwing out some clever economic formula. Politics and economics are intertwined, and the design of any reform package must pay close attention to that.

Rima is also candid, and combines diagnosis with prognosis—something often lacking in the dialogue on the region. Though good at analyzing and criticizing, we often fail to answer questions about what countries should do or where they should go from here. But this lecture points in concrete directions, both with the lessons that Rima mentions for Jordan and the outlines of a homegrown human development reform program for the region. The analysis ends with a call for reflection on how to effect the great transition required at these two levels, the national and the regional.

Jordan's story is a telling one, with external forces—whether related to conflict or to a need for resources to finance the country's development efforts—playing an important role. Ultimately, the question that arises is: how sustainable is the Jordanian model?

Looking at Jordanian development over the past 30 years shows that external factors have been extremely important in resolving its economic crises. The first wave

began with the tremendous migration of Jordanians to Gulf countries after the oil
price hike in the early 1970s. Then around 1985, when migration started to slow,
there was another wave from abroad due to the collapse of the Iraqi economy. Most
Iraqi business moved to Jordan, and there was another wave of resource injection to
the Jordanian economy. Finally, current foreign flows represent an important source
of finance for development.

Is this current pattern likely to continue? It is not just a question of how well the
economic program has been designed, whether by international financial institutions
or the Ministry of Planning, but of how the continuation and sustainability of this
model can be guaranteed with such heavy reliance on foreign resources. Rima is well
aware of this, and indicates that the jury is still out on Jordan's results.

I think a reflection for all of us here today is that here is a country trying its best
but still having serious difficulties, and how sustainable can that be? And are there
ways of continuing the success of its model? If external sources dry up, which is quite
possible, what are the alternatives? Is Jordan's economy strong enough to stand on its
own? That is really the first broad question I thought Rima's excellent lecture raised.

The second relates to the *Arab Human Development Reports*. Probably because I
have followed Rima's thinking over the years, I see continuity between her work in
Jordan and her work in the reports—the same vision, the same courage.

But there is considerable debate about the 2002 and 2003 *Arab Human Development Reports*, and I am sure the third will be no less controversial. The question that
has been raised, with some legitimacy, is what should the region's countries do? The
reports point out three major deficits in the pattern of development of the region's
countries, involving democracy, knowledge, and empowerment of women. As a
result the basis for creating a knowledge economy and society is not there.

Certainly, the question of democracy and freedom is very important. But what
should countries do? I remember, when sitting in Alexandria Library and helping to
write the Alexandria Declaration on reform in Arab countries, that was a paramount
question. And we concluded that there is no single approach for the entire region.

The differences between the region's economies are evident. Thus there is no way
to develop a recipe and say that it is the way to reform—to overcome the region's
problems with underperformance, whether in terms of growth, employment creation, trade openness, and so on. So, despite various proposals on how the region
should reform itself, questions remain: What is it concretely that the region should
do? Should it rely on a new approach of export-oriented growth? Should it rely
more on regional integration or subregional groups that could create power in international markets? If not these activities, then what?

A second area addressed by the *Arab Human Development Reports* is the importance of labor market behavior and employment. One of the major lacunae in the
development plans of the region's countries is that they took employment creation
as a residual, assuming that jobs would automatically be created as a result of other
activities and investments. But we all know that is not true. Thus we need to find a
paradigm that can be tailored to the needs of each country in the region, where creating employment is crucial.

Comment

Djavad Salehi-Isfahani

IT IS A PLEASURE TO DISCUSS RIMA KHALAF HUNAIDI'S LECTURE. BEFORE DOING SO, I'd like to express my gratitude to her for leading the effort to producing the 2002 and 2003 *Arab Human Development Reports*, several chapters of which are required reading for my students in "The Economic Development of the Middle East," a course I teach at Virginia Tech. Reading the current presentation was equally enjoyable and educational for me.

Jordan's Growth and Reform Patterns

The first part of her lecture summarizes events in Jordan since the 1973 oil shock, showing the pattern of boom and bust that has been the hallmark of economic growth in the Middle East and North Africa for the past half-century (Shafiq 1997). Jordan's economy is integrated enough with Arab oil-exporting countries to rise and fall with the price of oil. But there are significant differences between Jordan and the typical oil exporter, including that fact that Jordan has less control over its foreign exchange earnings. As Khalaf Hunaidi explains, much of the country's boom and bust pattern has been caused by changes in worker remittances. The oil price collapse of 1986 dealt a serious blow to the Jordanian economy, reducing GDP by 16 percent. Regional conflicts (in 1973 and 1990–91) have also adversely affected the country's economy. After 1991 Jordan's population increased by 10 percent as migrants returned from Persian Gulf countries, contributing to an increase in poverty from 3 to 14 percent.

Jordan's economy lacked the flexibility needed to permit soft landings after such downturns. In the late 1980s the government started the reform process, accepting conditions defined by the International Monetary Fund (IMF) and World Bank. The result was political unrest—with rioting driven by a hike in the price of gasoline—and the fall of the reform government.

The key point in the first part of Khalaf Hunaidi's lecture is the role of democratic institutions in helping reforms succeed. She blames lack of democracy, including limited popular participation in decisionmaking, for the failure of the first reform program. She contrasts this with a program introduced in the mid-1990s that gave opponents a stronger ostensible case—higher bread prices—yet they did not bring down the reforms. The conclusion she draws is that in the first case the people had no say in implementing the reforms, while in the second parliament approved them.

Khalaf Hunaidi does not explain the complex connections between individual decisions to riot (or not) and parliamentary participation. No matter how optimistic one likes to be about democracy's ability to help a society move along an imaginary efficient frontier as circumstances change, it would be useful to have some analytical support for these insights. The complexity of the links between democracy and successful reforms is evident from her account of the crisis resulting from the elimination of bread subsidies, where "some ministers distanced themselves from the measure in front of their constituencies and covertly lobbied members of parliament to introduce amendments to the suggested scheme."

Not being a political economist, I will not try to make sense of the complexity implicit in her interesting account of reform and democracy. Her explanation of why democratic participation made the decision to increase bread prices more palatable than the less socially costly gasoline price increase is certainly plausible, and has strong appeal. But the judgment on the effect of democracy on reform also depends on how it affects the likelihood of a decision to remove a subsidy in the first place. Does democratic decisionmaking help or hinder making tough, unpopular decisions? The answer could go either way. In thinking about this question, I find the concept of accountability more useful than democracy, which is broader and therefore less precise analytically. Accountability ensures that leaders consider the consequences of their actions on the populace but, unlike democracy, does not disperse the responsibility for decisionmaking.

To illustrate this point, let me offer an example of reform from family planning in Iran, an area of policy with which I am more familiar. In 1989 the government of Iran made a complete turnaround in its pro-natal policies to promote family planning. At the time, with the war with Iraq over and the time to deliver on revolutionary promises of a better life nearing, accountability rather than democracy was the primary motivating factor. The need for family planning was obvious, because earlier high fertility—especially in the early 1980s—had swelled the number of children of primary school age from 5.5 million at the start of the 1980s to 9.3 million at the end. Influential clergy and theologians were enlisted to argue the difficult case for family planning. And over the next 10 years fertility fell by half, making the program the most important reform taken by the Islamic government in its 25-year history.

I think that accountability in Iran, now as when the family planning reform was implemented, is better explained by political competition than by democracy. As Acemoglu and Robinson (2002, p. 1) observe, "Elites are unlikely to block development when there is a high degree of political competition." Interestingly, over the past 10 years neither accountability nor the expansion of democracy have helped the implementation of another important reform in Iran: the removal of energy subsidies, the most important of which is the gasoline subsidy—the same reform that in 1989 brought down Jordan's first reform government. The main difference was the redistributive nature of energy subsidy reform. As Esfahani and Taheripour (2002) argue, the Iranian government's inability to commit to redistributing the proceeds from energy reforms (worth about 10 percent of GDP) back to the population, in terms of current or future consumption, created a serious obstacle in reducing opposition to the reform.

Iran's reform experience offers another useful lesson. Unlike most family planning reforms around the world, Iran's was accomplished without aid from international institutions. Nothing helps discredit a reform more than the impression that it was dictated from the outside, by those who by assumption will not bear its primary burden. Perhaps the important difference between the gasoline and bread subsidy reforms in Jordan was that the parliamentary debate helped convince people that the reform was locally decided even though it was part of an agreement with Washington institutions. The feeling that a reform decision is made by the players in the game of social and economic change—the local population who by the mere fact of living in the country will endure its consequences—rather than by an outside power, is critical for the success of reforms with strong redistributive implications.

Iran's macroeconomic reforms in the 1990s were less successful than the family planning program for many reasons. But the fact that they came to be popularly— though wrongly—regarded as the work of the IMF and World Bank played a role in their faltering. One would think that Middle Eastern and North African countries, with their histories of socialist redistribution, are in a better position than fledging democracies to deal with the politics of redistribution and reform. On the other hand, the region's states are now too weak to undertake redistribution and too undemocratic to credibly explain or justify it.

In the final analysis, democracy may be regarded as a value in and of itself, with little need for justification on grounds of its value in implementing reforms. In that case one would have to be willing to pay its price in terms of delaying reforms, for a state powerful enough to redistribute is also capable of curtailing freedoms.

Labor Market Reform

I will conclude with a comment on the second part of Khalaf Hunaidi's lecture, on human development in the Arab world. Both *Arab Human Development Reports* (2002 and 2003) focus on human capital and correctly highlight the serious problems of youth unemployment and the mismatch between what schools teach and employers need. But in drawing policy implications they focus exclusively on the education system, with little attention to labor market reform. As Khalaf Hunaidi notes, Middle Eastern and North African labor markets are far from competitive and efficient. Various labor regulations and job guarantees in the private and public sectors have created strong incentives to seek diplomas rather than productive skills.

In a recent paper I argue that labor market reform should precede education reform because in a labor market that sends distorted signals to young people to emphasize memorization, test scores, and formal schooling, education reform is an uphill battle (Salehi-Isfahani and Murphy 2004). But reversing the sequencing implicit in the *Arab Human Development Reports* is no simple matter, and has a strong political economy implication. Unlike education reform, which is not primarily redistributive, the most obvious type of labor market reform—which reduces job security—affects the fortunes of older, employed workers differently than it does the young unemployed. Will a democracy where job holders outnumber new entrants be likely to support an increase in labor market flexibility?

Neither *Report* takes a serious look at the difficult issue of labor market reform as part of human capital policy for the Arab world. This comes as a surprise to those of us who think of human development as primarily the result of family decisions, and believe that millions of such decisions made with distorted incentives arising from poorly functioning labor markets can be hugely wasteful. But then it is much easier to discuss education reform, where all can be winners, than labor reform, which has many losers—perhaps the majority of current employees.

This is not the place to discuss the *Arab Human Development Reports*; the reason I raise the issue of labor market reform here is because it is related to the main conclusion of the first part of Khalaf Hunaidi's lecture, on the importance of democracy for reform. I believe that democracy (much more than accountability) can assist initiation and implementation of labor market reform. It is well understood that for labor market reform to succeed, social protection programs tailored to local cultural norms (family and community life) must be in place. Open debate and democratic decision-making help raise the credibility of social programs and dispel the popular impression that capitalism is being imposed not just from above but also from the outside.

Labor market reform is no panacea for the dreadful employment prospects in the Middle East and North Africa, which are well documented in a recent World Bank study, *Unlocking the Employment Potential in the Middle East and North Africa* (2004). Such reform is particularly difficult to push in countries that started their modernization in the last century displaying deep hostility to the Western model of capitalism. Knowing how specific market reforms have fared in particular political and social environments is an important step in finding the way forward. For that reason alone we should all be grateful to have Khalaf Hunaidi's insights from her experiences in implementing difficult market reforms—including privatization and subsidy reform—and on the role of democracy in making them succeed in Jordan.

References

Acemoglu, D., and J. Robinson. 2002. "Economic Backwardness in Political Perspective." MIT Working Paper 02-13. Massachusetts Institute of Technology, Cambridge, Mass.

Esfahani, H. S., and F. Taheripour. 2002. "Hidden Public Expenditures and Economic Performance in Iran." *International Journal of Middle East Studies* 34: 691–718.

Salehi-Isfahani, D., and Russell D. Murphy Jr. 2004. "Labor Market Flexibility and Investment in Human Capital." Virginia Tech, Department of Economics, Blacksburg, Va. [http://www.econ.vt.edu/%7Esalehi/research/creativity.pdf].

Shafiq, Nemat. 1997. "Rents, Reform and Economic Malaise in Middle East and North Africa." *Research in Middle East Economics* 2: 221–45.

World Bank. 2004. *Unlocking the Employment Potential in the Middle East and North Africa: Toward a New Social Contract.* Middle East and North Africa Region, Washington, D.C.

Eduardo Aninat

Assistant Secretary General, United Nations Development Programme; Former Minister of Planning, Jordan

Born in 1948, Eduardo Aninat has an M.A. and Ph.D. in economics from Harvard University. He has taught Public Finance and Economic Development at the Pontificia Universidad Católica de Chile and was an Assistant Professor of economics at Boston University. From 1981 to 1994, he was a principal in Aninat, Méndez and Associates, one of the largest consulting firms in Latin America. He has been a consultant for such international institutions as the World Bank and the Inter-American Development Bank, and he has advised a number of governments on matters ranging from tax policy to debt restructuring. He has been a member of the Boards of Directors of several private companies and institutions in Chile and abroad, including serving as the cofounder and first Chairperson of the Social Equity Forum, a panel of Latin American social policy experts sponsored by the Inter-American Development Bank.

Mr. Aninat has served in a range of economic positions in the Chilean Government; these included chief senior negotiator for the bilateral Canada-Chile trade agreement, and chief debt negotiator and senior advisor of the Central Bank of Chile and the Ministry of Finance. Most notably, Mr. Aninat was the Finance Minister of Chile from March 1994 to December 1999. He was the Chairman of the Board of Governors of the IMF and World Bank in 1995-96, representing Chile, Argentina, Bolivia, Peru, Uruguay, and Paraguay. In that capacity, Mr. Aninat has been involved in the discussions on initiatives ranging from international policies for heavily-indebted poor countries to the proposals for reform of international financial architecture. As Chile's Finance Minister, he helped to channel Chile's strong economic growth into social progress, including an ambitious reform of the public education system.

After his tenure as Finance Minister, Mr. Aninat served as Deputy Managing Director of the IMF from 1999 to 2003. He currently is CEO of Anisal International Consultants, a firm based in Santiago, Chile.

14 Options and Outcomes of Chile's Education Reforms, 1990–2000

Eduardo Aninat

IN EARLY 1990 A CENTER-LEFT COALITION OF CHRISTIAN DEMOCRATS AND SOCIAL-ist parties known as the Concertación—led by President Patricio Aylwin—came to power in Chile, having defeated an opponent associated with Augusto Pinochet's 17 years of authoritarian rule. One of the key issues on the coalition's agenda, as well as for economic analysts and decisionmakers, was addressing the so-called social debt accumulated during the Pinochet years.

So, in addition to ensuring sound macroeconomic policies, the newly democratic governments elected in the 1990s focused on expanding the social safety net and increasing public investment in human capital. The adoption of such policies was based on the strong conviction that Chile's market-oriented development strategy—inherited from the military rule but endorsed by the democratic administrations—should be augmented by policies that spread the benefits of economic growth more widely. A stronger focus on social policies was appropriate not only on moral grounds but also to ensure the political, social, and economic sustainability of the market-based development strategy.

The backlog of unsatisfied social demands involved areas such as education, health care, unemployment benefits, old age pensions, and wages for public workers providing social services. Though there was broad social consensus on the need to address this backlog, there were uncertainties about the time needed for such a recovery, the means of financing it, and the macroeconomic effects. In addition, there were concerns about whether the new political system was capable of dealing with the competing demands of different interest groups—including unions, political parties, and other lobbies—and about how to establish a rational institutional process for resolving them.

Given the equity and efficiency considerations involved, the incoming administration knew that it could not dismiss or postpone the resolution of these demands. Indeed, part of the Concertación's electoral success had been due to its pledges to resolve such social issues. With Chile's high economic growth rates, low-income groups strongly expected to reap—sooner rather than later—the benefits of public social spending. Moreover, many academic studies at the time argued that higher, better-focused social spending—if sustained over time—would generate a fairer distribution of income.

At the same time, there were legitimate concerns among economic advisers to private corporations and among technocrats working with political leaders (see, for example, Arellano and Cortázar 2000). These analysts feared that the expected size and speed of the new social programs deemed necessary to satisfy the social debt exceeded the Treasury's financing capacity. There were also concerns about how such potentially large programs would affect domestic absorption (inflation, external balances).

In late 1989 there were many discussions where the economic experts of the Concertación placed numerous provisos on the coalition's campaign promises to revamp social services, as well as on the capacity of Aylwin's administration (1990–94) to deliver on them. There were fears that acting too boldly and quickly would generate enormous pressures, risking unbalanced public budgets, higher inflation (which was still in the double digits), lower growth, and external imbalances. A few economists liked to refer to two other debts in addition to the social debt—external debt and domestic debt held by corporations—thereby highlighting the looming challenges for macroeconomic equilibrium.

The discussion here analyzes these issues in the context of an important social policy reform, providing a first-hand account of the process of public choice involved in education reforms. Attention is given to the challenges of designing reforms, providing financing, phasing in benefits, developing the right macroeconomic context, and managing the proponents of reform and the political supporters needed for new legislation.

Chile's education reforms are an important example of public policymaking for structural reforms in the context of Latin American development—except that they occurred in a context of high economic growth. This factor adds special interest to the analysis here, because high growth paradoxically generated more, not less, complexities in the reform negotiations.

Structural Elements of Chile's High Growth Rate— and Related Reforms

Academic, institutional, and empirical research on Chile's economic evolution between 1980 and 2000 points to two widely shared conclusions about the structural explanations for its much higher growth than its Latin American neighbors (see, among others, Hurtado Ruiz-Tagle 1988; Foxley in this volume; and Ffrench-Davis 2002). The first is the early, consistent approach that Chile took in opening its economy to trade. Since the first wave of sweeping liberalization of foreign trade policies in 1975–79, and their consistent deepening and broadening in the late 1980s and the 1990s, Chile's growth rate has been largely determined by the net contributions of the trade account and the current account to the balance of payments.

For centuries copper and a few other traditional commodities had been important influences on the structure of the economy and the generation of quasi-rents for various domestic and foreign economic agents, including the state. But it was the structural shift in the resource allocation process brought about by trade liberalization that set the economy on a different (and, on average, higher) growth path. Accordingly, most Chilean economists point to the push and pull factors derived from the (now very open) trade regime as the prime source of economic growth.

The country's success in opening the economy to deeper trade in goods, inputs, services, and foreign capital has also made the economy more subject and elastic to foreign economic cycles (booms and busts, recoveries and slowdowns). The issue of interest here is not a comparison of cyclicality with other advanced developing countries. Rather, it is why that cyclicality has not—for the most part—generated reversals in Chile's policies and medium-term growth patterns, as it has done in several of its Latin America neighbors.

That point leads to the second structural explanation for Chile's high economic growth: domestic institution building. Chile is a small, open economy that has generally been careful about and respectful of its economic institutions. Even during the turbulent years of its political shakeup (1969–74), policymakers and economic analysts generally observed issues of legality, constitutionality, and consolidation when several institutions were undertaking enormous changes. Such behavior is extremely rare in processes of revolutions and deep socioeconomic shifts, whether in Latin America, Asia, or Africa. Thus for several decades Chilean reformers have acted with an eye on acceptance of legal forms and (at least some) institutional procedures, and with some concern for how their actions would be viewed by historians.

Such deep concern for institutional consistency can be a blessing or a curse. Consider, for example, the institutional corruption entrenched in many Caribbean and Central American countries. The big difference in Chile is the pervasive support that an evolving society has provided to social and other institutions. Moreover, Chile has one of the oldest social safety nets in Latin America, and this social support has been promoted and protected by the state no matter what type of government has been in power.

For the analysis here the most salient part of this long institutional buildup has involved education, with efforts dating to Chile's early years as an independent republic in the 19th century. Early, strong, consistent efforts to foster the development of social institutions have provided an anchor to the country as a whole, particularly in times of stress provoked by cyclical external forces. For many years, whenever policymakers have had to address macroeconomic shocks, they have usually been able to secure support from this network of social institutions, which are widely respected by the general public. Because education is one of the main components of Chile's grid of social institutions, it seems logical to focus on it and to analyze the nature, incidence, feedback, and results of the sector reforms launched in 1995 by Eduardo Frei Ruiz-Tagle's administration (1994–2000), the Concertación team that followed Aylwin.

The Story of Chile's Education Reforms

A deep recession in 1982–84, coupled with flawed and unsupportive domestic policies for most of the 1980s, considerably lowered the living standards of poor and middle-class Chileans. As noted, the resulting social debt helped generate support for the Concertación, which promised to address unfulfilled needs. Accordingly, in 1991 Parliament approved significant tax reform aimed at redressing the absolute and relative drop in social spending. Changes in the bases and rates of specific direct and indirect taxes were intended to finance a gradual but systematic increase in social transfers and support.[1]

But these efforts were deemed insufficient—as became clear when extensive new social reforms were demanded of Frei, the second candidate of the Concertación, by a vocal and varied group of unions and civil society organizations. These reforms were also supported by a wide range of political actors. Given the economy's rapid growth (averaging 7 percent a year between 1989 and 1993), many analysts believed that Chile could do more for recipients of education, health, and other social benefits, especially since such groups were overwhelmingly poor or middle class. In addition, there was strong evidence that social returns to investments in these areas were not only positive, but also made an enormous contribution to Chile's stock of human capital.

It was clear that these issues would have to be addressed in a coherent way—one that would not undermine macroeconomic equilibria and that was also politically visible. After months of discussion inside the Cabinet and with experts from the Concertación, the ministries of finance and education suggested that President Frei make education reforms a priority, and focus on them early in his term. The reason was not only that these reforms had important equity and efficiency effects but also that they, if well advertised and managed, could provide a rallying point for social and political support.

Thus in mid-1994 I, as minister of finance, gave a public speech to explain the importance and objectives of the education reforms. The speech stated that within eight years the government sought to increase education spending to 7 percent of GDP—the same level as in Britain and Germany. I also said that achieving that goal would require shared efforts by the public and private sectors, given that the proposed changes were aimed at both (Aninat 1994).

I believe that education reforms were well chosen given the structural challenges facing Chilean society. But while the reform program generally worked well, it was not exhaustive. The discussion below describes the design and decisionmaking process for the reforms, based on accounts provided by those responsible for implementing them. The insights obtained are most valuable for purposes of learning about the political economy of social reform in the context of a growing developing country.

The reform dialogue

The National Commission of Modernization for Education (Comisión Nacional de Modernización para la Educación), created early in the Frei presidency, consisted of 18 professionals and academics from diverse backgrounds. The commission was charged with providing a complete diagnosis of the education system, including its main weaknesses. The resulting report (issued in September 1994) was an essential reference for efforts to develop a responsive legislative agenda.[2]

In early 1996 an interdepartmental government team began studying how to organize the various reforms initiatives. Some had already started, and provided a useful base for the more extensive reform program. As finance minister I was assigned to coordinate the design of the reforms along with Sergio Molina, the education minister.[3] The overriding goal of the reforms was to increase the quality and fairness of Chile's education system. Reforms focused on extending school hours, increasing support for teachers, and improving management of the education system. All three efforts involved long-term actions, and reform implementation would require several years and additional resources before they could take off on a steady state regime.

The advantages of extending school hours—over the course of the day or the year—were clear. Doing so would provide significant educational benefits and have positive social effects—especially for low-income households, where both parents increasingly work outside the home. A longer school year would also improve school management because it would enable teachers to focus on individual schools, making their efforts more cohesive by avoiding the established practice of teachers working in multiple schools. Moreover, these efforts were to be supported by improvements to school buildings, which would help nearby communities by making classrooms available for complementary activities (such as socialization and sports) after school hours, strengthening human capital.

Different approaches were considered for the transition to an extended school schedule, referred to as the Complete Journey at School (Jornada Escolar Completa, or JEC) program. Options included adding general hours throughout the school year, extending the school day by adding courses, and expanding academic and nonacademic activities (sports, workshops, and so on). Preference for any of these options, or some combination, was to give budget priority to institutions with the greatest needs, as determined by objective data on education standards. In the end all three options were used, varying by region and type of school.

The number of weeks of classes was increased from 37 to 40 a year, with a gradual phase-in period starting in 1998. In addition, primary school increased from 30 to 38 pedagogical hours a week, while secondary school increased from 36 to 42 pedagogical hours. (One pedagogical hour is equivalent to 45 minutes.) As a result students who receive all their primary and secondary education under the Complete Journey at School program will attend two more years of classes than they would have under the previous system. (In addition, in 1995 support was provided for students who need extra instruction.) The use of the additional hours depends on the education program designed by each school, reaffirming the pedagogical decentralization of recent years and the goals of projects to improve education (Arellano 2000).

Reforms also included a teacher improvement program that, along with increased field practice, provided massive benefits to teaching staff. Bonuses were created to reward the best teachers. In addition, a support program was created for university professors, and scholarships were provided to outstanding students. Many of these reforms covered various cohorts of beneficiaries, and continue to be implemented.

Finally, education reforms included the Montegrande Program, which fostered and supported secondary schools that were shining examples of the subsidized education system. The program also targeted elite secondary students, preferably from poor or middle-class families.

President Frei announced the education reforms to Congress in mid-1996, emphasizing their importance for increasing efficiency and equity. Congress then discussed the reforms, which received broad public support, and included them in the 1998 government budget.

Following a proposal from the Treasury, Frei's administration decided to use the value added tax (VAT) to finance the core new spending required by the reforms. The VAT rate had been 16 percent when the Concertación came to power in 1990. But it was raised to 18 percent that year, and remained at that level until 2003 thanks to a series of complex—and crucial—political negotiations, including a 1996 agreement in which I played a key role. (See below for further discussion of public finances.)

Reform issues

The reforms raised several issues. First, some experts in the private education system strongly opposed making the Complete Journey at School program mandatory, leading to heavy debate. These experts argued that private schools needed more freedom in organizing the education process. This debate reflected a long tradition in Chile's private education system, which has always fought strongly for its freedom in providing education. Paradoxically, most if not all the principals of private and public schools wanted to move to full-day schedules as soon as possible.

A second issue involved how to finance the investment in additional classrooms: through an increase in the monthly public subvention or through a one-time contribution. (The subvention is the equivalent of a voucher for students attending public schools or subsidized private schools.) The second approach allowed schools to enroll all their students in the new scheme at the same time, and ultimately prevailed. But it raised the costs of the reforms in their early years.

A third subject of discussion was the size of the increase in the monthly subvention. The increase had to be large enough to pay teachers for longer working days and to cover other expenses related to the Complete Journey at School program. The increase allocated ended up representing a bigger permanent increase in government spending than did the contribution for school construction, with the basic subsidy growing by a third for each student who entered the program. Under the final legislation for the reforms, issued in the first half of 1997, the subvention included resources for two hours a week of additional coordination among teachers, to help improve education quality.

Securing support

How did the government secure support for the education reforms from key politicians and labor unions? Discussions inside the Frei administration in 1994–95 favored presenting the reforms as a "wave of change" in education, rather than a piecemeal approach based on partial technical changes. It was not that technical issues did not matter. But the idea was to encompass them inside a broader umbrella: of shifting to a different scale of daily functioning in Chile's schools, starting in 1996. The core concept of a longer school day, based on the Complete Journey at School program, became the mobilizing banner for the education reforms.

Thus in 1995–96 President Frei, Minister of Finance Aninat, and Minister of Education Molina went to television, print media, political forums, Congress, and labor unions to sell the reforms—advocating a complete overhaul of primary and secondary schooling. The Ministry of Finance announced its commitment to permanently increase education spending by 0.5 percent of GDP starting in 1996. As discussed below, it was proposed that much of this financing come from keeping the VAT at 18 percent.

Financing the Reforms: Options and Results

The design of the education reforms and their financing in early 1996 occurred against a background of rapid economic growth (with Chile's real GDP having expanded by an average rate of nearly 8 percent in 1990–95), sound government finances (with fiscal accounts having been in balance or surplus in 1990–95), and strong revenue from the VAT (though the VAT rate was poised to fall from 18 to 17 percent in 1997).

The permanent cost of the proposed reforms was projected to reach 0.5 percent of GDP once they were fully implemented, which was expected to take up to five years. Most of the cost came from the move toward the longer school day. The reforms also implied temporary costs in their early years, mainly to put in place the infrastructure needed to allow for extended schooling.

Financing sources and approaches

From the outset, implementation of more active social policies was subordinated to an overarching commitment to macroeconomic stability. So, to avoid major macroeconomic imbalances, any expansion in the government's social agenda had to be matched by available fiscal resources. In principle these resources could come from three sources:

- *Increased revenue from strong GDP growth,* referred to as the growth dividend.

- *Reallocated budget resources,* such as from the reduced public debt service that had resulted from fiscal surpluses and macroeconomic stability.

- *Increased revenue from higher taxes.* Taxes accounted for 17 percent of GDP in the 1990s, enabling a moderate broadening of the tax base without placing an undue burden on private sector growth. These increases focused on indirect taxes (VAT, tariffs, specific levies) and direct incomes taxes.

Efforts to finance the reform costs initially focused on the first two sources. Indeed, the opposition in Congress claimed that the government could obtain the needed resources from the growth dividend alone. But a number of considerations indicated that such an approach would have been inconsistent with the government's long-term commitment to prudent fiscal policies and macroeconomic balance.

First, it was unlikely that Chile's rapid growth would continue indefinitely. Thus a prudent assessment of the resources that could be generated from GDP growth had to be based on a rate lower than the 7–8 percent that the economy had experienced for most of the 1990s. The scope for using the growth dividend to finance education reforms was further reduced by the so-called vegetative growth of social spending. This refers to spending requirements, not under the control of the economic authorities, associated with the evolution of social and demographic variables and the feedback from economic growth itself.

Public salaries were an important element of these spending requirements. In Chile's competitive job market, salaries in the public sector were in direct competition with private salaries, and strong real wage growth in the private sector—fueled by high GDP growth—inevitably fed into the public sector wage bill. This situation was exacerbated by the need for some parts of the public sector to narrow the salary differential with the private sector in order to attract qualified personnel.

Second, while there was room to reallocate resources to the social sector, they were unlikely to be sufficient to finance the education reforms. Moreover, significant reallocations had already occurred, with social spending having risen from 58 percent of public spending in 1989 to 66 percent in 1996. Thus there was less scope for further reallocations from infrastructure and other areas.

Finally, financing was needed for many other important policy initiatives in the social arena (such as raising the minimum welfare pension) and elsewhere (such as mitigating the fiscal costs of trade liberalization). Thus, taking resources from the growth dividend and using budget reallocations to finance education reforms would only have postponed the broader question of how to finance the government's policy agenda. All these considerations argued against going ahead with the education reforms purely on the basis of available fiscal resources or possible revenue gains from growth.

Thus the government had to explore alternative permanent financing sources for the reforms. For several reasons, maintaining the VAT at 18 percent (instead of reducing it to 17 percent, as had been planned) appeared to be the most sensible option:

- *Revenue generation.* Each percentage point of the VAT yielded revenue equal to 0.45 percent of GDP—close to the estimated permanent cost of the education reforms. In addition, maintaining the VAT at 18 percent from late 1997 onward would contribute to the high one-time investment needs in the early stages of the reforms.

- *Efficiency.* Because of its broad base and uniform rate, the VAT was one of the government's most efficient revenue instruments, and was the least distorting tax source that the government could tap to finance the reforms. Indeed, Chile's VAT was cleaner than most or all Latin American VATs.

- *Political economy.* Although the government anticipated strong support for the education reforms, an explicit tax increase would likely have encountered heavy resistance from the opposition and so could have complicated the passage of the reforms in Congress.[4] By contrast, the loss of scheduled tax relief for consumers through the VAT seemed to be a small sacrifice to ask for in return for better schooling and stronger human capital.

- *Equity.* The changes in social policy introduced in 1996 were guided by a political and economic vision for increasing equity.

The approach advanced by the Ministry of Finance was simple and appealing: the Frei government would ask consumers to contribute about 0.5 percent of GDP a year to achieve—through earmarked public spending—longer school hours in primary and secondary schools, both private and public. The reforms also involved improvements in the quality of education. Thus Chilean society was asked to accept a slight reduction in current consumption (through the higher VAT) in exchange for a marked increase in the country's human capital—with better education of its young citizens contributing to future productivity gains for Chile's emerging democracy. These basic arguments generated strong backing for the reform package, from both efficiency and equity perspectives. The reforms also increased support for the Concertación.

Potential impacts on public finances

In recent years some economists have argued that the financing of Chile's education reforms did not go far enough. They have claimed that because the financing arrangements did not generate new resources (the level of tax revenue was only maintained, not increased) but imposed additional expenses, an imbalance was on the make—implying a structural weakening of public finances. None of these arguments were made when the reforms were first discussed in Congress in the mid-1990s. On the contrary, at the time Treasury staff had to focus on convincing senators from the opposition that the growth dividend would not provide sufficient financing for the reforms.

This backward-looking view of education reform financing is also based on the premise that the VAT could have been maintained at 18 percent even if the reforms had not been introduced. But that view is flawed, because it is unlikely that Congress would have supported standalone legislation to keep the VAT at 18 percent or to compensate the revenue loss from the planned VAT decline through an increase in other taxes (such as income taxes).

It is possible to build counterfactual scenarios that could dispel some or all of the points made above. But while revisionist history can be entertaining for academic purposes, the fact is that none of these structural policy arguments were raised by any of the many participants in the decisionmaking debates of 1996–97.

Lessons and Areas for Further Research

It is too early to draw hard conclusions on the results of Chile's education reforms. Doing so would require a comprehensive cross-sectional database describing the skills gained by primary and secondary students who have gone through the new

Complete Journey at School system and graduated from reformed schools. The reforms were implemented gradually, and in many communities it took years for schools to achieve the longer hours sought by the reforms. Just six years have passed since the reforms were introduced, and several of the reforms' transitional elements are still under way. So, although some preliminary evidence is available on student achievements under the reformed education system, the findings are neither reliable nor representative. Thus this is a fruitful area for future research, especially for specialists with access to relevant education databases.

Still, Chile's experience with education reforms offers several useful lessons—not just for Chile, but for many developing countries. The first lesson relates to fiscal policy choices in the context of rapid economic growth. Looking back on what has contributed to the sustainability of high growth in Chile—as well as in small and medium-size developing countries in Latin America, the Caribbean, Africa, and Asia—one of the most crucial public policy choices has been to opt for social services linked to human capital formation. In such countries it is essential that the growth dividend be increasingly geared toward financing public social services (including education) not only for equity reasons but also to respond to the challenges of globalization, and to catch up to higher global standards of knowledge. When considered from a historical perspective, human capital formation (including education) usually carries among the higher social returns to developing country investments. That is especially the case for countries that have opted for deeper integration with the world economy, such as many Latin American and Asian countries.

The second lesson is more subtle. It involves the issues arising from the day-to-day pressures of recent political and economic changes in Latin America: what to do where there had been prior neglect of social concerns, the economy was achieving reasonable growth, the distribution of income had historically been highly unequal, and the public was demanding more and faster solutions from the government? High economic growth rates (around 7–8 percent a year) increased social demands, as various neglected groups saw the private sector booming. What to do, in this context, to be open to the voices of democracy and responsive to the public—while also maintaining macroeconomic balance? In many countries, including Chile in 1993–96, this has been a difficult path to travel, given vocal demands to expand social services.

Under such circumstances it is important to avoid two extreme, yet common, scenarios. The first is a "lone ranger" approach, where government technocrats in a developing country become distrustful and fearful of political parties, congress members, private lobbies, labor unions, and civil society organizations. Accordingly, they act with a defensive esprit de corps, rallying around one or two technocratic ministers (one of whom is usually the head of the treasury), hiding important economic information from the public, and developing an "aggressive-defensive" communications strategy. Then, when panicked by demands for more government spending on social and other services, such technocrats replicate the "lonely cowboy's syndrome" of pulling all the (technocrat) wagons into a circle and preparing all the "defensive ammunition" that can be collected for a prompt defense of the public war chest. I call this scenario the "panicking syndrome."

In the 1980s and 1990s this scenario became a self-fulfilling prophecy for country after country in Central and South America: technocrat ministers were fired, advisers were lost, and replacement teams would later belong to a second- or even third-best sourcing, with final subsequent worsening on fiscal, external, and inflation fronts. Today the region is sufficiently mature in its institutions and socioeconomic rules of the game to avoid such approaches to economic reform.

The second scenario is the opposite: the temptation for gradual populism. In this case pressure groups inside and outside the government attract the favor of technocrats in less visible and more complex ways. There is a broad literature on populism, corruption, log-rolling lobbying, and similar features, applied to developments in actual policymaking in Latin America and Asia. I will not repeat it here. To summarize this second point, consider the many sudden transformations of economic and policy leaders into populist political leaders, including examples from Argentina, Bolivia, Chile, Colombia, Ecuador, Honduras, Mexico, Nicaragua, Venezuela, and many other countries. The dangers for sound economic and fiscal management are evident.

A third lesson involves the importance of maintaining strong macroeconomic policies. Without credible, well-structured public finances, no major social reforms can be undertaken. Many Latin American countries have learned this lesson only after many experiences in the wrong direction.

Fourth, planners of social reforms must pay close attention to the organization of labor markets. The organization of employers and employees has an enormous impact on the political economy of the labor process (strikes, lobbies, demands made of political actors) and the way that the final delivery (productivity) of services is achieved.

In the case of reforms and "big push" strategies promoting more resources for social services, governments are generally acting over more labor-intensive sectors. But the quality of final outcomes and delivery to beneficiaries may run counter to the enhanced spending patterns. The economic final incidence of many spending programs can end up raising the wages of teachers or other workers at a pace incommensurate with what the original reforms intended. As such, truncated reform processes can distort the aims of policy reformers and produce heavy frustration among citizens—laying the seeds for taxpayer revolts (such as tax evasion or erosion of the tax base).

Of special importance are the connections between adding fiscal resources to a particular social sector (which always creates tensions) and the productivity gains resulting from the incentives created for the actors in the reform process (teachers, principals, experts). Better analysis of this issue is needed to secure better results.

The final lesson involves the need for clear, well-communicated prioritization schemes. When a government initiates action in an area—say, education—and signals its intention to increase spending there, the most likely public response is that unions and interest groups working in other public areas will become more restless and demanding. Thus the government must be firm that the chosen area is the top priority, and that other needs must be postponed or restructured. Of crucial importance is how the strategy for a prioritization process is established and explained to the public. The sooner and simpler this is done, the better. But it is also essential to have a clear political discussion on how and by whom the priority has been chosen, to secure support for legislative changes and budget reallocations.

Public choices on social policies are fascinating, and generally rewarding. But the scope and depth of strategic challenges surrounding implementation of these issues in developing countries should not be minimized. Political economy is not only a scientific matter—it is also an art.

Notes

1. This section draws heavily on chapter 2 in Arellano (2000, pp. 34–42), a book by a minister who oversaw education reforms in 1998–99.

2. This refers to the so-called Brünner Commission Report, guided by sociologist José Joaquín Brünner. The report provided many of the framework ideas that served as background for specific reform issues.

3. We headed the interdepartmental team, which also included the Treasury's budget director (Arellano) and representatives from other public agencies.

4. The government in Chile did not command a majority in Congress and was thus forced to seek agreement with at least one opposition party to get its legislative initiatives approved. The voting practices of conservative, unelected "institutional senators" also had to be managed to win a vote in the Senate.

References

Aninat, Eduardo. 1994. "Transcripción del discurso pronunciado en televisión abierta nacional por el Ministro de Hacienda." Santiago.

———. 1999. "Exposición de la Hacienda Pública." Congreso Nacional, Ministerio de Hacienda, Santiago.

Aninat, Eduardo, Andreas Bauer, and Kevin Cowan. 1999. "Addressing Equity Issues in Policymaking: Lessons from the Chilean Experience." In Vito Tanzi and others, eds., *Economic Policy and Equity*. Washington, D.C.: International Monetary Fund.

Arellano, José Pablo. 2000. *Reforma educacional: Prioridad que se consolida.* Editorial Los Andes, Chile.

Arellano, José Pablo, and Julio Cortázar. 1982. "Del milagro a la crisis: Algunas reflexiones sobre el momento económico." *Colección de Estudios 8.* CIEPLAN, Chile.

Atkinson, A. B. 1999. *The Economic Consequences of Rolling Back the Welfare State.* Cambridge, Mass.: MIT Press.

Aylwin, Patricio. 1994. *Crecimiento con equidad: Discursos escogidos 1992–1994.* Editorial Andrés Bello, Chile.

Buchanan, James M., and Richard A. Musgrave. 2000. *Public Finance and Public Choice: Two Contrasting Visions of the State.* Cambridge, Mass.: MIT Press.

CIEPLAN (Corporación de Investigaciones Económicas para Latinoamérica). 1986. *Colección de Estudios 19*. Santiago: Alfabeta Editores.

Eyzaguirre Guzmán, Nicolás. 2003. *Estado de la Hacienda Pública 2003*. Santiago: Gobierno de Chile, Ministerio de Hacienda.

Ffrench-Davis, Ricardo. 2001a. *Entre el neoliberalismo y el crecimiento con equidad: Tres décadas de política económica en Chile*. 2ª ed. Dolmen Ediciones S.A.

————. 2001b. *Financial Crisis in Successful Emerging Economies*. Washington, D.C.: Brookings Institution and Economic Commission for Latin America.

————. 2002. *Economic Reforms in Chile: From Dictatorship to Democracy*. University of Michigan Press.

Foxley, Alejandro, Eduardo Aninat, and José Pablo Arellano. 1980. "Las desigualdades económicas y la acción del estado." Estudio preparado para el Programa Mundial del Empleo de la Organización Internacional del Trabajo, Fondo de Cultura Económica, México.

Hurtado Ruiz-Tagle, Carlos. 1988. *De Balmaceda a Pinochet,* Ediciones Logos, Chile.

Ministerio de Hacienda, Gobierno de Chile. 1997. "Informe financiero: Proyecto de ley que crea régimen de Jornada Escolar Completa diurnal." Despachado por la Comisión de Educación, Cultura, Ciencia y Tecnología del Senado, Santiago.

Miranda, Marcela, and José Piñera. 2003. "La nueva revolución." *Revista qué pasa* 32 (1697): 54–56.

Musgrave, Richard A. 2000. *Public Finance and Public Choice*. 3rd printing. Cambridge, Mass.: MIT Press.

Oppliger, Marcel, and Patricia Matte. 2003. "La pasión por educar." *Revista qué pasa* 32 (1697): 50–53.

Paehlke, Robert C. 2003. *Democracy's Dilemma: Environment, Social Equity, and the Global Economy*. Cambridge, Mass.: MIT Press.

Persson, Torsten, and Guido Tabellini. 2002. *Political Economics: Explaining Economic Policy*. Cambridge, Mass. MIT Press.

Comment

Carol Graham

FOR SEVERAL REASONS IT IS A REAL PLEASURE TO COMMENT ON EDUARDO ANINAT'S lecture. The first is that Eduardo is a committed reformer: a former finance minister who has always had a genuine dedication to social equity as well as a good sense of political reality. This is a rare combination of traits, particularly among finance ministers.

The second reason is that his lecture describes yet another forward-looking innovation in social policy from Chile. As Eduardo notes, Chile's commitment to social policies came early in its and Latin America's histories, and since then it has been a leader in developing new approaches and programs. Each new set of policies and innovations builds on lessons from the past—both achievements and mistakes—so there is constant learning and adaptation. The targeted safety nets and reorientation of social spending to the poorest citizens in the 1970s and 1980s, for example, were a reaction to a universal system of benefits that had grown unwieldy and left out the poorest. Similarly, the democratic administrations that came to power starting in 1990 committed to improving access to and quality of public services for a much broader portion of the population. Although they maintained the Pinochet regime's focus on targeted services for the poorest, they also tried to address the plight of the near poor and the middle class—who did not benefit from the targeted services and relied on deteriorating services from the public sector, yet ultimately paid the tax for the targeted approach.

The third reason it is such a pleasure to comment is that Chile's recent education reforms are an excellent example of how well-designed social service reforms can enhance both equity and efficiency. These were the framing themes for the Concertación and have served Chile remarkably well. Indeed, the joining of these two themes in the design of social policy distinguishes the Chilean "miracle" as much as do its high growth rates.

Lessons from Chile

Eduardo identifies several issues that were key to the success of the education reforms. Chile's experience also provides lessons that can be applied in a wide range of other policy contexts. The first is that reformers must walk a fine line between populism and defensive technocratic insulation. Both strategies have a history of backfiring in Chile, with more populists in the 1960s and 1970s leading to more insulated technocrats in the 1980s and 1990s—though this could swing back. Thus close attention must be paid to both political concerns and public communication. (I have seen this in many contexts besides Chile and with many kinds of reform, from privatization to pension reform to macroeconomic stabilization.)

Of equal importance is managing public expectations. Allowing these to outpace a government's ability to deliver can create big problems, because few things are worse for political stability than unmet expectations. My research shows that people are very happy when they get more than they expected—but are much more unhappy when they get less than they expected or, even worse, lose benefits. Thus policymakers must combine good communication with prudent management of expectations.

As Eduardo emphasizes, it is enormously helpful to have broad public consensus and support for a reform, with a goal that virtually everyone agrees is good for society as well as for equity and efficiency. Education is a much easier sell in this regard than, say, pension or other reforms. But the point is that the packaging and marketing of a reform can affect its odds of success nearly as much as can its content.

Another major issue is that reforms must be crafted and presented within a sustainable public financing framework. This was crucial for Chile's education reforms, which were greatly aided by having a large growth dividend to provide much of the needed financing. The decision to ensure that the reform received funding from the higher value added tax (VAT) was also critical to grounding it in sustainable public finances. Indeed, the reformers deserve enormous credit for insisting on grounding the reforms in sustainable fiscal policy in addition to a growth boom that was unlikely to continue at the same rate.

Finally, Eduardo notes that careful attention must be paid to the labor market and service delivery, as this was perhaps the most difficult aspect of reform in Chile. That is not surprising, yet this is the area where analysts have the least experience and fewest recommendations for change. How can a country improve public services when there is a monopsony in the supply of labor? This is an extremely difficult issue, and not surprisingly one where Eduardo does not suggest any possible solutions, such as subcontracting with the private sector. It would have been useful to have some thoughts or recommendations on this issue.

A related point involves Eduardo's references to raising teacher productivity. He does not discuss the tradeoffs and constraints to raising the productivity of existing teachers; the underlying assumption seems to be that productivity can be increased with additional resources. A bigger, more contentious question is, what are the marginal returns to investing in productivity under the current labor market structure relative to those associated with more systemic (and controversial) changes in that structure? I am not implying that this question could have been addressed when the education reforms were introduced, as doing so could have jeopardized the entire process. But I would have liked to see some discussion of the question, now that Eduardo is reflecting on the experience.

Other Points about Chile's Reforms

I think that Chile's education reforms were great for many reasons. They addressed major structural constraints, such as the length of the school day, even though doing so was costly and complicated. Moreover, the reformers were careful to emphasize the benefits that the reforms would provide for large numbers of beneficiaries, making it easier to secure support for incurring their costs. In addition, the special programs for the poorest students and the incentive programs for the best students, teachers, and schools provide an important balance in objectives and mirror the larger framework of achieving equity and efficiency. I was also pleased to learn that the reformers relied on studies by the Brookings Institution to evaluate the positive effects of extra time spent in school!

I will conclude with a more general point. Underlying the rationale of the education reforms—as well as the goals of increasing equity and efficiency—is an objective that I think is the only feasible way to permanently address the inequitable income distribution in Chile and Latin America, and that is enhancing social mobility. My work on social mobility, some conducted with Nancy Birdsall, suggests that there is more mobility in the region than many observers expect, and that opportunities for upward mobility are closely linked to having higher levels of education (see, among others, Birdsall and Graham 2000). But the region also harbors considerable vulnerability to downward mobility and poverty—and people who finish secondary school but do not achieve higher levels of education are the most vulnerable to falling from the middle or near middle class into poverty.

These findings highlight the importance of making more progress on education reforms, and the contribution that Chile's reforms can make by setting an example. It is too early to evaluate how the reforms have affected academic performance. But once those data are available and if they are very positive (as expected), Chile could provide a model for other countries—something it has already done in many other areas, from social security reform to macroeconomic management.

Reference

Birdsall, Nancy, and Carol Graham. 2000. *New Markets, New Opportunities? Economic and Social Mobility in a Changing World*. Washington, D.C.: Brookings Institution and Carnegie Endowment for International Peace.

Comment

Roberto Junguito

I CONGRATULATE THE WORLD BANK FOR HAVING CHOSEN EDUARDO ANINAT TO deliver one of the lectures in this series. Aninat has distinguished himself as an economist, academic researcher, and policymaker in Latin America, and in recent years has made a significant contribution as deputy managing director of the International Monetary Fund (IMF).

For his lecture Aninat chose one of the central topics in development theory, public policies for investing in human capital, and applied it to Chile in the 1990s. In sum, the Bank chose the right lecturer from the right country to discuss the right subject at the right time.

Chile—Latin America's Top Performer in the 1990s

During the 1990s Chile outperformed all other Latin American economies, particularly in terms of GDP growth. Indeed, during the decade Chile had the world's fourth-highest GDP growth. This rapid growth was accompanied by a gradual lowering of inflation—an outcome attained without major costs in terms of exchange rate appreciation, as occurred in many other Latin American countries. Chile also achieved the region's largest drop in poverty rates, showing that countries that grow strongly for a sustained period can significantly reduce poverty.

These achievements were accompanied by, and to some extent due to, the following developments:

- Chile's governance index is above its expected level given its GDP per capita.
- Its corruption index is below the average for both Latin America and other emerging market economies.
- Public debt was cut to 34 percent of GDP by the end of the 1990s.
- Chile has the region's highest tax pressure and highest value added tax (VAT) productivity index.

- During the 1990s it achieved significant financial deepening, including the region's highest level of stock market capitalization.

- Strong bank performance indicators—such as low operating costs, low non-performing loans, and high profitability—also distinguish Chile from its neighbors.

- Chile also has the highest savings rate in Latin America, as well as a low index of dollarization.

- Finally, it is one of the most open economies of the region.

Many economists, in Chile and around the world, have been analyzing the reasons for Chile's success, which go beyond issues of factor shares and total factor productivity. Aninat offers two major explanations: trade openness and strong institutions. After hearing his lecture, a third reason comes to mind: the importance attached to investing in human capital.

Lessons for Other Countries

Using the example of investment in human capital, Aninat shows how successful policymaking is achieved in Chile. A basic but important lesson for other Latin American countries is that no new spending, no matter how important, should be approved unless there is additional public revenue to support it. Another institutional lesson from Chile's experience is that ministries of finance must involve themselves in allocating resources across sectors.

In addition, Aninat's lecture highlights the fact that high and sustained economic growth can result in much higher social spending, because growth provides a revenue dividend that can be used to cancel social debt. It also shows that increasing the tax burden—which in Chile involved raising the VAT to 18 percent—is easier when it is linked to a specific public expenditure with a high internal rate of return, such as education.

The lecture also indicates the importance of investing in human capital in the developing world. Finally, Chile shows that strong macroeconomic policies are crucial to economic and social success.

About the Editors

Timothy Besley is professor of economics and political science at the London School of Economics and director of its Suntory and Toyota International Centres for Economics and Related Disciplines (STICERD). He previously taught at Princeton University. He is a fellow of the British Academy, Econometric Society, and European Economics Association. His research interests include political economy, development economics, and public economics. He has been coeditor of *American Economic Review* and managing editor of *Economic Journal*. Besley holds an undergraduate degree and a Ph.D. in Economics from Oxford University.

Roberto Zagha is senior economic adviser in the Poverty Reduction and Economic Management Network at the World Bank. While at the Bank, Zagha has been an economist, sector manager, and director in the Latin America and Caribbean and South Asia regions. Most recently he led the Bank's study of development lessons from the 1990s, of which this volume is part. Before joining the Bank, Zagha was assistant professor of economics at the University of São Paolo, where he also pursued doctoral studies in economics.

About the Discussants

Montek S. Ahluwalia is profiled on p. 187.

Alice Amsden is Barton L. Weller Professor of Political Economy in the Department of Urban Studies and Planning at the Massachusetts Institute of Technology. She has published numerous works on the economic development and political economy of East Asia and Eastern Europe, including *Asia's Next Giant: South Korea and Late Industrialization* (Oxford University Press, 1989) and *The Market Meets Its Match: Restructuring the Economies of Eastern Europe* (with Jacek Kochanowicz and Lance Taylor, Harvard University Press, 1994). She has won the Leontief Prize for Advancing the Frontiers of Economic Thought, among other awards. Amsden holds a Ph.D. from the London School of Economics.

Anders Åslund is director of the Russian and Eurasian Program at the Carnegie Endowment for International Peace, a position he has held since 2003. He joined the Endowment as senior associate in 1994. He is also adjunct professor at Georgetown University. Åslund has been an economic adviser to the governments of Russia and Ukraine, and since 1998 has advised President Askar Akaev of the Kyrgyz Republic. He has also been a professor at the Stockholm School of Economics and director of the Stockholm Institute of East European Economics. He is chairman of the Economics Education and Research Consortium and of the Advisory Council of the

Center for Social and Economic Research (Warsaw, Poland). He has edited ten books and has been widely published in *Foreign Affairs, Foreign Policy, New York Times, Washington Post, Financial Times, Wall Street Journal* and others. Åslund holds a Ph.D. in Modern Economic History from Oxford University.

C. Fred Bergsten has been director of the Institute for International Economics since its creation in 1981. He is also chairman of the "Shadow G-8," which advises the G-8 countries on their annual summit meetings, and co-chairman of the TransAtlantic Strategy Group, created by the Bertelsmann Foundation. He was chairman of the U.S. Competitiveness Policy Council, created by Congress, throughout its existence from 1991 to 95, and chairman of the Asia–Pacific Economic Cooperation (APEC) Eminent Persons Group throughout its existence from 1993 to 95. He was also assistant secretary for international affairs of the U.S. Treasury in 1977 to 1981, assistant for international economic affairs at the National Security Council in 1969 to 71, and senior fellow at the Carnegie Endowment for International Peace in 1981, the Brookings Institution in 1972 to 76, and the Council on Foreign Relations in 1967 to 68. He is the author, coauthor, or editor of numerous books on international economic issues, including *The United States and the World Economy: Foreign Economic Policy for the Next Decade* (2005), *Dollar Adjustment: How Far? Against What?* (2004), and *Dollar Overvaluation and the World Economy* (2003). Bergsten holds a Ph.D. from the Fletcher School of Law and Diplomacy at Tufts University.

Nancy Birdsall is founding president of the Center for Global Development, a think tank based in Washington, D.C. Before launching the center, she served for three years as senior associate and director of the Economic Reform Project at the Carnegie Endowment for International Peace. From 1993 to 98 Birdsall was executive vice president of the Inter-American Development Bank (IADB). Before that she spent 14 years in research, policy, and management positions at the World Bank, most recently as director of the Policy Research Department. She holds a Ph.D. in economics from Yale University.

Eliana Cardoso is visiting professor at the Fundação Getúlio Vargas in São Paulo. In 1993 she became William Clayton Professor of International Economic Affairs at the Fletcher School at Tufts University. She has also been visiting associate professor of economics at the Massachusetts Institute of Technology (MIT), Yale University, and Georgetown University. She has been a sector manager at the World Bank, adviser in the Research Department of the International Monetary Fund (IMF), president of the New England Council of Latin American Studies, a member of the advisory board of the *Journal of Latin American Studies*, and a member of the editorial boards of *Nova Economia* and *The World Bank Research Observer*. She has published more than 100 papers on economic development, inflation, and international finance, and currently writes a weekly column for the Brazilian publication *Valor Econômico*. Cardoso holds a Ph.D. in economics from MIT.

Agustín Carstens is deputy managing director of the IMF. Before taking his current position, he was Mexico's deputy secretary of finance. From 1999 to 2000

Carstens was an executive director at the IMF, representing Costa Rica, El Salvador, Guatemala, Honduras, Mexico, Nicaragua, Spain, and Venezuela. Prior to that he held various positions at the Banco de México (central bank), including director general of economic research and chief of staff in the Governor's office. He has also written articles for volumes published by the Federal Reserve Bank of Boston, University of London, Organisation for Economic Co-operation and Development (OECD), the IMF, and the World Bank, as well as for *Columbia Journal of World Business, American Economic Review, Journal of Asian Economics, Journal of International Finance, Cuadernos Económicos del ICE* (Spain), and *Gaceta de Economía del ITAM* (Mexico). He holds a Ph.D. in economics from the University of Chicago.

Michael Chege is director of the Center for African Studies at the University of Florida at Gainesville, where he is also associate professor of political science. He has taught at the University of Nairobi (Kenya) and the Graduate Institute of International Studies at the University of Geneva (Switzerland). From 1988 to 1994 he worked for the Ford Foundation in Harare, Zimbabwe, as program officer in charge of public policy and international affairs programs in Eastern and Southern Africa. Chege holds a Ph.D. from the University of California at Berkeley.

J. Bradford DeLong is professor of economics at the University of California at Berkeley. He is also co-editor of the *Journal of Economic Perspectives*, research associate at the National Bureau of Economic Research, and visiting scholar at the Federal Reserve Bank of San Francisco. From 1993 to 1995 he served in the U.S. government as deputy assistant secretary of the treasury for economic policy, reporting to Assistant Secretary Alicia Munnell. Before that he was Danziger Associate Professor in the Department of Economics at Harvard University. He has also been John M. Olin Fellow at the National Bureau of Economic Research, assistant professor of economics at Boston University, and lecturer in the department of economics at the Massachusetts Institute of Technology. DeLong holds a Ph.D. in economics from Harvard University.

Richard Eckaus is Ford International Professor of Economics Emeritus at MIT and a member of the National Advisory Council on Environment and Technology Policy for the U.S. Environmental Protection Agency. He has been a professor of economics at MIT since 1962, and has served as a consultant to many countries as well as the United Nations, World Bank, and Asian Development Bank, among other organizations. Eckaus has written several books and numerous articles on the economics of development, technology, education, and other topics. He holds a Ph.D. in economics from MIT.

Roque B. Fernández is professor of macroeconomic analysis at the Center for Macroeconomic Studies of Argentina (CEMA) in Buenos Aires. During 1996 to 1999 he was Argentina's minister of economy and public works, and from 1991 to 1996 president of its Central Bank. In addition, he has written several articles published in internationally renowned academic journals, including *American Economic Review* and *Journal of Political Economy*. He holds a Ph.D. in economics from the University of Chicago and a doctorate in economic sciences from the National University of Córdoba (Argentina).

Stanley Fischer is Citigroup's vice chairman, chairman of its Country Risk Committee, and head of its Public Sector Group. From 1994 to 2001 he was first deputy managing director of the IMF. Before that he was Killian Professor and head of the department of economics at MIT. In 1988 to 1990 he was vice president of development economics and chief economist at the World Bank. Fischer has also held consulting appointments with the U.S. State Department, U.S. Treasury, and Bank of Israel. He holds a Ph.D. in economics from MIT.

Ricardo Ffrench-Davis has been principal regional adviser at the Economic Commission for Latin America and the Caribbean since 1992. Before that he was professor of Graduate Programs at the Institute of International Studies and Department of Economics at the University of Chile. He is also co-founder of the Center for Research on Latin America, for which he served as vice president from 1976 to 90. Ffrench-Davis has written 17 books and about 100 articles on international economics, development strategies, foreign financing, and Latin American economies. He holds a Ph.D. in economics from the University of Chicago.

Carol Graham is senior fellow in economic studies and co-director of the Center on Social and Economic Dynamics at the Brookings Institution. She is also visiting professor of economics at the Johns Hopkins University. She has written numerous books, including *Happiness and Hardship: Opportunity and Insecurity in New Market Economies* (with Stefano Pettinato, Brookings, 2002) and *Private Markets for Public Goods: Raising the Stakes in Economic Reform* (Brookings, 1998), as well as several journal articles on the political economy of reform. Graham has served as special adviser to the deputy managing director of the IMF and been a consultant at the IADB, World Bank, United Nations Development Programme (UNDP), and Harvard Institute for International Development (HIID). She holds a Ph.D. in economics from Oxford University.

Ricardo Hausmann is professor of the practice of economic development at the Kennedy School of Government at Harvard University. From 1994 to 2000 he was the first chief economist of the IADB, where he created the Research Department. In 1992 to 1993 he was Venezuela's minister of planning and a board member of its Central Bank. He also served as chair of the IMF to World Bank Development Committee. From 1985 to 1991 he was professor of economics at the Instituto de Estudios Superiores de Administracion (IESA) in Caracas, where he founded the Center for Public Policy. In addition, in 1988 to 91 he was a visiting fellow at Oxford University. Hausmann holds a Ph.D. in economics from Cornell University.

Jeffrey Herbst is Chair üat the Woodrow Wilson School of Public and International Affairs at Princeton University. Herbst has taught at Princeton since 1987, and has studied as a Fulbright Scholar in South Africa and Zimbabwe. He has written several books and numerous articles on African politics and development, including *States and Power in Africa: Comparative Lessons in Authority and Control* (Princeton University Press, 2000) and *The Politics of Reform in Ghana: 1982 to 1991* (University of California at Berkeley Press, 1992). Herbst holds a Ph.D. in Political Science from Yale University.

Enrique V. Iglesias began his fourth five-year term as president of the Inter-American Development Bank in 2003. In 1985 to 1988 he was Uruguay's minister of foreign relations, in 1972 to 1985 executive secretary of the United Nations Economic Commission for Latin America and the Caribbean, in 1986 chairman of the conference that launched the Uruguay Round of international trade negotiations (in Punta del Este, Uruguay), and in 1981 secretary general of the United Nations Conference on New and Renewable Sources of Energy (Kenya). Iglesias has also taught economic development at Uruguay's Universidad de la República and served as director of its Institute of Economics. He graduated from the Universidad de la República with degrees in economics and business administration in 1953 and pursued specialized programs of study in France and the United States.

Nurul Islam is Research Fellow Emeritus at the International Food Policy Research Institute (IFPRI), which he joined in 1987 as senior policy adviser to the director general. during his more than three-decade career, Islam has held academic appointments at Dhaka University, Oxford, and Yale, and been founder and director of the Bangladesh Institute of Development Studies, minister and deputy chairman of the first Bangladesh Planning Commission, and assistant director general of the United Nations Food and Agriculture Organization. He has written extensively on trade, development, food security, and public policy. His publications include *Looking Outward: Bangladesh in the World Economy* (University Press Limited, 2004), *Explorations in Development Issues: Selected Articles of Nurul Islam* (Ashgate, 2003), and *Foodgrain Price Stabilization in Developing Countries* (IFPRI, 1996). Islam holds a B.A. and M.A. in economics from Dhaka University and an M.A. and Ph.D. in economics from Harvard University.

Roberto Junguito is research fellow at Fedesarrollo, a think tank based in Bogotá, Colombia. Before joining Fedesarrollo, he held various positions in the Colombian government, including minister of economy and public credit, member of the governing board of the Central Bank, and Ambassador to France. From 1991 to 1999 Junguito was executive director for Colombia at the IMF. He holds degrees in economics from the University of the Andes (Colombia) and Princeton University.

Vijay Kelkar is adviser to India's minister of finance, in the rank of a minister of state. From 1999 to 2002 he was an executive director at the IMF. Before that he held various positions in the government of India, including finance secretary. In addition, in 1991 to 94 he was director of the International Trade Division of the United Nations Conference on Trade and Development. He holds a Ph.D. in economics from the University of California at Berkeley.

Pedro Malan has been chairman of the board of directors of Unibanco (Brazil) since 2004, after serving as vice chairman since 2003. He served as Brazil's minister of finance from 1995 to 2002, president of Brazil's Central Bank from 1993 to 1994, special consultant and chief external debt negotiator for Brazil's ministry of finance from 1991 to 1993, World Bank executive director from 1986 to 1990 and 1992 to 1993, IADB executive eirector from 1990 to 1992, director of the United Nations Department of International Economic and Social Affairs from 1985 to 1986, and director of the United Nations Center of Transnational Corporations from 1983 to 1984. Malan holds a Ph.D. in economics from the University of California at Berkeley.

Michael Mussa is senior fellow at the Institute for International Economics. From 1991 to 2001 he was economic counselor and director of the Department of Research at the IMF. By appointment of President Ronald Reagan, Mussa was a member of the U.S. Council of Economic Advisers in 1986 to 1988. From 1976 to 1991 he was a faculty member at the Graduate School of Business at the University of Chicago, and from 1971 to 1976 was on the faculty of the Department of Economics at the University of Rochester. During this period he also served as a visiting faculty member at the Graduate Center of the City University of New York, London School of Economics, and Graduate Institute of International Studies (Geneva, Switzerland). Mussa has written extensively on international economics, macroeconomics, monetary economics, and municipal finance for professional journals and research volumes. Mussa holds a Ph.D. in economics from the University of Chicago.

Mario Nuti is professor of comparative economic systems at the University of Rome, a position he has held since 1993. He has been an economic adviser to the European Union and the governments of Belarus, Poland, and Uzbekistan, as well as a consultant at several international organizations, including the World Bank, IMF, International Labour Organization, and UNDP. He has also written numerous publications on postcommunist economic transition. Nuti holds a Ph.D. in economics from Cambridge University.

Gur Ofer is Harvey M. and Lyn P. Meyerhoff Emeritus Professor of Soviet Economics at the Hebrew University of Jerusalem. Until recently he was chair of the International Advisory Board of the New Economic School of Moscow and one of its founders, and head of the Israel National Institute for Health Policy and Health Services Research. An expert on the Russian economy, he has held academic positions at Yale, Harvard, Columbia, University of California at Los Angeles, Northeastern, and Boston College. In addition, he has been a guest research fellow at the RAND Corporation, Brookings Institution, and World Bank, among other organizations, and written a number of books and articles on the Soviet economy and post-Soviet transition. Ofer holds a Ph.D. in economics from Harvard University.

Steven Radelet is senior fellow at the Center for Global Development, where he works on issues related to foreign aid, developing country debt, economic growth, and trade between industrial and developing countries. From 2000 to 2002 he was deputy assistant secretary of the U.S. Treasury for Africa, the Middle East, and Asia. From 1990 to 2000 he was on the faculty of Harvard University, where he was a fellow at HIID, director of the Institute's Macroeconomics Program, and a lecturer on economics and public policy. During 1991 to 1995 he lived in Jakarta, Indonesia, where he was HIID's resident adviser on macroeconomic policy to the ministry of finance. From 1986 to 1988 he served in a similar capacity for the ministry of finance and trade in the Gambia. He holds a Ph.D. in economics from Harvard University.

Samir Radwan is managing director of the Economic Research Forum (ERF), a Cairo-based think tank focused on economic issues facing the Middle East and North Africa. Before joining the ERF, he was adviser on development policies to the director general and counselor on Arab countries at the ILO. Radwan has also been adviser to the prime minister of Egypt on the development of a National Employment Program (2000 to 01) and director of the Development and Technical Cooperation Department (1994 to 96) and Development Policies Department (1996 to 99) at the ILO. Widely published on development issues, particularly employment policies and poverty, Radwan has also been visiting professor on the faculty of economics and political sciences at Cairo University and the American University of Cairo. Radwan holds a Ph.D. in economics from London University.

Djavad Salehi-Isfahani is professor of economics at Virginia Polytechnic Institute and State University, where he has taught since 1984. Salehi-Isfahani has also held academic positions at the Institute for Research in Planning and Development in Tehran, Oxford University, and the University of Pennsylvania. From 1979 to 1980 he was economist in the Central Bank of Iran. Salehi-Isfahani has written numerous publications on the oil market, labor market, and Iranian economy. He holds a Ph.D. in economics from Harvard University.

Jan Svejnar is Everett E. Berg Professor of Business Administration at the University of Michigan Business School and Professor of Economics at the University of Michigan. He has served as economic adviser to Czech Republic President Vaclav Havel and as director of the Economics Institute at the Academy of Sciences of the Czech Republic, and has held academic positions at the University of Pittsburgh and Cornell University. He has also written numerous works on transition economies and international business. Svejnar holds a Ph.D. in economics from Princeton University.

Index

Note: n and *nn* indicate *note* and *notes.*